THE ANATOMY OF ADMINISTRATIVE LAW

This book seeks to further our understanding of the nature of administrative law doctrine and adjudication. It has three main aims. The first is to improve understanding of administrative law's 'anatomy' by pulling the subject apart and exploring the nature of the legal structures at play in adjudication. In doing so, the book emphasises three main ways in which administrative law's anatomy is both complex and diverse, namely:

- administrative law doctrine interacts with a broad array of legislative frameworks;
- administrative law adjudication seeks to accommodate a variety of legal values; and,
- administrative law is concerned with legal relationships of different kinds.

The second aim is to illustrate the importance of recognising the complexity and variety of administrative law's anatomy in three particular doctrinal contexts: procedural review, legitimate expectations and standing.

The third and final aim is to raise an important but under-explored question: is it plausible and useful to attempt to make sense of administrative law doctrine by reference to a singular organising concept or principle?

The overarching message of the book is one of cynicism. The complexity and variety of administrative law's legal structures probably means that attempts to explain the field 'monistically', while they may capture important themes, will be unhelpfully reductionist. Ambitious and thought-provoking, this is an important new statement on administrative law.

The Anatomy of Administrative Law

Joanna Bell

•HART•
OXFORD • LONDON • NEW YORK • NEW DELHI • SYDNEY

HART PUBLISHING
Bloomsbury Publishing Plc
Kemp House, Chawley Park, Cumnor Hill, Oxford, OX2 9PH, UK
1385 Broadway, New York, NY 10018, USA
29 Earlsfort Terrace, Dublin 2, Ireland

HART PUBLISHING, the Hart/Stag logo, BLOOMSBURY and the Diana logo are trademarks of Bloomsbury Publishing Plc
First published in Great Britain 2020

First published in hardback, 2020
Paperback edition, 2021

A catalogue record for this book is available from the British Library.

Library of Congress Cataloging-in-Publication Data

Names: Bell, Joanna, 1990- author.

Title: The anatomy of administrative law / Joanna Bell.

Description: Oxford ; New York : Hart, 2020. | Based on author's thesis (doctoral - University of Oxford, 2017) issued under title: Against monism and in favour of an anatomical approach to administrative law. | Includes bibliographical references and index.

Identifiers: LCCN 2020001978 (print) | LCCN 2020001979 (ebook) | ISBN 9781509925339 (hardback) | ISBN 9781509925346 (Epub)

Subjects: LCSH: Administrative law—Great Britain. | A dministrative law—Philosophy.

Classification: LCC KD4879 .B45 2020 (print) | LCC KD4879 (ebook) | DDC 342.41/06—dc23

LC record available at https://lccn.loc.gov/2020001978

LC ebook record available at https://lccn.loc.gov/2020001979

ISBN: HB: 978-1-50992-533-9
PB: 978-1-50994-392-0
ePDF: 978-1-50992-535-3
ePub: 978-1-50992-534-6

Typeset by Compuscript Ltd, Shannon

For my nephew Albert

ACKNOWLEDGEMENTS

People say that writing a book is never easy. I am not in a position to know if this is right. It is certainly true, however, that writing this particular book was not easy. The chapters contained here have gone through a great many drafts. The ideas are the product of many years of research and reflection. The writing process has also spanned a number of important stages of my life and the challenges which have come with those. The process of writing has, however, been made vastly easier by the presence of some truly wonderful people in my life. I owe each of them an immeasurable debt of gratitude.

My first and most utmost thanks go to Liz Fisher, Professor of Environmental Law at the University of Oxford. Liz supervised the doctoral work from which this book developed. She is a truly remarkable supervisor, scholar and friend. Her scholarly fervour is matched only by her warmth and humility. I will be forever grateful for all of the support she has given me.

My doctoral research was generously funded by a full studentship from the Arts and Humanities Research Council. This was a life-changing opportunity and opened doors which would not otherwise have been available. I feel very fortunate to have been a recipient.

My doctoral work was examined by a number of leading scholars, each of whom command my utmost respect and admiration. Professor Timothy Endicott (Oxford) and Professor Peter Cane (Cambridge) served as final examiners. Their input not only improved the quality of my ideas but changed my attitude to writing. I remain immensely grateful to them. Professor Rebecca Williams (Oxford) and Professor Paul Craig (Oxford) served as examiners at other stages of my doctoral studies. I learnt a great deal from them and their feedback helped me immeasurably through the early stages of the work.

The production team at Hart have been a delight to work with. Kate Whetter has overseen a very smooth publication process. Victoria Broom has been endlessly patient and thorough in copy-editing.

During the course of writing, I have worked at a number of institutions. At each, I had the privilege of working with an array of supportive and inspiring people. My three years as a College Associate Lecturer at St John's College, Cambridge were enjoyable and edifying in equal measure. Professor Albertina Albors-Llorens, Professor David Fox, Dr Jodi Gardner and Professor Christine Gray were truly wonderful colleagues and I continue to value their friendship enormously. The broader public law community at Cambridge also provided an inspirational place to develop my ideas. I am particularly grateful to Professor Mark Elliott, Professor David Feldman and Professor Alison Young for the time and opportunities they afforded me.

I am grateful to everyone at Keble College, Oxford who made my time as a student and, later, as a lecturer so rewarding. Professor Edwin Peel has been endlessly encouraging and kind. Professor James Edelman (now Honorable Justice Edelman) was a major influence on my decision to pursue an academic career. Amy Barker, Katie Blake, Abbie Cooper, Natasha Holcroft-Emmess, Anjoli Maheswaran Foster and Natalie Wallen made my early years of studying the law rich and enjoyable. I count myself very lucky to have them in my life.

My greatest debt of gratitude of all is owed to my family who have provided me with a seemingly endless supply of love and support. I will never be able to repay my parents, Mark and Deborah, for everything they have done for me. They have supported my ambitions selflessly and completely. My sister Emma is one of the strongest women I know and a constant source of both comfort and inspiration. My wonderful partner Nick has uncomplainingly rearranged his life, multiple times, to enable me to pursue my academic career. He has celebrated my small successes and talked me through moments of doubt. He has been my rock throughout the process of writing both doctorate and book. I cannot express in words how thankful I am for everything he has done for me.

Finally, I would like to take the opportunity to thank you, the reader. There is a great mass of interesting things to read in this world and it is humbling to think that you have chosen to read my book. I hope its arguments will convince you. At the very least I hope you will find in here much which prompts you to question and to reflect.

Joanna Bell
Jeffrey Hackney Tutorial Fellow in Law, St Edmund Hall
Associate Professor, Oxford Law Faculty

TABLE OF CONTENTS

TABLE OF CASES

TABLE OF LEGISLATION

Statutes

Statutory Instruments etc

United States of America Legislation

European Material

1

Introduction

I. What is 'Administrative Law'?

This book is about the nature of administrative law and the approaches scholars use to make sense of it. Before outlining the book's arguments, it is useful to outline what 'administrative law' means for the purposes of this book.

Administrative law is difficult to define, but in much conventional thought and for the purposes of this book it refers to the legal doctrines developed by the domestic courts for the purpose of overseeing the activities of public administration. That is not to say that administrative law includes every legal doctrine capable of being applied to the acts of public administrators. The liability of administrative decision-makers in contract, tort and property law,[1] under the Human Rights Act 1998[2] and European Union law,[3] for example, all fall outside the scope of this book. The book's focus is more specific: it is concerned with the body of doctrine developed by the courts of England and Wales in order to provide appropriate oversight of decision-making within institutions of public administration.[4]

It has become common, at least in the English and Welsh legal context,[5] to imagine administrative law as a set of judicially-created legal doctrines, commonly

[1] Mark Elliott and Jason Varuhas, *Administrative Law*, 5th edn (Oxford University Press, 2016) Ch 15; William Wade and Christopher Forsyth, 11th edn (Oxford University Press, 2014) Ch 20; Carol Harlow, 'Public and Private Law: Definition Without Distinction' (1980) 43 *MLR* 241; Anne Davies, *The Public Law of Government Contracts* (Oxford University Press, 2008).

[2] Human Rights Act 1998, especially section 6.

[3] European Union law is of significant practical importance in many areas including, for instance, planning administration.

[4] This book does not address the ongoing, difficult, question of how far outside of the context of public administration the principles of administrative law are relevant. See: *Nagle v Fielden & Others* [1966] 2 QB 633 (CA); *R v Panel on Take-overs and Mergers, ex parte Datafin Plc* [1987] QB 815 (CA); *R v Panel on Take-overs and Mergers, ex parte Guinness Plc* [1990] 1 QB 146 (CA); *R v Football Association, ex parte Football League* [1993] 2 All ER 833 (QB); *R v Disciplinary Committee of the Jockey Club, ex parte Aga Khan* [1993] 1 WLR 909 (CA); *R v Jockey Club, ex parte RAM Racecourses Ltd* [1993] 2 All ER 225 (QB); *Braganza v BP Shipping Ltd* [2015] UKSC 17, [2015] 1 WLR 1661, especially [23]–[32]. For academic literature, see contributions in Michael Taggart (ed), *The Province of Administrative Law* (Hart Publishing, 1997); Dawn Oliver, 'Common Values in Public and Private Law and the Public/Private Divide' [1997] *PL* 630; Colin Campbell, 'Monopoly Power as Public Power for the Purposes of Judicial Review' (2009) 125 *LQR* 491; Mark Elliott, 'Judicial Review's Scope, Foundations and Purposes: Joining the Dots' [2012] *New Zealand Law Review* 75; Ernest Lim and Cora Chan, 'Problems with *Wednesbury* Unreasonableness in Contract Law: Lessons from Public Law' (2019) 135 *LQR* 88.

[5] Dean Knight suggests the position is similar in New Zealand: Dean Knight, *Vigilance and Restraint in the Common Law of Judicial Review* (Cambridge University Press, 2018), especially Ch 3.

referred to as the 'principles of administration'[6] or 'grounds of review,'[7] which apply generally across all areas of administrative decision-making.[8] An overview of these doctrines can therefore serve as a useful guide to the book's subject-matter. Supplying a list of the grounds of review, however, is not a straightforward task for at least two reasons. In the first place, judges and scholars asked to list the grounds of review would undoubtedly disagree about whether certain principles ought to be included.[9] Administrative law does not stand still; courts may come to recognise new grounds and there is sometimes room for disagreement about whether a new candidate has acquired this status.[10] In the second place, there is also ongoing disagreement both about how certain grounds ought to be formulated[11] and how the principles of administration as a whole are to be arranged or 'classified'.[12] Lord Diplock, for instance, famously suggested that there are three main heads of review – illegality, procedural impropriety and irrationality[13] – thereby suggesting that other grounds are to be understood as emanations of these basic ideas, while others have proposed much lengthier, non-hierarchical lists.[14]

While these complexities ought not to be underestimated, there is a core cluster of grounds of review which would find their way on to the lists of most English and Welsh practitioners and commentators, at least in some form, and can therefore serve as a rough guide to the books' subject-matter. According to these principles, administrative decision-makers must do the following:

- Comply with the requirements stipulated in the statutes which allocate their functions.[15]
- Act on a proper understanding of the law.[16]

[6] Language used throughout by Dawn Oliver, 'The Underlying Values of Public and Private Law' in Taggart (n 4).

[7] Knight (n 5) Ch 3; Timothy Endicott, *Administrative Law*, 3rd edn (Oxford University Press, 2015) 70.

[8] Knight (n 5); *Endicott*, ibid. For a striking example, see Wade and Forsyth (n 1) 26. See also Prevention of Terrorism Act 2005, s3(11): 'in determining [the appeal] … the court must apply the principles applicable in an application for judicial review'. (Since repealed by the Terrorism Prevention and Investigation Measures Act 2011). A similar formulation is used in Tribunals, Courts and Enforcement Act 2007, s15(4).

[9] For a recent example, see *R (Gallaher) v Competition and Markets Authority* [2018] UKSC 25, [2018] 2 WLR 1583 (discussed in Mark Elliott, 'A "Principle" of Consistency? The Doctrinal Configuration of the Law of Judicial Review' (2018) 77(3) *CLJ* 444).

[10] A modern example concerns open justice. See: *Kennedy v Information Commissioner* [2014] UKSC 20, [2015] AC 455; *Dover DC v Campaign to Protect Rural England (Kent)* [2017] UKSC 79, [2018] 1 WLR 108; Joanna Bell, '*Dover DC v CPRE Kent*: Legal Complexity and Reason-Giving in Planning Law' (2018) 23(1) *Judicial Review* 25; Joanna Bell, 'Reflections on Open Justice and the Status of the General Common Law Duty to Give Reasons' (2018) 77(2) *CLJ* 240.

[11] The most obvious example is the ongoing debate concerning the governing principles of substantive review. For a useful overview, see Hanna Wilberg and Mark Elliott (eds), *The Scope and Intensity of Substantive Review* (Hart Publishing, 2015) Ch 2.

[12] *Council of Civil Service Unions (CCSU) v Minister for the Civil Service* [1985] AC 374 (HL), 410.

[13] *Ibid.*

[14] See for instance the list in Paul Craig, *Administrative Law*, 8th edn (Sweet & Maxwell, 2016) 17.

[15] *R v Secretary of State for the Home Department, ex parte Fire Brigades Union* [1995] 1 AC 513 (HL).

[16] *R v Lord President of the Privy Council, ex parte Page* [1993] AC 682 (HL).

- Act to promote the 'policy and objects'[17] of the legislation which confers their power and not for some other illegitimate purpose.[18]
- Take into account all relevant considerations[19] and ignore those which are irrelevant.[20]
- Not delegate their powers unlawfully[21] nor fetter[22] their discretion by adopting an unduly rigid policy.
- Act and maintain the appearance of acting impartially.[23]
- Make decisions in a manner which is procedurally fair[24] including by allowing those whose rights and interests[25] are affected by the decision a fair opportunity to participate.[26]
- Sometimes offer reasons for their decisions[27] and ensure those reasons are legally adequate.[28]
- Not disappoint legitimate expectations unlawfully.[29]
- Refrain from exercising their powers in ways which are unreasonable[30] and, in some circumstances,[31] disproportionate.[32]

In addition to imagining administrative law as a set of generally-applying 'grounds of review', it has also become common in the English and Welsh legal context to think of administrative law as something which is applied primarily in the context of an 'application for judicial review'.[33] The 'application'[34] or 'claim'[35] for the judicial

[17] *Padfield v Minister of Agriculture, Fisheries and Food* [1968] AC 997 (HL), 1030.

[18] *Roberts v Hopwood* [1925] AC 578 (HL); *Wheeler v Leicester CC* [1985] AC 1054 (HL).

[19] *Tesco Stores Ltd v Secretary of State for the Environment* [1995] 1 WLR 759 (HL).

[20] *Associated Provincial Picture Houses Ltd v Wednesbury Corporation* [1948] 1 KB 223 (CA).

[21] *Barnard v National Dock Labour Board* [1953] 2 QB 18 (CA). For refinement of this rule see especially *Carltona Ltd v Commissioners of Works* [1943] 2 All ER (HL); *R v Secretary of State for Social Security, ex parte Sherwin* [1996] 2 WLUK 301; *DPP v Haw* [2008] 1 WLR 379; Mark Freedland, 'The Rule Against Delegation and the *Carltona* Doctrine in an Agency Context' [1996] *PL* 19.

[22] *British Oxygen Co Ltd v Minister of Technology* [1971] AC 610 (HL).

[23] *Porter v Magill* [2001] UKHL 67, [2002] 2 AC 357.

[24] *In Re HK (An Infant)* [1967] 2 QB 617 (CA).

[25] *R v Secretary of State for the Home Department, ex parte Al Fayed (No 1)* [1998] 1 WLR 763 (CA).

[26] *Ridge v Baldwin* [1964] AC 40 (HL).

[27] *R v Secretary of State for the Home Department, ex parte Doody* [1994] 1 AC 531 (HL).

[28] *South Buckinghamshire DC v Porter* [2004] UKHL 33, [2004] 1 WLR 1953.

[29] *R v North & East Devon Health Authority, ex parte Coughlan* [2001] QB 213 (CA).

[30] 'Unreasonableness' seems increasingly to be the courts' preferred formulation over 'irrationality'. See especially *Pham v Secretary of State for the Home Department* [2015] UKSC 19, [2015] 1 WLR 1591; *R (Keyu) v Secretary of State for Foreign and Commonwealth Affairs* [2015] UKSC 69, [2016] AC 1355.

[31] *Keyu* (n 30).

[32] *R (Daly) v Secretary of State for the Home Department* [2001] 2 AC 532 (HL); *Pham* (n 30) (discussed in Thomas Adams, 'Stumbling towards the Constitution' (2016) 75(1) *CLJ 1*); Paul Craig, 'The Nature of Reasonableness Review' (2013) 66 *Current Legal Problems* 131.

[33] *O'Reilly v Mackman* [1983] 2 AC 237; William Wade, 'Procedure and Prerogative in Public Law' (1985) 101 *LQR* 180.

[34] Senior Courts Act 1981, s31.

[35] Civil Procedure Rules 1998, Part 54.

review procedure will be discussed in chapter two. Explained briefly, this procedure was introduced in the course of major reforms in the late 1970s[36] and now constitutes one of the main legal processes by which challenges to administrative decision-making can be brought.

It is certainly the case that many administrative law issues are brought to the courts' attention via the judicial review process. Judicial review, however, is not an exclusive forum for hearing administrative law issues in the sense in which they are understood by this book.[37] This is so for two main reasons. First, the judicial review procedure is a relatively modern creation in the English and Welsh legal system. Prior to its introduction, however, judges had been developing what have come to be known as the grounds of review for centuries and it is important not to exclude these cases from consideration.[38] Second, even following the procedural reforms, the courts continue to engage with the grounds of review both inside and outside of the application for judicial review process.[39] It is common for statutes to provide for appeals on a point of law in relation to specific aspects of administration,[40] and the courts have stressed the central role the grounds of review play in determining whether an error of law has been made out in that context.[41] It may also be possible for parties to rely on the grounds of review collaterally in criminal[42] or tortious[43] proceedings.[44] Administrative law as it is understood here is therefore, in an important sense, wider than the judicial review procedure.[45]

It will be apparent from the above that this book adopts a highly 'court-centred'[46] understanding of administrative law, in that its focus is on *legal* techniques used by *courts*. In that sense, the focus of the book might be described as being on *doctrinal* administrative law, rather than administrative law in a broader sense. It is important to recognise explicitly both that this is to proceed from an understanding

[36] Rules of the Supreme Court (Amendment No 3) 1977 (SI 1977/1955).

[37] See further Elliott and Varuhas (n 1) Ch 13.

[38] In the context both of applications for a prerogative writ and ordinary claims for declaration of injunction. See further Paul Craig, *UK, EU and Global Administrative Law: Foundations and Challenges* (Cambridge University Press, 2015) Ch 1.

[39] In addition to the points made below, it should also be noted that tribunals play an important role in applying the grounds of review under the Tribunals, Court and Enforcement Act 2007, s15.

[40] Well-known examples include Town and Country Planning Act 1990, ss286–90; Roads (Scotland) Act 1984, Sch 2, para 2 (relied on in *Walton v Scottish Ministers* [2012] UKSC 44, [2013] PTSR 51); Tribunals, Courts and Enforcement Act 2007, s13; Investigatory Powers Act 2016, s242.

[41] Note Carnwath LJ's observation that 'the history of remedies in administrative law has seen the gradual assimilation of the various forms of review, common law and statutory' (*E v Secretary of State for the Home Department* [2004] EWCA Civ 49, [2004] QB 1044 at [41]).

[42] *Boddington v British Transport Police* [1999] 2 AC 143, [1998] 2 WLR 639 (HL).

[43] *Cooper v Wandsworth Board of Works* (1863) 143 ER 414 which proceeded as a claim in trespass.

[44] For general discussion of collateral challenge, see Christopher Forsyth, 'Collateral Challenge and the Rule of Law' [1999] *Judicial Review* 165; Mark Elliott, 'Boddington: Rediscovering the Constitutional Logic of Administrative Law' [1998] *PL* 92.

[45] It is also narrower in the sense that the judicial review application can be used to raise other kinds of issue. See for instance Human Rights Act 1998, s7.

[46] Michael Taggart, 'A Prolegomanon to an Intellectual History of Administrative Law in the Twentieth Century: The Case of John Willis and Canadian Administrative Law' (2005) 43 *Osgoode Hall Law Journal* 223, 232.

of administrative law which is both traditional and narrow and that there have long been influential calls urging scholars to embrace a broader understanding of administrative law.[47] For some, for instance, administrative law (or perhaps 'administrative justice'[48]) is properly conceived as the study of *any* mechanism by which public administration is regulated.[49] On this view, judicial decisions constitute one small portion of the materials to be incorporated into our purview; the operation of mechanisms such as tribunals[50] and ombudsmen[51] must also be prioritised.[52] Others would go further still and suggest that the centre-point for studying administrative law must be *inside* institutions of public administration.[53] For such scholars, the aim of administrative law is to understand how administration functions in order that it can be bettered.[54] From this perspective, judicial decisions supply an extremely small part of this much bigger picture.[55]

[47] For a strong version of this idea, see Allan C Hutchinson, 'The Rise and Ruse of Administrative Law and Scholarship' (1985) 48(3) *MLR* 293. See also John Willis (ed), *Canadian Boards at Work* (MacMillan, 1941); John Willis, 'What I like and What I Don't Like About Lawyers' (1969) 76 *Queen's Q* 1; Harry Arthurs, 'Mechanical Arts and Merchandise: Canadian Public Administration in the New Economy' (1997) 42 *McGill Law Journal* 29; Harry Arthurs, 'Woe Unto You, Judges' (2002) 29 *Journal of Law and Society* 657.

[48] For general discussion, see Joe Tomlinson, 'The Grammar of Administrative Justice Values' (2017) 39(4) *Journal of Social and Family Law* 524.

[49] Carol Harlow and Richard Rawlings, *Law and Administration*, 3rd edn (Cambridge University Press, 2009) Ch 1; Michael Adler, *Administrative Justice in Context* (Hart Publishing, 2010); Richard Kirkham, 'Administrative Justice in Context: A Manifesto for Further Study' (2011) 74(4) *MLR* 617.

[50] Genevra Richardson and Hazel Genn, 'Tribunals in Transition: Resolution of Adjudication?' [2007] *PL* 116; Peter Cane, *Administrative Tribunals and Adjudication* (Hart Publishing, 2009); Robert Thomas and Joe Tomlinson, 'Mapping Current Issues in Administrative Justice: Austerity and the "More Bureaucratic Rationality" Approach' (2017) 39(3) *Journal of Social Welfare and Family Law* 380; Robert Thomas, 'Current Developments in UK Tribunals: Challenges for Administrative Justice' in Sarah Nason (ed), *Administrative Justice in Wales and Comparative Perspectives* (Cardiff University of Wales Press, 2017); Robert Thomas and Joe Tomlinson, 'A Different Tale of Judicial Power: Administrative Review as a Problematic Response to the Judicialisation of Tribunals' (forthcoming in *Public Law*).

[51] Mary Seneviratne, *Ombudsmen: Public Services and Administrative Justice* (Butterworths, 2002); Trevor Buck, Richard Kirkham and Brian Thompson, 'Putting the Ombudsman into Constitutional Context' (2009) 62(4) *Parliamentary Affairs* 600; Trevor Buck, Richard Kirkham and Brian Thompson, *The Ombudsman Enterprise and Administrative Justice* (Routledge, 2010); Richard Kirkham and Jane Martin, 'Designing an English Public Services Ombudsman' (2014) 36(3) *Journal of Social Welfare and Family Law* 330.

[52] Indeed, in terms of capacity to impact administrative practice, their study might be regarded by some as more important. For general discussion see Simon Halliday, *Judicial Review and Compliance with Administrative Law* (Hart Publishing, 2004); Marc Hertoghe and Simon Halliday, *Judicial Review and Bureaucratic Impact: International and Interdisciplinary Perspectives* (Cambridge University Press, 2004); Carol Harlow, 'Striking Back and Clamping Down: An Alternative Perspective on Judicial Review' in John Bell, Mark Elliott, Jason Varuhas and Philip Murray (eds), *Public Law Adjudication in Common Law Systems* (Hart Publishing, 2016).

[53] Nicholas Parillo, *Administrative Law from the Inside Out: Essays on Themes in the Work of Jerry L Mashaw* (Cambridge University Press, 2018).

[54] David Cowan et al, *The Appeal of Internal Review: Law, Administrative Justice & The Non-Emergence of Disputes* (Hart Publishing, 2003); Jerry Mashaw, 'Bureaucratic Justice: Managing Social Security Disability Claims' (Yale University Press, 2009); Bernardo Zacka, *When the State Meets the Street: Public Service and Moral Agency* (Harvard University Press, 2017).

[55] It has often been urged, for instance, that the 'number of cases [heard by the courts] is infinitesimal compared with the millions of decisions taken daily by public authorities' (Harlow and Rawlings (n 49) 537).

This book does not seek to challenge the legitimacy of these broader understandings of administrative law. Nor does it aim to cast doubt on the value of incorporating the study of tribunals, ombudsman and the internal workings of administration into scholarly research and teaching agendas.[56] To the contrary, the promotion of collective knowledge of these phenomenon is deeply important both for its own sake and because our understanding of the courts' role can be enriched by it.[57] Quite simply, however, this book seeks to develop understanding in a different direction. It has long been argued that classic approaches to administrative law miss important nuances by disregarding the activities and perspectives of bodies other than courts. This book makes a different argument. It draws attention to important nuances *within* the case law which are too often overlooked and makes a case for paying greater attention to them.

II. The Book's Three Main Aims

With this broad sketch of administrative law in mind, it is useful next to outline the three main aims of the book. In doing so, it is helpful to begin with a story which may at first sight seem unrelated but which neatly captures many of the book's overarching themes.

In 1981, Nobel prize-winning physicist Richard Feynman took part in a series of interviews with the BBC entitled 'The Pleasure of Finding Things Out'.[58] Over the course of one of these interviews Feynman offered a monologue which has since come to be known as his 'Ode to a Flower'. The following passage is taken from that monologue:

> I have a friend who's an artist and has sometimes taken a view which I don't agree with very well. He'll hold up a flower and say 'look how beautiful it is,' and I'll agree. Then he says 'I as an artist can see how beautiful this is but you as a scientist take this all apart and it becomes a dull thing,' and I think that he's kind of nutty. First of all, the beauty that he sees is available to other people and to me too … At the same time, I see much more about the flower than he sees. I could imagine the cells in there, the complicated actions inside, which also have a beauty. I mean it's not just beauty at this dimension, at one centimetre; there's also beauty in the smaller dimensions, the inner structure, also the processes. The fact that the colours in the flower evolved in order to attract insects to pollinate it is interesting; it means that insects can see colour. It adds a question: does this aesthetic sense also exist in lower forms? Why is it aesthetic? All kinds of interesting

[56] For a more cynical view, see Christopher Forsyth, 'Book Reviews' (1996) 55(3) *CLJ* 621 (reviewing Denis Galligan, *A Reader on Administrative Law* (Oxford University Press, 1996) and Lee Bridges, George Meszoras and Maurice Sunkin, *Judicial Review in Perspective*, 2nd edn (Cavendish Publishing, 1995).

[57] Sidney Shapiro and Elizabeth Fisher, '*Chevron* and the Legitimacy of "Expert" Public Administration' (2013) 22(2) *William and Mary Bill of Rights Journal* 465.

[58] Professor Richard Feynman, 'The Pleasure of Finding Things Out' (*BBC*, 1981–1982) available at: www.bbc.co.uk/programmes/p018dvyg.

questions which the science knowledge only adds to the excitement, the mystery and the awe of the flower. It only adds. I don't understand how it subtracts.

Two important points are worth noting about this monologue. The first is that, for Feynman, the key to understanding an object such as a flower is to recognise that it is made up of many small components and complex processes. In order to understand the flower fully, for Feynman therefore, it is important that it is 'taken apart' and its minutiae explored. The second is that this means that the flower cannot be neatly summed up in terms of a singular idea. Feynman is deeply cynical of his artist friend's suggestion that the only thing one needs to grasp about the flower is that it is beautiful.[59] It is both possible and important, for Feynman, to recognise that the flower is beautiful. This, however, ought not to be allowed to dominate understanding and to lead to other important truths about the flower being overlooked.

What has 'Ode to a Flower' to do with administrative law? As will be explained now, this story captures in a neat and striking way the major arguments of this book.

A. The 'Anatomy' of Administrative Law: Three Core Senses of Complexity and Variety

In order to explain the first main aim of the book, it is useful to return to the first important point about Feynman's monologue. For Feynman, in order to understand an object such as a flower it is necessary to take the object apart in order to examine both its 'inner structure'[60] and its processes. In the case of the flower, what this reveals is that the flower is made up of many intricate components which interact in complex ways. The first main aim of this book is to make a similar argument in the context of administrative law. If one engages in an exercise in 'pulling apart' case law dealing with administrative law issues, it becomes clear that the legal structures in play in adjudication are both complex and varied. The book calls attention to three more particular senses in which this is so.

First, legislative detail matters enormously in administrative law adjudication.[61] In England and Wales the vast majority of systems of administrative decision-making are constituted by a statutory framework.[62] These frameworks are often

[59] Feynman's artist friend's reaction to the flower is reminiscent of the suggestion by 20th century American modernist Georgia O'Keeffe that 'details are confusing … [and that] it is only by selection, by elimination, by emphasis that we get to the real meaning of things'. (See Jonathan Stuhlman and Barbara Buhler Lynes, *Georgia O'Keeffe: Circling Around Abstraction* (Hudson Hill Press, 2007) 22.)

[60] Feynman (n 58).

[61] This is not to suggest that legislative detail matters less in other fields of law. See discussion below.

[62] There continue to be examples of unusual systems of public administration which are not constituted by a primary Act of Parliament, because they have been introduced through prerogative or common law powers. See, eg: *R v Criminal Injuries Compensation Board, ex parte A* [1999] 2 AC 330 (HL); *Page* (n 16) and discussion in section IV below.

dense and detailed, being constituted by many layers of law[63] and, perhaps increasingly, soft law.[64] The administrative frameworks which legislation creates, furthermore, are not of one kind. Partly because of the Government's role as initiator of the majority of legislation,[65] statutes are passed in order to create administrative schemes which perform different kinds of task and pursue a variety of aims. The details of these administrative frameworks should not be lightly glossed over. They play an extremely important role in administrative law adjudication in shaping[66] how grounds of review apply to a given sets of facts.[67]

Second, administrative law pursues a variety of different normative goals.[68] Despite repeated attempts to identify an overarching 'meta-value'[69] towards which the field oriented, when the courts adjudicate on administrative law matters they seek to accommodate and protect an array of different values, policies and interests.[70] There are, furthermore, at least two more specific senses in which this is true. First, the *legal origins* of administrative law's values are varied;[71] administrative law is neither concerned exclusively with protecting values regarded as embedded in the common law[72] nor with uncovering and promoting the policy goals underlying statutes.[73] The courts when adjudicating seek to accommodate both. Second, the *beneficiaries* of administrative law are also varied. Administrative law is neither primarily 'public-regarding'[74] nor 'individual-regarding'.[75] The courts, rather, are

[63] Including both primary Acts of Parliament and, often, secondary legislation, especially in the form of Regulations. For discussion, see chapters two and three.

[64] Greg Weeks, *Soft Law and Public Authorities* (Hart Publishing, 2016).

[65] Adam Tomkins, 'What is Parliament For?' in Nicholas Bamforth and Peter Leyland (eds), *Public Law in a Multi-Layered Constitution* (Hart Publishing, 2003).

[66] To borrow a term from Paul Daly, the grounds of review are not 'self-applying' (Paul Daly, 'The Language of Administrative Law' (2016) 94 *Canadian Bar Review* 519, 522). See further, Trevor Allan, 'The Constitutional Foundations of Judicial Review: Conceptual Conundrum or Interpretative Inquiry?' (2002) 61(1) *CLJ* 87.

[67] See chapters four, five and six.

[68] Peter Cane, 'Theory and Values in Public Law' in Paul Craig and Richard Rawlings (eds), *Law and Administration in Europe: Essays in Honour of Carol Harlow* (Oxford University Press, 2003), especially at 10; Sarah Nason, *Reconstructing Judicial Review* (Hart Publishing, 2017) 15; Paul Craig, 'Taxonomy and Public Law: A Response' [2019] *PL* 281.

[69] Joe Tomlinson, 'The Narrow Approach to Substantive Legitimate Expectations and the Trend of Modern Authority' (2017) 17(1) *Oxford University Commonwealth Law Journal* 75, 81 (citing Paul Daly, 'A Pluralist Account of Deference and Legitimate Expectations' in Matthew Groves and Greg Weeks (eds), *Legitimate Expectations in the Common Law World* (Hart Publishing, 2017)).

[70] Paul Daly, 'Administrative Law: A Values-Based Approach' in Bell, Elliott, Varuhas and Murray (eds) (n 52); Paul Daly, 'Administrative Law: Characteristics, Legitimacy, Unity' in Mark Elliott, Jason Varuhas and Shona Wilson Stark, *The Unity of Public Law?* (Hart Publishing, 2018).

[71] Thomas Adams, 'Ultra Vires Revisited' [2018] *PL* 31.

[72] Oliver (n 6); Oliver (n 4).

[73] A binary reflected, for instance, in the famous comparison drawn in Harlow and Rawlings (n 49) Ch 1, between 'red light' and 'green light' theory. For critique of this binary and related work, see Cane (n 68) and Elizabeth Fisher, 'Law and Energy Transitions: Wind Turbines and Planning Law in the UK' (2018) 38(3) *OJLS* 528.

[74] Jason Varuhas, 'The Public Interest Conception of Public Law: Its Procedural Origins and Substantive Implications' in Bell, Elliott, Varuhas and Murray (eds) (n 52) 52.

[75] *Ibid.*

concerned in adjudication to protect and promote the interests of both the public and the individual.[76]

Third and finally, applicants sit in different kinds of relationship with the administrative decision-makers they seek to challenge. There has been an influential way of thinking[77] according to which the 'shape' of an administrative law case is fundamentally different from that of legal challenges in other fields such as human rights law[78] or strands[79] of private law.[80] According to this view, claimants in human rights law and private law go before courts in order to assert legal rights which *they personally hold* against the defendant.[81] Administrative law challenges, by contrast, are said to be characterised differently. Thus, it has sometimes been said that applicants in administrative law seek to enforce legal duties which administrative decision-makers owe, not to them personally, but to the *public at large* or a cross-section of it.[82] This book argues, however, that this purported distinction is overly simplistic. Applicants in administrative law challenges bear different sorts of relationship with decision-makers. Some challenges can properly be characterised as cases which involve a duty owed to the public as a collectivity.[83] Not every case, however, fits this pattern. Indeed in many instances, administrative law challenges can look much more like the private law or human rights law case paradigm of an individual asserting a personal legal right against a defendant.[84]

The first main aim of this book, then, is to suggest that administrative law adjudication in this field is inherently legally complex in at least three core senses. Another way of expressing this aim is through the image of 'anatomy'. Merriam-Webster defines 'anatomy' as the 'art of separating the parts of an organism in order to ascertain their position, relations, structure and function'.[85] This captures neatly the exercise. What the book shows is that if we pull administrative

[76] See further, Cane (n 68); Joanna Bell, 'Judicial Review of Executive Action & Common Law Constitutional Rights' in Mark Elliott and Kirsty Hughes, *Common Law Constitutional Rights* (forthcoming in Hart Publishing).

[77] See chapters three and seven.

[78] Jason Varuhas, 'Against Unification' in Wilberg and Elliott (eds) (n 11).

[79] Jason Varuhas, for instance, draws a distinction between 'vindicatory' and 'compensatory' torts which is important to his overall conception of the relationship between administrative law, human rights law and private law: Jason Varuhas, *Damages and Human Rights* (Hart Publishing, 2016) Ch 2.

[80] Lord Woolf, 'Public Law – Private Law: Why the Divide? A Personal View' [1986] *PL* 220; Nicholas Bamforth, 'Hohfeldian Rights and Public Law' in Matthew Kramer (ed), *Rights Wrongs & Responsibilities* (Palgrave, 2001).

[81] The book does not address the question of whether this provides too simplistic an account of private law and human rights law. There is, however, reason to believe that it does. See for instance *Coventry v Lawrence* [2015] UKSC 50, [2015] 1 WLR 3485; Joanna Miles, 'Standing under the Human Rights Act 1998' (2000) 59(1) *CLJ* 133; Joanna Miles, 'Standing in a Multi-Layered Constitution' in Bamforth and Leyland (n 65); Craig (n 68).

[82] See citations at (n 80).

[83] A considerable amount of environmental protection legislation maps onto this description. See for instance the discussion of the Countryside and Rights of Way Act 2000 in chapter three.

[84] See discussion of *R (Conville) v Richmond-upon-Thames LBC* [2006] EWCA Civ 718, [2006] 1 WLR 2808 in chapter three.

[85] www.merriam-webster.com/dictionary/anatomy.

law apart and examine the basic legal structures which are in play in adjudication, what we will see is that those legal structures are both complex and varied in at least three core senses.

B. Administrative Law's Complex and Varied Anatomy in Context: Three Case Studies

The first main aim of this book is important and valuable in itself. As Jason Varuhas has observed,[86] although there are aspects of the administrative law, such as the law on substantive review,[87] which have received a great amount of scholarly attention in recent years,[88] there has been comparatively little written on administrative law at a more 'architectural'[89] level, at least outside of the long-standing 'ultra vires debate'.[90] This, very fortunately, is beginning to change with excellent and thought-provoking contributions having been published in recent years by, for example, Varuhas himself,[91] Sarah Nason,[92] Dean Knight,[93] Paul Daly[94] and

[86] Jason Varuhas, 'Taxonomy and Public Law' in Elliott, Varuhas and Wilson Stark (eds) (n 70).

[87] Wilberg and Elliott (n 11). In addition see: Lord Irvine, 'Judges & Decision-Makers: The Theory & Practice of *Wednesbury* Review' [1996] *PL* 59; John Laws, '*Wednesbury*' in Christopher Forsyth and Ivan Hare (eds), *The Golden Metwand and the Crooked Cork* (Oxford University Press, 1998); Murray Hunt, 'Sovereignty's Blight: Why Public Law Needs a Concept of Due Deference' in Bamforth and Leyland (eds) (n 65); Trevor Allan, 'Human Rights and Judicial Review: A Critique of "Due Deference"' (2006) *CLJ* 671; Julian Rivers, 'Proportionality & Variable Intensity Review' [2006] *CLJ* 174; Paul Daly, *A Theory of Deference in Administrative Law: Basis, Application and Scope* (Cambridge University Press, 2012); Murray Hunt, 'Against Bifurcation' in David Dyzenhaus, Murray Hunt and Grant Huscroft (eds), *A Simple Common Lawyer: Essays in Honour of Michael Taggart* (Oxford University Press, 2009); David Mead, 'Outcomes Aren't All: Defending a Process-Based Review of Public Authority Decisions Under the HRA' [2012] *PL* 61.

[88] By contrast, other administrative law doctrines, such as review for purpose and relevancy, have received relatively little academic attention.

[89] To borrow an image used in a number of places in the literature. See for instance: Kenneth Culp Davis, 'The Future of Judge-Made Public Law in England: A Problem of Practical Jurisprudence' (1961) *Columbia Law Review* 201, 220; Andrew Halpin, 'Review Article: The Theoretical Controversy Concerning Judicial Review' (2001) 64(3) *MLR* 500, 509; Mark Aronson, 'The Growth of Substantive Review: The Changes, Their Causes and Their Consequences' in Bell, Elliott, Varuhas and Murray (eds) (n 52) 114.

[90] At least outside of the context of the long-standing 'ultra vires' debate. See: Dawn Oliver, 'Is Ultra Vires the Basis of Common Law Judicial Review?' [1987] *PL* 543; Christopher Forsyth, 'Of Fig Leaves and Fairy Tales: The Ultra Vires Doctrine, The Sovereignty of Parliament and Judicial Review' (1996) 55(1) *CLJ* 12; Mark Elliott, 'The Ultra Vires Doctrine in a Constitutional Setting: Still the Central Principle of Administrative Law' (1999) 58(1) *CLJ* 129; Paul Craig, 'Competing Models of Judicial Review' [1999] *PL* 428; Mark Elliott, *The Constitutional Foundations of Judicial Review* (Bloomsbury, 2001); Paul Craig and Nicholas Bamforth, 'Constitutional Analysis, Constitutional Principle & Common Law Judicial Review' [2001] *PL* 763; Trevor Allan, 'The Constitutional Foundations of Judicial Review: Conceptual Conundrum or Interpretative Inquiry?' (2002) *CLJ* 87; Adams (n 71).

[91] See Varuhas (n 74), Varuhas (n 78) and Varuhas (n 86).

[92] Nason (n 68).

[93] Knight (n 5).

[94] Daly, 'Administrative Law: A Values-Based Approach' (n 70); Daly 'Administrative Law: Characteristics' (n 70).

Janina Boughey.[95] The point remains, however, that the broader picture is relatively under-explored.[96]

The first aim of the book focuses on advancing understanding in this direction. By exploring the complex and varied anatomy of administrative law, one hope is to develop a further understanding of the nature of administrative law adjudication in a general sense. The second aim of the book, by contrast, is to demonstrate the importance of these arguments at a lower, more focused, level. An understanding of the complex and varied anatomy of administrative law is valuable not only because it furthers understanding of administrative law *as a whole*. It also sheds useful light on a series of *specific aspects* of administrative law. Chapters four, five and six of the book use three case studies by which to demonstrate this. Chapter four is concerned with procedural review, chapter five with legitimate expectations and chapter six with standing.

The arguments of chapters four, five and six are detailed and difficult to summarise succinctly here. It is therefore useful to discuss one example by way of illustration. The example chosen is procedural review, the subject of chapter four. It will be seen in chapter four that, following the erosion of the idea that procedural review focuses on controlling exercises of judicial (as opposed to administrative power) in the 1960s, many attempts have been made to identify a 'master idea or principle'[97] capable of making sense of procedural review. Many of the accounts which have emerged, however, have suffered from difficulties. According to the dominant way of thinking since the landmark decision in *Ridge v Baldwin*[98] the purpose of procedural review is to ensure that decision-making power is exercised fairly. This understanding, however, is not without its difficulties.[99] Most importantly, it paints a picture of procedural review whereby courts form what is 'essentially an intuitive judgment'[100] as to what is 'fair' in a given context. Attempts, however, to develop a 'thicker' account of procedural review, such as by isolating a singular normative goal review towards which it is orientated,[101] or by pinpointing an 'irreducible core'[102] of process rights which are protected in all instances, have not been consistently borne out in the case law.

All of this gives rise to at least two important questions. First, why it is proving so difficult to develop an overarching account of procedural review? Second, do

[95] Janina Boughey, *Human Rights and Judicial Review: The Newest Despotism?* (Hart Publishing, 2017).

[96] As Kenneth Culp Davis put it, English and Welsh administrative law tends to focus on the 'tasks of bricklayers' at the expense of 'architecture' (Davis (n 89) 201).

[97] Stephen Smith, *Contract Theory* (Oxford University Press, 2004) 11.

[98] Ridge (n 26); *Re HK* (n 24).

[99] See especially discussion by Beatson LJ in *R (L) v West London Mental Health NHS Trust* [2014] EWCA Civ 47, [2014] 1 WLR 3103.

[100] *R (Forest Heath DC) v Electoral Commission Boundary Committee* [2009] EWCA Civ 1296 at [39].

[101] See, eg, Denis Galligan, *Due Process and Fair Procedures* (Oxford University Press, 1997); Trevor Allan, 'Procedural Fairness and the Duty of Respect' (1998) 18(3) *OJLS* 497.

[102] See especially *R v Secretary of State for the Home Department, ex parte AF* [2009] UKHL 28, [2010] 2 AC 269.

these difficulties lead inevitably to the conclusion that procedural review is little more than an inherently discretionary exercise in determining what 'feels'[103] fair in a given context?

The core argument of chapter four is that the complex and varied anatomy of administrative law helps to shed light on these issues. In the case of the first issue, recognising the complexity and variety of the legal structures in play in adjudication helps to explain why an overarching account of procedural review is proving elusive. The three core senses of complexity and variety to which the earlier chapters draw attention are in play in the procedural review context as much as they are across administrative law adjudication more broadly. Each in turn supplies a reason why procedural review is not easily explained by reference to an overarching 'master idea or principle'.[104]

The complex and varied anatomy of administrative law also illuminates the second issue of whether it is right to think of procedural review as involving an 'intuitive judgment'[105] in deciding what is fair. A close reading of the recent case law on procedural review, with the various sense of administrative law's complexity in mind, suggests that judicial reasoning is characterised by greatly more legal structure than this account suggests. That legal structure takes at least two main forms. First, many procedural review challenges now arise against the background of a detailed legislative or policy-based procedural code. The questions which arise in adjudication are therefore often relatively narrow questions of construction which the courts deal with primarily by navigating the code in order to understand its aims. This, however, is not to downplay the importance of the common law in procedural review. Common law continues to play an important role in supplementing legislative and policy codes. The second source of legal structure in procedural review is a series of established patterns in how the common law performs this role.

C. Questioning Monism

The first and second aims of this book are positive in nature. They seek to add something to our understanding, first, by calling attention to the variety of legal structures in play in administrative law adjudication and, second, by demonstrating how recognition of this complexity illuminates specific doctrinal issues. The third aim of the book, by contrast, is negative in nature. Its focus is on casting doubt on the utility of an explanatory exercise which is often undertaken in the administrative law literature. This exercise can be termed 'monism'.

[103] To borrow an idea, from a different context, see Core Hoexter, 'A Matter of Feel? Public Powers and Functions in South Africa' in Elliott, Varuhas and Wilson Stark (eds) (n 70).
[104] Smith (n 97) 11.
[105] *Forest Heath* (n 100) at [39].

In order to explain this aim, it is useful to begin by returning to Feynman's 'Ode to a Flower'. As explained above, in this monologue Feynman takes significant issue with his artist friend's suggestion that, in order to understand the flower, it is sufficient to grasp only the single most important thing about it: that it is beautiful. Feynman's problem with this way of thinking is not that he thinks his friend is wrong to say that the flower is beautiful. It is, rather, that emphasising only the flower's beauty offers only a partial account of the flower and obscures many details which are essential to a thorough understanding.

The approach of Feynman's artist friend in understanding the flower has its analogues in the administrative law literature. This commentary is replete with examples of the search for a singular overarching 'organising concept'[106] capable of explaining doctrines within this field. Among the most influential,[107] for instance, is the idea that administrative law aims to keep administrative decision-makers within the boundaries of their 'jurisdiction',[108] and that in administrative law adjudication the courts aim to promote the public, as opposed to individual, interest.[109]

The third aim of this book is to raise the question of whether this approach to understanding administrative law is plausible or useful. The overarching message, ultimately, is one of cynicism. It is important to be clear in what sense this book aims to cast doubt on monism. As emphasised above, Feynman's problem with his artist friend's account of the flower is not that he believes him to be *wrong* in observing that the flower is beautiful. In a similar way, this book does not seek to argue that the monistic accounts of administrative law discussed throughout are fundamentally *incorrect*. On the contrary, many usefully call attention to a significant theme which characterises administrative law adjudication or has characterised its development.[110] The book's aim, rather, is to suggest that monistic accounts of administrative law doctrine are likely to be partial only. By reducing administrative law to a singular, unifying principle or idea, such accounts fail to equip us with the full set of intellectual tools which are needed to understand administrative law adjudication.

To briefly summarise, this section has introduced the three main aims of the book. The first aim is to explore the 'anatomy' of administrative law by pulling apart the case law in order to explore the legal structures which are in play. When this is done, the book argues, it becomes clear that administrative law adjudication is complex and varied in at least three core senses. The second aim of the book is to argue that recognition of this complexity and variety is important not only

[106] Christopher Forsyth, 'The Rock and the Sand: Jurisdiction and Remedial Discretion' (2013) 18(4) *Judicial Review* 360 [27].

[107] See discussion in chapter seven.

[108] Forsyth (n 106); Philip Murray, 'Judicial Review of the Upper Tribunal: Appeal, Review and the Will of Parliament' (2011) 70(3) *CLJ* 487; Philip Murray, 'Process, Substance and the History of Error of Law Review' in Bell, Elliott, Varuhas and Murray (eds) (n 52).

[109] Varuhas (n 74).

[110] See discussion in chapter seven.

for its own sake but because it sheds considerable light on particular doctrinal issues, including in the context of procedural review, legitimate expectations and standing. Finally, the third aim of the book is to draw out an important, negative implication of these positive arguments: the complex and varied anatomy of administrative law gives us reason to question the plausibility of isolating a singular 'organising principle'[111] capable of lending unity to administrative law.

III. The Trajectory of Argument: An Overview of the Book's Chapters

With this overview of the book's three main aims in mind, it is helpful next to offer a more detailed outline of the content of each chapter. Most of those chapters can be broadly divided into three clusters, each corresponding to one of the book's core aims. Chapters two and three concern the complex and varied anatomy of administrative law in a general sense. Chapters four, five and six discuss specific case studies which illustrate the importance of embracing this complexity and variety. Chapter seven focuses on the plausibility and utility of monistic analysis in making sense of administrative law.

Chapter two begins with an outline of the evolution of administrative law in England and Wales, taking the publication of Albert Venn Dicey's *Lectures Introductory to the Study of the Law of the Constitution*[112] in 1885 as its starting point. One purpose in outlining this recent history is scene-setting; it is useful to provide the reader, especially the reader less familiar with English and Welsh administrative law and its evolution, with an introductory account of the subject. More fundamentally, however, the historical analysis in this chapter is closely connected to the arguments of the book. Thus, in the course of exploring administrative law's evolution, chapter two will draw out two main lessons. The first is that administrative law's modern history is multifaceted and messy. There is therefore considerable reason to regard with cynicism attempts to present the subject as having grown up around, or having been deliberately created to comply with, a singular 'organising concept'.[113] The second lesson of chapter two is that an exploration of administrative law's modern history tends to bring to the surface a number of important senses in which the legal structures which are in play in adjudication are both complex and varied. The historical analysis in chapter two, in other words, offers a first glimpse of the administrative law's 'anatomy.'

Chapter three is concerned directly with administrative law's complex and varied 'anatomy'. This chapter 'pulls administrative law apart' in order to examine

[111] Christopher Forsyth, 'Blasphemy against Basics: Doctrine, Conceptual Reasoning and Certain Decisions of the UK Supreme Court' in Bell, Elliott, Varuhas and Murray (eds) (n 52) 155.
[112] Albert Venn Dicey (edited by John Allison), *The Law of the Constitution (Oxford Edition of Dicey)* (Oxford University Press, 2013).
[113] Forsyth (n 106) [27].

the legal structures which are in play in adjudication. The bulk of discussion will be divided into three main parts, each of which elaborates on one of the core senses in which the book argues administrative law is an inherently legally complex field. Section I discusses the importance of legislative detail in legal adjudication. Section II explores the array of legal values, policies and interests the courts seek to accommodate when adjudicating on administrative law issues. Section III, finally, discusses the variety legal relationships which can subsist between applicant and administrative decision-maker.

In chapters four, five and six the book changes focus from thinking generally about the nature of administrative law to discussing specific doctrinal issues. Each uses a doctrinal case study through which to illustrate the importance of the book's broader themes.

Chapter four is concerned with procedural review. This chapter has already been discussed in some depth above. For present purposes it therefore suffices to note that the bulk of discussion in this chapter is divided into four main parts. Section I explains what is meant by 'procedural review'. Section II explores the evolution of procedural review since the landmark decision in *Ridge*,[114] highlighting some of the most astute difficulties scholars have faced in developing an overarching account of the ground. Sections III and IV then discuss the considerable light which recognition of administrative law's complex and varied anatomy can shed on two issues. Section III explores why it is proving so difficult to provide a unified account of procedural review. Its central argument is that the three core senses of complexity and variety to which the book calls attention are in play in the procedural review context as much as they are across administrative law adjudication more broadly. Each provides a reason why procedural review cannot be easily explained by reference to a singular 'organising principle'.[115] Section IV addresses the question of whether procedural review is best understood as involving an 'intuitive judgment'[116] as to what fairness requires in a particular case. It argues that a close reading of the recent procedural review case law, keeping in mind the three core senses in which administrative law is complex and varied, reveals judicial reasoning to be characterised by more legal structure than this way of thinking suggests. This structure takes the form of both particularised procedural codes created by legislation and policy and a series of established patterns in the way the common law supplements these codes.

Chapter five focuses on the book's second case study: legitimate expectations. The chapter has four main parts. Section I explains what is meant by a 'legitimate expectations' case and section II offers a broad outline of the development of the law and literature on legitimate expectations. Post-*Coughlan*,[117] many attempts have been made to develop a general account of legitimate expectations. This task

[114] *Ridge* (n 26).
[115] Forsyth (n 111) 155.
[116] *Forest Heath* (n 100) [39].
[117] *Coughlan* (n 29).

has, however, proven challenging. One difficulty has been that the early case law and literature tended to rely on highly abstract concepts which were incapable of providing meaningful guidance on a case-by-case basis as to when the courts would intervene. 'Thicker' accounts have not, however, been consistently borne out in case law. These difficulties have led to many having a cynical view of the ground. According to this view, legitimate expectation lacks predictability, coherence and insufficiently constrains judges.[118]

These developments lead to at least two important questions. First, why has it proven so difficult to develop a general account of the law on legitimate expectations?[119] Second, do these difficulties indicate that the case law on legitimate expectations lacks predictability, coherence and judicial restraint? Sections III and IV argue that embracing the complex and varied anatomy of administrative law helps to shed light on these questions.

Section IV argues that, much like procedural review, the legitimate expectations case law is characterised by the same three core senses of complexity and variety discussed in chapter three. Each suggests a reason why the legitimate expectations case law is not easily explained in general, overarching terms. Section IV then turns to the question of whether it is correct to assume that, in the absence of an overarching theory, the law therefore lacks structure, predictability and restraint. A close reading of recent legitimate expectations case law, with the complex and varied anatomy of administrative law specifically in mind, suggests that there is a good deal more predictability, coherence and judicial restraint than has sometimes been imagined. Section IV, in particular, will suggest that there are four broad kinds of scenario in play in the legitimate expectations case law and that clear, discernible patterns can be observed in how the courts conduct review in each of them.

The final case study, considered in chapter six, is standing. The bulk of the discussion in this chapter is divided into three main parts. Section I overviews the development of standing in English and and Welsh administrative law.[120] Its core argument is that standing's evolution has been beset by a tension. On the one hand, judges and scholars have sometimes offered general propositions concerning how the courts resolve issues of standing. For instance it is common to read that the courts used the opportunity presented by the procedural reforms of the late 1970s[121] to introduce an increasingly 'liberal'[122] approach to standing, which

[118] Swati Jhaveri, 'The Doctrine of Substantive Legitimate Expectations: The Significance of *ChiuTeng@ Kallang Pte Ltd v Singapore Land Authority*' [2016] *PL* 1; Cameron Stewart, 'The Doctrine of Substantive Unfairness and the Review of Substantive Legitimate Expectations' in Matthew Groves and HP Lee (eds), *Australian Administrative Law* (Cambridge University Press, 2007).

[119] Mark Elliott, 'From Heresy to Orthodoxy: Substantive Legitimate Expectations in the United Kingdom' in Groves and Weeks (n 69).

[120] Elliott and Varuhas (n 1) Ch 14.

[121] Rules of the Supreme Court (Amendment No 3) 1977 (SI 1977/1955).

[122] See, eg, John McGarry, 'The Importance of an Expansive Test of Standing' (2014) 19(1) *Judicial Review* 60.

is fundamentally different in nature from the essentially 'rights-based standing rules'[123] of private law[124] and human rights law.[125] On the other hand, the case law continues to resist explanation in these terms. The leading case law continues to emphasise that what counts as a sufficient interest varies according to context.

As in previous chapters, the development of thinking on standing gives rise to at least two important questions. First, why has a singular approach to standing not emerged? Second, if the courts are not guided by a uniform and clear conception of standing, how do they determine whether an individual has a 'sufficient interest'[126] to bring a challenge? Chapter six argues that significant light is shed on these questions by the complex and varied anatomy of administrative law. Section II argues that, as in other contexts, the three senses of complexity and variety inherent in administrative law adjudication are in play in the standing case law and that each explains why a singular 'test' of standing has not emerged. Section III then begins to address the question of how the courts determine whether an applicant has standing, if not by reference to a singular overarching approach. For a number of reasons, this is a very difficult question to address in categorical terms. Section III however draws attention to three overlooked aspects of the case law. Taken collectively, these three aspects of the judicial approach can be encapsulated in the idea that standing, in England and Wales, is 'ground-dependent' in nature.

Having demonstrated the importance of recognising the complexity and variety of administrative law's anatomy in a series of specific doctrinal contexts, chapter seven turns to a final issue: the plausibility and utility of 'monism'. As explained above, whereas the first and second main aims of this book advance positive arguments, the book's third aim is negative in nature. The goal is to raise the question of whether it continues to be plausible or useful to try to explain administrative doctrine by reference to an overarching 'organising concept'.[127] The overarching message is one of cynicism.

Chapter seven casts doubt on the plausibility of monism in two ways. Section I discusses a series of influential attempts to explain administrative law at a general level by reference to a singular 'organising concept'.[128] Two will be discussed in detail: 'the public interest conception'[129] and jurisdiction theory.[130] Section I draws attention to a series of deficiencies in these accounts of administrative law. It argues that, while both capture important truths about administrative law adjudication, they offer ways of thinking which are partial only.

Section II then turns to the appeals of monism. In order to cast doubt on the utility of monistic analysis, it is not enough to merely point out that the main

[123] Varuhas (n 11).
[124] *Brushmoor UK Ltd v BP Raffinaderij Rotterdam BV*, 24 February 2014 (QB) (unreported).
[125] Human Rights Act 1998, s7; Miles 'Standing under the Human Rights Act' (n 81).
[126] Senior Courts Act 1981, s31(3).
[127] Forsyth (n 106) [27].
[128] Forsyth (n 106) [27].
[129] Varuhas (n 74).
[130] See citations at n 108.

monistic accounts of administrative law which have been developed are deficient. It is necessary also to explore the extent to which there are good reasons for trying to understand the field by reference to an overarching 'master idea'.[131] That is the task of section II. This section introduces four considerations which help to explain why scholars have often been drawn to the idea that administrative law should be understood by reference to an 'organising concept'.[132] Introduced briefly, they are:

a) the kernel of truth which lies at the centre of many of the major monistic approaches to administrative law;
b) the tendency to equate three notions: the ideas of intelligibility, coherence and unity;[133]
c) the assumption that locating an 'organising principle'[134] which grounds administrative law is the most effective way to ensure that judges are properly constrained; and
d) the long-standing sense in which administrative law has suffered from an 'identity crisis'.[135]

The core argument of section II is that while these considerations provide superficially appealing arguments for explaining administrative law in monistic terms, the force of these arguments weakens under closer consideration.

The final chapter of the book, chapter eight, then offers the book's conclusions. The discussion in this chapter is divided into three parts. The first briefly outlines the territory covered in earlier chapters. The second draws out some practical, future implications of the book's arguments for administrative law and its study. The third offers some closing reflections.

IV. Scope

Before moving on from introductory matters, it is important to add four important clarifications concerning the book's scope. The first concerns its jurisdictional focus. This book is focused on administrative law doctrine as it has been developed, and is applied, in the English and Welsh legal system.[136] The book,

[131] Smith (n 97), 11.
[132] Forsyth (n 106) [27].
[133] Ernest Weinrib, *The Idea of Private Law* (Oxford University Press, 1995).
[134] Forsyth (n 111) 155.
[135] Something which is often said of the study of public administration but which applies to the study of administrative law also. See for instance Kent Aiken Kirawan, 'The Crisis of Identity in the Study of Public Administration' (1977) 9(3) *Polity* 321; Gerald Frug, 'The Ideology of Bureaucracy in American Law' (1983) 97 *Harvard Law Review* 1276; Jos CN Raadschelders, *Public Administration: The Interdisciplinary Study of Government* (Oxford University Press, 2011) Ch 1.
[136] For discussion of administrative law in Wales, see specifically Sarah Nason (ed), *Administrtaive Justice in Wales and Comparative Perspectives* (University of Wales Press, 2017).

that is, is singular in its choice of jurisdiction, is not comparative in nature and is certainly not an exercise in exploring the possibility of global administrative law.[137]

With that said, it is hoped that the book and its arguments will be of interest to administrative law scholars and practitioners within other common law jurisdictions. The book's suggestion that, in the English and Welsh legal system, administrative law's basic legal and normative components are inherently complex and that, as a result, the subject cannot be plausibly reduced to a singular 'organising concept'[138] raises interesting and important questions about whether the same thing is true in other jurisdictions. Is monistic analysis, for instance, of greater utility in jurisdictions which have codified the grounds of review,[139] which have written constitutions[140] or in which formalism is more deeply embedded into the legal culture than it is in England and Wales?[141] Is the complexity and variety of basic legal and normative components of administrative law reflected in the experience of all common law systems? Are there important differences in terms of the specific causes and symptoms? Questions such as these unfortunately fall beyond its immediate scope. One hope in writing this book, however, has been to prompt consideration of them.

The second important issue concerns the extent to which this book contributes to the extensive literature concerning the relationship between administrative law and human rights law.[142] This book deals explicitly with only the administrative law side of this relationship, and contains no detailed consideration of human rights law. It is, however, likely that the arguments in this book have important implications for the proper way of understanding the relationship between the two. An example will suffice to illustrate. Chapter three will explain how some commentators[143] have sought to erect a clear boundary between the two fields of law, based on the idea that while administrative law is inherently 'public-regarding',[144] human rights law is inherently 'individual-regarding'.[145]

[137] See Craig (n 38) Chs 5 and 6.

[138] Forsyth (n 106) [27].

[139] Administrative Procedure Act 1946 (US), s10(e).

[140] Boughey (n 95) Chs 2 and 3.

[141] Michael Taggart, '"Australian Exceptionalism" in Judicial Review' (2008) 36(1) *Federal Law Review* 1; Thomas Poole, 'Between the Devil and the Deep Blue Sea: Administrative Law in an Age of Rights' in Linda Pearson, Carol Harlow and Michael Taggart (eds), *Administrative Law in a Changing State (Essays in Honour of Mark Aronson)* (Hart Publishing, 2008); Janina Boughey, 'Reconsidering *R (Cart) v Upper Tribunal* and the Rationale for Jurisdictional Error' [2017] *PL* 592; Knight (n 5) Ch 2.

[142] Michael Taggart, 'Reinventing Administrative Law' in Bamforth and Leyland (eds) (n 65); David Dyzenhaus (ed), *The Unity of Public Law* (Hart Publishing, 2004); Hunt, 'Against Bifurcation' (n 87); Thomas Poole, 'The Reformation of English Administrative Law' (2009) 68(1) *CLJ* 142; Thomas Poole and Sangeeta Shah, 'The Law Lords and Human Rights' (2011) 74(1) *MLR* 79; Varuhas (n 78); Varuhas (n 86); Beverly McLachlin, 'The Role of the Supreme Court of Canada in Shaping the Common Law' and Jason Varuhas, 'Administrative Law and Rights in the UK House of Lords and Supreme Court' both in Paul Daly (ed), *Apex Courts and the Common Law* (University of Toronto Press, 2019).

[143] Thereby 'bifurcating' the law: Hunt, 'Against Bifurcation' (n 87).

[144] Varuhas (n 74) 52.

[145] Varuhas (n 74) 52.

Certain practical implications have been said to follow from this distinction, including that the proportionality doctrine is properly confined to human rights adjudication only.[146] The argument will not be fully developed here, but one important implication of this book is that at least one side of this picture presents an overly simplistic view of the law. Administrative law, at least, cannot be said to be concerned purely with either the interests of the public or the individual. It appears a difficult argument, therefore, to say that there can be no space in administrative law for the proportionality doctrine because it is a field concerned with protecting the public as opposed to the individual.

The third and final matter concerns the extent to which this book is about the so-called 'public/private divide'.[147] Again, this book is focused explicitly on only one side of this relationship and does not offer a detailed analysis of private law doctrine. The book, furthermore, does not engage in discussion of a series of important issues – such as the liability of public authorities in tort[148] and contract,[149] the scope of application of the grounds of review,[150] the doctrine of 'procedural exclusivity'[151] and the legacy of the 'new management' movement[152] on public administration – which a reader might reasonably expect from a comprehensive discussion of the public-private divide. Again, however, the book has a series of important implications for our understanding of the relationship between public and private law.

One important message of the book is that, in a similar way to the relationship between administrative law and human rights law, it is not possible to draw a neat divide between administrative law and private law[153] on the basis that while the latter is concerned with the relationship between individuals, the former is concerned with the interests of the public.[154] Such a view, it will be seen, proceeds

[146] Varuhas (n 78).

[147] Harlow (n 1).

[148] On negligence see for instance: *X v Bedfordshire County Council* [1995] 2 AC 633 (HL); *Gorringe v Calderdale Metropolitan Borough Council* [2004] UKHL 15, [2004] 1 WLR 1057; *Mitchell v Glasgow City Council* [2009] UKHL 11, [2009] AC 874; *Robinson v Chief Constable of West Yorkshire* [2018] UKSC 4, [2018] AC 736; *Michael v Chief Constable of South Wales Police* [2015] UKSC 2, [2015] AC 1732. See Donal Nolan, 'The Duty of Care After *Robinson v Chief Constable of West Yorkshire Police*' (2017–2018) 9 *UK Supreme Court Yearbook* 174; Jonathan Morgan, 'Nonfeasance and the End of Policy? Reflections on the Revolution in Public Authority Liability' (2019) 35(1) *Professional Negligence* 32.

[149] See especially *Ayr Harbour Trustees v Oswald* (1883) 8 App Cas 623; *Birkdale District Electic Supply Co Ltd v Southport Corporation* [1926] AC 355 (HL).

[150] See citations at n 4.

[151] *O'Reilly* (n 33); Wade (n 33).

[152] Gavin Drewry, 'The Executive: Towards Accountable Government and Effective Governance?' in Jeffrey Jowell and Dawn Oliver (eds), *The Changing Constitution*, 7th edn (Oxford University Press, 2011).

[153] Or at least parts of it. Varuhas, for instance, differentiates between vindicatory and compensatory torts: Varuhas (n 79).

[154] Bamforth (n 80); Woolf (n 80). See further discussion in chapter three.

from too simplistic an understanding of the normative groundings of, at least, administrative law.

Another important implication of the book for the relationship between public law and private law is more buried but no less important: it is important that administrative and private law scholars pay attention to each other's legal fields and that they talk to each other. There is much to be gained from such a dialogue by both sides. One reason for this is that on both sides of the line, judges and scholars are increasingly having to grapple, in what has been called an 'age of statutes',[155] with difficult legal questions concerning the relationship between legislation and common law. One major theme which runs throughout this book is the way in which, in adjudicating on administrative law issues, judges seek to accommodate and promote both the policy goals underlying a given statutory scheme and values regarded as inherent in the common law. In a similar way, James Goudkamp and John Murphy[156] have stressed that the prevalent view that tort law, for instance, 'is essentially a common law subject',[157] is now outdated; legislation has come to play a more significant role in tort law,[158] and other private law, regimes and it is not plausible to continue to treat 'common law and statute [as] very separate bodies of law'.[159] Any scholar seeking to further his or her understanding of the relationship between common law and legislation,[160] therefore, would benefit greatly from increased dialogue between public and private law academics and practitioners.

A fourth and final clarification concerns the book's engagement with prerogative powers.[161] It was noted above that the vast majority of administrative schemes operating in the English and Welsh legal system have been constituted by statute. One consequence of this is that most administrative law challenges also

[155] Guido Calabresi, *A Common Law for the Age of Statutes* (Harvard University Press, 1985). Lord Bingham also noted the 'legislative hyperactivity' of the modern age: Tom Bingham. 'The Rule of Law' (2007) 66 *CLJ* 67, 70. For a useful discussion of the centrality of legislation in the environmental law context, see Eloise Scotford and Jonathan Robinson, 'UK Environmental Legislation and its Administration in 2013 – Achievements, Challenges and Prospects' (2013) 25(3) *Journal of Environmental Law* 383.

[156] James Goudkamp and John Murphy, 'Tort Statutes and Tort Theories' (2015) 131(1) *LQR* 133. See also James Goudkamp and John Murphy, 'The Failure of Universal Theories of Tort Law' (2015) 21(2) *Legal Theory* 47; John Murphy, 'The Heterogeneity of Tort Law' (forthcoming in *OJLS*).

[157] Goudkamp and Murphy 'Tort Statutes and Tort Theories', *ibid*, 133.

[158] Jack Beatson, 'Has the Common Law a Future?' (1997) 56(2) *CLJ* 291, 301. TT Arvind and Jenny Steele (eds), *Tort Law and the Legislature* (Hart Publishing, 2012).

[159] Andrew Burrows, 'The Relationship between Common Law and Statute in the Law of Obligations' (2012) 128 *LQR* 232, 233.

[160] See generally Patrick Atiyah, 'Common Law and Statute Law' (1985) 48 *MLR* 1; Jack Beatson, 'The Role of Statute in the Development of Common Law Doctrine' (2001) 117 *LQR* 247. Andrew Burrows, *Thinking About Statutes: Interpretation, Interaction, Improvement (The Hamlyn Lectures)* (Oxford University Press, 2018).

[161] For excellent recent discussion, see Anne Twomey, *The Veiled Sceptre: Reserve Powers of Heads of State in Westminster Systems* (Cambridge University Press, 2018).

arise against the background of, often highly detailed and particularised, legislative frameworks. There are, however, a small number of important administrative schemes, and thus administrative law challenges relating to such schemes,[162] which have been established through the use of prerogative powers. One important example, for instance, is the scheme for the issuance and withdrawal of passports.[163]

The continued existence of these prerogative schemes gives rise to a host of difficult questions about whether and how administrative law adjudication is different in prerogative, as opposed to legislative, contexts. In some ways the apparent difference may be less stark than might be expected. One factor which might have softened the distinction, for instance, is the publication of detailed bodies of policy outlining how decisions are to be taken within prerogative schemes. This development may mean that courts often have to grapple with questions of construction[164] in prerogative cases, in much the same way as they do in many challenges in the context of statutory schemes.[165] Challenging questions nonetheless persist. Does, for instance, the notion of 'non-justiciability' have any continued role in the context of schemes introduced by the prerogative as opposed to statute?[166] If judicial review is available, does review take place on all of the otherwise applicable grounds, or do some grounds only function when there is a statute in the picture?[167] Do the courts, and ought they, subject decisions of this kind to the same degree of scrutiny as they would if they originated from a statute?[168]

Questions such as these are deserving of specific attention and cannot be addressed in this book. It is important to note, however, that the book's references to the importance of legislative frameworks in administrative law adjudication should not obscure the continued existence of prerogative schemes. Nor should they be understood as implying that questions about how judicial review functions in the prerogative context are easy or unimportant.

[162] Usually arising in judicial review proceedings because, in the absence of a statute, it is unlikely that a route of appeal would be available.

[163] *R (XH) v Secretary of State for the Home Department* [2017] EWCA Civ 41, [2018] QB 355.

[164] The courts maintain that questions concerning interpretations of policy are subject to review in much the same way as interpretations of statute. See, eg, *Tesco Stores Ltd v Dundee CC* [2012] UKSC 13, [2012] PTSR 983, especially [18]–[19] (although note also *Hopkins Homes Ltd v Secretary of State for Communities and Local Government* [2017] UKSC 37 in which Lord Carnwath emphasises the need to have due regard to the reasoning and expertise of administrative decision-makers, in that case planning inspectors).

[165] See, eg, *R (Project Management Institute) v Minister for the Cabinet Office* [2016] EWCA Civ 21, [2016] 1 WLR 1737.

[166] *R v Criminal Injuries Compensation Board, ex parte Lain* [1967] 2 QB 864 (QB); *CCSU* (n 12); Paul Daly, 'Justiciability and the "Political Question" Doctrine' [2010] *PL* 160.

[167] *R (Sandiford) v Secretary of State for Foreign and Commonwealth Affairs* [2014] UKSC 44, [2014] 1 WLR 297; Adam Perry, 'The Flexibility Rule in Administrative Law' (2017) 76 *CLJ* 375.

[168] *R (Bancoult) v Secretary of State for Foreign and Commonwealth Affairs* [2008] UKHL 61, [2009] 1 AC 453.

V. Conclusion

By way of conclusion, it is helpful to offer a brief sketch of the three main aims of this book, explained in more detail above.

The first main aim of this book is to explore the 'anatomy' of administrative law. The legal structures in play in administrative law adjudication, it argues, are both complex and varied in at least three core senses. First, legislative and policy detail matters enormously in administrative law adjudication. Most administrative law challenges arise against the background of a detailed legislative and policy framework and these frameworks vary significantly from one to the next. A major focus of administrative law adjudication is on making sense of this legislative background and its details therefore play a major role in legal reasoning. Second, administrative law protects a plurality of legal values, interests and policies. These include at least the following: the policy aims underlying the relevant legislative scheme, values regarded as fundamental by the common law, the rights of the individual and goods or ideals in which the public as a collectivity, or a subsection of it, is regarded as having an especially important interest. Third, applicants sit in different kinds of relationship with the administrative decision-makers they seek to challenge. It is far from the case that a neat line can be drawn between adjudication in administrative law and private law on the basis that, while in the latter the applicant goes to court to assert a personal legal right which she alleges has been infringed,[169] in the former the applicant appears to draw the attention of the judge to a public 'wrong'[170] said to have taken place.[171] Administrative law cases, rather, take different 'shapes'. While some cases undoubtedly fit this public law paradigm,[172] others can closely resemble the conventional image of a private law case.[173]

The second aim of the book is to show that all of this matters deeply, and not only because it furthers understanding of the general nature of administrative law. An understanding of the three core senses in which administrative law's anatomy is complex and varied is also important because it illuminates certain specific doctrinal issues within the field. A series of chapters in this book illustrate this through a detailed discussion of doctrinal case studies. The areas considered are procedural review, legitimate expectations and standing. In each case, the book argues that its broader themes shed useful light on some important questions concerning the ways in which doctrine functions.

[169] Wesley Hohfeld, *Fundamental Legal Conceptions as Applied in Judicial Reasoning* (The Law Book Exchange, 2010).

[170] *R v Somerset CC, ex parte Dixon* [1998] Env LR 111 (QB).

[171] Bamforth (n 80); Woolf (n 80).

[172] *R v Inspectorate of Pollution ex parte Greenpeace (No 2)* [1994] 2 CMLR 548 (QB).

[173] *Conville* (n 84).

The third and final aim is to cast doubt on the plausibility of a prevalent approach to understanding administrative law which the book terms 'monism'. Attempts to reduce administrative law to a singular 'organising concept'[174] which is capable of lending it unity are prevalent in legal scholarship at both the general and specific level. In the end, however, the book suggests that there is reason to regard this approach cynically. Administrative law adjudication is legally complex and involves the application of a varied array of legal structures. There is therefore reason to doubt that an account of administrative law which presents the field as being organised around a singular 'master principle or idea'[175] will be able to supply the full array of intellectual tools needed to understand case law.

[174] Forsyth (n 106) [27].
[175] Smith (n 97) 11.

2

The Development of Modern Administrative Law

The previous chapter introduced the main arguments of this book. As explained there, this book has three main aims. The first is to explore the 'anatomy' of administrative law, calling attention to three core senses in which the basic legal structures in play in adjudication are both complex and varied. The second is to demonstrate the importance of recognising this complexity in a series of specific doctrinal contexts. The third is to cast doubt on the plausibility of explaining administrative law doctrine by reference to a singular 'organising concept'.[1]

This chapter introduces the field of administrative law in greater detail and begins to take some steps in developing these arguments. Its focus is on the development of modern administrative law, primarily across the twentieth century. The reasons for beginning with a discussion of this history are broadly threefold. First, there is an important 'scene-setting' purpose to this chapter. Readers of this book will have different levels of familiarity with English and Welsh administrative law. An outline of administrative law's recent history serves as a useful introduction for students and those who work primarily in other jurisdictions or legal fields. Second, even among those familiar with English and Welsh administrative law, an understanding of the subject's history is often thinner than of other dimensions. As Stephen Sedley[2] has noted, the panoptic history of English and Welsh public law has not yet been written. This chapter makes no claim to offer the missing volume on the twentieth century. One hope, however, is that the chapter will draw attention to a number of important, but sometimes overlooked, aspects of the field's modern history.

Third and most fundamentally, there are important connections between the historical analysis in this chapter and the broader arguments of the book. Indeed, a central aim of this chapter is to emphasise two important lessons about administrative law which emerge from consideration of its modern history and which

[1] Christopher Forsyth, 'The Rock and the Sand: Jurisdiction and Remedial Discretion' (2013) 18(4) *Judicial Review* 360 [27].

[2] Stephen Sedley, *Lions Under the Throne: Essays on the History of English Public Law* (Cambridge University Press, 2015) 1.

are of wider importance.[3] These lessons will be drawn out and discussed in greater detail in section II. It is useful however to very briefly describe them here.

The chapter's first core lesson is that administrative law's history is both complex and multifaceted. The tale of administrative law's development is far from a linear story of the subject growing up, or being deliberately constructed, around a singular 'master principle or idea'.[4] There is, therefore, considerable reason to be cynical of narratives which present the field in this way.[5] The book's second lesson concerns the nature of the legal structures at play in administrative law adjudication. An exploration of administrative law's history, the book argues, is important because it brings to light a number of important ways in which these legal structures are both complex and diverse. The modern history of administrative law, in other words, offers a first glimpse of the subject's complex and varied 'anatomy'.

The bulk of the discussion in this chapter will take place in section I. This section explores the modern development of administrative law, primarily across the twentieth century, taking a critical discussion of Albert Venn Dicey's *Lectures Introductory to the Study of the Law of the Constitution* (here '*Lectures*') as its entry-point.[6] The analysis will be divided into a consideration of six time-periods:

a) the publication of Dicey's *Lectures* in 1885;
b) the 1910s;
c) the 1920s and 1930s;
d) the 1940s;
e) the 1950s and 1960s; and
f) the 1970s onwards.

Section II returns to the chapter's two core lessons, briefly sketched above, and fleshes them out in detail. Section III finally concludes.

I. Administrative Law's Modern History

The aim of this section is to explore some of the major landmarks in the modern history of administrative law. The focus is primarily on the twentieth century and a critical discussion of Dicey's *Lectures*,[7] published in 1885, is used as an entry-point. In the course of discussing Dicey's writings, the discussion will allude to some important developments from earlier centuries. The primary focus, however,

[3] In that sense, the chapter can be thought of as an exercise in what John Allison has termed 'history to understand': John Allison, 'History to Understand, and History to Reform, English Public Law' (2013) 72(3) *CLJ* 526.

[4] Stephen Smith, *Contract Theory* (Oxford University Press, 2004) 11.

[5] See chapter 7.

[6] Albert Venn Dicey (edited by John Allison), *The Law of the Constitution (Oxford Edition of Dicey)* (Oxford University Press, 2013).

[7] *Ibid.*

is on the 1900s. No claim is made to chronical exhaustively every important development across the twentieth century. The aim, rather, is to give a flavour of the complexity of administrative law's modern history by discussing just some of the most important landmarks.

Before turning to this history, two points should be noted. First, that this chapter focuses primarily on the twentieth century and engages only briefly with prior developments, but should not be taken to indicate that there is nothing of importance to be learnt by looking further back. As Paul Craig has stressed, and as will be seen below, 'we have had [in England and Wales] a body of legal rules concerned directly with the legal constraints that should be placed on administration … for at least 400 years'.[8] The popular idea that administrative law is a modern creation is therefore highly misleading.[9] Furthermore, Craig's work,[10] and the work of others including especially Edith Henderson,[11] Stephen Sedley[12] and Philip Murray,[13] is illustrative of the light which can be shed on modern administrative law doctrine by exploring earlier centuries.[14] It is nonetheless appropriate for this chapter to confine its focus primarily to the twentieth century. The complexity of administrative law's history and nature can be amply demonstrated by focusing on this modern history. Looking further back would undoubtedly supply further evidence of administrative law's complex origins. It is not, however, necessary for the purposes of this chapter. It is also important that the historical exercise undertaken here is manageable in a chapter of reasonable length in the context of a book which is not, of itself, historical in nature. Broadening the time period would create the risk that the account offered would be of insufficient detail.[15]

Second, that this chapter takes the work of Dicey as its entry-point might, at first sight, seem an odd choice. Jeffrey Jowell has written of a temptation to 'found a club based around a resolution no longer to quote Dicey when beginning a lecture on English public law'[16] and Jowell's impulse is very easy to understand.

[8] Paul Craig, *UK, EU and Global Administrative Law: Foundations and Challenges* (Cambridge University Press, 2015) 26.

[9] *Ibid*, 25.

[10] *Ibid*.

[11] Edith Henderson, *Foundations of English Administrative Law: Certiorari and Mandamus in the Seventeenth Century* (Harvard University Press, 1963).

[12] Sedley (n 2); Stephen Sedley, *Ashes and Sparks* (Cambridge University Press, 2011); Stephen Sedley, *Law and the Whirligig of Time* (Hart Publishing, 2018).

[13] Philip Murray, 'Judicial Review of the Upper Tribunal: Appeal, Review and the Will of Parliament' (2011) 70(3) *CLJ* 487; Philip Murray, 'Process, Substance and the History of Error of Law Review' in John Bell, Mark Elliott, Jason Varuhas and Philip Murray (eds), *Public Law Adjudication in Common Law Systems: Process and Substance* (Hart Publishing, 2016).

[14] See also Janet McLean, *Searching for the State in British Legal Thought* (Cambridge University Press, 2012); Peter Cane, *Controlling Administrative Power: An Historical Comparison* (Cambridge University Press, 2016).

[15] For discussion of earlier centuries see citations above.

[16] Jeffrey Jowell, 'Restraining the State: Politics, Principle and Judicial Review' (1997) 50(1) *Current Legal Problems* 189, 189.

Dicey's *Lectures* have been subject to the most rigorous of critique, leading Felix Frankfurter in 1938, for instance, to write in an oft-cited passage,[17] that Dicey's work was striking proof that 'many a theory survives long after its brains are knocked out'.[18] Many of the core propositions of Dicey's work have been criticised by commentators[19] and, as will be seen, even Dicey himself came to revisit and revise some of the core propositions in his earlier works.[20]

Few would doubt there is much to criticise in Dicey's writing. There are, however, two main reasons why Dicey's *Lectures* form a useful entry-point into thinking about the evolution of modern administrative law. First, critically reviewing the account Dicey developed in 1885 provides a useful opportunity to reflect on the state of administrative law in England and Wales at the close of the nineteenth century. By this time the courts had long been grappling with what would now be regarded as issues of administrative law. As will be seen however, many of these important developments received little or no discussion in, or risked being obscured by, Dicey's early writings. Second, Dicey's work formed an intellectual starting-point for thinking about public law issues throughout much of the twentieth century.[21] His writings reflected the first major attempt to look at the mass of case law, legislation and political practice which touched on public law issues, and to filter it down to the most important themes.[22] In undertaking this task, Dicey effectively put in place a set of ideas[23] which were treated by many as orthodoxy.[24] It is not possible, therefore, to understand much of the thinking

[17] Harry W Arthurs, 'Rethinking Administrative Law: A Slightly Dicey Business' (1979) 17(1) *Osgoode Hall Law Journal* 1, 4 and Dame Sian Elias, 'The Unity of Public Law?' in Mark Elliott, Jason Varuhas & Shona Wilson Stark (eds), *The Unity of Public Law?* (Hart Publishing, 2018) 16.

[18] Felix Frankfurter, Foreword to 'Discussion of Current Developments in Administrative Law' (1938) 47 *Yale Law Journal* 515, 517.

[19] Arthurs (n 17); WI Jennings, *The Law and the Constitution*, 5th edn (University of London Press, 1959); RFV Heuston, *Essays in Constitutional Law*, 2nd edn (Stevens and Sons, 1964); Lord Bingham, 'Dicey Revisited' [2002] *PL* 39; Rivka Weill, 'Dicey was not Diceyan' (2003) 62(2) *CLJ* 474; Martin Chamberlain, 'Immigration Appeals and the Rule of Law: A Very Dicey Argument' [2004] 9(2) *Judicial Review* 112; Iain McLean and Alistair McMillan, 'Professor Dicey's Contradictions' [2007] *PL* 435; Michael Gordon, 'The Conceptual Foundations of Parliamentary Sovereignty: Reconsidering Jennings and Wade' [2009] *PL* 519; Mark Walters, 'Dicey on Writing the "Law of the Constitution"' (2012) 32(1) *OJLS* 21; Dylan Lino, 'Albert Venn Dicey and the Constitutional Theory of Empire' (2016) 36(4) *OJLS* 751; Dylan Lino, 'The Rule of Law and the Rule of Empire: AV Dicey in Imperial Context' (2018) 81(5) *MLR* 739.

[20] Albert Venn Dicey, 'The Development of Administrative Law in England' (1915) 31 *LQR* 120.

[21] Graham Gee and Gregoire Webber, 'A Grammar of Public Law' (2013) 14(12) *German Law Journal* 2137, 2150.

[22] For useful discussion of the 'pedagogical beginnings' of these lectures, see discussion by John Allison at Dicey (n 6) xxiv–xlii.

[23] Dicey (n 6), Introduction by John Allison.

[24] As FH Lawson put it in 'Dicey Revisited' [1959] *Political Studies* 109 at 109, Dicey's works became 'a phantom to replace the reality in the memory of those who have finished their university course, even if they then go on to teach'. See also David Sugarman, 'The Legal Boundaries of Liberty: Dicey, Liberalism and Legal Science' (1983) 46 *MLR* 102; David Sugarman, 'Legal Theory, the Common Law Mind and the Making of the Textbook Tradition' in William Twining (ed), *Legal Theory and the Common Law* (Oxford University Press, 1986).

and writing surrounding administrative law, especially in the early decades of the twentieth century, without understanding the picture Dicey painted in 1885. Dicey's account supplied a distortive simplification of a more complex reality.[25] Much writing in the early decades of the twentieth century, however, regarded it as a starting-point to either be assumed or responded to.[26]

A. 1885: The Early Views of Albert Venn Dicey

With these introductory points in mind, the chapter can now turn to its entry-point into the modern history of administrative law: a critical discussion of Dicey's *Lectures*, published in 1885.[27] The first edition of *Lectures* was published three years after Dicey returned to the University of Oxford,[28] to take up the Vinerian Professorship. As Dicey explained, the aims of this volume were those of 'stat[ing] what the laws are which form part of the [English] constitution, … arrang[ing] them in their order …. explain[ing] their meaning and exhibit[ing] where possible their logical connection'.[29]

There are a number of different ways to introduce the picture of the constitution Dicey painted in these lectures. Dicey himself famously divided his lectures into a discussion of, what he saw as, the constitution's 'three … guiding principles':[30] the sovereignty of Parliament;[31] the rule of law[32] and the role played by constitutional conventions.[33] For present purposes it is useful to take a different approach and to explore the answers Dicey offered to three main questions. First, to what extent did bodies other than the courts and Parliament exercise public decision-making power in the English and Welsh legal system? Second, what mechanisms were available to the courts for the purpose of controlling such power? Third, to what extent was it proper to say that English and Welsh law had a body of 'administrative law'?

[25] Elizabeth Fisher, Pasky Pascual and Wendy Wagner, 'Understanding Environmental Models in their Legal and Regulatory Context' (2010) 22(2) *Journal of Environmental Law* 251.

[26] Dicey (n 6) xiv–xv and John Allison, *A Constitutional Distinction in the Common Law: A Historical and Comparative Perspective on English Public Law* (Oxford University Press, 2000) 18–23; N Johnson, 'Dicey and his Influence on Public Law' [1985] *PL* 717.

[27] Dicey (n 6) xi–xlii.

[28] Having attended the University of Oxford as a student.

[29] Dicey (n 6) 24. See further Albert Venn Dicey, 'Can English Law Be Taught at the Universities?' (Inaugural Lecture, All Souls College, Oxford, 21 April 1883. Helpfully reproduced in Dicey (n 6), Appendix I).

[30] *Ibid*, 5.

[31] *Ibid*, Lecture 2. For notable works inspired by Dicey's writings on parliamentary sovereignty, see: William Wade, 'The Basis of Legal Sovereignty' (1955) 13 *CLJ* 72; William Wade, 'Sovereignty – Revolution or Evolution?' (1996) 112 *LQR* 568; Jeffrey Goldsworthy, *Parliamentary Sovereignty: Contemporary Debates* (Cambridge University Press, 2010); Nick Barber, 'The Afterlife of Parliamentary Sovereignty' (2011) 9(1) *International Journal of Constitutional Law* 144.

[32] Dicey (n 6), Ch 4. For discussion see Paul Craig, 'Formal and Substantive Conceptions of the Rule of Law: An Analytical Framework' [1997] *PL* 467.

[33] Dicey (n 6) Chapter 14.

i. Public Decision-Making Power Outside of Parliament and the Courts

On the subject of public decision-making power exercised by bodies other than the courts and Parliament, Dicey had surprisingly little to say,[34] at least in the first edition of *Lectures*.[35] Indeed, what Dicey did offer on this matter was largely in the way of stressing, what Dicey saw as, inherent limitations on their extent.[36]

Two examples will suffice to illustrate. The first concerns Dicey's offerings on delegated legislative powers.[37] By the time Dicey was writing, there was a centuries-old parliamentary practice of delegating broad rule-making powers to both the Crown and specially created statutory bodies. As Cecil Carr stressed,[38] the history of delegated legislation can be traced back until at least[39] the reign of Henry VIII.[40] The most famous example in the Tudor period[41] is undoubtedly the Statute of Proclamations[42] which empowered the King 'with the advice of a majority of his Council, to set forth proclamations … of such sort as to His Majesty and his said council should seem necessary and requisite'.[43] This was, however, far from a lone example. The office of Commissioner of Sewers, for instance, was first put on a permanent statutory basis in 1531.[44] As Paul Craig has noted, the Commissioners had an array of powers including 'the power to make statutes, ordinances and provisions as might be required for the safeguarding, conservation and redress of the constructs that fell within their jurisdiction'.[45]

Despite this lengthy and important history, the subject of delegated law-making powers received relatively little discussion in Dicey's *Lectures* beyond a few references.[46] In his second lecture,[47] Dicey did recognise a practice on the part of Parliament of empowering 'the Privy Council, the judges or some other body to make rules … for the determination of details which cannot be settled by Parliament'.[48] The observation, however, was not unpacked in any detail. It was

[34] See the Introduction by Allison to Dicey (n 6).
[35] This changed in Dicey's later writings. See discussion below.
[36] Dicey (n 6) xxxvii–xxxviii; Dicey (n 29).
[37] Dicey paid greater attention to legislation in overseas territories (whether enacted by the UK Parliament or by a national legislature) than to delegated legislation within England and Wales. See Dicey (n 6), Chs 2 and 3.
[38] Cecil Carr, *Delegated Legislation: Three Lectures* (Cambridge University Press, 1921).
[39] The *Committee on Ministers' Powers Report* (HM Stationery Office, 1932) ('Donoughmore Report') traces the history further back, 12–15.
[40] Carr (n 38), Ch 6 describes the eight years between the coming into effect of the Statute of Proclamations and the death of Henry VIII as the 'golden age of delegated legislation'.
[41] Donoughmore Report (n 39) 12–15.
[42] Proclamation by the Crown Act 1539.
[43] Carr (n 38) 50. See further Cane (n 14).
[44] Bill of Sewers 1531.
[45] Craig (n 8), 86.
[46] See also Dicey (n 6), Ch 3.
[47] Dicey (n 6), Ch 2.
[48] Dicey (n 6) 34.

instead followed by a bemoaning of, what Dicey saw as, an unjustified limit on the legislative powers of central government. According to Dicey:

> The cumbersomeness and prolixity of English statute law is due in no small measure to futile endeavours of Parliament to work out the details of large legislative change …. the law would, it is probable, be a good deal improved if the executive government of England could, like that of France, by means of decrees ordinances or proclamations having the force of law, work out the detailed application of the general principle embodied in the Acts of the legislature.[49]

Although *Lectures*, in other words, recognised the existence of delegated legislative power, Dicey's main contribution was the suggestion that these powers were more limited than they ought to be. In this regard Dicey regarded the *Case of Proclamations*,[50] and the establishment of the principle that 'royal proclamations have in no sense the force of law',[51] as having placed an undue restriction on the legislative powers of central government.

A second, and more important, example of Dicey emphasising what he saw as inherent limitations on the decision-making power of bodies other than Parliament and courts concerns, what Dicey termed, the 'first … feature'[52] of the rule of law. According to Dicey, the rule of law in the English and Welsh context was fundamentally opposed to the notion that officials could exercise discretionary power, permitting them to interfere with person or property in the absence of a finding, by the ordinary courts, that they had breached the law. For Dicey, the rule of law therefore meant that:

> …. no man is punishable or can be lawfully made to suffer in body or goods except for a distinct breach of law established in the ordinary legal manner before the ordinary courts of the land … [and] in this sense [English law could be] contrasted with every system of government based on the exercise by persons in authority of wide, arbitrary or discretionary powers of constraint.[53]

There are different ways of interpreting this passage. One possible reading is that, while public authorities were granted the power to interfere with the person or property of the individual, these decisions were subject to strict oversight by the 'ordinary courts.' Another is that such powers of interference, in the absence of a finding of unlawfulness by the ordinary courts, did not exist on a significant scale in the English and Welsh legal system. This aspect of Dicey's account is difficult to accept as a description of the position by the late-1800s. By the time Dicey was writing, English and Welsh law contained many examples of decision-makers being empowered to interfere with both the body and property of individuals without

[49] Dicey (n 6) 34.
[50] *Case of Proclamations* (1611) 12 Co Rep 74.
[51] Dicey (n 6) 13.
[52] Dicey (n 6), Ch 4.
[53] Dicey (n 6), Ch 4.

any finding of unlawfulness by the ordinary courts. An older example is again the Commissioners of Sewers. It was emphasised above that the Commissioner wielded broad legislative powers.[54] As Paul Craig has stressed, the Commissioners also:

> … had extensive judicial authority … [including] judicial discretion to fine or imprison those who committed offences wilfully … while those who were guilty of neglect … could be made to bear the cost of repair, or have their goods distrained.[55]

A second example is provided by the statutory backdrop to the well-known nineteenth century decision in *Cooper*.[56] *Cooper* arose against the background of a major slum housing crisis in London. Parliament's response to this crisis had been to pass the Metropolis Local Management Act 1855[57] which, among other things, created a new hierarchy of administrative authorities[58] empowered to prevent the building of new and dangerous properties. Most significantly, section 76 empowered relevant authorities to 'cause … to be demolished'[59] properties erected without seven days' notice being given or in breach of an order. Importantly, there was, under section 76, no need for the breach of the law to have been established in the 'ordinary courts'. The authority, rather, acted on its own assessment of the conduct of the person intending to build.

ii. Legal Mechanisms for the Control of Power

Dicey's emphasis on the perceived limits of the decision-making powers of bodies other than Parliament and the courts perhaps shaped his engagement with a second issue: the techniques which were available to the courts in overseeing such power. Two main points are important.

The first is that Dicey painted a particular picture of the legal techniques deployed by judges. According to this picture, the courts' techniques were the same as those wielded by the courts in claims against private individuals or organisations. What Dicey called 'ordinary law' was, therefore for him, the courts' primary defence against misuse of administrative power.[60] This was a state of affairs, furthermore, which for Dicey was deeply appealing.[61] According to Dicey, the rule of law would be undermined if officials were subject to different legal obligations

[54] Craig (n 8) 86.

[55] Craig (n 8) 85.

[56] *Cooper v Wandsworth Board of Works* (1863) 143 ER 414.

[57] Metropolis Local Management Act 1855.

[58] At the top of this hierarchy was the Metropolitan Board of Works which sat above a tier of vestries and District Board of Works.

[59] Metropolis Local Management Act 1855, s76.

[60] Jason Varuhas has described this as the idea that 'public law *is* private law': Jason Varuhas, 'The Public Interest Conception of Public Law: Its Procedural Origins and Substantive Implications' in Bell, Elliott, Varuhas and Murray (eds) (n 13).

[61] See also Paul Craig, 'Dicey: Unitary, Self-Correcting Democracy and Public Law' (1990) 106 *LQR* 105.

than the private citizen. The rule of law required commitment to the principle of equality and the idea that 'every man, whatever be his rank or condition, is subject to the ordinary law of the realm and amenable to the ordinary jurisdiction of the ordinary tribunals'.[62] Dicey also praised the 'the inseparable connection between the means of enforcing a right and the right to be enforced'[63] which he saw as inherent in the 'ordinary law' of England and Wales. For Dicey, the 'ordinary law' of England and Wales not only identified the content of a particular right[64] but coupled it with a series of legal processes and remedies.[65]

There is an important element of truth in Dicey's observations. It was certainly the case, for example, that the courts had been hearing, what would now be regarded as private law cases involving administrative decision-makers. There are, for instance, countless examples of the courts dealing with trespass claims against Justices of the Peace.[66] The second important point, however, is that, as Matthew Lewans has stressed,[67] there is much of significance which at best was not explicitly discussed, and at worst was obscured, by Dicey's *Lectures*. By 1885, a number of highly significant lines of case law, in which the courts grappled with questions concerning the role they should play in overseeing administrative decision-making, had emerged. Many of these important lines of case law however received little or no discussion in *Lectures*. They also risked being obscured by Dicey's assertion that official and citizen alike were subject to the same law.

Two examples will suffice to illustrate.[68] The first concerns a line of case law dealing with the writ of mandamus. Mandamus, like certiorari and prohibition, had originated as a mechanism by which the King's Court could issue directions to and control the activities of lower courts.[69] Over the course of the seventeenth, eighteenth and nineteenth centuries, the courts were invited to put these writs to use in new contexts in order that they could play a greater role in the oversight of the exercise of power by bodies *other* than courts. Important steps forward had been taken. Over the course of these centuries, mandamus evolved from being a mechanism 'used by the central courts to protect their officers and litigants from arrest by the numerous local courts'[70] into, what Paul Craig has described as, a 'more general purpose tool for the remedying of administrative error'[71] by bodies

[62] Dicey (n 6) 114.
[63] Dicey (n 6) 117.
[64] As Dicey saw being done in other states: Dicey (n 6), Ch 3.
[65] Dicey discussed specific examples such as the right to personal liberty.
[66] See discussion in Murray, 'Process, Substance and the History of Error of Law Review' (n 13) of *Brittain v Kinnaird* 129 ER 789 and *Cave v Mountain* 133 ER 330. See also *Cooper* (n 56).
[67] Matthew Lewans, 'Rethinking the Diceyan Dialectic' (2008) 58(1) *University of Toronto* 75.
[68] For another interesting dimension to the story of administrative law's evolution across the nineteenth century, see Kevin Costello, 'Drink and the Development of Administrative Law 1820–1910' [2018] *PL* 224.
[69] Stanley De Smith, 'The Prerogative Writs' (1951) 11(1) *CLJ* 40.
[70] Henderson (n 11) 49.
[71] Craig (n 8) 51.

beyond courts. *Bagg's Case*[72] is commonly taken as a landmark decision in this regard. In this case the King's Bench made use of mandamus to restore the plaintiff to the office of burgess, following his removal by the Mayor of Plymouth.

This line of case law, and mandamus more broadly, however, received no discussion in Dicey's *Lectures*. In retrospect, this is particularly problematic because there are important cases in the late-nineteenth century which grappled with the question of mandamus' precise limits. *Lewisham Union Guardians*[73] is a deeply interesting case in this regard. This case is worth exploring in some detail because it has important lessons for the law on standing, discussed in chapter six.

Lewisham Union Guardians arose against the background of the Vaccination Act 1871.[74] This Act placed local authorities known as 'guardians of the poor' under statutory duties to take steps to prevent the spread of infectious disease. The applicant in *Lewisham Union Guardians* was itself a statutory authority[75] which sought to argue that the guardians of the poor in its area had failed to fulfil its legal duties and requested relief in the form of mandamus. The Divisional Court refused to grant relief. The difficulty the plaintiff faced was that the major cases on mandamus which had emerged by that time, including *Bagg's Case* itself,[76] concerned a specific type of legal relationship. The applicant in these classic cases argued that an office or liberty to which she had a *personal* entitlement had been denied or violated. As Stanley De Smith has explained, mandamus had therefore usually been deployed as a means of 'compelling [the] restitution [of individuals] to offices and liberties'.[77]

The difficulty was that *Lewisham Union Guardians* concerned a legal relationship of a very different kind. Here were a series of statutory duties which were designed, not to protect any one identifiable individual who in turn could be said to have a 'right'[78] to their performance but, to promote the interests of the *public as a collectivity* in the management of disease. The applicant in *Lewisham Union Guardians*, therefore, was asking the Court to expand the remit of mandamus. The Divisional Court refused. Putting the point in very strong terms, Wright J opined that the Court would be:

> … far exceeding its function if it were to assume jurisdiction to enforce the performance by public bodies of all their statutory duties without requiring clear evidence that the person who sought its interference *had a legal right* to insist upon such performance.[79]

[72] *Bagg's Case* (1615) 11 Co Rep 93b.

[73] *R v Guardians of the Lewisham Union* [1897] 1 QB 498 (DC).

[74] Vaccination Act 1871.

[75] *R v Secretary of State for Employment, ex parte Equal Opportunities Commission & Another* [1995] 1 AC 1 (HL).

[76] *Bagg's Case* (n 72).

[77] De Smith (n 69).

[78] See discussion in Wesley Hohfeld, *Fundamental Legal Conceptions as Applied in Judicial Reasoning* (The Law Book Exchange, 2010).

[79] *Lewisham Union Guardians* (n 73) 500 (emphasis added).

While deeply important, the expanding role of mandamus and the struggles the courts were incurring in defining its outer limits received no explicit discussion in *Lectures*. Perhaps more importantly, Dicey's suggestion that all persons, whether officials or citizens, were subject to the same law arguably obscured the important role being played by prerogative writs, including mandamus, in controlling administrative decision-making by the late-nineteenth century.

A second example of an important line of case law which received no discussion in *Lectures* concerned procedural review. By 1885 a mass of case law[80] had emerged in which plaintiffs argued that they ought to have been given notice prior to an administrative decision being taken. A landmark case, and a useful way into the case law, is *Capel v Child*.[81] Parliament had[82] conferred on bishops responsibilities for the administration of the Church of England. Section 50 of the relevant Act created the power to require vicars to appoint curates at their own expense in circumstances where the 'ecclesiastical duties of [that vicar were being] inadequately performed'.[83] In *Capel*, the bishop had made use of this power, and had done so without giving Capel notice and an opportunity to address his concerns.

The Court held that the bishop had acted unlawfully. Two main lines of reasoning run through the judgments. The first is that it is a basic principle of the common law that both sides of an argument must be heard before a judgment is rendered. As Bayley B put it, it is 'an invariable maxim of law that you cannot proceed against a party without his having the opportunity to be heard and without his appearing in court before a judgment shall be pronounced on him'.[84] The Court considered that this maxim was as applicable to the decision of the bishop as it was to the actions of the courts themselves. The second line of reasoning focused on the statutory background to the case. This statutory background, Bayley B emphasised,[85] permitted the bishop to appoint a curate only where it appeared 'to the satisfaction' of the bishop that the vicar's ecclesiastical duties were being inadequately performed. The Court considered that hearing from the vicar, prior to rendering a decision, could only enhance the bishop's ability to perform this role. The Court found it difficult to see how a bishop who had heard from only one side could meaningfully be said to be 'satisfied' of neglect.[86]

A substantial body of case law followed *Capel* in which the courts considered how far these lines of reasoning applied outside of its specific context.[87] A question

[80] *Bagg's Case* (n 72); *R v University of Cambridge* (1723) 1 Stra 557 ('*Dr Bentley's Case*'); *Brutton v Vestry of St George's Hanover Square* (1871–1872) LR 13 Eq 339; *Cheetham v Mayor of Manchester* (1874–1875) LR 10 CP 249; *London & South Western Railway Co v Cyril Flower* (1875) 1 CPD 77; *Masters v Pontypool Local Government Board* (1878) 9 Ch D 677; *Hopkins v Smethwick Local Board of Health* (1890) 24 QBD 712.

[81] *Capel v Child* 149 ER 235 (1833).

[82] 57 Geo 3, c99.

[83] *Ibid*, 50.

[84] *Capel* (n 81). See also the related case of *The King v Benn & Church* 6 Term Rep 198 (1795).

[85] *Capel* (n 81).

[86] *Capel* (n 81).

[87] For a further example, see *R v Archbishop of Canterbury* (1859) 1 E and E 545.

which arose time and again was whether *Capel* required the involvement of affected parties where decision-making took place under a different statutory scheme. A key determining factor came to be the extent to which involving the individual in decision-making would undermine the purposes for which Parliament had established the scheme in question.

It is useful to contrast *Re Hammersmith Rent-Charge*[88] with *Cooper*.[89] The former arose against the background of section 82 of the Tithe Commutation Act[90] which permitted courts to order local sheriffs to undertake an 'inquisition'[91] into unpaid rent. The applicant in the case argued that, in light of *Capel*, it would be unlawful for the Court to take such a decision ex parte. The Court rejected this argument. The scheme in play in *Re Hammersmith Rent-Charge* was very different to the one at issue in *Capel*. A key aim was to put in place a speedy decision-making procedure to which landlords, to whom rent was overdue, could turn in order to recover rent. Permitting the tenant to appear at the preliminary stage, where no final decision would be produced, would simply result in further delay and thereby unacceptably compromise the aims of this scheme.[92]

In *Cooper*, by contrast, the Court applied *Capel* to require the Boards of Works, prior to exercising the power to demolish property under section 82 of the Metropolis Local Management Act 1855, to supply the property owner with notice. Central to the judges' reasoning was that hearing from the property owner would only enhance the Boards' ability to realise the aims of the background statutory scheme. As Erle CJ put it:

> I cannot conceive any harm that could happen to the district board from hearing the party ... but I can conceive a great many advantages which might arise in the way of public order, in the way of doing substantial justice, and in the way of fulfilling the purposes of the statute ...[93]

Like the evolution of mandamus, however, this important line of procedural review case law received no explicit discussion in Dicey's *Lectures*. While, therefore, there was much truth in Dicey's suggestion that officials and citizens are subject to the 'ordinary law' applied by the 'ordinary courts', *Lectures* also overlooked, or at least did not explicitly engage with, a number of important legal developments taking place at the time. In retrospect these developments can be seen as earlier examples of the courts developing the techniques of modern administrative law.

[88] *Re Hammersmith Rent-Charge* 154 ER 1136 (1849).
[89] *Cooper* (n 56).
[90] Tithe Commutation Act, 6 & 7 Will 4.
[91] *Ibid*, s82.
[92] *Hammersmith* (n 88).
[93] *Cooper* (n 56).

iii. 'Administrative Law' in England and Wales

Turning now to the final question: to what extent did Dicey think it proper to describe the English and Welsh legal system as having a system of 'administrative law'? Dicey's view in this regard is well-known:

> *Droit administratif* is a term known under one form or another to the law of most continental states … it is one for which English legal phraseology supplies no proper equivalent. The words 'administrative law,' which are the most natural rendering of *droit administratif*, are unknown to English judges and counsel, and are in themselves hardly intelligible without further explanation.[94]

The contrast Dicey drew between England and Wales and the French system of *droit administratif* of course contained an important element of truth. There were, and continue to be, important differences between the two jurisdictions. Most obviously, French law, like many continental systems, operates a distinct court system for the hearing of challenges against public administrators. Although English and Welsh law now has a specialist Administrative Division in the High Court,[95] at the appellate level courts are non-specialist and hear challenges from all areas of law. Private law claims are also frequently brought against public bodies in the civil courts.

Dicey's contrast between the law of France and that of England and Wales, however, went beyond recognising such differences. What Dicey set up was a contrast between the English conception of the rule of law, on the one hand, and the notion of administrative law, on the other. Dicey's work could be read as suggesting that the two were *fundamentally opposed* to one another[96] such that to accept one was to therefore reject the other. As Dicey reportedly said elsewhere, in his view, the centrality of the notion of the rule of law meant that the English 'know nothing of administrative law; and [that] we wish to know nothing.'[97]

The creation of this rule of law/administrative law binary was problematic for at least two reasons. The first has already been discussed in some detail. By 1885, bodies other than courts were exercising significant public decision-making power. The courts were developing important lines of case law which developed techniques in order to oversee the use of such power. If administrative law is understood in the sense of a set of mechanisms used by courts to oversee the activities of public administration then, contrary to Dicey, the courts of the English and Welsh

[94] Dicey (n 6) 101.

[95] In addition to a system of administrative tribunals. See Tribunals, Courts and Enforcement Act 2007 (discussed in Robert Carnwath, 'Tribunal Justice – A New Start' [2009] *PL* 48).

[96] Dicey (n 6) 102.

[97] A quotation taken from a conversation reported to have taken place between Dicey and M Barthelemy. See William Robson, 'The Report of the Committee on Ministers' Powers' (1932) 3 *Political Quarterly* 346.

legal system had been developing it for centuries.[98] The second problem is that the longer-term effect of juxtaposing the rule of law with administrative law was to render administrative law a 'dirty word'[99] for much of the twentieth century. The implication of this binary was that the recognition of a branch of administrative law entailed displacing of the rule of law. Characterising administrative law as something which could only be embraced while abandoning the rule of law had a significant delaying effect on the emergence of administrative law as a distinct subject of study.[100]

B. 1910s: The Liberal Reforms, Dicey's Later Works and the First World War

Having set out in some detail Dicey's early views in 1885, it is helpful next to turn to a pivotal decade in the modern history of administrative law: the 1910s. Four developments in this decade are especially worthy of discussion.

The first is the general election of 1910 in which Henry Asquith was elected to the office of Prime Minister (an office which he had held since 1908 and would hold until 1916). During this time, Asquith's Government passed a broad array of legislation, introducing administrative schemes, the likes of which had not been seen before.[101] The passage of the Government's legislation in this time period was not always straightforward – indeed, it was under Asquith's Government that the infamous Parliament Act 1911[102] was passed in order to ease the passage of Bills through the House of Lords – but the product of this era was a series of substantial welfare reforms dealing with a broad variety of subject-matters. These included, among others, pensions,[103] national insurance,[104] education,[105] workers' rights[106] and probation.[107]

This development did not pass unnoticed by Dicey. In 1915 Dicey wrote that:

> During the last fifty years, and notably since the beginning of the twentieth century, the nation as represented in Parliament has undertaken to perform a large number of duties with which before the Reform Act of 1832 no English Government had any concern whatever. This assertion is so obviously and admittedly true that it is hardly

[98] Craig (n 8), Ch 1.

[99] Otto Kahn-Freund, 'The Legal Framework of Society' in William Robson (ed), *Man and the Social Sciences* (London: Allen & Unwin, 1972) 212.

[100] Prem Lata Sharma, *Modern Methods of Teaching Political Science* (Sarup & Sons, 2002) 164–69.

[101] Based on a campaign manifesto known as the 'People's Budget' of 1909.

[102] Parliament Act 1911. See discussion of the background to that legislation and its constitutional implications in *R (Jackson) v Attorney-General* [2005] UKHL 56.

[103] Old Age Pensions Act 1908.

[104] National Insurance Act 1911; National Insurance Act 1913.

[105] Education Act 1914.

[106] Trade Disputes Act 1906; Workers Compensation Act 1906; Merchant Shipping Act 1906.

[107] Probation Act 1907.

> necessary to produce evidence in its support. If any critic doubts its substantial accuracy he should study the long line of Elementary Education Acts dating from 1870, the Old Age Pensions Acts 1908 and 1911 and the National Insurance Acts 1911 and 1913.[108]

It is worth pausing to reflect on the variety of the administrative schemes which are discussed in this passage. Compare, for instance, the Old Age Pensions Act 1908 with the Elementary Education Act 1870. The former enactment, a creation of the Asquith Government, was a scheme which purported to confer a series of legal rights on individuals.[109] Sections 2 and 3, for instance, conferred on individuals who met relatively clearly defined statutory criteria[110] what is described in the Act as a personal 'entitlement'[111] or 'right to receive [an] old age pension'.[112] The later sections of the Act enacted a machinery for making decisions about whether individuals met those criteria in borderline cases and for delivering pensions to those who were entitled to them under the legislation.[113] The Elementary Education Act 1870,[114] by contrast, had a rather different structure. The centrepiece of the Act was a broad and public-facing legal duty, imposed on the central Education Department, which required the Department to ensure that a sufficient supply of schools was 'provided for every school district'.[115]

A second important development in the 1910s concerned a series of cases in which applicants challenged the implementation of these new schemes.[116] One particularly important case which is worth considering in some detail is *Arlidge*.[117] *Arlidge* arose against the background of the Housing, Town Planning, &c. Act 1909.[118] This Act replicated a pre-existing power on the part of local authorities to order the closure of properties deemed unfit for human habitation[119] and replaced the previous appeal route to the quarter sessions with a new right of appeal to the Local Government Board.[120] In *Arlidge* the applicant challenged a refusal by the Local Government Board to overturn a closure order. The Board, Arlidge argued, should have given him access to a report compiled by an inspector and an opportunity to make representations on it.

Arlidge is an important case because it marked the beginning of a different approach to procedural review. As explained above, across cases such as *Capel*[121]

[108] Dicey (n 20) 149.
[109] See discussion of *R (Conville) v Richmond-upon-Thames LBC* [2006] EWCA Civ 718, [2006] 1 WLR 2808 in chapter 3.
[110] Old Age Pensions Act 1908, ss2 and 3.
[111] *Ibid*, s1.
[112] *Ibid*.
[113] *Ibid*, ss7 and 8.
[114] Elementary Education Act 1870.
[115] *Ibid*, s5.
[116] *Board of Education v Rice* [1911] AC 179 (HL); *Dalziel Parish School Board v Scotch Education Department* [1913] 1 SLT 457.
[117] *R v Local Government Board, ex parte Arlidge* [1915] AC 120 (HL).
[118] Housing, Town Planning, &c. Act 1909.
[119] *Ibid*, s17.
[120] *Ibid*, s39.
[121] *Capel* (n 81).

and *Cooper*[122] the courts had insisted that the individual had a right to participate in decision-making to the extent that participation would not undermine the aims of the background statutory scheme.[123] This was the approach taken by the Court of Appeal when deciding *Arlidge*.[124] The House of Lords, however, took a different, and more deferential, approach. In circumstances where Parliament had chosen to give a right of appeal, not to the courts but to the Local Government Board, it was said, it must be taken to be the case that Parliament regarded the relevant decision as being administrative, rather than judicial, in nature. The courts should therefore afford to the Board a greater degree of latitude in designing its own procedures. As Lord Moulton put it, the procedural rules used by the Board, were therefore to be regarded as, for the most part, 'beyond the criticism of the Courts' which had no 'business [in seeking] to add or take away from them'.[125]

Why did the House of Lords alter its reasoning in such a significant way at this time? It is likely that there were a number of different factors in play.[126] One especially important consideration concerned complications caused by the procedural route by which *Arlidge* had brought his challenge. In the absence of a purpose-built procedural route for challenging the decision of the Board, Arlidge had applied for a writ of certiorari. Like the writ of mandamus discussed above, certiorari had originated as a mechanism by which the King's Court could oversee the activities of lower courts.[127] Over the course of earlier centuries, the courts had expanded the remit of the remedy, putting it to use in the context of bodies other than courts. Judges, however, continued to struggle with identifying the outer boundaries of the remedy. In *Arlidge* and a handful of cases decided shortly after,[128] this complication manifested in a particular idea: that a line was to be drawn between 'judicial' functions, where certiorari was available to correct breaches of natural justice, and 'administrative' functions, where certiorari did not give the courts the same scope to interfere.[129]

A third important development in the 1910s concerns the later works of Dicey. Over the course of the early-twentieth century Dicey revisited his earlier views a number of times,[130] and most notably in an article published in the *Law Quarterly*

[122] *Cooper* (n 56).

[123] *Hammersmith* (n 88).

[124] *R v Local Government Board, ex parte Arlidge* [1914] 1 KB 160 (CA).

[125] *Arlidge* (n 117) 150.

[126] For a cynical view, see the discussion in Sedley (n 2) Ch 1.

[127] Murray, 'Process, Substance and the History of Error of Law Review' (n 13).

[128] See especially *R v Electricity Commissioners, ex parte London Electricity Joint Committee* [1924] 1 KB 171 (CA); *R v Legislative Committee of the Church Assembly, ex parte Haynes-Smith* [1928] 1 KB 411 (KB).

[129] For criticisms, see LG Baxter, 'Fairness and Natural Justice in English and South African Law' (1979) 96 *South African Law Journal* 607; Ian Holloway, 'Natural Justice and the New Property' (1999) 25 *Monash University Law Review* 85.

[130] See Albert Venn Dicey, 'Droit Administratif in Modern French Law' (1901) 17 *LQR* 302; Albert Venn Dicey, *An Introduction to the Study of the Law of the Constitution*, 8th edn (Macmillan, 1915), Preface to the Eighth Edition.

Review in 1915.[131] In this article Dicey refined his position on each of the core questions discussed in subsection A above.

In the first place, as discussed above, in this article and other works,[132] Dicey dedicated much more discussion to the existence and significance of administrative decision-making power which he saw as rapidly expanding features of the legal system.[133] In the second place, Dicey also had a good deal more to say in these later works on the legal techniques which were being developed by judges for the oversight of administrative power. Dicey, for instance, wrote in 1915 that recent case law[134] had seen the concretisation of two 'clear and distinct principle[s] by which any department of the Government … must be guided in the exercise of powers conferred upon it by statute'.[135] According to the first, 'any power conferred upon a government department by statute must be exercised in strict conformity with the terms of that statute'.[136] According to the second, 'a government department when it exercises judicial or quasi-judicial jurisdiction under a statute is bound to act with judicial fairness and equity, but is not in any way bound to follow the rules of procedure in English courts'.[137] In the third place, Dicey in these later works also indicated a change of heart on the place of 'administrative law' in the English and Welsh legal context. The courts, Dicey wrote, had taken 'a considerable step towards the introduction among us of something like the *droit administrative* of France'.[138]

A fourth and final noteworthy development in the 1910s was the First World War. On 8th August 1914, Parliament passed the Defence of the Realm Act 1914.[139] This Act was enacted with minimal scrutiny[140] and originally contained one substantive section providing that the Government had power 'during the continuance of the … war to issue regulations as to the powers and duties of the Admiralty and Army Council … and other persons acting [on its] behalf for securing the public safety and defence of the realm'.[141] In subsequent months, the Act was amended a number of times[142] and with each amendment the legislative powers of the Government expanded. The requirement in the original Act that the Government issue regulations 'as to the powers and duties' of military actors and government employees was removed in 1914.[143] The amended Act instead

[131] Dicey (n 20).
[132] See especially Albert Venn Dicey, *Lectures on the Relation between Law and Public Opinion in England During the Nineteenth Century*, 2nd edn (Macmillan, 1914).
[133] See especially *ibid* and the discussion of what Dicey referred to as the 'period of collectivism'.
[134] *Arlidge* (n 117).
[135] Dicey (n 20) 148.
[136] Dicey (n 20) 148.
[137] Dicey (n 20) 149.
[138] Dicey (n 20) 152.
[139] Defence of the Realm Act 1914.
[140] Cecil Carr, *Concerning English Administrative Law* (Oxford University Press, 1941) Ch 1.
[141] Defence of the Realm Act, s1.
[142] See especially Defence of the Realm Consolidation Act 1914.
[143] *Ibid*, s1(1).

provided that the Government 'ha[d] power …. to issue regulations for securing the public safety and defence of the realm'[144] more broadly.

As Cecil Carr noted, the powers conferred by the Defence of the Realm Acts were used broadly. Using them, central government introduced such diverse provisions as:[145]

> … restrictions affecting dangerous drugs, firearms, celluloid storage and the preservation of official secrets; there were obligations to carry wireless apparatus on ships, to close shops early and to sell tea by net weight … Regulations under DORA dealt not only with food control, war supplies and State management of the liquor trade, but even with the prohibition of dog shows and of whistling for cabs in London.

The consequence of all of this was that the 1910s were a pivotal decade in the modern history of administrative law. The reforms of Asquith's Liberal Government coupled with the outbreak of the First World War resulted in a substantial expansion in the statutory powers of governmental bodies and the introduction of administrative schemes of a scale and nature not seen before. This, and a number of important cases which were decided in this decade, also led Dicey to revisit his earlier antipathy to the idea of administrative law.

C. 1920s and 1930s: The Aftermath of the War, Making Sense of the Enlarged Administrative State and the Donoughmore Report

Turning next to the 1920s and 1930s, three main points fall to be made. The first is that, while it might have been expected that, following the conclusion of the First World War in 1918, the UK would have seen a stripping back of the legislative and administrative functions accumulated by central government, no such thing happened. Cecil Carr noted that little effort was made on the part of the Government 'after the last shot was fired'[146] to disarm itself of the extensive powers it had acquired during the war effort. As Carr put it, the broad powers of the central Government which had been 'tolerated while the guns were still firing' therefore long 'outstayed [their] welcome, as abnormal departmental activity so often does'.[147]

The second important point is that the 1920s and 1930s were crucial decades in the modern history of administrative law because numerous writers in this era recognised the considerable growth in central governmental power and began to

[144] *Ibid.*
[145] Cecil Carr, 'Administrative Law' (1935) 51 *LQR* 58, 60.
[146] Carr (n 140) 25.
[147] Carr (n 140) 25.

think conscientiously what was to be done about it.[148] Different approaches to this issue can be seen. As David Williams observed, while for some the time had come to rethink the traditional English antipathy towards 'administrative law', for others Dicey's:

> .... suggestion that a system of administrative law ... was inconsistent with ... 'the rule of law' was easily converted ... into the superficial view that the growing powers of the administration and indeed any concept of administrative law, were inconsistent with 'the rule of law'.[149]

A comparison between two important texts, both published in the year 1929, neatly illustrates the point. The first is FJ Port's *Administrative Law*,[150] the first book published under that title in English and Welsh law.[151] The second is Lord Hewart's *The New Despotism*.[152]

These books were, in a sense, motivated by similar concerns. Both Port and Hewart argued that the growth of the administrative state meant it was now necessary to explore whether changes needed to be made in order to provide better oversight of decision-making power. Port, for instance, wrote that:

> Conditions have so changed during the past fifty years or so, that much to which exception might well have been taken under the earlier and simpler system of government must now be admitted as inevitable ... [These developments] make it imperative that there shall be as little delay as possible in setting our house in order. To delay reforms further would be to endanger the well-being of the whole system of administrative law in this country.[153]

Relatedly, both Port and Hewart expressed concern about particular phenomena which they saw as increasing, but worrying, features of the English and Welsh legal system. Both, for instance, expressed antipathy towards the proliferation of legislative finality clauses.

Although, however, there were commonalities between Port and Hewart's texts, there were also major differences between them. The main disparity concerned the use the authors made of the Diceyan dichotomy between the rule of law and administrative law. To the extent that Port engaged with this dichotomy,

[148] William Robson, *Justice and Administrative law* (Macmillan & Co, 1928) (for discussion see William Robson, *Justice and Administrative law Reconsidered* (1979) 32(1) *Current Legal Problems* 107; TS Simey, *Justice and Administrative Law* (1948) 58 *The Economic Journal* 264); Carleton Kemp Allen, *Bureaucracy Triumphant* (Oxford University Press, 1931) (for discussion see HDH, *Bureaucracy Triumphant* (1932) 4(3) *CLJ* 399; Harold Laksi, *Bureaucracy Triumphant* (1931–1932) 45(4) *Harvard Law Review* 754)); John Willis, *The Parliamentary Powers of English Government Departments* (Cambridge University Press, 1933).

[149] David Williams, 'The Donoughmore Report in Retrospect' (1982) 60 *Public Administration* 273, 275.

[150] FJ Port, *Administrative Law* (Longmans & Sons, 1929).

[151] Carol Harlow and Richard Rawlings, 'Administrative Law in Context: Restoring a Lost Connection' [2014] *PL* 28.

[152] Lord Gordon Hewart of Bury, *The New Despotism* (Ernst Benn Ltd, 1929).

[153] Port (n 150), author's foreword, xii.

his approach was to challenge it. For Port, it was time to abandon the idea that 'the subject of administrative law .... connotes a state of affairs which is in conflict with the principles of our common law'.[154] For him the developments of recent decades did not:

> ... in any sense justify the plea that the whole modern development of administrative law [was] wrongly conceived ... [but did] make it imperative that there [should] be as little delay as possible in setting our house in order.[155]

The time had come for Port, in other words, to rethink the idea that the rule of law and administrative law were fundamentally opposed phenomena. It was essential that scholars embraced the notion of administrative law and began studying public administration and its legal oversight specifically and critically.[156]

Hewart, by contrast, did not argue for a collapse of the rule of law/administrative law binary. His argument, rather, focused on returning English and Welsh law to the position Dicey had described in his earlier works. The narrative Hewart offered in *The New Despotism* was one in which English and Welsh law had moved unjustifiably away from its traditional rule of law roots[157] into a state of 'administrative lawlessness'.[158] Hewart sought to draw to the attention of the public what he described as the 'systematic .... [and] well thought out plan'[159] on the part of central government to 'clothe the department[s] with despotic power'.[160] The solution to this state of affairs, according to Hewart, was heightened public awareness of this phenomenon and a collective demand that the worst of the excesses be stripped back.[161]

A third and final development in the 1920s and 1930s which is worthy of discussion is the publication in 1932 of the Donoughmore Report.[162] The Donoughmore Report was, to a large degree, a response to the publication of Hewart's *The New Despotism*.[163] David Williams has described the 'appointment of the Committee on Ministers' Powers' as a 'pre-emptive strike'.[164] 'The Government had been alerted', according to Williams, 'to the forthcoming publication of *The New Despotism* and

[154] Port (n 150), author's foreword.
[155] Port (n 150), author's foreword.
[156] This was closely reflected in the book's content. Port, for instance, looked abroad to both France and the US for ideas about how to develop an effective system of administrative law.
[157] Hewart (n 152) Ch 2.
[158] Hewart (n 152) Ch 4.
[159] Hewart (n 152) 153.
[160] Hewart (n 152) 153.
[161] Hewart (n 152) Ch 8.
[162] Donoughmore Report (n 39). See discussion in Robson (n 97).
[163] The Committee wrote that while it regarded *The New Despotism* 'as a warning against possible dangers of great gravity' and regarded Hewart as having done the public a 'service' in offering his 'outspoken criticism', it wished to stress that there was 'no ground for public fear if the right precautions [were] taken'.
[164] David Williams, 'The Donoughmore Report in Retrospect' (1982) 60 *Public Administration* 273, 281.

by publication date the Lord Chancellor, Lord Sankey, had prepared the membership of the Committee'.[165]

Perhaps unsurprisingly, a major focus of the Donoughmore Report was therefore on rejecting some of the premises of *The New Despotism*. The Donoughmore Report challenged the backwards-looking tone of Hewart's text and urged the importance of looking forwards. The enlarged administrative state, it stressed, was here to stay[166] and the focus ought therefore to be on identifying the 'safeguards' required to ensure that the country was able to 'continue to enjoy the advantages of the practice'.[167] The Donoughmore Report also challenged Hewart's characterisation of the English and Welsh legal system as having weakened the rule of law. The Committee acknowledged that the increasing allocation to Ministers of responsibility for taking decisions 'which determine the rights of private persons' entailed a 'prima facie … infringement'[168] of the rule of law. It argued, however, that, as long as proper safeguards were introduced, such developments could be regarded as perfectly consistent with the constitution. To that end, the Committee recommended a series of reforms including the limitation of Henry VIII and ouster clauses, the creation of Standing Committees within Parliament for the purpose of scrutinising the delegation of legislative power and a more rigorous judicial approach to procedural review.

While the Committee distanced itself from the premises of Hewart's *The New Despotism*, it did not go as far as FJ Port. In particular, it continued to resist the idea that it was appropriate to use the language of 'administrative law' in the English and Welsh legal context. The Committee, like Dicey's early writings, saw administrative law as inherently linked with the continental model of separate court systems. It did not think that there was a need to introduce this model in the English and Welsh legal context, regarding the High Court's 'supervisory jurisdiction'[169] under the prerogative writs as largely capable of ensuring proper judicial oversight. The continued antipathy to the language of administrative law later led William Robson to evocatively describe is as having 'started life with the dead hand of Dicey lying frozen on its neck'.[170]

D. 1940s: The Second World War and the Atlee Government

The 1920s and 1930s, then, were a time when commentators, prompted by a major expansion of governmental power in the 1910s, started to think conscientiously about the legal oversight of public administration. The outbreak of the Second

[165] *Ibid*.
[166] Donoughmore Report (n 39).
[167] Donoughmore Report (n 39).
[168] Donoughmore Report (n 39).
[169] Donoughmore Report (n 39).
[170] Robson (n 97) 315.

World War in 1939 rather put the brakes on this project. As David Williams has written, the effects of the Second World War were, from an administrative law perspective, twofold.[171] On the one hand, the War further perpetuated the growth in central governmental power. From 1939 both administrative power and 'delegated legislation continued to grow in volume',[172] in large part due to the passage of a series of further defence Acts.[173] On the other, the collective appetite for exploring and developing forms of oversight to counterbalance this growth significantly weakened. As Williams put it, 'the Second World War ensured … the relegation of the search for … safeguards to a low priority'.[174]

Liversidge[175] is a classic illustration of Williams' point. The Emergency Powers (Defence) Act 1939 conferred on His Majesty's Government the broad power to 'by Order in Council make such regulations … as appear … to be necessary and expedient for securing … the defence of the realm'.[176] This included the power to make 'provision for … the detention of persons whose detention appears to the Secretary of State to be expedient'.[177] The Government used this power to pass the Defence (General) Regulations 1939[178] which stated, equally broadly, that 'if the Secretary of State ha[d] reasonable cause to believe any person to be of hostile origin or association … he may make an order against that person directing that he be detained'.[179]

Liversidge challenged his detention under the Regulations as a claim in trespass. A central question which arose in the case was how the term 'if the Secretary of State has reasonable cause to believe' ought to be interpreted. For Lord Atkin, who offered a dissenting judgment, the answer to the case was clear: it was a long-established principle of the common law that the courts should 'stand between the subject and any attempted encroachment on his liberty by the executive'.[180] This principle required the courts to proceed from the position that 'every imprisonment is prima facie unlawful'[181] and go on to ask whether the Secretary of State had articulated lawful grounds for his decision to detain. When this was asked in Liversidge's case, Lord Atkin concluded, the Secretary of State had clearly acted unlawfully: the Secretary of State had refused to 'justify with particulars'[182] the basis of his decision.

[171] Williams (n 164) 290.
[172] Williams (n 164) 290.
[173] Emergency Powers (Defence) Act 1939; Emergency Powers (Defence) Act 1940. Carr (n 140) said of this Act at 20 'that Act was passed in one afternoon, with no warning … all that anybody said was that the Act ought to have been passed much earlier'.
[174] Williams (n 164) 289–90.
[175] *Liversidge v Anderson* [1942] AC 206 (HL).
[176] Emergency Powers (Defence) Act 1939 Act, s1(1).
[177] *Ibid*, s1(2).
[178] Defence (General) Regulations 1939.
[179] *Ibid*, reg 18b.
[180] *Liversidge* (n 175) 244.
[181] *Liversidge* (n 175) 245.
[182] *Liversidge* (n 175) 246.

The majority in *Liversidge*, by contrast, considered that while it was proper for the common law to afford strong legal protection to liberty in times of peace, this common law starting-point was not applicable to war-time legislation.[183] As Viscount Maugham put it, the 'suggested rule' that 'legislation dealing with the liberty of the subject must be construed, if possible, in favour of the subject'[184] had '"no relevance in dealing with an executive measure by way of preventing a public danger" when the safety of the state is involved'.[185]

Apart from the Second World War, with its dual effect of both expanding governmental power and of relegating 'the search for .... safeguards to a low priority',[186] a second major development in the 1940s was the election of the first majority Labour Government, headed by Clement Atlee, in 1945. Atlee's Government was elected on a manifesto of extensive post-war social reform. The implementation of this manifesto, like Asquith's 'People's Budget'[187] agenda in the 1910s, saw the creation of new administrative schemes, the shape and size of which had not been introduced before. These reforms included the laying of the foundations of the National Health Service,[188] the introduction of a host of social security benefits[189] including unemployment and sickness benefits[190] and a retirement pension,[191] the creation of regulatory schemes in relation to the coal industry,[192] the provision of utilities,[193] and the maintenance of railways,[194] the introduction of the general requirement to obtain planning permission before developing land[195] and the creation of a scheme to protect aspects of the countryside in which the public was deemed to have an especially important interest.[196]

[183] Another factor which seemed to influence the decision was a belief in the effectiveness of ministerial responsibility to Parliament (see for instance *Liversidge* (n 175) at 222 and discussion in JDB Mitchell, 'The Causes and Effects of the Absence of a System of Public Law in the United Kingdom' [1965] *PL* 95, 100). For more cynical discussion see: Gavin Drewry, 'The Executive: Towards Accountable Government and Effective Governance?' in Jeffrey Jowell and Dawn Oliver (eds), *The Changing Constitution*, 7th edn (Oxford University Press, 2011); Tony Wright, 'The Politics of Accountability' in Mark Elliott and David Feldman (eds), *The Cambridge Companion to Public Law* (Cambridge University Press, 2015); Philip Norton, 'Parliament: A New Assertiveness' in Jeffery Jowell and Dawn Oliver (eds), *The Changing Constitution*, 8th edn (Oxford University Press, 2015).

[184] *Liversidge* (n 175) 218.

[185] *Liversidge* (n 175) 219, citing *R v Halliday* [1917] AC 260, 270.

[186] Williams (n 149) 289–90.

[187] See discussion above.

[188] National Health Service Act 1946.

[189] National Insurance Act 1946. See discussion in WA Robson, 'The National Insurance Act 1946' (1947) 10(2) *MLR* 171.

[190] National Insurance Act 1946, s11.

[191] National Insurance Act 1946, s20.

[192] Coal Industry Nationalisation Act 1946.

[193] Electricity Act 1947.

[194] Transport Act 1947.

[195] Town and Country Planning Act 1947. See especially discussion in Elizabeth Fisher, Bettina Lange and Eloise Scotford, *Environmental Law* (Oxford University Press, 2013) 791–94.

[196] National Parks and Access to the Countryside Act 1949.

As with the schemes introduced by Asquith's Government, one striking feature of these reforms is that the legislation which created them varied considerably in terms of aim and structure. Consider in the first place the National Parks and Access to the Countryside Act 1949. A major purpose of this Act was to designate areas of scientifically interesting[197] or especially beautiful land as being of particularly important public interest[198] and, in doing so, to confer on it a variety of special legal protections. The National Insurance Act 1946, by contrast, is notably different. Like the Old Age Pensions Act[199] discussed above, a major purpose of this Act was to lay down the conditions in which certain classes of individual were to be regarded as personally entitled to various forms of statutory benefit. Take, for instance, the following section which deals with widow's allowance:

> (1) … A widow *shall be entitled* to widow's benefit if the husband satisfied the relevant contribution conditions.[200]

The effect of this section is to confer on individuals who meet certain conditions a statutory entitlement to receive a specified benefit.

Perhaps unsurprisingly, what followed the introduction of the Labour Government's new initiatives were a series of cases concerning the proper implementation of these schemes.[201] One important case is *Franklin*.[202] This case arose against the backdrop of the New Towns Act 1946.[203] This Act gave power to the Minister for Housing to 'make an order designating [an] area as the site of a proposed new town' when satisfied 'that it [would be] expedient in the national interest'.[204] The Minister had used the power to designate Stevenage as such a site. The order was however challenged by the applicant on the ground that the Minister, in delivering a speech in which he had insisted that 'the project will go forward, because it must go forward',[205] had shown himself to be biased. The House of Lords rejected the challenge. Drawing on the line of reasoning which had been developed in cases such as *Arlidge*,[206] the Court reasoned that the common law's concern with bias and its appearance applied primarily in relation to bodies exercising judicial power, something which could not be said of the Minister for Housing.

[197] *Ibid*, s23.
[198] *Ibid*, ss87–88.
[199] Old Age Pensions Act 1908.
[200] National Insurance Act 1946, s17.
[201] *R v Northumberland Compensation Appeal Tribunal, ex parte Shaw* [1952] 1 KB 338 (CA).
[202] *Franklin v Minister of Town and Country Planning* [1948] AC 87 (HL).
[203] New Towns Act 1946.
[204] *Ibid*, s1(1).
[205] *Franklin* (n 202) 90.
[206] *Arlidge* (n 117).

E. 1950s and 1960s: The First Major Textbooks and the 'Holy Trinity' of Cases but Still no Administrative Law?

Turning now to the 1950s and 1960s, something of a tension underlies the developments of this time. On the one hand, administrative law flourished, both in the sense that the first major textbooks on the subject were published and that the House of Lords decided a number of acclaimed cases[207] which were heralded as taking major steps in the development of administrative law.[208] On the other hand, it is possible to find repeated statements throughout these decades in both case law[209] and the literature[210] to the effect that, English and Welsh law lacked a 'developed system of administrative law'.[211]

Three main points should be elaborated. First, the 1950s and early 1960s saw the publication of the first major textbooks on the subject of administrative law.[212] John Griffith and Harry Street's *Principles of Administrative Law*[213] came first in 1952. As noted in a review by Owen Hood Phillips,[214] the aim of this book was to fill a significant gap in the literature by providing 'the first textbook to be published on English Administrative Law'.[215] The view of the authors was that the time had come to afford administrative law the 'status of a compulsory subject in legal education'[216] and a suitable text was therefore required to provide a framework for such courses. *Principles of Administrative Law* is an interesting book to look back on in retrospect. The text is not organised around a discussion of generally applying 'grounds of review'.[217] Rather, much like FJ Port's text of 1929, the book explores the *different kinds of power* exercised by government and the available techniques for controlling them. In this regard the authors distinguished broadly between the 'legislative powers of the administration'[218] on the one hand and the 'administrative and judicial powers of the administration' on the other.[219]

[207] *Anisminic Ltd v Foreign Compensation Commission* [1969] 2 AC 147 (HL); *British Oxygen Co Ltd v Minister of Technology* [1971] AC 610 (HL).

[208] A further important development was the *Report of the Committee on Administrative Tribunals and Enquiries* (1957) ('Franks Report') (discussed in Geoffrey Marshall, 'The Franks Report on Administrative Tribunals and Enquiries' (1957) 35(4) *Public Administration* 347).

[209] *Ridge v Baldwin* [1964] AC 40 (HL).

[210] Mitchell (n 183).

[211] *Ridge* (n 209) 72.

[212] Port (n 150).

[213] John Griffith and Harry Street, *Principles of Administrative Law* (Pitman & Sons, 1952).

[214] Owen Hood Phillips, '*Principles of Administrative Law* by JAG Griffith and H Street' (1953) 16(2) *MLR* 248. See also TCT, '*Principles of Administrative Law* by JAG Griffith & H Street' (1953) 11(3) *CLJ* 501.

[215] Although note Port (n 150).

[216] Griffith and Street (n 213), Preface.

[217] Compare the structure to, for instance, Mark Elliott and Robert Thomas, *Public Law*, 3rd edn (Oxford University Press, 2017) Ch 12.

[218] Griffith and Street (n 213), Chs 2 and 3.

[219] Griffith and Street (n 213), Chs 4 and 5.

Seven years after the publication of Griffith and Street's text came Stanley De Smith's *Judicial Review of Administrative Action*,[220] and two years after that, William Wade's *Administrative Law*.[221] As Carol Harlow and Richard Rawlings[222] and Denis Galligan[223] have observed, these texts have had a long-standing and formative impact on thinking about administrative law. A major change of direction taken in both texts was the arrangement of the subject around the notion of generally applying 'grounds of review'. Whereas the earlier texts of both Port[224] and Griffith and Street[225] focused on different kinds of power, the bulk of De Smith's *Judicial Review of Administrative Action* explores such topics as review for 'vires, jurisdiction, law and fact', 'natural justice: the right to a hearing', 'natural justice: interest and bias' and 'review of discretionary power'. As noted in the introductory chapter, this way of imagining administrative law has become dominant in the English and Welsh legal context.[226]

The second point in need of elaboration is that a series of important cases were decided across the 1960s which helped, as Lord Diplock later put it, to 'liberate English law from the fetters that the courts had [hitherto] imposed upon themselves'.[227] The most well-known of these – the 'holy trinity of cases of the '60s',[228] as Thomas Poole has termed them – were *Ridge*,[229] *Padfield*[230] and *Anisminic*.[231] It is useful to discuss the first two of these in some detail.

In *Ridge*[232] the House of Lords returned to a legal question the courts had been grappling with for centuries: when must an individual be given notice and an opportunity to participate prior to an administrative decision being taken? As explained above, across a course of cases in the nineteenth century the courts had insisted on the provision of notice to affected individuals[233] to the extent that this was consistent with the aims of the background statutory scheme.[234] From the

[220] Stanley De Smith, *Judicial Review of Administrative Action* (Stevens & Sons, 1959). The textbook is now in its eighth edition: Lord Woolf, Jeffrey Jowell, Catherine Donnolly and Ivan Hare, *De Smith's Judicial Review*, 8th edn (Sweet & Maxwell, 2018). A useful overview of the evolution of this textbook can be found in Dean Knight, *Vigilance and Restraint in the Common Law of Judicial Review* (Cambridge University Press, 2018), Ch 1.

[221] William Wade, *Administrative Law* (Oxford University Press, 1961). The textbook is now in its eleventh edition: William Wade and Christopher Forsyth, *Administrative Law*, 11th edn (Oxford University Press, 2017).

[222] Harlow and Rawlings (n 151).

[223] Denis Galligan, 'Judicial Review and the Textbook Writers' (1982) 2 *OJLS* 257.

[224] Port (n 150).

[225] Griffith and Street (n 213).

[226] Knight (n 220).

[227] *O'Reilly v Mackman* [1983] 2 AC 237, 278.

[228] Thomas Poole, 'The Reformation of English Administrative Law' (2009) 68(1) *CLJ* 142, 142.

[229] *Ridge* (n 209).

[230] *Padfield v Minister of Agriculture, Fisheries and Food* [1968] AC 997 (HL).

[231] *Anisminic* (n 207).

[232] *Ridge* (n 209).

[233] *Capel* (n 81); *Cooper* (n 56).

[234] *Hammersmith* (n 88).

early twentieth century, however, a more restrictive approach had emerged. The courts confined themselves to intervening only where the decision was judicial, as opposed to administrative, in nature.[235] Complications resulting from the use of the writ of certiorari were part of the reason for this shift.

Stephen Bailey[236] has observed that while *Ridge* is often 'regarded as having decided that … natural justice can apply to administrative as well as judicial'[237] decisions, this proposition more accurately 'reflects how *Ridge* was subsequently treated'[238] than what it decided. Part of the significance of *Ridge*, however, lies in the fact that their Lordships, and especially Lord Reid, cast enough doubt on the suitability of the distinction that commentators and subsequent case law[239] could convincingly argue that the case had removed it. Lord Reid[240] undertook a comprehensive review of the case law. His Lordship suggested that great assistance could be drawn from older cases such as *Cooper*[241] and that some of the newer case law ought to be treated with caution. One issue was that some of these cases[242] concerned war-time legislation. Another was that issues of natural justice had become intermingled with those concerning the availability of certiorari, resulting in the unsatisfactory distinction between judicial and administrative power gaining prominence.[243]

Another major decision of the 1960s, *Padfield*,[244] arose against an unusual administrative scheme which regulated the production and sale of milk.[245] Under the scheme, producers were required to sell milk to a body known as the Milk Marketing Board. One of the tasks of this Board was to determine the price which was to be paid to producers within the various regions based on such considerations as transportation costs. When the Board refused to increase the price to be paid to producers in the South-East of England, representatives of these producers requested the Minister for Agriculture to use her statutory power to establish a committee of investigation.[246] When she refused, the producers initiated legal proceedings. The essence of their argument was that the refusal to use the statutory power threatened to undermine the aim of the statutory scheme to ensure

[235] *Nakkuda Ali v MF de Jayaratne* [1951] AC 66 (PC); *R v Metropolitan Police Commissioners, ex parte Parker* [1953] 1 WLR 1150 (DC).

[236] Stephen Bailey, '*Ridge v Baldwin* [1964]: "Nuff Said"' in Maurice Sunkin and Satvinder Juss (eds), *Landmark Cases in Public Law* (Hart Publishing, 2017).

[237] *Ibid*, 10.

[238] *Ibid*.

[239] See especially *In Re HK (An Infant)* [1967] 2 QB 617 (CA).

[240] Stanley De Smith, 'The Right to a Hearing in English Administrative Law' (1955) 68(4) *Harvard Law Review* 569; William Wade, 'The Twilight of Natural Justice?' (1955) 67 *LQR* 103.

[241] *Cooper* (n 56).

[242] For instance *Nakkuda Ali* (n 235).

[243] Baxter (n 129).

[244] *Padfield* (n 230) (discussed in Maurice Sunkin, '*Padfield v Ministry of Agriculture, Fisheries and Food* [1968]: Judges and Parliamentary Democracy' in Sunkin and Juss (eds) (n 236)).

[245] Agricultural Marketing Act 1958.

[246] *Ibid*, s19.

that farmers across the UK were not prejudiced by location. The House of Lords accepted this argument. More importantly, in doing so, they explicated an important principle: that public authorities, in exercising statutory power, are obligated to exercise those powers in order to 'promote the policy and objects of the Act'[247] rather than for another peripheral purpose.

Running counter to these developments, however, is a third important point: despite the proliferation of textbooks and landmark cases, it was common to read in the 1950s and 1960s that English law lacked a body of administrative law.[248] Lord Devlin wrote extra-judicially in 1956, for instance, that in his view 'the common law ha[d] now … no longer the strength to provide any satisfactory solution to the problem of keeping the executive … under proper control'.[249] Kenneth Culp Davis in 1961 observed that, in his view, the English courts had too long confined their role in adjudication to that of 'brick-laying' and had neglected their role as 'architects' of administrative law.[250] JDB Mitchell similarly complained in 1965 that, in England, public law was 'too often regarded as a series of unfortunate exceptions to the desirable generality or universality of the rules of private law, and [was] not seen as a rational system'.[251]

How can this tension be explained? One important factor[252] was the continued absence of a purpose-built procedure for the bringing of legal challenges against administrative decision-makers. In the absence of such a procedure applicants had made use of processes – including applications for prerogative writs and private law claims in trespass[253] – which had originated to solve other problems. There was therefore a sense of square pegs being made to fill round holes. In many instances the solution had been adequate. As explained above, for instance, across the sixteenth century and onwards the courts had expanded the role of mandamus from its original context in order to provide relief in instances where an individual had unlawfully been denied an office or status.[254] In other contexts, however, difficulties had emerged. As explained above, for instance, in the context of procedural review, the use of certiorari had resulted in the courts carving a difficult distinction between judicial and administrative functions.

The courts of the 1960s had begun the process of removing some of the technical difficulties which had emerged. In *Ridge*,[255] for instance, the House

[247] Padfield (n 230) 1030.

[248] Lord Denning, *Freedom under Law* (Stevens, 1949) 126.

[249] Patrick Devlin, 'The Common Law, Public Policy and the Executive' (1956) 9(1) *Current Legal Problems* 1, 14.

[250] Kenneth Culp Davis, 'The Future of Judge-Made Public Law in England: A Problem of Practical Jurisprudence' (1961) *Columbia Law Review* 201.

[251] Mitchell (n 183).

[252] In addition, Kenneth Culp Davis argued that English judges conceived of their role in developing public law too narrowly: Davis (n 250).

[253] *Cooper* (n 56); *Liversidge* (n 175).

[254] *Bagg's Case* (n 72).

[255] *Ridge* (n 209).

of Lords laid the foundation for eradicating the judicial-administrative power distinction. Other difficulties, however, proved much more difficult to solve. One was especially problematic: the issue with which the Court had been faced in *Lewisham Union Guardians*,[256] discussed above. The problem is this: say a statute places a public body under a legal duty designed to protect, not one individual but, the public as a whole. How, if at all, can the duty be enforced in court?

In *Lewisham Union Guardians*, the Court had felt itself unable to expand mandamus to provide a remedy in such a case. By the 1960s, the courts had not got much further. Access to mandamus continued to be controlled by the notion[257] that the writ would not be issued in the absence of 'clear evidence that the person who sought its interference *had a legal right* to insist upon such performance'.[258] There were instances where courts had applied this idea in a rather artificial way, by holding, for example, that an individual ratepayer had a personal right to have a public-facing statutory duty performed.[259] There was, however, a good deal of uncertainty in the case law. The application for mandamus also did not allow the applicant to make the legal argument which she wished to make: namely, that the public authority was failing to fulfil a legal duty which had been enacted for the *public* benefit. The courts had also closed off the option of obtaining a declaration that such duties were being unlawfully breached or an injunction mandating their performance. These remedies, the courts had determined, were only applicable in cases where the claimant was able to show that she possessed an *individual* legal right to have the public authority's duty performed.[260]

The effect of all of this was that, even by the late 1960s, there continued to be important gaps in judicial oversight of administrative decision-making. In the absence of a purpose-built legal process, the courts continued to struggle to carve out a method for holding administrative decision-makers to 'public-regarding'[261] statutory duties. This led some, such as Lord Diplock writing extra-judicially in 1974,[262] to argue that until a streamlining of the procedural law took place, English and Welsh lawyers could not 'claim to have a fully developed system of administrative law'.[263]

[256] *Lewisham Union Guardians* (n 73).

[257] *R v Russell ex parte Beaverbrook Newspapers Ltd* [1969] 1 QB 342 (DC); *R v Commissioners of Customs & Excise, ex parte Cook* [1970] 1 WLR 450 (QB).

[258] *Lewisham Union Guardians* (n 73).

[259] *R v Hereford Corporation, ex parte Harrower* [1970] 1 WLR 1424 (QBD).

[260] *Gregory v Camden LBC* [1966] 1 WLR 899 (QB), 909. See further *Boyce v Paddington BC* [1903] 1 Ch 109 (Ch); *Gouriet v Union of Post Office Workers* [1978] AC 435 (HL).

[261] Varuhas (n 60) 52.

[262] Lord Diplock, 'Judicial Review Revisited' (1974) 33(2) *CLJ* 233.

[263] *Ibid*, 245.

F. 1970s Onwards: Procedural Reform and the Evolution of the Grounds of Review

Turning now to administrative law's evolution from the 1970s onwards, three main developments are worth discussing. The first is the procedural reforms of the late 1970s. Following the prompts of such writers as Lord Diplock,[264] the Law Commission in 1976 published an influential report on remedies and procedures in administrative law. The Commission recommended substantial change.[265] At the heart of the proposals was the introduction of a streamlined process, known as the 'application for judicial review'[266] ('AJR'). The AJR would provide a major procedural route by which challenges to administrative decision-making could be brought before the courts. Via it, applicants would be able to request any one, or any combination, of the mandatory order, prohibiting order, quashing order,[267] declaration and injunction. The AJR process would have two stages. First, the applicant would apply to the High Court for permission. Second, if permission were granted, a substantive hearing of the issues would take place. The Law Commission recommended that, in order to be granted permission, an applicant would need to demonstrate that she had a 'sufficient interest in the matter'[268] to which her application related. The Commission's recommendations proved influential. The application for judicial review procedure was created in 1977, through an amendment to the Supreme Court Rules.[269] The process was eventually incorporated into primary legislation in the Senior Courts Act 1981.[270]

The effects of the reforms were substantial. One of the most important consequences of the reforms was that they provided an opportunity for the courts to develop the law so that a remedy was available in cases where administrative decision-makers failed to comply with statutory duties designed to benefit the public as a collectivity.[271] Admittedly the path towards achieving this was not straightforward. One complication was that the first case in which the House of Lords had reason to consider the meaning of the new 'sufficient interest'[272] test of standing was *Fleet Street Casuals*.[273] *Fleet Street Casuals* arose against the

[264] Davis (n 250).
[265] Law Commission, 'Report on Remedies in Administrative Law' (Law Comm No 73, 1976).
[266] *Ibid*, [43]–[44].
[267] To use the modern labels.
[268] Law Commission (n 265) [48].
[269] Rules of the Supreme Court (Amendment No 3) 1977 (SI 1977/1955).
[270] Senior Courts Act 1981.
[271] Although the procedural reforms helped to eradicate certain technicalities from the law, it ought also to be noted that they also led to the (at least temporary) introduction of others, including the idea of procedural exclusivity. See especially *O'Reilly* (n 227) and William Wade, 'Procedure and Prerogative in Public Law' (1985) 101 *LQR* 180.
[272] Senior Courts Act 1981, s31(3).
[273] *R v Inland Revenue Commissioners, ex parte National Federation of Self-Employed* [1982] AC 617 (HL).

background of the tax administration system. For a number of their Lordships hearing the case, a significant feature of the legislation which created this system[274] was a strong emphasis on preserving the privacy of the tax affairs of the individual. This feature of the legislation was pivotal to the majority's[275] application of the 'sufficient interest' test in *Fleet Street Casuals*. The centrality of privacy to the tax administration system, the House of Lords emphasised, meant that it must be only in very exceptional circumstances that an individual or organisation[276] could be recognised as having a 'sufficient interest' to challenge the quantum of tax paid by another.

In *Fleet Street Casuals*, then, the detail of the background legislative framework played a major role in how the majority applied the new 'sufficient interest' test of standing. Unfortunately, however, this was sometimes overlooked in subsequent case law. In the often criticised[277] *Rose Theatre*[278] case, for instance, Schiemann J[279] treated *Fleet Street Casuals* as having established a *general* approach to standing. According to Schiemann J, in any AJR the court now needed to look closely at 'the statute under which the decision was taken … and decide whether that statute gives that individual expressly or impliedly *a greater right or expectation than any other citizen of this country* to have the decision taken lawfully'.[280] This was an unfortunate decision. Its effect would have been to once again prevent the courts from issuing a remedy in contexts where a statute created a legal duty designed to protect the public as a collectivity. Returning again to *Lewisham Union Guardians*,[281] for instance, no applicant would have been able to show that the Vaccination Act 1871[282] conferred on them a 'greater right or expectation than any other citizen'[283] that the guardians of the poor would take steps to prevent the spread of disease.

A major breakthrough arrived in a series of cases[284] from the 1980s onwards, including *Dixon*,[285] *World Development Movement*[286] and *Greenpeace*.[287] Collectively

[274] Especially Inland Revenue Act 1890; Taxes Management Act 1970.

[275] Ironically, the case is probably best known for the judgment of Lord Diplock who dissented.

[276] Discussed in Dominic de Cogan, '*CIR v National Federation of Self-Employed and Small Businesses* 1981: All Grievances Converging on Tax Law' in John Snape and Dominic de Cogan (eds), *Landmark Cases in Revenue Law* (Hart Publishing, 2019).

[277] *R v Somerset CC, ex parte Dixon* [1998] Env LR 111 (QB).

[278] *R v Secretary of State for the Environment, ex parte Rose Theatre* [1990] 1 QB 504 (QB).

[279] Konrad Schiemann, 'Locus Standi' [1990] *PL* 342.

[280] *Rose Theatre* (n 278) 522 (emphasis added).

[281] *Lewisham Union Guardians* (n 73).

[282] Vaccination Act 1871.

[283] *Rose Theatre* (n 278) 522.

[284] *R v HM Treasury, ex parte Smedley* [1985] QB 657 (CA); *R v Secretary of State for Foreign and Commonwealth Affairs, ex parte Lord Rees-Mogg* [1994] QB 552 (DC).

[285] *Dixon* (n 277).

[286] *R v Secretary of State for Foreign and Commonwealth Affairs, ex parte World Development Movement* [1995] 1 WLR 386 (QB).

[287] *R v Inspectorate of Pollution ex parte Greenpeace (No 2)* [1994] 2 CMLR 548 (QB).

these decisions concretised the notion of 'representative standing'.[288] According to this idea, in contexts where a statutory duty protects or promotes a good in which the public as a collectivity has a strong interest, an individual or organisation will be permitted to mount a legal challenge to enforce the duty, provided that they are qualified to act in a representative capacity.[289] This development has enabled the courts to provide a remedy in statutory contexts where promotion of the public interest, as opposed to the conferral of individual benefits, is the central concern.[290]

A second development from the 1970s onwards follows on from a point made earlier. As explained above, the publication of two key textbooks, De Smith and Wade, in the late-1950s[291] and early 1960s[292] introduced a new way of conceptualising administrative law. Under this approach, the field was imagined as a cluster of legal standards which apply *generally* across all areas of public administration. From the 1970s onwards this way of imagining the legal field has acquired the status of orthodoxy in the English and Welsh context.[293] This can be seen in at least two places. First, the 1980s and 1990s have seen the publication of further textbooks on administrative law, including texts by Paul Craig[294] and Peter Cane.[295] It is striking that these new texts have generally[296] organised the subject in much the same way as both De Smith and Wade. Second, certain judges also began to speak of administrative law in such terms. Most famously, Lord Diplock[297] in *CCSU*[298] engaged in a highly influential attempt to categorise the major developments in the field around a series of 'heads'[299] of review. His Lordship, for instance, famously opined that administrative law had:

> .... developed to a stage … [where] one can conveniently classify under three heads the grounds upon which administrative action is subject to control … The first ground I would call 'illegality,' the second 'irrationality' and the third 'procedural impropriety'.[300]

[288] Peter Cane, 'Standing up for the Public' [1995] *PL* 276; David Feldman, 'Public Interest Litigation and Constitutional Theory in Comparative Perspective' (1992) 55 *MLR* 44.

[289] Mark Elliott and Jason Varuhas, *Administrative Law*, 5th edn (Oxford University Press, 2017) Ch 14.

[290] This is not to deny that there were pre-1977 cases where the courts intervened to enforce duties of this kind. See for instance *R v Greater London Council, ex parte Blackburn* [1976] 1 WLR 550 (CA).

[291] De Smith (n 220).

[292] Wade (n 221).

[293] Knight (n 220).

[294] Paul Craig, *Administrative Law*, 8th edn (Sweet & Maxwell, 2016).

[295] Peter Cane, *Administrative Law*, 5th edn (Clarendon Law Series, 2011).

[296] An important exception is Carol Harlow and Richard Rawlings, *Law and Administration*, 3rd edn (Cambridge University Press, 2009).

[297] Richard Wilberforce, 'Lord Diplock and Administrative Law' [1986] *PL* 6.

[298] *Council of Civil Service Unions v Minister for the Civil Service* [1985] AC 374 (HL).

[299] *Ibid*, 410.

[300] *Ibid*.

The third and final development to be discussed concerns the emergence and concretisation of a cluster of further legal principles.[301] In recent decades a series of new principles have come to be added to the conventional list of grounds. In *Coughlan*,[302] for instance, the Court of Appeal spoke of legitimate expectations having 'emerged as a distinct application of the concept of abuse of power'.[303] This ground will be the subject of detailed discussion in chapter five. Briefly, however, in *Coughlan* the Court of Appeal explained that the law had reached the position where it could now be said that

> where the court considers that a lawful promise or practice has induced a legitimate expectation … the court will in a proper case decide whether to frustrate the expectation is so unfair that to take a new and different course will amount to an abuse of power.[304]

Much has been written on the contours and rationale of the legitimate expectation ground. Very broadly, however, the ground places restrictions on the ability of administrative decision-makers to go back on a prior assurance when it considers that there are good policy reasons for doing so. In *Coughlan* itself, for instance, the Court of Appeal found that the local health authority had acted unlawfully when it closed a residential care facility in contravention of an assurance to the applicant that she would have a 'home for life' there.

The 1980s and 1990s also saw courts placing renewed emphasis[305] on the 'principle of legality'.[306] As explained by Lord Hoffmann in *Simms*,[307] this legal mechanism enables the courts to identify values which are taken to be inherent in the common law and to protect them by invoking the presumption that Parliament is intended to legislate consistently with such values. This principle has been invoked in a series of well-known cases in order to provide protection for such values as access to court,[308] non-retrospectivity of punishment[309] and privacy of legal correspondence.[310]

[301] See also *Bugcayday v Secretary of State for the Home Department* [1987] AC 514; Paul Craig, 'Judicial Review and Anxious Scrutiny: Foundations, Evolution and Application' [2015] *PL* 60; *Pham v Secretary of State for the Home Department* [2015] UKSC 19, [2015] 1 WLR 1591.

[302] *R v North & East Devon Health Authority, ex parte Coughlan* [2001] QB 213 (CA).

[303] *Ibid*, [71].

[304] *Ibid*, [57].

[305] For an earlier example, see *Smith v East Elloe Rural DC* [1956] AC 736, especially Lord Reid's judgment.

[306] David Dyzenhaus, Murray Hunt and Michael Taggart, 'The Principle of Legality in Administrative Law: Internationalisation as Constitutionalisation' (2001) *Oxford University Commonwealth Law Journal* 5.

[307] *R v Secretary of State for the Home Department, ex parte Simms* [2000] 2 AC 115 (HL).

[308] *R v Lord Chancellor, ex parte Witham* [1998] QB 575 (CA). *R (UNISON) v Lord Chancellor* [2017] UKSC 51, [2017] 3 WLR 409.

[309] *R v Secretary of State for the Home Department, ex parte Pierson* [1998] AC 539 (HL).

[310] *R v Secretary of State for the Home Department, ex parte Leech* [1994] QB 198 (CA); *R (Daly) v Secretary of State for the Home Department* [2001] 2 AC 532 (HL).

To summarise, in the decades following the procedural reforms, administrative law has developed considerably. The introduction of the AJR provided the courts with an opportunity to develop representative standing, a notion which enables judges to more straightforwardly provide remedies in statutory contexts where the central focus is the promotion of the public, as opposed to individual, interest. Post-1977, the mode of thinking about administrative law as a generally-applying cluster of grounds has acquired considerable influence, especially in textbooks and the thinking of certain judges. Finally, grounds or principles, such as legitimate expectations and the principle of legality, have been added to the list.

II. Two Core Lessons

The previous section explored the evolution of administrative law across the twentieth century, taking a critical discussion of Dicey's *Lectures*[311] as an entry-point. As explained in the Introduction, there are a number of reasons for telling this story at this early stage of the book. First, the historical analysis above offers a useful introduction to some of the main features of English and Welsh administrative law for the unfamiliar reader. Second, even among scholars and practitioners well-versed in English and Welsh administrative law, historical understanding is often thinner than other dimensions. Third and most fundamentally, there are important connections between the historical account in section I and the broader aims of this book. The aim of this section is to draw out two core lessons which have wider significance.

A. Lesson 1: The Complexity of Administrative Law's History

The first core lesson of this chapter is that the story of the development of administrative law in England and Wales is far from a neat and linear tale. Even a fairly brief exploration of some of the key landmarks reveals that administrative law's history is one which is both multifaceted and messy.[312] Administrative law in England and Wales was not deliberately concocted at a particular moment in time so as to conform with a singular vision of the field. Nor did it gradually crystallise around a singular 'organising principle'.[313] There is therefore considerable reason to regard cynically any historical narrative which presents administrative law's development in neat and linear terms. Narratives of this kind may often capture

[311] Dicey (n 6).

[312] Michael Taggart, 'Prolegomenon to an Intellectual History of Administrative Law in the Twentieth Century: The Case of John Willis and Canadian Administrative Law' (2005) 43 *Osgoode Hall Law Journal* 223, 232.

[313] Christopher Forsyth, 'Blasphemy against Basics: Doctrine, Conceptual Reasoning and Certain Decisions of the UK Supreme Court' in Bell, Elliott, Varuhas and Murray (eds) (n 13) 155.

important themes. They will, however, present an overly simplistic account of the law and overlook a great deal of important historical nuance.

It is useful to illustrate this point with an example. Chapter seven will discuss in some depth an influential way of thinking about administrative law known as the 'public interest conception'.[314] It is useful to very briefly introduce it here. At the heart of the public interest conception is a purported distinction between two types of normative aim an area of law might have. On the one hand, an area of law might be focused on protecting individuals by affording strong forms of legal protection to rights and interests regarded as especially fundamental. On the other, an area of law might be 'public-regarding'[315] in the sense that it focuses centrally on promoting collective interests. According to the public interest conception, at least the bulk of administrative law doctrine falls into the second camp. As Jason Varuhas has put it, the public interest conception understands administrative law as being centrally concerned 'with ensuring public power [is] exercised properly – that is, in accordance with precepts of good administration – for the good of the public as a whole'.[316]

Chapter seven will discuss the public interest conception in far greater detail. For now, the important point is that, related to the public interest conception, is a particular way of thinking about the *evolution* of administrative law. The public interest conception, in particular, presents English and Welsh administrative law as having been deliberately formulated at a particular moment in time in order to comply with an overarching normative logic. According to Varuhas, more particularly, the public interest conception is the result of a group of influential judges harnessing the opportunity presented by the procedural reforms of 1977 to fashion the new understanding of administrative law around a concern to promote the public interest.

There is undoubtedly an element of truth in this account.[317] As explained in section I, it is certainly the case that, following the procedural reforms of the late-1970s, the courts successfully carved out for themselves a greater role in enforcing statutory duties enacted to promote the collective interests. Due to a variety of reasons, pre-1977, enforcement of statutory duties of this kind was at best sporadic. One of the most important developments following the 1977 procedural reforms has been the concretisation of the concept of 'representative standing'. This development gives courts greater scope to provide remedies for the breach of such duties at the bequest of concerned individuals and organisations.

The problem with historical narrative offered by the public interest conception, however, is that despite capturing this important theme, there are other dimensions in administrative law's development which are missed or obscured.

[314] Varuhas (n 60).
[315] Varuhas (n 60) 52.
[316] Varuhas (n 60) 52.
[317] Joanna Bell, 'Judicial Review of Executive Action & Common Law Constitutional Rights' in Mark Elliott and Kirsty Hughes, *Common Law Constitutional Rights* (forthcoming in Hart Publishing).

The picture painted by this mode of thinking, in other words, is a partial one only. Two particular deficiencies are worth drawing out.

First, by focusing centrally on the courts' achievement in carving out for themselves a greater role in promoting the *public-regarding* purposes which underlie administrative schemes, the historical narrative offered by the public interest conception obscures a series of *individual-regarding* dimensions to the field. By focusing, in other words, on important post-1977 developments, such as the evolution of representative standing, this narrative obscures the long-standing role the courts have played in intervening to protect the interests of the individual. The early case law on procedural review provides a good example. As explained, across the nineteenth century the courts decided a series of cases which established that individuals whose rights were at stake in a decision should be given notice to the extent that doing so would not significantly undermine statutory aims.[318] Due to a combination of factors, this approach changed over the course of the early twentieth century.[319] The landmark decision in *Ridge*[320] in 1964, however, provided a foundation on which later courts could build[321] to restore something more akin to the earlier approach.

Other examples can be given. Recent decades have, for instance, seen the crystallisation of the doctrine of legitimate expectations.[322] This ground will be discussed in chapter five. It is important to note briefly here, however, that it has important individual-regarding elements. A central concern of the court is to protect individuals both from the moral harms which result when a decision-maker reneges on a promise[323] and from the material harms which are suffered when an administrative decision-maker changes its policy position without making provision for transition.[324]

A second deficiency is closely related to the first: the historical narrative offered by public interest conception obscures the historically complex origins of the grounds of review.[325] The impression this account creates is one in which the courts took the opportunity presented by the procedural reforms to introduce a new conception of administrative law, organised around a concern to promote the interests of the public. This carries the risk, in turn, that the grounds of review are presented as a cluster of doctrines specifically developed in the 1980s in order to further this aim. Jason Varuhas, for instance, has explained that

[318] *Capel* (n 81); *Hammersmith* (n 88).
[319] De Smith (n 240); Wade (n 240).
[320] *Ridge* (n 209).
[321] *Re HK* (n 239).
[322] *Coughlan* (n 302).
[323] *R (Bibi) v Newham LBC* [2001] EWCA Civ 607, [2002] 1 WLR 237, [55]. See discussion of 'category 1' cases in chapter 5.
[324] *R (Patel) v General Medical Council* [2013] EWCA Civ 237, [2013] 1 WLR 2801. See discussion of 'category 3' cases in chapter 5.
[325] Craig (n 8); Paul Craig, 'Taxonomy and Public Law: A Response' [2019] *PL* 281.

it was a 'short step'[326] from the premise that administrative law is centrally 'public-regarding'[327] in nature, to the major grounds. There are different ways of reading this suggestion. It is important, however, to be clear that the 'grounds of review' are not the product of conscientious design, nor were they created at a single moment in history. As the discussion above illustrates, their origins are diverse. Some, such as legitimate expectations, are relatively modern creations.[328] Others, however, such as the law on procedural review, have origins in case law which is centuries old.

B. Lesson 2: Three Senses of Complexity and Variety in Administrative Law's 'Anatomy'

The first core lesson which emerges from a consideration of administrative law's modern history then, is that administrative law is not the product of conscientious design. The field developed organically and its evolution has been characterised by complexity. This leads neatly on to the second lesson. One reason for the complexity of administrative law is that there is considerable variety in terms of the legal structures with which courts engage in adjudication. There are, furthermore, at least three important senses in which this is true.

First, as can be seen throughout the discussion above, administrative law challenges do not arise in a legal vacuum. Rather, they usually arise against the backdrop of a legislative framework. These frameworks vary considerably in terms of their purposes and structure and their details play an important role in how administrative law doctrine is applied. This can be seen in much of the discussion above. As explained, for instance, the twentieth century saw at least two major expansions of the legislative frameworks which constitute administrative schemes: the first during the Asquith Government in the 1910s and the second during the Atlee Government of 1945 – giving rise to significant bodies of administrative law case law. It was seen that, within these periods of growth, the legislative frameworks which were enacted varied considerably from one to the next. Some focused on defining the circumstances in which individuals have a personal right to state assistance. Others set up institutional frameworks for safeguarding collective interests, such as those in the preservation of scientifically interesting or especially beautiful land.[329]

The discussion above also began to illustrate how the outcome of a legal challenge can turn on the aims or detail of the legislative framework. In the nineteenth-century decision *Hammersmith Rent-Charge*,[330] for instance, the Court

[326] Varuhas (n 60).
[327] Varuhas (n 60) 52.
[328] See discussion in chapter 5.
[329] National Parks and Access to the Countryside Act 1949.
[330] *Hammersmith* (n 88).

held that the individual had no right to notice because requiring notice would undermine the effectiveness of the background legislative scheme. Similarly, in the important *Fleet Street Casuals*[331] case, the majority of the House of Lords concluded that the applicant lacked a 'sufficient interest'[332] because permitting individuals or organisations to bring challenges in the tax context was thought to be inconsistent with the emphasis on privacy in the legislative framework.

Second, it is also clear from the above that administrative law doctrine has not been developed with a singular normative vision of the purposes of administrative law in mind. In developing administrative law judges, rather, have sought to strive to work out how to accommodate a plurality of purposes, values and interests. This is so, furthermore, in at least two senses.

In the first place, in developing administrative law the courts have sought to accommodate legal values with different *origins*. Aspects of administrative law doctrine have, for instance, been developed in order to ensure that decision-makers act so as to promote the purposes underlying the legislative schemes to which Parliament has leant it approval. The clearest example of this is probably the principle concretised in *Padfield*.[333] This doctrine requires administrative decision-makers to have specific regard to the aims of the background legislative framework and to act with those purposes in mind. Correlatively, when adjudicating under it, the courts focus centrally on understanding the objectives of the legislative scheme in order to determine whether a decision has been taken in line with them. That said, the discussion above also draws attention to aspects of administrative law doctrine which are centrally concerned with safeguarding common law values. The principle of legality, for instance, ensures that common law values regarded as 'fundamental' can only be overridden by clear legislative words. The early case law on procedural review, furthermore, emphasised the importance of protecting the long-established common law principle that affected individuals should be given notice of a decision prior to their rights being infringed.

In the second place, in developing administrative law doctrine the courts have sought to afford protection to both the interests of the public and the individual. Again the discussion above illustrates this very clearly. The relationship between administrative law doctrine and the promotion of the public interest is best illustrated in the case law which develops 'representative standing'. As explained above, this notion enables the courts to more straightforwardly provide remedies in cases where an administrative decision-maker acts contrary to a statutory duty enacted to benefit the public as a collectivity. Other aspects of the discussion, however, also illustrated the courts' longstanding preoccupation with ensuring that individuals,

[331] *Fleet Street Casuals* (n 273).
[332] Senior Courts Act 1981, s31(3).
[333] *Padfield* (n 230).

whose rights and interests are at stake, are meaningfully protected. A good example is again provided by the case law on procedural review.

Third, the discussion above also illustrates that administrative law case law has required the courts to engage with different kinds of legal relationships. The Divisional Court in deciding *Lewisham Union Guardians*, for instance, formed the view that it is inappropriate to issue a writ of mandamus to enforce a statutory duty enacted to benefit the public as a collectivity, as opposed to upholding the rights of an individual applicant to hold an office or a licence. In later case law, however, the courts developed the notion of representative standing which enables them to provide relief in cases precisely of this kind. This is not to say, however, that administrative law is concerned only with duties owed to the public at large, and that challenges are never concerned with the rights of individuals. As will be emphasised in the next chapter, such an understanding is overly simplistic. One reason for this is that the legislative schemes which sit in the background of administrative law challenges are not of one kind. Some frameworks, especially those in the social welfare context, purport to define the circumstances in which individuals acquire 'rights' or 'entitlements' to receive particular forms of treatment from administrative decision-makers.

To summarise, this chapter has been concerned with the evolution of administrative law across the course of the twentieth century. This history is significant and interesting of itself. Furthermore, at least two important lessons of broader importance can also be drawn out from it. The first lesson is that administrative law in England and Wales has not developed in a neat and linear way. Administrative law was not crafted at a particular moment in time to conform to an overarching logic. Its evolution, rather, has been both multifaceted and messy. The second lesson, and one reason for this, is that the legal structures in play in administrative adjudication are both complex and varied. Administrative law challenges arise against an array of different legislative frameworks; the courts seek to accommodate a variety of different legal values and administrative law challenges concern legal relationships of different kinds. An exploration of the field's modern history, in other words, offers a first glimpse of what this book terms administrative law's complex and varied 'anatomy'.

III. Conclusion

This chapter has offered an overview of the development of administrative law since the late nineteenth century. The purpose in doing so has not been to provide an exhaustive chronical of every important development over this period. The aim, rather, has been to call attention to some of the most important landmarks in order to give a sense of the complexity of the field's modern history.

After exploring this history, the chapter has drawn out two main lessons of broader importance. The first is that administrative law's modern history is far from a neat and linear tale. There is, therefore, considerable reason to be cynical of attempts to present the field as having grown up around, or been deliberately crafted around, an 'organising concept'.[334] The second is that even a broad exploration of just some of the core stages in administrative law's development offers a first glimpse of, what the book terms, the complex and varied 'anatomy' of administrative law. That 'anatomy' is the focus of the next chapter.

[334] Forsyth (n 1) [27].

3

The Anatomy of Administrative Law

In its introductory chapter, this book discussed a monologue which was offered by Nobel Prize-winning physicist Richard Feynman in the course of an interview with the BBC. Feynman's 'Ode to a Flower' tells the story of a disagreement between Feynman and a friend of his who worked as an artist. Feynman's artist friend explains that he does not see why a scientist would 'take … apart'[1] an object such as a flower in order to understand it. Understanding the flower is simple: one needs to grasp only the most important thing about it, namely that it is beautiful. Feynman, however, fundamentally disagrees. For him, the flower is an inherently complex and detailed object, characterised by an intricate 'inner structure.' Pulling apart the flower is necessary in order to examine this structure and to build a thorough understanding of it.

As explained in chapter one, the first main aim of this book is to make a similar argument in relation to administrative law. There is a great deal to be learnt by 'pulling apart' administrative law case law and observing the legal structures which are in play in legal adjudication. What becomes apparent when this is done is that those legal structures are both complicated and diverse in at least three core senses. In other words, much like the flower, the 'anatomy' of administrative law is characterised by important sources of complexity and variety.

The book began to develop this argument in the previous chapter. Chapter two explored the development of modern administrative law, primarily focusing on the twentieth century. It drew out from that history two important lessons. First, the modern history of administrative law is both multifaceted and messy. There is, therefore, considerable reason to be cynical of attempts to present administrative law as having grown up or been deliberately created around a singular 'organising concept'.[2] Second, an exploration of administrative law's modern history highlights at least three senses in which the legal structures in play in adjudication are complex and varied: (i) administrative law challenges usually arise against the background of legislative frameworks and there is considerable diversity across these frameworks; (ii) courts seek to accommodate a plurality of legal values, interests and

[1] Professor Richard Feynman, 'The Pleasure of Finding Things Out' (*BBC*, 1981–1982) available at: www.bbc.co.uk/programmes/p018dvyg.

[2] Christopher Forsyth, 'The Rock and the Sand: Jurisdiction and Remedial Discretion' (2013) 18(4) *Judicial Review* 360 [27].

purposes when adjudicating on administrative law issues and (iii) administrative law challenges concern legal relationships of different kinds.

The core aim of this chapter is to unpack each of those senses of complexity in more detail. The chapter can therefore be thought of as an exercise in 'pulling apart' administrative law case law. Or, to put it another way, in exploring the 'anatomy' of administrative law. The bulk of the discussion is divided into three sections. Section I is concerned with the centrality of legislative frameworks in administrative law adjudication. Section II focuses on the plurality of legal values, interests and purposes the courts seek to accommodate when determining administrative law challenges. Section III explores the varieties of legal relationship administrative law case law can concern. The final section then concludes.

I. First Sense of Complexity and Variety: The Interrelationship of Administrative Law Doctrine and the Legislative Framework in the Background of the Case

The central argument of this chapter is that the legal and normative structures which are in play in administrative law adjudication are both complex and varied in three core senses. The aim of sections I, II and III is to work through, and explain, each in turn.

This section is focused on a first source of complexity and variety. This sense can be introduced in the following terms: the grounds of review do not function as a series of freestanding legal tests[3] which apply directly to the facts of the case and mechanistically determine the proper legal outcome.[4] On the contrary, administrative law doctrine often interacts closely with the particular legislative framework in the background of the challenge. The legislative frameworks with which administrative law doctrine interacts, furthermore, are not of one kind. Rather they vary significantly, in their aims, structure and detail, from one to the next.

This brief description of administrative law's first sense of complexity and variety is in need of significant unpacking. It is worth expanding on three points in particular.

The first is that administrative law doctrine interacts closely with the particular legislative framework in the background of a legal challenge. The close interaction of grounds of review and legislation is a phenomenon which characterises

[3] Trevor Allan, 'The Constitutional Foundations of Judicial Review' (2002) 61(1) *CLJ* 87; Trevor Allan, 'Doctrine and Theory in Administrative Law: An Elusive Quest for the Limits of Jurisdiction' [2003] *PL* 429.

[4] As Daly has put it, the grounds of review are not 'self-applying': Paul Daly, 'The Language of Administrative Law' (2016) 94 *La Revue Du Barreau Canadien* 520, 522.

adjudication under all of the grounds of review. There is not, however, one monolithic way in which administrative law doctrine interacts with legislation, meaning that talk of '*the*' relationship between the grounds of review and legislation in this field is very difficult.[5]

It is useful to illustrate this point with a brief discussion of a few examples. A broad (and imperfect) distinction has been drawn elsewhere between grounds of review which are 'thin' and grounds which are 'thicker'.[6] Grounds which are thin create frameworks which refer the court to the legislative scheme in the background of the case with a particular set of queries in mind. These grounds, in other words, do relatively little of the 'legal work'[7] in determining the outcome of a case. Rather, their function in many cases is to provide a framework around which inquiries concerning legislation can be organised.

The clearest example[8] is the '*Padfield* principle'.[9] As explained in chapter three, this ground places administrative decision-makers under a duty to exercise discretionary powers in order to 'promote the policy and objects of the Act'[10] which conferred them. The principle by itself, however, will rarely provide a determinate answer to the kinds of legal disputes which arise before the courts. The role of the *Padfield* principle is often to direct administrative decision-makers and reviewing courts to engage in close analysis of the background legislative scheme. It is, after all, only following a careful reading of this regime, with the aim of uncovering its underlying purposes, that the courts can go on to ask whether the administrative decision-maker has acted with its 'policy and objects'[11] sufficiently in mind.[12]

Other grounds of review cannot be characterised as 'thin' in this sense. This is true, for instance, of aspects of the law of procedural review.[13] Consider the question of when an individual must be given access to the 'gist' of the case against them. The courts have come to recognise a strong common law presumption that individuals must be informed of, at least, an outline of the arguments and evidence before an adverse decision is made against them.[14] The principle in favour of gisting

[5] Thomas Adams, 'Ultra Vires Revisited' [2018] *PL* 31.

[6] Joanna Bell, 'Judicial Review of Executive Action & Common Law Constitutional Rights' in Mark Elliott and Kirsty Hughes, *Common Law Constitutional Rights* (forthcoming in Hart Publishing).

[7] Joanna Bell, '*ClientEarth (No 2)*: A Case of Three Legal Dimensions' (2017) 29(2) *Journal of Enivonmental Law* 343.

[8] See further discussion in Adams (n 5); Joanna Bell, 'Rethinking the Story of *Cart v Upper Tribunal* and its Implications for Administrative Law' (2019) 39(1) *OJLS* 74.

[9] Language used throughout, for instance, *Patel v Secretary of State for the Home Department* [2013] UKSC 72, [2014] AC 651; *R (Britcits) v Secretary of State for the Home Department* [2017] EWCA Civ 368.

[10] *Padfield v Minister of Agriculture, Fisheries and Food* [1968] AC 997 (HL) 1030.

[11] *Ibid.*

[12] It is for this reason that judgments which *Padfield* challenges often read, primarily, as a very detailed consideration of the statutory background to the case: *Bromley LBC v Greater London Council* [1983] 1 AC 768 (HL).

[13] See discussion of the importance of procedural codes in chapter 4.

[14] *Bank Mellat v HM Treasury* [2013] UKSC 39, [2014] AC 700.

does more than supply a frame around which questions concerning legislation are to be organised. In circumstances where legislation is silent on the issue of whether relevant evidence ought to be disclosed to them, the common law presumption in favour of gisting may supply a clear answer to the case.[15] Engagement with the specific statutory framework in the background of a challenge is, nonetheless, of central importance in procedural review adjudication.

One reason for this is that the common law principle in favour of gisting has presumptive force only. Where an administrative decision-maker can successfully demonstrate that the purposes of the specific legislative scheme at the background of the case would be significantly compromised by permitting the individual access to the gist of the case, this may be capable of displacing the common law starting-point.[16] As a result, judicial reasoning in many procedural review cases focuses to a large extent on understanding the underlying policy aims of the background legislative framework.[17]

The second important point to be stressed under this heading concerns the diversity of the legislative schemes with which the grounds of review interact. The statutory frameworks which Parliament creates are not of one kind. There are, rather, many different kinds of legislative framework. This chapter cannot provide an exhaustive taxonomy. Indeed, it is highly doubtful that the compilation of such a taxonomy is even possible. Instead, it will suffice to discuss three broad categories of scheme by way of illustration.

The first category of administrative scheme which is particularly worthy of discussion consists of regimes which are designed to regulate the making of individualised decisions. It seems prudent to discuss this category of case first because Sarah Nason has suggested that approximately half of the Administrative Court's workload is made up of legal challenges based on administrative regimes of this kind.[18] The hallmark of this category of administrative scheme is its structure: schemes of this kind are designed primarily to regulate the taking of decisions about whether an individual ought to be subjected to a particular burden, or granted a benefit. Individualised administrative schemes thus tend to prescribe a number of things. They very often set out the criteria against which the individual's case will be determined. They also often lay down stipulations as to the procedure to be followed in determining whether those criteria are fulfilled.[19]

[15] *R (Rowe) v Revenue and Customs Commissioners* [2017] EWCA Civ 2105, [2018] 1 WLR 3039 (discussed in chapter 5).

[16] *R (Haralambous) v St Albans Crown Court* [2018] UKSC 1, [2018] AC 236.

[17] *Ibid.*

[18] Nason terms them 'individual grievance cases': Sarah Nason, *Reconstructing Judicial Review* (Bloomsbury, 2016) 143.

[19] Including by providing for the possibility of review. See: *Begum v Tower Hamlets LBC* [2003] UKHL 5, [2003] 2 AC 430; *Ali v Birmingham CC* [2010] UKSC 8, [2010] AC 39; *Ali v United Kingdom* (40378/10) (2016) 63 EHRR 20; *Poshteh v Kensington and Chelsea RLBC* [2017] UKSC 36.

There are a number of classic examples of individualised schemes of this kind. Consider, for instance, a licensing scheme[20] such as that which regulates the issuance of television licences.[21] The central functions of this scheme include the identification of the circumstances in which the BBC, using its statutory power,[22] will 'see fit'[23] to confer a licence for the 'installation and use'[24] of a television. The legislative framework also lays down a procedure through which individuals who fail to obtain such a licence may be penalised.[25] Other clear examples of individualised decision-making schemes include many social security or housing regimes.[26] Consider, for example, the Welfare Reform Act 2012[27] and its accompanying legislation.[28] A central function of this scheme is to prescribe circumstances in which an individual applicant[29] will be regarded as having an 'entitlement'[30] to 'a benefit known as universal credit'.[31] The scheme also equips such individuals with procedural rights entitling them to have their application decided by a particular method.[32] Further examples of individualised schemes include those relating to professional discipline[33] and tax.[34]

Another category of scheme which is worth emphasising bears some similarity to the first, although it is importantly different. Schemes of this second kind are in part designed to regulate the making of decisions about how individuals ought to be treated. They also, however, feature inbuilt, often procedural, safeguards designed to protect other interests which will be particularly acutely affected by the decision.

[20] For examples of challenges see: *Nakkuda Ali v MF de Jayaratne* [1951] AC 66 (PC); *R v Metropolitan Police Commissioners, ex parte Parker* [1953] 1 WLR 1150 (DC); *McInnes v Onslow Fane* [1978] 1 WLR 1520 (Ch); *R (Raphael) v Highbury Corner Magistrates' Court* [2011] EWCA Civ 462, [2012] PTSR 427; *Peerless Ltd v Gambling Regulatory Authority* [2015] UKPC 29, [2015] LLR 539.

[21] Communications Act 2003, Part 4; Communications (Television Licensing) Regulations 2004 (SI 2004/692); Communications (Television Licensing) (Amendment) Regulations 2017 (SI 2017/221). Note that a predecessor of the current scheme relating to TV licensing was in issue in the classic case of *Congreve v Home Office* [1976] QB 629 (CA).

[22] Communications Act 2003, s364.

[23] *Ibid.*

[24] *Ibid*, s363.

[25] See especially *ibid*, s366.

[26] Paul Craig, 'Taxonomy and Public Law: A Response' [2019] *PL* 281, 283–91. See, eg: *R (Wiles) v Social Security Commissioners* [2010] EWCA Civ 258; *R (Hardy) v Sandwell MBC* [2015] EWHC 890 (Admin), [2015] PTSR 1292.

[27] Welfare Reform Act 2012.

[28] Universal Credit Regulations 2013 (SI 2013/376).

[29] Or couple: Welfare Reform Act 2012, s1.

[30] *Ibid*, s3.

[31] *Ibid*, s1.

[32] Social Security Act 1998, s12.

[33] See, eg: *Cronin v Greyhound Board of Great Britain Ltd* [2013] EWCA Civ 668; *R (Hill) v Institute of Chartered Accountants in England and Wales* [2013] EWCA Civ 555, [2014] 1 WLR 86; *R (Chief Constable of Thames Valley Police) v Police Appeals Tribunal* [2016] EWCA Civ 1315.

[34] *R v Inland Revenue Commissioners, ex parte National Federation of Self-Employed* [1982] AC 617 (HL).

The clearest example of a scheme of this kind is the planning regime,[35] which forms the background to many well-known administrative law challenges.[36] This regime is in part a scheme for determining whether individuals who apply for permission to 'develop land'[37] ought to be granted authorisation. That is, one of its functions is to lay down criteria against,[38] and a process by,[39] which an individual's application for planning permission will be determined. Importantly, however, another major feature of the planning regime is the conferral of a series of protections on individuals or groups whose interests are likely to be affected by development. Take, for instance, section 61W of the Town and Country Planning Act 1990. This provision requires persons applying for planning permission to 'publicise the proposed application in such manner as the person reasonably considers is likely to bring the proposed application to the attention of a majority of the persons who live at … premises in the vicinity of the land'.[40] The central aim of this provision is to provide a form of procedural protection to the interests of those who reside close to planned development.

The planning regime is not the only administrative scheme which has this dual aspect. A further example[41] is administrative regimes relating to the grant of economic advantages. Schemes of this kind, like the planning regime, often have two broad limbs.[42] In the first place, they lay down criteria by which companies or individuals applying will be determined. In the second place, they also often put in place safeguards for those who will be most acutely affected by the grant of the benefit, namely economic competitors. A scheme of this kind was in play, for instance, in the Court of Appeal decision in *Project Management Institute*.[43]

[35] Town and Country Planning Act 1990; Town and Country Planning (General Permitted Development Order) 1995 (SI 1995/418); Planning and Compulsory Purchase Act 2004; Planning Act 2008; Localism Act 2011. See discussion in Elizabeth Fisher, Bettina Lange and Eloise Scotford, *Environmental Law* (Oxford University Press, 2013) Ch 18; *R (Alconbury Developments Ltd) v Secretary of State for the Environment, Transport and the Regions* [2001] UKHL 23, [2003] 2 AC 295, especially [68].

[36] *Tesco Stores Ltd v Secretary of State for the Environment* [1995] 1 WLR 759; *R v Somerset CC, ex parte Dixon* [1998] Env LR 111; *South Bucks DC v Porter* [2003] UKHL 26, [2003] 2 AC 558; *Oakley v South Cambridgeshire DC* [2017] EWCA Civ 71, [2017] 1 WLR 3765; *Dover DC v Campaign to Protect Rural England (Kent)* [2017] UKSC 79, [2018] 1 WLR 108.

[37] Town and Country Planning Act 1990, s57.

[38] *Ibid*; *Stringer v Minister for Housing and Local Government* [1970] 1 WLR 1281.

[39] Town and Country Planning Act 1990, ss61, 65, 70–74, 77–79.

[40] *Ibid*, s61W(2).

[41] Some licensing regimes fall more naturally into this category, ie the regime relating to licensing for the sale of alcohol. See especially: Licensing Act 2003; Licensing Act 2003 (Personal licences) Regulations 2005 (SI 2005/41); Licensing Act 2003 (Premises licences and club premises certifications) Regulations 2005 (SI 2005/42); Licensing Act 2003 (Licensing authority's register) (other information) Regulations (SI 2005/43); *R (Albert Court Residents' Association and Others) v Westminster CC* [2011] EWCA Civ 430, [2012] PTSR 604.

[42] The public procurement regime might be included within this category. See: Public Contracts Regulations 2015 (SI 2015/102) (implementing Directive 2014/24/EU of the European Parliament and of the Council of 26 February 2014 on public procurement and repealing Directive 2004/18/EC Text with EEA relevance [2014] OJ L94/65); *R (Chandler) v Secretary of State for Children, Schools and Families* [2010] PTSR 749, [2009] EWCA Civ 1011.

[43] *R (Project Management Institute (PMI)) v Minister for the Cabinet Office* [2016] EWCA Civ 21, [2016] 1 WLR 1737.

The background to this case was an administrative regime[44] which regulated the grant of Royal Charter status. One function of this scheme was to lay down criteria by which individual applications would be processed.[45] The scheme also put in place a number of inbuilt safeguards, designed to protect the interests of applicant companies' economic competitors.[46] Cabinet Office policy, for instance, provided that Chartered status would not usually be granted to a company if there was a 'significant overlap'[47] between its interests and those of an economic rival. Similarly, the same policy also placed applicants for Chartered status under a requirement to 'take soundings'[48] from their commercial rivals prior to making an application.

A third category of administrative regime which is worthy of discussion is substantially different from the first two. Schemes falling within this category are in no sense designed to regulate the taking of decisions about the treatment of individuals. Their focus, rather, is on collective or public interests. Very broadly, such schemes put in place frameworks which regulate decisions about how such interests are best protected or promoted.

Two examples will suffice to illustrate. First, consider administrative schemes relating to the protection of certain aspects of the environment[49] such as that which designates and preserves Areas of Outstanding Natural Beauty ('AONBs'). At the core of the AONB scheme is section 82 of the Countryside and Rights of Way Act 2000.[50] This provision confers on Natural England, a statutory body[51] whose purpose is that of ensuring that 'natural environment is conserved, enhanced and managed',[52] the power to designate certain rural regions as being of 'such outstanding natural beauty that it is desirable'[53] that a special status should be attached. The effect of such a designation is that a cluster of special legal and policy protections bite when decisions are being taken about the land. One, for instance, is section 84(4) of the 2000 Act. This provision places planning authorities under a statutory duty to 'take all such action as appears to them expedient for the

[44] Note that the regime is unusual as it did not have a legislative footing, but was introduced through prerogative powers. See discussion in chapter 1, section IV.

[45] The Cabinet Office had published on its website a list of five criteria which would guide its decision as to whether to grant Chartered status in a given case: *PMI* (n 43) [9].

[46] This was a central reason why the Court of Appeal regarded the applicant as having a 'sufficient interest' to bring the challenge. (See *PMI* (n 43) [37] and *R (Project Management Institute) v Minister for the Cabinet Office* [2014] EWHC 2438 (Admin) in which Mitting J reached the opposite conclusion.)

[47] *PMI* (n 43) [9].

[48] *PMI* (n 43) [9].

[49] Further examples include Air Quality Standards Regulations 2010 (SI 2010/1001) (implementing Directive 2008/50/EC of the European Parliament and of the Council of 21 May 2008 on ambient air quality and cleaner air for Europe [2008] L152/1); Conservation of Habitats and Species Regulations 2010 (SI 2010/490) (implementing the Council Directive 92/43/EEC of 21 May 1992 on the conservation of natural habitats and of wild fauna and flora [1992] L206/7); Wildlife and Countryside Act 1981, ss28–33.

[50] Countryside and Rights of Way Act 2000.

[51] Created by the Natural Environment and Rural Communities Act 2006, s107.

[52] *Ibid*, s2(1).

[53] Countryside and Rights of Way Act 2000, s81(1) (as amended by Natural Environment and Rural Communities Act 2006, s107).

accomplishment of the purpose of conserving and enhancing the natural beauty of the area'.[54] Another, is that central government planning policy stipulates that 'planning permission should be refused for major developments [on the land] … except in exceptional circumstances'.[55]

As this discussion illustrates, the AONB framework will often interact with another administrative scheme, namely the planning regime.[56] In particular, when making decisions about whether a particular applicant should be granted planning permission, planning authorities must have regard to the desirability of conserving AONBs. At its heart, however, the AONB scheme is not concerned with defining the circumstances in which individuals should be made subject to burdens or granted benefits. Its driving logic, rather, is the idea that there are regions of countryside which, due to their beauty, ought to be subject to special protection.[57] The AONB regime affords this protection by creating designation powers and structuring administrative decision-making about developing on land of this type.

By way of a second example of a scheme of this kind, consider also the legislative background to *World Development Movement*:[58] the Overseas Development and Co-operation Act 1980.[59] Section 1 of this Act empowered the Secretary of State to take certain actions 'for the purpose of promoting the development or maintaining the economy of a country or territory outside the United Kingdom or the welfare of its people'.[60] Like the AONB regime, the focus of this scheme is not on regulating the taking of particularised decisions about how individual applicants ought to be treated. The idea underlying the scheme, rather, would seem to be that the public as a collectivity has an interest in seeing assistance provided to foreign states. The Overseas Development and Co-operation Act therefore created a framework which empowered the Secretary of State to take steps to promote this interest and regulated how decisions could be taken.

So far the discussion in this section has developed two main points. The first is that the administrative law doctrine interacts closely with the aims, structure and detail of statutory schemes and that there is not a singular way in which the grounds of review do this. The second is that legislative frameworks are not of one

[54] *Ibid*, s84(1).

[55] Department for Communities and Local Government, 'National Planning Policy Framework' ('NPPF') (February 2019) [116].

[56] *R (Hillingdon LBC) v Transport Secretary* [2010] EWHC 626, (Admin); Lord Carnwath, 'Judges and the Common Laws of the Environment – At Homes and Abroad' (2014) 26(2) *Journal of Environmental Law* 177; Elizabeth Fisher, 'Law and Energy Transitions: Wind Turbines and Planning Law in the UK' (2018) 38(3) *OJLS* 528.

[57] This is not to suggest that there is a monolithic view on why land should be regarded as valuable: see Elizabeth Fisher, Bettina Lange and Eloise Scotford, *Environmental Law*, 2nd edn (Oxford University Press, 2019) Ch 20.

[58] *R v Secretary of State for Foreign and Commonwealth Affairs, ex parte World Development Movement Ltd* [1995] 1 WLR 386 (DC).

[59] Overseas Development and Co-operation Act 1980 (since repealed by International Development Act 2002).

[60] *Ibid*, s1(1).

kind, but vary significantly, in terms of their aims, detail and structure. Before moving on from this first sense of complexity and variety, it is worth discussing a third and final issue: the level of detail in which administrative schemes are expressed.

It is very difficult to be categorical about this issue. Administrative law legislation is an under-researched subject, at least in general terms.[61] There is, however, reason to think that the administrative schemes which form the background of many administrative law challenges are increasingly rich in detail.[62] Two developments, which have attracted some scholarly attention, are especially worthy of discussion.

In introducing the first, it is useful to return to a cluster of points discussed in chapter two. This chapter emphasised that one of the important themes which has characterised administrative law's development since 1885 is the assumption by central government, due to a variety of factors,[63] of a series of new administrative functions. Chapter two, for instance, explained that the 1910s saw central government assume important roles in the distribution of state pensions[64] and the delivery of universal state education.[65] In a similar way, the 1940s witnessed the introduction of a host of new administrative schemes including those relating to planning,[66] environmental protection,[67] social security[68] and the creation of a National Health Service.[69] These developments have had many important consequences.[70] For present purposes, however, the most important concerns delegated legislation. Delegated legislation in England and Wales has a long and interesting history.[71] Many have suggested,[72] however, that, as the Government began to take on a greater array of administrative roles over the course of the twentieth century, the quantity and density of secondary legislation increased.

[61] Discussion of legislation tends to focus on particular developments of regimes. For instance, for useful discussion of legislation relating to environmental regulation, see Eloise Scotford and Jonathan Robinson, 'UK Environmental Legislation and Its Administration in 2013 – Achievements, Challenges and Prospects' (2013) 25(3) *Journal of Environmental Law* 383.

[62] A development perhaps connected to the creation of specialist administrative First-tier Tribunals (Tribunals, Courts and Enforcement Act 2007) and the Planning Court (Mr Justice Lindblom, 'The Planning Court: One Year On' [2015] *Journal of Planning and Environmental Law* OP3).

[63] Chapter 2.

[64] Old Age Pensions Act 1908.

[65] Education Act 1914.

[66] Town and Country Planning Act 1947.

[67] National Parks and Access to the Countryside Act 1949.

[68] National Insurance Act 1946.

[69] National Health Service Act 1946.

[70] Many of the legal implications, including increased academic interest in administrative law, were discussed in chapter 2.

[71] Cecil Carr, *Delegated Legislation: Three Lectures* (Cambridge University Press, 1921).

[72] *Ibid*; Lord Gordon Hewart of Bury, *The New Despotism* (Ernst Benn Ltd, 1929); The *Committee on Ministers' Powers Report* (HM Stationery Office, 1932) ('Donoughmore Report'); Nick Barber and Alison Young, 'The Rise of Prospective Henry VIII Clauses and their Implications for Sovereignty' [2003] *PL* 112.

If this is correct, it will naturally have had implications for the courts. In particular, it will have meant that the legal landscapes in which courts are adjudicating have changed considerably.[73] In order to illustrate this point, it is useful to consider two examples. First, the well-known case of *Cooper*.[74] As chapter two explained, *Cooper* was a landmark case in the evolution of thinking about procedural review.[75] The Court held that, prior to demolishing an individual's property, the Board of Works was required to supply them with notice. For present purposes, however, the most interesting point about *Cooper* concerns the background legislative framework: the Metropolis Local Management Act 1855.[76] The Act was enacted in order to respond to London's slum-housing crisis during the mid-nineteenth century. It created a new hierarchy of administrative decision-makers and equipped them with powers to manage unsafe properties. The Act was, however, 'skeletal'[77] in nature. On the subject of the procedures to be followed by a Board prior to demolishing property, for instance, the Act provided only that this power was triggered where a house 'be begun, erected, made or provided in any respect contrary to any Order'.[78] The Act was completely silent on whether, prior to exercising this power, there were any procedural steps the Board of Works was required to follow, or not follow. When Erle CJ described the Court as 'supply[ing] the omission of the legislature',[79] therefore, he was capturing an important feature of the case. *Cooper* concerned a statutory scheme which specified relatively little. The task of the Court was therefore to work within a legislative vacuum and to draw on common law principles to identify the proper legal solution to the issue at hand.

Fast-forwarding, however, to another landmark procedural review case – *Ridge*[80] decided in 1964 – it is notable that the legal landscape in which the courts were operating was rather different. The background to *Ridge* was a series of detailed Regulations[81] which dealt specifically with the issues of procedure. It is often overlooked that one of the legal questions which arose in *Ridge* was whether the applicant's case fell within the scope of the Regulations which dealt with the

[73] One development, of course, is that courts have had to consider challenges to Regulations themselves: *R (Reilly) v Secretary of State for Work and Pensions* [2013] UKSC 68, [2014] AC 453.

[74] *Cooper v Wandsworth Board of Works* (1863) 143 ER 414.

[75] Timothy Endicott, *Administrative Law*, 4th edn (Oxford University Press, 2018) Ch 4.

[76] Metropolis Local Management Act 1855.

[77] House of Lords Select Committee on the Constitution, *The Legislative Process: The Delegation of Powers* (16th Report of Session 2017–2019) 17–19.

[78] Metropolis Local Management Act 1855, s76.

[79] *Cooper* (n 74) 194.

[80] *Ridge v Baldwin* [1964] AC 40 (HL).

[81] Police Discipline Regulations 1952 (SI 1952/1705); Police (Discipline) (Deputy Chief Constables, Assistant Chief Constables and Chief Constables) Regulations 1952 (SI 1952/1706); Police (Discipline) (Deputy Chief Constables, Assistant Chief Constables and Chief Constables) Regulations 1954 (SI 1954/1688).

dismissal of senior police officers.[82] Four of five Law Lords concluded that the watch committee had unlawfully failed to comply with the process they laid out.[83]

A comparison of these cases draws attention to a phenomenon which has been explained by Carol Harlow and Richard Rawlings in the following terms:

> … far from the Victorian prototype of the common law supplying 'the omission of the legislature' in sparse statutes, [procedural review challenges often involve] judges navigating, evaluating and commenting on, whole thickets of legislatively sanctioned administrative procedure.[84]

The legal landscapes in which procedural review challenges arise, in other words, seem to have changed significantly across the twentieth century. Unlike *Cooper*, *Ridge* was far from a case in which a legislative framework conferred power and made little provision for procedural questions. There were, on the contrary, a series of detailed regulations setting out the steps the watch committee ought to take prior to exercising its powers. As chapter four will explain, *Ridge* is far from a lone example. Many procedural review challenges now require judges to 'navigate, evaluate and comment on whole thickets of legislatively sanctioned administrative procedure',[85] rather than address procedural questions which have been given no explicit consideration elsewhere.

A second development worth discussing is the role played by 'soft law'[86] in supplementing primary and secondary legislation.[87] There is a common belief that governmental guidance and administrative policy play a much greater role in structuring administrative discretion and making provision for issues such as procedure than they once did.[88] In the absence of systematic research into the subject, it is difficult to know with certainty whether, and the degree to which, this is the case. There are, however, certainly examples in recent years of the courts actively encouraging the increased use of administrative policies.[89] It is also clear

[82] Stephen Bailey, '*Ridge v Baldwin* [1964]: "Nuff Said"' in Maurice Sunkin and Satvinder Juss (eds), *Landmark Cases in Public Law* (Hart Publishing, 2017).

[83] By contrast, only Lords Reid, Morris and Hodson decided in Ridge's favour on the natural justice ground.

[84] Carol Harlow and Richard Rawlings, 'Proceduralism and Automation: Challenges to the Values of Administrative Law' in Elizabeth Fisher, Jeff King and Alison Young (eds), *The Foundations and Future of Public Law (in Honour of Paul Craig* (forthcoming in Oxford University Press) (a pre-publication version of the chapter is available as *LSE Legal Studies Working Paper No 3/2019*).

[85] *Ibid.*

[86] Greg Weeks, *Soft Law and Public Authorities* (Hart Publishing, 2018).

[87] Kenneth Culp Davis, *Discretionary Justice: A Preliminary Inquiry* (University of Illinois Press, 1971); Denis Galligan, 'The Nature and Function of Policies Within Discretionary Power' [1976] *PL* 332; Yoav Dotan, 'Why Administrators Should Be Bound By Their Policies' (1997) 17(1) *OJLS* 23.

[88] Robert Baldwin and John Houghton, 'Circular Arguments: The Status and Legitimacy of Administrative Rules' [1986] *PL* 239; Aileen McHarg, 'Administrative Discretion, Administrative Rule-Making and Judicial Review' (2017) 70(1) *Current Legal Problems* 267; House of Lords Constitution Committee (n 77) 21–23.

[89] *Nzolameso v Westminster CC* [2015] UKSC 22, [2015] PTSR 549 [39]–[41].

that published policy plays a very substantial role in a number of areas of administrative decision-making, such as planning[90] and immigration.[91]

Again, if it is right that administrative policy is becoming more prevalent, this naturally has consequences for the courts and judicial doctrine. It would mean, in particular, that policy and guidance is increasingly forming part of the administrative landscape against which legal challenges arise. This gives rise to a host of important questions. One, for instance, is whether new grounds of review should be developed in order to ensure responsible use of policy and guidance. The Supreme Court began to grapple with this question in *Lumba*[92] and *Mandalia*.[93] The effect of these cases is to concretise a general principle to the effect that public authorities must generally 'follow [their] published policy … unless there are good reasons for not doing so'.[94] Another cluster of questions concerns the extent to which review under established grounds is changing in light of the fact that policy is increasingly used to supplement legislative frameworks. Chapter four touches on this question in the context of procedural review. As will be seen there, there have been numerous procedural review challenges in recent years which have turned centrally on the proper construction of a policy document which has been introduced for the specific purpose of specifying a decision-making procedure to be followed.

It is useful to conclude the discussion in this section by offering a brief summary of the points developed herein. The aim of this section has been to draw attention to a first core sense in which administrative law's basic legal and normative components are both complex and varied. Three main points have been stressed. First, the grounds of review do not operate as freestanding legal tests which mechanistically determine the outcomes of challenges. Administrative law doctrine, rather, often interacts closely with the particular legislative framework which arises in the background of a case. Second, the legislative schemes which constitute systems of administration are not of one type and vary considerably, in terms of their aims, structure and detail from one to the next. Third, there is reason to think that the legislative frameworks which form the background of administrative law challenges have become richer in detail in recent decades. There is a popular view that delegated legislation became more prevalent across the twentieth century and that more recent years have seen a growth in reliance on supplementary policy and guidance. If this is right, the legal and policy landscape against which administrative law challenges arise may be growing in density, and this may have implications for judicial doctrine.

[90] NPPF (n 55). Town and Country Planning Act 1990, Part 2 (on local plans).
[91] Immigration Rules: www.gov.uk/guidance/immigration-rules.
[92] *R (Lumba) v Secretary of State for the Home Department* [2011] UKSC 12, [2012] 1 AC 245.
[93] *Mandalia v Secretary of State for the Home Department* [2015] UKSC 59, [2015] 1 WLR 4546.
[94] *Lumba* (n 92) [26]; see further McHarg (n 88).

II. Second Sense of Complexity and Variety: Administrative Law Protects an Array of Different Values, Purposes and Interests

The previous section discussed a first sense in which the legal structures in play in administrative law adjudication are complex and varied. This section is concerned with a second: diversity in the values, interests or purposes which the courts seek to accommodate when adjudicating on administrative law issues. The short point is that administrative law's values are not of one kind. The courts, rather, seek to accommodate and promote a plurality of different normative considerations. There are at least two important senses in which this is so.

First, administrative law's values are diverse in terms of their *origins*. It is a vast oversimplification to suggest[95] that administrative law is concerned exclusively with either ensuring that administrative decision-makers act so as to promote the aims of Parliament or protecting common values. On the contrary, administrative doctrine is focused on accommodating and protecting both legislative purpose and values 'highly regarded'[96] by the common law.

It is useful to illustrate this point by drawing again on a handful of examples. The courts' concern with ensuring that the aims underlying legislation are promoted can be neatly illustrated by referring again to two examples discussed above. Section I discussed the '*Padfield* principle'. As explained, this ground regards administrative decision-makers as required to act so as 'to promote the policy and objects of the Act'[97] which confers their power. One consequence is that the *Padfield* principle carves out for the courts an important role in intervening to ensure that administrative decision-makers exercise discretionary powers in ways which are directed towards the policy aims which underlie legislative frameworks. Section I also discussed the question of when an individual is entitled to be given at least the 'gist' of the case against them. As stressed above, the case law on 'gisting' shows that the courts are careful to ensure that the obligation to disclose an outline of arguments and evidence to an individual is not imposed in a way which would significantly undermine the policy aims underlying the legislative framework in the background of the case.[98]

To conclude from these examples, however, that administrative law is therefore exclusively, or even primarily, concerned with promoting the policy aims

[95] Jeffrey Jowell, 'Restraining the State: Politics, Principle and Judicial Review' (1997) 50(1) *Current Legal Problems* 189, 196.

[96] *R v Higher Education Funding Council, ex parte Institute of Dental Surgery* [1994] 1 WLR 242 (DC) 263.

[97] *Padfield* (n 10) 1030.

[98] *Haralambous* (n 16). See also discussion of *Re Hammersmith Rent-Charge* 154 ER 1136 (1849) in chapter 2.

which underlie legislation would fail to accommodate other important parts of the picture.[99] On the contrary, the courts have also developed administrative law doctrine so as to accommodate interests or values regarded as especially important by the common law.

Procedural review is, again, a good illustration. It was seen throughout chapter two that the courts have used different approaches to procedural review across administrative law's recent history. At all stages, however, the courts reserved for themselves a role in intervening to protect interests or values regarded as especially important by the common law. Even, for instance, during what has been termed the 'long sleep'[100] of public law from the 1930s until the 1960s the courts made clear that administrative decision-makers, when exercising 'judicial' or 'quasi-judicial'[101] functions, were required to comply with the common law principle of natural justice. Another clear example of the judicial preoccupation with promoting values regarded as inherent in the common law is the case law developing the 'principle of legality'.[102] As explained in chapter two, this principle protects certain values considered to be especially fundamental by the common law by invoking a presumption that Parliament intends to legislate compatibly with them. As chapter two explained, this principle has been invoked to protect such interests as access to court,[103] the privacy of legal correspondence[104] and non-retrospectivity in punishment.[105]

On the subject of the origins of administrative law's values, a final point worth noting is that none of this is to suggest that a clear line can be drawn in all contexts between the purposes which underlie legislation and common law values. The more complex reality is that legislative purpose and common law values interact in complex and diverse ways. One example was discussed above. Section I explained that it is now fairly common for legislative frameworks to make extensive provision for procedural issues. The procedures which these frameworks create, furthermore, often include requirements – such as the disclosure of information[106] and provision of reasons[107] – which are also often imposed by the common law. It

[99] Craig (n 26).

[100] Stephen Sedley, *Lions Under the Throne* (Cambridge University Press, 2015) Ch 2.

[101] LG Baxter, 'Fairness and Natural Justice in English and South African Law' (1979) 96 *South African Law Journal* 607.

[102] *R v Secretary of State for the Home Department, ex parte Simms* [2000] 2 AC 115 (HL).

[103] *R v Lord Chancellor, ex parte Witham* [1998] QB 575 (CA). *R (UNISON) v Lord Chancellor* [2017] UKSC 51, [2017] 3 WLR 409.

[104] *R v Secretary of State for the Home Department, ex parte Leech* [1994] QB 198 (CA); *R (Daly) v Secretary of State for the Home Department* [2001] 2 AC 532 (HL).

[105] *R v Secretary of State for the Home Department, ex parte Pierson* [1998] AC 539 (HL).

[106] See, eg, General Medical Council (Fitness to Practise) Rules Order of Council 2004 (2004/2608) rule 16.

[107] For examples in the planning context see: Town and Country Planning (Inquiries Procedure) (England) Rules 2000 (SI 2000/1624) rule 11; Town and Country Planning (Development Management Procedure) (England) Order 2015 (SI 2015/595) art 35(1); Openness of Local Government Bodies Regulations 2014 (SI 2014/2095), reg 7(2); Town and Country Planning (Environmental Impact Assessment) Regulations 2017 (SI 2017/571).

is very difficult to state precisely the nature of the relationship between common law values and legislative purpose in this context. One possible interpretation is that the development of common law doctrine in the courts has resulted in important common law values coming to be taken seriously by Parliament and government. Arguably, however, such an account presupposes that judicial rulings have a greater impact on administrative practice than they, in reality, do.[108] Other possible readings are that Parliament and government have come to embrace these values independently or value procedural requirements of this kind for different reasons. Whatever the precise nature of the link, the core point is that there is not always a neat divide between legislative purpose and common law values.

In addition to variety in terms of legal origin, there is at least one further sense in which the values protected by administrative law are varied. This sense addresses an important question: who are the *beneficiaries* of administrative law doctrine? Or, to put it another way, *whose interests* does administrative law seek to protect?

Chapter two briefly introduced a way of thinking which will be discussed in detail in chapter seven labelled the 'public interest conception'.[109] Explained briefly, the public interest conception seeks to draw a line between two different categories of value and interests.[110] On the one hand, it is said, there are *individualistic* values. These are goods and interests which are to be regarded as fundamental to the individual. These are said to be the concern of branches of law outside of administrative law, such as human rights law[111] and certain strands of tort law.[112] On the other hand, however, there are goods in which the *public* as a collectivity is taken as having an especially important interest. Administrative law's distinctiveness, the public interest conception asserts, lies in its primary normative orientation towards interests of this kind.

As chapter two discussed, there is an important element of truth in the public interest conception. *One* of the important functions of modern administrative law is certainly the promotion of the vision of the public good which underlies the legislative scheme in the background of a challenge. *World Development Movement*,[113] for instance, fits this description well. As explained in section I, *World Development Movement* arose against the background of a legislative scheme[114] which empowered the governmental Minister to take steps to promote

[108] Carol Harlow, 'Striking Back and Clamping Down' in John Bell, Mark Elliott, Jason Varuhas and Phillip Murray (eds), *Public Law Adjudication in Common Law Systems* (Hart Publishing, 2015); Maurice Sunkin, '*Padfield v Ministry of Agriculture, Fisheries and Food*' [1968]: Judges and Parliamentary Democracy' in Sunkin and Juss (eds) (n 82).

[109] Jason Varuhas, 'The Public Interest Conception of Public Law: Its Procedural Origins and Substantive Implications' in John Bell, Mark Elliott, Jason Varuhas and Philip Murray (eds), *Public Law Adjudication in Common Law Systems: Process and Substance* (Hart Publishing, 2016).

[110] Jason Varuhas, 'Taxonomy and Public Law' in Mark Elliott, Jason Varuhas and Shona Wilson Stark (eds), *The Unity of Public Law?* (Hart Publishing, 2018).

[111] Jason Varuhas, 'Against Unification' in Mark Elliott and Hanah Wilberg (eds), *The Scope and Intensity of Substantive Review: Traversing Taggart's Rainbow* (Hart Publishing, 2015).

[112] Jason Varuhas, *Damages and Human Rights* (Hart Publishing, 2016).

[113] *World Development Movement* (n 58).

[114] Overseas Developments and Co-operation Act 1980.

'the development or maintaining the economy of a country or territory outside the United Kingdom or the welfare of its people'.[115] In *World Development Movement* the Administrative Court clarified that this meant that the Secretary of State could not make use of these statutory powers to fund 'economically unsound' projects.[116] The basis of judicial intervention, in other words, was that, in the courts' view, the Secretary of State exercising statutory power in a way which would seriously compromise, rather than enhance, the public interest which the legislative scheme was introduced to protect.[117]

Importantly, however, there are at least two problems with the suggestion that administrative law is centrally, or even primarily,[118] concerned with promoting the interests of the public as opposed to those of any one individual. One is that this way of thinking obscures the courts' established and important role in developing the common law so as to afford legal protection to *individual* rights and interests. A series of examples of this role have been discussed in this and the previous chapter. They include the creation of a common law presumption entitling the individual to be given notice[119] and access to at least the gist of the arguments and evidence[120] and the 'principle of legality'.[121]

A second difficulty with characterising administrative law doctrine as concerned centrally with the promotion of public, as opposed to individual, interests is that this mode of thinking overlooks the variety inherent in the legislative schemes which form the background of many administrative law challenges. Section I emphasised that the legislative frameworks which confer functions on administrative decision-makers are not of one kind. Administrative schemes vary significantly in their aims, detail and structure. Thus, while there are important examples of legislative schemes, such as many environmental schemes,[122] which structure decision-making regarding collective interests, not every legislative framework can be so characterised. Many licensing, housing and social security schemes, for instance, confer a series of entitlements on *individuals* who, perhaps due to a particular vulnerability, are taken to be deserving of state assistance.

Where courts adjudicate on administrative law issues in the context of a scheme of this kind, it will often be difficult to characterise judicial intervention as being oriented towards the promotion of the public interest, as distinct from that of the individual. A good example is *Conville*.[123] *Conville* arose against the

[115] *Ibid*, s1(1).
[116] *World Development Movement* (n 58) 402.
[117] For critique, see Jonathan Sumption, 'The Limits of Law' reproduced in Richard Ekins, Paul Yowell and Nick Barber (eds), *Lord Sumption and the Limits of Law* (Hart Publishing, 2016).
[118] Jason Varuhas suggests the individual is a 'subsidiary' concern in administrative law: Varuhas (n 111) 101.
[119] *Bank Mellat* (n 14).
[120] *R (L) v West London Mental Health NHS Trust* [2014] EWCA Civ 47, [2014] 1 WLR 3103.
[121] *Simms* (n 102).
[122] See citations at n 49.
[123] *R (Conville) v Richmond-upon-Thames LBC* [2006] EWCA Civ 718, [2006] 1 WLR 2808.

background of section 190 of the Housing Act 1996[124] which places local housing authorities under a statutory obligation to provide individual applicants with a 'reasonable opportunity'[125] to secure accommodation.[126] The housing authority in *Conville* had adopted a reading of 'reasonable opportunity' which permitted it to take into account budgetary considerations. On the basis of this reading, it argued that offering bed-and-breakfast accommodation to the applicant was 'reasonable'. The Court of Appeal concluded that the authority's interpretation of section 190 was not permissible because budgetary constraints ought to be disregarded in determining what was 'reasonable'.

The most interesting feature of this case, for present purposes, is that it is very difficult to describe it as one in which the court intervened to promote the interests of the public, as opposed to those of the individual. To borrow language from Paul Craig, there is a 'reductionist'[127] sense in which *Conville* can be characterised this way: the Housing Act 1996 reflected the decision of a 'duly elected legislature'[128] that a particular scheme of housing assistance was in the interests of the general public and the Court of Appeal intervened in order to preserve the integrity of that scheme. There is, however, also a clear sense in which *Conville* is a case in which the Court of Appeal sought to safeguard individuals by ensuring that they received the full strength of the entitlements which, on what the Court took to be the proper reading of the legislation, Parliament had conferred on them.

It is useful to conclude the discussion in section II with a brief summary of the points developed and by drawing out some further implications. The main argument developed across this section has been that the values, purposes and interests which administrative law protects are complex and varied and this is so in at least two important senses. First, the origins of administrative law's values are diverse. When adjudicating on administrative law issues, the courts seek both to accommodate and promote the aims underlying the relevant legislative scheme and to afford legal protection to values regarded as especially important by the common law. Second, the beneficiaries of administrative law are also varied. Administrative law is neither wholly, or even primarily, 'public-regarding'[129] nor 'individual-regarding'.[130] Its doctrine rather seeks to promote both sets of interests and, in many contexts, it may not be possible to draw a clear line between them.

Before moving on, it is worth noting that this analysis has important implications for a series of common tendencies within administrative law scholarship. Two in particular are worth drawing out. The first is that the discussion in this section offers reason to be cynical about attempting to 'list' the values or purposes

[124] Housing Act 1996, s190.
[125] *Ibid.*
[126] *Conville* (n 123) [36].
[127] Craig (n 26) 284.
[128] Craig (n 26) 284.
[129] Varuhas (n 109) 52.
[130] Varuhas (n 109) 52.

which are promoted by administrative law. This exercise has sometimes been attempted in the literature. Dawn Oliver, for example, has drawn out five 'common law values' which she suggests underlie adjudication in both private and public law.[131] Paul Daly, similarly, has suggested that the most useful way of understanding administrative law is as an endeavour by the courts to accommodate four key values: the rule of law, the separation of power, democracy and good administration.[132]

Arguments such as these are often accompanied with the caveat that the supplied list ought not to be taken as exhaustive. There is an important reason for this: any assumption that administrative law can be reduced to a fixed set of values is very difficult indeed. One major problem is that, as explained above, a major focus of administrative law adjudication is on uncovering and promoting the aims underlying legislative frameworks. Legislative policy, however, does not stand still. As new governments, responding to new issues, obtain control of the legislative agenda,[133] legislation is passed in order to advance different objectives.[134] It is, in other words, important not to imagine that the values which shape administrative law doctrine at a given moment in time are fixed.

A second important implication of the complexity and variety of administrative law's values is that it is difficult to see how grounds of review could be 'taxonomised'[135] or categorised by reference to their purpose. In a recent work,[136] Varuhas has argued that 'without good legal taxonomy … rigorous analysis and coherent legal development may be impossible'.[137] He urges public law scholars to take taxonomy more seriously and suggests the most effective way to do this may be to organise public law doctrines by 'function'.[138] Varuhas' intuition is that, at least the bulk of[139] the grounds of review could be classified as doctrines 'relating to the regulation of public power in the public interest',[140] as opposed to much of

[131] Dawn Oliver, 'Common Values in Public and Private Law and the Public/Private Divide' [1997] *PL* 630; Dawn Oliver, 'The Underlying Values of Public and Private Law' in Michael Taggart (ed), *The Province of Administrative Law* (Hart Publishing, 1997).

[132] Paul Daly, 'Administrative Law: A Values-Based Approach' in Bell, Elliott, Varuhas and Murray (eds) (n 109); Paul Daly, 'A Pluralist Account of Deference and Legitimate Expectations' in Matthew Groves and Greg Weeks (eds), *Legitimate Expectations in the Common Law World* (Hart Publishing, 2017); Paul Daly, 'Administrative Law: Characteristics, Legitimacy, Unity' in Elliott, Varuhas and Wilson Stark (n 110).

[133] Adam Tomkins, 'What is Parliament For?' in Nicholas Bamforth and Peter Leyland (eds), *Public Law in a Multi-Layered Constitution* (Hart Publishing, 2003).

[134] See for instance *R (Cart) v Upper Tribunal* [2011] UKSC 28, [2012] 1 AC 663; Mark Elliott and Robert Thomas, 'Tribunal Justice and Proportionate Dispute Resolution' (2012) 71(2) *CLJ* 297; Bell (n 8).

[135] Varuhas (n 110).

[136] To a degree, Adams (n 5) can be read as proposing a divide between two kinds of ground, some focused on giving effect to the intentions of Parliament and others on protecting common law values.

[137] Varuhas (n 110) 40.

[138] Varuhas (n 110) 61–62.

[139] Varuhas (n 110) 64. Varuhas seems to regard legitimate expectations as an exception: Jason Varuhas, 'In Search of a Doctrine: Mapping the Law of Legitimate Expectations' in Groves and Weeks (eds) (n 132).

[140] Varuhas (n 110) 64.

human rights law which is properly characterised as concerning the 'protection and vindication of basic personal rights'.[141]

The analysis in this section, however, suggests that administrative law doctrine is not so easily categorised. An attempt to allocate grounds of review to different categories by reference to the legal values which they serve to promote may obscure more than it will reveal. One reason is that, as has been stressed above, it is difficult to draw neat lines between different categories of legal value; there is, for instance, no clear distinction between values derived from the common law and those which underlie legislation, nor between the interests of the public and those of the individual. Another is that, as has been emphasised throughout this chapter, administrative law doctrine interacts closely with different kinds of legislative scheme. This has important implications for the taxonomical endeavour. It means that a singular ground of review might serve as the basis of judicial intervention for the protection of different interests depending on the legislative context in which a challenge arises.[142]

III. Third Sense of Complexity and Variety: Administrative Law Adjudication Concerns Different Kinds of Legal Relationship

The third and final sense of complexity and variety to which this book draws attention is the plurality of legal relationships with which courts grapple when adjudicating on administrative law issues. In explaining this argument, it is helpful to begin by taking something of a detour into the literature on private law theory and introducing in some detail a concept which has dominated thinking about the nature of legal relationships in that context:[143] the notion of 'individual right-duty correlativity'.[144]

The idea of 'individual right-duty correlativity' is most often associated with the writings of Wesley Hohfeld.[145] Hohfeld's central concern was that judges tend

[141] Varuhas (n 110) 64.

[142] *Conville* (n 123).

[143] Ernest Weinrib, 'Corrective Justice in a Nutshell' (2002) 52 *University of Toronto Law Journal* 349; Rob Stevens, *Torts and Rights* (Oxford University Press, 2007).

[144] For examples within the context of privity of contract see: *Tweddle v Atkinson* (1861) 121 ER 762; *Dunlop Pneumatic Tyre Company Ltd v Selfridge & Co Ltd* [1915] AC 847 (HL); *Shanklin Pier v Detel Products Ltd* [1951] 2 KB 854 (KB); *Scruttons Ltd v Midland Silicones Ltd* [1962] AC 446 (HL); *Beswick v Beswick* [1968] AC 58 (HL); *Alfred McAlpine Construction Ltd v Panatown Ltd* [2001] 1 AC 518 (HL).

[145] Wesley Hohfeld, *Fundamental Legal Conceptions as Applied in Judicial Reasoning* (The Law Book Exchange, 2010). See: Andrew Halpin, *Rights & Law: Analysis & Theory* (Hart Publishing, 1997) especially Ch 2; Leif Wenar, 'The Nature of Rights' (2005) 33 *Philosophy and Public Affairs* 223; Robert Stevens, 'Rights and Other Things' (26 July 2010) available at SSRN: http://ssrn.com/abstract=1648954; Peter Cane, 'Rights in Private Law' in Andrew Robertson and Donal Nolan (eds), *Rights and Private Law* (Hart Publishing, 2011).

to use the term 'right' 'indiscriminately'[146] to refer to a number of conceptually distinct legal statuses including 'privileges',[147] 'powers'[148] and 'immunities'.[149] Hohfeld was highly critical of this 'chameleon-hued'[150] use of the term, considering it to be a 'peril both to clear thought and to lucid expression'.[151] Rather, he argued, the term 'right' is only used in its 'strictest'[152] and most appropriate sense to refer to an individual right correlative to a duty. Hohfeld explained this idea in the following terms:

> What clue do we find, in ordinary legal discourse, toward limiting the word [right] to a definite and appropriate meaning? That clue lies in the correlative 'duty' for it is certain that even those who use the word and the conception of 'right' in the broadest possible way are accustomed to thinking of 'duty' as the invariable correlative. As said in *Lake Shore & M.S.R. Co v Kurtz*: 'A duty or a legal obligation is that which one ought or ought not to do. "Duty" and "right" are correlative terms. When a right is invaded, a duty is violated.'[153]

In other words, for Hohfeld, the ideas of 'individual right' and 'duty' are flipsides of one coin. Where an individual has a right that another do X (such as a right that that other stay off her land[154]) it must be the case that that other is under a legal duty, a duty which she owes to the right-holder, to do the same. Similarly, where an individual is under a duty to do Y it must be the case that there is some other individual to whom the duty is owed and who thus holds a right entitling her to have Y done. For Hohfeld, then, we ought not to think of 'individual right' and 'duty' separately for it is not possible to make sense of one without the other. The reason for this is that, simply, these terms are just different ways of describing exactly the same phenomenon – that of a legal doctrine creating a special relationship of correlativity between two individuals whereby one becomes bound to the other to behave in a particular way.

This explanation of individual right-duty correlativity is highly abstract. It is accordingly helpful to concretise the discussion a little. Although it rather anticipates the argument of this chapter to the effect that this idea plays an important role in administrative law as well as private law, the most helpful way of doing so is to discuss an example of a legislative provision, arising within the field of administrative law. For that purpose is it useful to return again to section 190(2) of the

[146] Hohfeld, *ibid*, 36.
[147] Hohfeld, *ibid*, 38–50.
[148] Hohfeld, *ibid*, 50–60.
[149] Hohfeld, *ibid*, 60–63.
[150] Hohfeld, *ibid*, 35.
[151] Hohfeld, *ibid*.
[152] Hohfeld, *ibid*, 36.
[153] Hohfeld, *ibid*, 38 citing *Lake Shore & MSR Co v Kurtz* (1894) 37 NE 303, 304.
[154] To use Hohfeld's example: Hohfeld (n 145) 38.

Housing Act 1996 which, as explained above, supplied the legislative background to the *Conville*[155] case. Section 190(2) reads as follows:

> 2) If the authority is satisfied that the applicant has a priority need they shall –
>
> a) secure that accommodation is available for his occupation for such period as they consider will give him a reasonable opportunity of securing accommodation for his occupation ...[156]

As the Court of Appeal's judgment in *Conville*[157] illustrates, it is plausible to understand this provision as creating a relationship of 'individual right-duty correlativity' between an individual applicant and her local housing authority. The Court explained that:

> The *duty* with respect to accommodation is that it be made available for such period as the authority consider will give the applicant a 'reasonable opportunity of securing accommodation for his occupation.' That is something *conferred on the applicant*; a *right he acquires coterminous with the extent of the duty*.[158]

The idea being expressed by Pill LJ, speaking for the Court of Appeal, in this passage is as follows: section 190(2) creates a special relationship of correlativity between an individual applicant and a local housing authority. This relationship can be looked at from two angles. On the one hand, one can see the provision as placing the local housing authority under a duty, *owed to the individual applicant*, to make accommodation available for her for a sufficient period of time. On the other hand, one can see the provision as conferring on *the individual* applicant a statutory right entitling her to be given the same by the authority. Ultimately, however, because duty and right are 'coterminous' with one another, these are merely different ways of saying the same thing: that, as a result of section 190, a legal relationship pertains between a local housing authority and an individual applicant such that the former is bound to treat the latter in certain ways.

With this understanding of individual right-duty correlativity in mind, it is now important to return to its significance for administrative law. There has been an influential way of thinking about administrative law according to which a neat line can be drawn between it and other legal fields, such as private law[159] on the basis of the relevance of the notion of individual right-duty correlativity. According to this way of thinking, while individual right-duty correlativity plays an important role in the field of private law, it does not play a significant role

[155] *Conville* (n 123).
[156] Housing Act 1996, s190(2) (as amended by Homelessness Act 2002, Sch 1, para 9).
[157] *Conville* (n 123).
[158] *Conville* (n 123) [36] (my emphasis).
[159] And human rights law: Varuhas (n 111).

in the context of administrative law. Legal duties which arise in this field, rather, are said to be characterised by '*collective* right-duty correlativity'.[160] The idea can be put another way: whereas legal duties arising in private law are, at least very often,[161] owed to some individual who in turn holds a correlative right entitling her to have the duty performed, the legal duties with which administrative law is concerned function differently. They are, more particularly, owed to the public as a collective. The public thus, in turn, holds a collective right entitling it to have the duty performed.

The influence of this way of thinking can be seen in a number of places. Take, for instance, the following passage, written by Nicholas Bamforth:[162]

> In public law the primary concern of the courts, analytically speaking, is to remedy breaches of a duty owed by public authorities either *to society at large* or to sections of society … public law *does not involve any direct correlative* between a right held by the individual litigant and the duty owed to that litigant.[163]

The clear assertion of this passage is that there is an important structural difference between administrative law and private law doctrine in terms of the legal relationships with which these legal fields are concerned. Thus, according to Bamforth, while much of private law creates relationships of right-duty correlativity between individuals, administrative law doctrine defines the legal relationship between public authorities and the public as a collective. In a similar way, consider the following passage written, again, extra-judicially by Lord Woolf:[164]

> I regard public law as being the system which enforces the proper performance by public bodies of the duties which they *owe to the public*. I regard private law as being the system which protects the private rights of private individuals or the private rights of public bodies.[165]

Again, Lord Woolf's clear suggestion is that administrative law and private law are structurally distinct. While the former gives rise to legal duties 'owe[d] to the public',[166] the latter recognises legal duties which correlate with an individual personal right.

More recently, this way of thinking can also be traced in some of Jason Varuhas' writings. In responding to the claims by some[167] that the introduction

[160] Jason Varuhas, 'The Reformation of English Administrative Law? "Rights", Rhetoric and Reality' (2013) 72 *CLJ* 369, 409 citing Matthew Kramer, 'Rights Without Trimmings' in Matthew Kramer, *A Debate Over Rights: Philosophical Enquiries* (Oxford University Press, 2000).

[161] For a cynical view see Ronen Perry, 'Correlativity' (2008) 28(6) *Law and Philosophy* 537.

[162] Nicholas Bamforth, 'Hohfeldian Rights and Public Law' in Matthew Kramer (ed), *Rights Wrongs & Responsibilities* (Palgrave, 2001).

[163] *Ibid*, 15 (my emphasis). See also 11.

[164] Lord Woolf, 'Public Law – Private Law: Why the Divide? A Personal View' [1986] *PL* 220.

[165] *Ibid*, 221.

[166] *Ibid*.

[167] Michael Taggart, 'Reinventing Administrative Law' in Bamforth and Leyland (eds) (n 133); Thomas Poole, 'The Reformation of English Administrative Law' (2009) 68(1) *CLJ* 142.

of the Human Rights Act[168] had resulted in the 'righting'[169] of administrative law, Varuhas carves out two different ways of understanding the basic common law duties 'to act reasonably, lawfully and with procedural fairness'.[170] According to the first, these duties are owed to some individual, such that in relation to each duty there will be some individual who holds a correlative right entitling her to have the duty performed.[171] According to the second, they are duties 'owed to the public at large'[172] and thus 'are correlative to claim-rights held by the public at large'. As explained by Varuhas:

> On this analysis the Home Office owes a duty to *the public as a whole* to perform [its] functions reasonably. The Home Office also owes a duty *to the public* to perform its public functions intra vires and another to perform those functions fairly. On this view, each public authority could be said to owe a discrete set of duties, to act reasonably, lawfully and with procedural fairness, in the exercise of its statutory functions, *each of which is correlative to a public right.*[173]

Varuhas argues that it is the latter way of thinking which is the more convincing,[174] a view which is consistent with his later writings.[175]

Against this background, this chapter stresses that the reality is more complex than this influential way of thinking suggests. Adjudication on administrative law issues requires the courts to grapple with legal relationships of different kinds. On the one hand, there are clear examples of cases which are most straightforwardly characterised as concerning the relationship of *collective* right-duty correlativity[176] which subsists between an administrative decision-maker and the public at large. On the other, however, there are also many instances of administrative law adjudication in which the courts are concerned which legal relationships of *individual* right-duty correlativity.

A good example of the former type of case is *Greenpeace*.[177] In this case, which will be discussed in some detail in chapter five, the Court held that the Secretary of State was under a legal duty to abide by her promise that no change would be made to the UK's nuclear energy policy without 'the fullest public consultation'.[178] Importantly, this legal duty cannot plausibly be analysed through the lens of individual right-duty correlativity. Public consultation would not have benefitted any

[168] Human Rights Act 1998.
[169] Sian Elias, 'Righting Administrative Law' in David Dyzenhaus, Murray Hunt and Grant Huscroft (eds), *A Simple Common Lawyer: Essays in Honour of Michael Taggart* (Hart Publishing, 2009).
[170] Varuhas (n 160) 409. Here Varuhas makes use of the Lord Diplock's well-known tripartite structure: *Council of Civil Service Unions v Minister for the Civil Service* [1985] AC 374 (HL) 410.
[171] Varuhas understands the rights contained in Human Rights Act 1998, Sch 1 as functioning in this way: Varuhas (n 160) 398–400.
[172] Varuhas (n 160) 409.
[173] Varuhas (n 160) 409 (emphasis added).
[174] Varuhas (n 160) 409–11.
[175] See citations at nn 109–112.
[176] Varuhas (n 160) 409.
[177] *R (Greenpeace) v Secretary of State for Trade & Industry* [2007] EWHC 311 (Admin), [2007] Env LR 29.
[178] *Ibid* [9].

one individual more than any other.[179] It was also clear that standing to enforce the duty was not confined to any singular person or organisation.[180] *Greenpeace*, on the contrary, is quite clearly a case most naturally analysed as a case in which the Secretary of State was found to be under a legal obligation which was owed to the public as a collectivity.

Not every administrative law case, however, can be characterised in this way. Indeed, there are many instances where the courts clearly regard themselves as concerned with the personal legal relationship which persists between an administrative decision-maker and the individual applicant. There are two main reasons for this. The first has already been alluded to at a number of points: it is not uncommon for the legislative framework in the background of the case to specifically create legal relationships of this kind.[181] Chapter two, for instance, discussed a number of examples of legislative frameworks, enacted throughout the course of the twentieth century, which specifically conferred on individuals who met certain criteria, for instance, the 'right to receive [an] old age pension'[182] or the 'entitlement'[183] to widow's benefit. Similarly, the discussion of *Conville*[184] above drew attention to a legislative provision which the Court of Appeal clearly regarded as having conferred on the applicant a 'right' to be given a reasonable opportunity to secure accommodation.

Second, and furthermore, there are also clear examples of the courts regarding the *common law* as manifesting in legal duties which are owed to the individual applicant. A good example is in the context of procedural review. There is a clear and consistent tendency of courts and academics speaking of the common law as conferring procedural rights on individuals. Take, for instance,[185] the following passage from Lord Reed's judgment in *Osborn*:[186]

> The *right of the prisoner* to request an oral hearing is not correctly characterised as a right of appeal. In order to justify the holding of an oral hearing … what he has to persuade the board is that an oral hearing is appropriate.[187]

[179] According to one influential theory of rights – 'interest' or 'benefit' theory – to say a duty is owed to an individual is to say that she is its beneficiary. See: Jeremy Bentham, *The Works of Jeremy Bentham published under the Superintendence of his Executor John Bowring* (William Tait, 1838–1843); Joseph Raz, 'Legal Rights' (1984) 4(1) *OJLS* 1; Jeremy Waldron, 'A Right to Do Wrong' (1981) 92 *Ethics* 21; Matthew Kramer 'Refining the Interest Theory of Rights' (2010) 55(1) *American Journal of Jurisprudence* 55(1), article 2; Matthew Kramer and Hillel Steiner, 'Theories of Rights: Is There a Third Way?' (2007) 27(2) *OJLS* 281; Nicholas Vrousalis, 'Between Insensitivity and Incompleteness: Against the Will Theory of Rights' (2010) 16(4) *Res Publica* 415.

[180] *Greenpeace* (n 177). According to a second influential theory of rights – 'will' or 'control' theory – to say an individual has a right is to say that she alone can choose to enforce it. See HLA Hart, *Essays on Bentham* (Clarendon, 1982); Siegfried Van Duffel, 'In Defence of the Will Theory of Rights' (2012) 18 *Res Publica* 321.

[181] *R v Birmingham CC, ex parte Millard & Connolly* (1994) 26 HLR 551.

[182] Old Age Pensions Act 1908, s1.

[183] National Insurance Act 1946, s17.

[184] *Conville* (n 123).

[185] See chapter 4 for further examples.

[186] *R (Osborn) v Parole Board* [2013] UKSC 61, [2014] AC 1115.

[187] *Ibid* [2] (emphasis added).

The clear idea underlying this passage is that the duty to which the Court gave effect in *Osborn* was one which was characterised by Hohfeldian 'individual right-correlativity'. That is, which was owed to the individual subject of the relevant decision and which thus correlated with a personal legal right entitling him to have the duty performed. By way of a similar second example, take the following passage from Lord Dyson's judgment in *Lumba*:[188]

> *The individual* has a *basic public law right* to have his or her case considered under whatever policy the executive sees fit to adopt.[189]

Again, the clear idea underlying this passage would seem to be that the duty on the part of a decision-maker to 'follow his published policy … unless there are good reasons for not doing so'[190] is, at least in many contexts,[191] a duty which is owed to an individual.

To summarise, this section has sought to draw attention to a third sense in which the basic legal and normative components of administrative law may be said to be both complex and varied: administrative law adjudication requires the courts to engage with legal relationships of different kinds. It is certainly true that certain cases, including for instance those which arise in the context of a 'public-regarding'[192] statutory duty, are incapable of being understood through the lens of individual right-duty correlativity. These cases are more naturally understood as giving rise to questions about what the public as a collectivity is entitled to. Not all administrative law cases, however, fit this pattern. There are many examples of challenges where the courts – perhaps because the legislative scheme in the background of a case purports to confer a personal 'entitlement' on an individual – regard themselves as adjudicating on the content of a legal duty which is owed directly to the individual applicant.

IV. Conclusion

It is useful to conclude this chapter by offering some closing reflections on the relationship between its arguments and the broader aims of the book. Chapter one explained that this book has three main aims. The first is to engage in an exercise in 'pulling apart' administrative law so as to explore the basic legal and normative components which are in play in legal adjudication. This exercise in deconstruction has been the central preoccupation of this chapter. The main argument has been that, when administrative law is dismantled in this way it becomes

[188] *Lumba* (n 92).
[189] *Lumba* (n 92) [35] (emphasis added).
[190] *Lumba* (n 92) [26].
[191] *Project Management Institute* (n 43) is perhaps an exception. As explained above, however, the policy provisions in that case sought to protect both the interests of the company applying for Royal Charter status and their business competitors.
[192] Varuha (n 109) 52.

clear that its basic components are both complex and varied and that this is so in three core senses. First, administrative law doctrine interacts closely with the particular legislative which sits in the background of a challenge and these schemes are not of one kind. Second, administrative law is concerned to protect and promote a variety of legal values. This is so both in the sense that the origins of administrative values are diverse and that the field can be characterised as neither public nor individual-regarding.[193] Third, it is too simplistic a view to suggest that administrative law can be neatly distinguished from other legal fields, such as private law, on the basis that while the notion of individual-right duty correlativity plays a central role in the latter it is irrelevant to the former.[194] The more complex reality is that adjudication on administrative law issues requires the courts to engage with a plurality of different kinds of legal relationship.

An understanding of administrative law's complex and varied anatomy is important for its own sake. As chapter one emphasised, there has been relatively little written[195] on administrative law's broader 'architecture'[196] in recent decades. A major aim of this book is to push thinking on this subject forward. The arguments of this chapter, however, are also valuable in a further sense. The second major aim of the book is to demonstrate that an awareness of the complex and varied 'anatomy' of administrative law is of substantial importance because it sheds light on a series of doctrinal issues within the legal field. It is to this aim which the book now turns. Chapters four, five and six make use of three case studies – procedural fairness, legitimate expectations and standing respectively – in order to illustrate the light which can be shed on specific doctrinal questions by an increased awareness of administrative law's complex 'anatomy'.

[193] Varuha (n 109) 52.
[194] Bamforth (n 162).
[195] At least outside of the long-standing 'ultra vires' debate: Adams (n 5).
[196] Kenneth Culp Davis, 'The Future of Judge-Made Public Law in England: A Problem of Practical Jurisprudence' (1961) *Columbia Law Review* 201, 220.

4

Procedural Review

As the introductory chapter explained, this book has three main aims. The first is to call attention to administrative law's complex and varied 'anatomy'. Chapters two and three have focused on this aim. Chapter two explored the evolution of administrative law since the late-nineteenth century and, in the course of doing so, offered a first glimpse of the inherent complexity of the field. Chapter three then 'pulled apart' administrative law and emphasised three core senses in which the legal structures in play in adjudication are complex and varied. These are, first, variety in the legislative schemes in the background of administrative law challenges and with which administrative law doctrine interacts; second, the plurality of interests, policies and purposes which courts seek to accommodate in administrative law adjudication and, third, the diversity of the legal relationships in play.

This chapter now moves from the book's first aim to its second: demonstrating the important light which a recognition of administrative law's complex and varied 'anatomy' can shed on a series of specific doctrinal questions. In doing so, the book's focus moves from the general to the specific. This and the next two chapters make use of three case studies by which to illustrate this aim. This chapter focuses on procedural review, chapter five on legitimate expectations, and chapter six on standing.

Before outlining the arguments of this chapter, it is useful to say something on why procedural review, legitimate expectations and standing supply suitable case studies. As Jason Varuhas has emphasised, any commentator seeking to advance understanding of 'the current state of administrative law as a whole … ought closely to examine a cross-section of administrative law doctrine'.[1] The three case studies have been chosen because they concern legal issues of different kinds. Procedural review concerns the courts' approach to overseeing the processes by which administrative decision-makers reach decisions. Legitimate expectations, at least post-*Coughlan*,[2] is commonly thought to go beyond procedural review and involve closer engagement with the substance of decisions. Standing concerns a different kind of question again, namely who can access the courts in order to challenge administrative conduct.

[1] Jason Varuhas, 'The Reformation of English Administrative Law? "Rights", Rhetoric and Reality' (2013) 72 *CLJ* 369, 376.

[2] *R v North & East Devon Health Authority, ex parte Coughlan* [2001] QB 213 (CA); Mark Elliott, 'From Heresy to Orthodoxy: Substantive Legitimate Expectations in the United Kingdom' in Matthew Groves and Greg Weeks, *Legitimate Expectations in the Common Law World* (Hart Publishing, 2017).

With these broader points in mind, it is useful next to turn to and introduce the focus of this chapter: procedural review. The discussion herein is divided into four main parts.

Section I briefly sketches what is meant by 'procedural review' for the purposes of this chapter. Section II then explores the recent development of procedural review in England and Wales. As will be explained, the House of Lords' seminal decision in *Ridge*[3] led to the erosion of the idea that procedural review aims to control 'judicial', as opposed to administrative, power. Following this development, both scholars and judges have sought a new, overarching explanation of procedural review. Developing an account has, however, been challenging. The most influential, and successful account in terms of achieving 'fit'[4] with the case law understands procedural review by reference to 'a flexible notion of overarching fairness'.[5] The difficulty with this understanding, however, is that it (at least) risks presenting judicial reasoning as an 'essentially intuitive'[6] exercise, which lacks structure and predictability.[7] In spite of this, attempts to develop 'thicker' accounts of procedural review, such as by identifying an 'irreducible core'[8] of process rights applicable in all contexts, have not been consistently borne out in the case law.

The discussion in section II gives rise to at least two important questions. First, why is it proving so difficult to develop a general, overarching account of procedural review?[9] Second, do the difficulties in developing such an account give rise to concerns that procedural review is no more than an inherently unstructured and discretionary exercise in deciding what is 'fair'?

Sections III and IV argue that significant light can be shed on these questions by the broader themes of the book. The argument in section III is that it is not especially surprising that it is proving difficult to build an overarching account of procedural review. The three senses of complexity and variety to which the book calls attention are in play in the procedural review case law as much as they are across administrative law adjudication more generally. These senses, in turn, suggest three reasons why the procedural review case law cannot be easily explained by reference to a single, overarching model.

Section IV argues, however, that these difficulties do not necessitate the conclusion that procedural review is therefore inherently unstructured and discretionary. This part is informed by an analysis of 127 recent cases decided by appellate courts between 2009 and 2018. A close reading of this case law, with the complex and varied anatomy of administrative law in mind, reveals that there is a good deal more structure to judicial reasoning than is sometimes assumed. This structure

[3] *Ridge v Baldwin* [1964] AC 40 (HL).
[4] Stephen Smith, *Contract Theory* (Oxford University Press, 2004) Ch 1.
[5] *R (L) v West London Mental Health NHS Trust* [2014] EWCA Civ 47, [2014] 1 WLR 3103 [69].
[6] *R (Forest Heath DC) v Electoral Commission Boundary Committee* [2009] EWCA Civ 1296 [39].
[7] *West London Mental Health NHS Trust* (n 5) [69]–[74].
[8] *Secretary of State for the Home Department v AF (No 3)* [2009] UKHL 28, [2010] 2 AC 269.
[9] Christopher Forsyth, 'The Rock and the Sand: Jurisdiction and Remedial Discretion' (2013) 18(4) *Judicial Review* 360 [27].

takes two main forms. First, many modern procedural review challenges now arise against the background of a rich legislative and policy framework. These frameworks commonly make detailed provision for administrative procedure.[10] One consequence is that the legal issues which now arise in modern procedural review challenges are often highly specific questions of construction. The courts commonly address these questions by navigating the background framework and seeking to resolve the ambiguity in the way which would best promote its purposes. This, however, is not to downplay the significance of the common law. Common law principles continue to play an important role in supplementing the procedural protections which are laid down in legislation and policy.[11] The second source of structure in judicial reasoning takes the form of a series of clear and consistent patterns in the ways in which the common law performs this role.

It is important to be clear at the outset that it is no part of the argument in section IV, or this chapter more broadly, that the current judicial approach to procedural review is perfect. Indeed, the final section of the discussion in section IV will point to a handful of underexplored questions concerning whether the courts' approach to certain issues is the right one. What section IV takes issue with, rather, is the notion that adjudication in the procedural review context is 'protean'[12] and 'infinitely flexible'.[13] This characterisation of procedural review, it argues, risks obscuring a number of considerations which lend meaningful structure to judicial reasoning.

I. What is 'Procedural Review'?

In building the chapter's arguments, it is useful to proceed slowly. The first thing to be done is to make clear what is meant by 'procedural review'. Aileen Kavanagh has written that:

> … the process by which the public body made the decision is the way in which it decided …. [but] the 'way in which a decision is made' could refer to the steps of the public authority's reasoning or to the things a public authority did to enable it to do that reasoning, such as consulting, hearing both sides, etc.[14]

This chapter is concerned with process in the second, more limited, sense. Its focus is on the steps which must be taken by administrative decision-makers to gather information and to involve individuals and groups, rather than with its reasoning process per se. The case law considered throughout this chapter therefore has

[10] Paul Craig, 'Perspectives on Process: Common Law, Statutory and Political' [2010] *PL* 275.

[11] *Bank Mellat v HM Treasury (No 2)* [2013] UKSC 39, [2014] AC 700.

[12] *R (Moseley) v Haringey LBC* [2014] UKSC 56, [2014] 1 WLR 3947 [24].

[13] *R (Daniel Johns Manchester Ltd) v Manchester CC* [2018] EWHC 464 (Admin) [45].

[14] Aileen Kavanagh, 'Reasoning about Proportionality under the Human Rights Act 1998: Outcomes, Substance and Process' (2014) 130 *LQR* 235.

an important shared feature: an individual or group challenges an administrative decision on the basis that they ought to have been permitted to play a larger role than they did in an administrative decision-making process.

This case law, in other words, sees courts grapple with questions about the extent to which individuals and groups are entitled, as a matter of law, to *participate* in administrative decision-making. Questions about participation take different forms. Sometimes the applicant argues that she ought to have been given notice that a decision was being contemplated and invited to make representations.[15] In others, the question is whether a consultation exercise ought to have been carried out in order to obtain the view of the public, or a subsection of it, before a general change in policy direction is made.[16] Other common issues include challenges to the nature of the information which is disclosed for comment,[17] the degree of specificity in which proposals for policy change are presented,[18] the amount of time given for comment[19] and the manner in which applicants are permitted to make representations.[20]

The understanding of 'procedure' deployed in this chapter is also restricted in a second sense. Procedural review is commonly thought of as having a number of strands.[21] In an oft-cited passage[22] in *Kanda*[23] for instance, Lord Denning said:

> The rule against bias is one thing. The right to be heard is another. Those two rules are the essential characteristics of what is often called natural justice.[24]

This chapter is concerned with the *audi alteram partem* 'pillar' only. Case law exploring the operation of the rule against bias[25] in the administrative law context[26]

[15] *Bank Mellat (No 2)* (n 11).

[16] *R (Seabrook Warehousing Ltd) v HMRC* [2010] EWCA Civ 140; *Abbassi v SSHD* [2011] EWCA Civ 814; *Government of the Republic of France v Royal Borough of Kensington and Chelsea* [2017] EWCA Civ 429.

[17] *R (Derrin Brothers) v Revenue and Customs Commissioners* [2014] EWHC 1152 (Admin), [2014] ACD 130; *R (British Sky Broadcasting Ltd) v Commissioner of Police of the Metropolis* [2014] UKSC 17; *Competition and Markets Authority v Concordia Int* [2018] EWCA Civ 1881, [2018] Bus LR 2452.

[18] *R (Sumpter) v SoS for Work and Pensions* [2015] EWCA Civ 1033; *R (Robson) v Salford CC* [2015] EWCA Civ 6, [2015] PTSR 1349.

[19] *Derwent Holdings Ltd v Trafford BC* [2011] EWCA Civ 832.

[20] *McKay v Secretary of State for Justice* [2011] EWCA Civ 522; *R (Sandler) v Office of the Independent Adjudicator* [2011] EWCA Civ 1614; *Perry v Nursing and Midwifery Council* [2013] EWCA Civ 145, [2013] 1 WLR 3423; *R (Naidu) v SSHD* [2016] EWCA Civ 156, [2016] 1 WLR 3775.

[21] William Wade and Christopher Forsyth, *Administrative Law*, 11th edn (Oxford University Press, 2014), Chs 12–14.

[22] *R (George Harrison (Whitby) Ltd) v Secretary of State for Environment, Transport and Regions* [2000] WL 1544724 [80]; *R (Davis) v West Sussex CC* [2012] EWHC 2152 (Admin), [2013] PTSR 494 [62].

[23] *Kanda v Malaya* [1962] AC 332 (PC).

[24] *Ibid*, 337.

[25] *Dimes v Proprietors of the Grand Junction Canal* 10 ER 301 (1852) (HL); *Locabail (UK) Ltd v Bayfield Properties Ltd* [2000] QB 451; Abimbola A Olowofoyeku, 'The Nemo Judex Rules: The Case Against Automatic Disqualification' [2000] *PL* 456.

[26] *R (Island Farm Development Ltd) v Bridgend CBC* [2006] EWHC 2189 (Admin); *Belize Bank Ltd v Attorney-General of Belize* [2011] UKPC 36.

is very worthy of study, but simply falls outside of the scope of this chapter. Similarly, while review of reason-giving is commonly classified as an aspect of procedural review,[27] challenges to failures to give,[28] or to the adequacy of,[29] reasons are not covered here.[30]

II. The Evolution of Procedural Review

With this understanding of procedural review in mind, the chapter can now turn to its second task: exploring the development of thinking about procedural review. The focus here is primarily on the evolution of procedural review case law and literature following the landmark House of Lords decision in *Ridge*.[31] It is, however, useful to briefly revisit the pre-*Ridge* history by way of introduction. A fuller account can be found in chapter two.

As chapter two emphasised, procedural review of administrative decision-making is hardly a modern phenomenon. English and Welsh courts have been grappling with questions concerning the rights of individuals to participate in decision-making processes for centuries.[32] Chapter two discussed a number of examples of this, including the important decisions of *Capel*[33] and *Cooper*.[34] In both of these cases, the courts emphasised a strong common law presumption in favour of supplying notice of a decision to significantly affected individuals.

Across the twentieth century, however, due to a variety of influences,[35] the courts began to take a more restrictive approach to procedural review than they had in the past. During this time, procedural review was commonly rationalised as a form of control on *judicial* power. The basic idea was that a distinction was to be drawn between administrative functions, on the one hand, and judicial or

[27] Timothy Endicott, *Administrative Law*, 4th edn (Oxford University Press, 2018) Ch 6. Whether this is the proper way to categorise review of reason-giving is open to question: David Dyzenhaus, 'Dignity in Administrative Law: Judicial Deference in a Culture of Justification' (2012) 17(1) *Review of Constitutional Studies* 87.

[28] *R v Secretary of State for the Home Department, ex parte Doody* [1994] 1 AC 531 (HL); *R v Civil Service Appeal Board, ex parte* Cunningham [1992] ICR 817 (CA); Paul Craig, 'The Common Law, Reasons and Administrative Justice' (1994) 53 *CLJ* 282.

[29] *South Bucks DC v Porter* [2003] UKHL 26, [2003] 2 AC 558; *Dover DC v Campaign to Protect Rural England (Kent)* [2017] UKSC 79, [2018] 1 WLR 108.

[30] Joanna Bell, 'Reason-Giving in Administrative Law: Where Are We and Why Have the Courts Not Embraced the "General Common Law Duty to Give Reasons?"' (forthcoming in MLR) (an early access version is available here: https://onlinelibrary.wiley.com/doi/10.1111/1468-2230.12457).

[31] *Ridge* (n 3).

[32] Paul Craig, *UK, EU and Global Administrative Law: Foundations and Challenges* (Cambridge University Press, 2015) Ch 1.

[33] *Capel v Child* 149 ER 235 (1833).

[34] *Cooper v Wandsworth Board of Works* 143 ER 414 (1863).

[35] See chapter 2.

'quasi-judicial'[36] functions, on the other.[37] In the former case, the decision-maker was treated as having responsibility to design its own procedures.[38] In the latter, procedural review was regarded as available in order to secure compliance with the basic requirements of natural justice. The writings of a cluster of influential scholars[39] across the 1950s and 1960s, however, encouraged the House of Lords to revisit this issue in the seminal decision of *Ridge*. Although *Ridge* itself did not abolish the distinction between administrative and judicial power,[40] Lord Reid drew attention to the doubtful origins of the idea that the applicability of natural justice should depend on the classification of the power.[41] The case itself, furthermore, signalled a more generous approach to the recognition of procedural rights.[42]

Overall then, pre-*Ridge* and for much of the twentieth century, it was common to imagine procedural review as being centrally concerned with the control of *judicial*, as opposed to *administrative*, power. *Ridge* and subsequent case law led to the erosion of this idea. Although this freed courts from having to grapple with the difficult distinction between judicial and administrative power,[43] it did open up a new and difficult question. Namely: if procedural review was no longer to be guided by reference to the divide between judicial and administrative power, how now was it to be understood?[44]

Post-*Ridge*, case law and literature has long grappled with this question and a considerable body of literature on procedural review has amassed. Supplying a clear answer has, however, proven challenging.

The most common way of conceptualising procedural review post-*Ridge* has relied on the idea that the courts now apply a 'flexible notion of overarching fairness'.[45] It is often said that *Ridge* led to the old schema being replaced by a new approach, under which the starting-point of procedural review is that every administrative decision-maker is under a general duty to exercise powers in a manner which is *fair*.[46] Perhaps the most famous example of this line of thinking

[36] LG Baxter, 'Fairness and Natural Justice in English and South African Law' (1979) 96 *South African Law Journal* 607; Ian Holloway, 'Natural Justice and the New Property' (1999) 25 *Monash University Law Review* 85.

[37] *R v Electricity Commissioners, ex parte London Electricity Joint Committee* [1924] 1 KB 171 (CA); *R v Legislative Committee of the Church Assembly, ex parte Haynes-Smith* [1928] 1 KB 411 (KB).

[38] *R v Local Government Board, ex parte Arlidge* [1914] 1 KB 160 (CA) 150.

[39] Stanley De Smith, 'The Right to a Hearing in English Administrative Law' (1955) 68(4) *Harvard Law Review* 569; William Wade, 'The Twilight of Natural Justice?' (1955) 67 *LQR* 103.

[40] Stephen Bailey, '*Ridge v Baldwin* [1964]: "Nuff Said"' in Maurice Sunkin and Satvinder Juss (eds), *Landmark Cases in Public Law* (Hart Publishing, 2017).

[41] *Ridge* (n 3) 71–79.

[42] Stanley De Smith, 'The House of Lords on Natural Justice' (1963) 26(5) *MLR* 543.

[43] Although some have drawn on the divide in other contexts: *Re Racal Communications Ltd* [1981] AC 374 (HL); Robert Craig, 'Ouster Clauses, Separation of Powers and the Intention of Parliament: From *Anisminic* to *Privacy International*' [2018] *PL* 570.

[44] De Smith (n 42).

[45] *West London Mental Health NHS Trust* (n 5) [69].

[46] *R v Gaming Board for Great Britain, ex parte Benaim and Khaida* [1970] 2 QB 417; DJ Mullan, 'Fairness: The New Natural Justice' (1975) 25(3) *University of Toronto Law Journal* 281.

is the judgment of Lord Parker CJ in *Re HK*[47] in which his Lordship explained that, following *Ridge*:

> … even if an immigration officer is not in a judicial or quasi-judicial capacity, he must at any rate give the immigrant an opportunity of satisfying him of the matters in the subsection … that is not, as I see it, a question of acting or being required to act judicially, *but of being required to act fairly*.[48]

The 'general duty of fairness' approach also appeared subsequently to obtain the approval of the House of Lords in *Wiseman*[49] where Lord Reid explained that:

> Natural justice requires that *the procedure before any tribunal should be fair in all the circumstances*, and I would be sorry to see this fundamental general principle degenerate into a series of hard and fast rules.[50]

This 'fairness account' of procedural review represents the most conventional way of thinking about procedural review since the late-1960s. In terms of achieving 'fit'[51] with the case law, it is also the most successful. The fairness account accords with the case law in the sense that courts commonly draw on the language of fairness.[52] The account is also capable of accommodating almost any outcome settled on by courts. This is because fairness is said to be a 'protean concept, not susceptible of much generalised enlargement'.[53] Its content has been said to be 'infinitely flexible'[54] and highly dependent 'on the circumstances of the case'.[55] It is therefore very difficult to point to a case outcome which the account cannot accommodate. Apparent differences across cases can be explained away by invoking the idea that the 'duty of fairness operates in a highly modulated and fact-sensitive way'[56] and therefore that 'different situations require different levels of fairness'.[57]

The flipside of this point, however, is that thinking in terms of a 'general duty of fairness' also has important weaknesses. The drawbacks were strongly emphasised by Beatson LJ in *West London Mental Health NHS Trust*:

> There are dangers in concentrating on a flexible notion of overarching fairness … Emphasising flexibility and saying no more … may lead to a modern version of Sir William Wade's nightmare of a Tennysonian 'wilderness of single instances'[58] in

[47] *In Re HK (An Infant)* [1967] 2 QB 617 (CA).

[48] *Ibid*, 630 (emphasis added).

[49] *Wiseman v Borneman* [1971] AC 297 (HL).

[50] *Ibid*, 308 (emphasis added).

[51] Smith (n 4) Ch 1.

[52] *Daniel Johns* (n 13) [45]; *San Vincente v Secretary of State for Communities and Local Government* [2014] EWCA Civ 1555 [19]; *R (United Company Rusal Plc) v London Metal Exchange* [2014] EWCA Civ 1271, [2015] 1 WLR 1375 [27]–[28]; *R (Foster) v Secretary of State for Justice* [2015] EWCA Civ 281 [30].

[53] *Moseley* (n 12) [24].

[54] *Daniel Johns* (n 13) [45].

[55] *R (Rowe) v Revenue and Customs Commissioners* [2017] EWCA Civ 2105, [2018] 1 WLR 3039 [106].

[56] *EK (Ivory Coast) v SSHD* [2014] EWCA Civ 1517, [2015] Imm AR 367 [40].

[57] Mark Elliott and Jason Varuhas, *Administrative Law*, 5th edn (Oxford University Press, 2017) 206.

[58] A phrase famously appearing in Lord Tennyson's *Aylmer's Field* (1793) and used often in legal scholarship: DM Gordon, 'The Relation of Facts to Jurisdiction' (1929) *LQR* 458, 459; Christopher

> which all the contextual factors will be relevant in considering what the requirements of procedural fairness are in a given situation without any factor or group of factors having decisive weight in shaping what is in practice required. The consequence may either risk obscuring the overarching principle or stating it at a level of generality which is not of use as a practical tool to decision-making.[59]

The problem is that thinking in terms of fairness alone is that it tells one little about how the courts *actually determine* what the procedural requirements are with which decision-makers are required to comply. The fairness account risks characterising procedural review as an exercise in which courts find answers to legal questions by applying a vague and open-ended 'test'[60] of fairness. It is, however, a short step from saying that procedural review entails the application of a 'flexible'[61] and 'case-sensitive'[62] duty of fairness to the idea that what is required by the law in any given context 'is essentially an intuitive judgment'.[63]

These difficulties have sometimes led commentators and judges to search for a 'thicker' account of procedural review. Such an explanation has, however, proven elusive. One example will suffice to illustrate: the idea of an 'irreducible core'[64] or 'minimum'[65] of process rights. This idea posits there is a basic cluster of rights lying at the heart of procedural review which are incapable of erosion. These rights entitle individuals whose rights and interests are at stake to be given at least notice, the 'gist' of the case against her and an opportunity to make representations. A procedure which falls below this floor of basic rights is to be regarded as unlawful.

The notion of the irreducible core received strong judicial approval in a number of high-profile cases in the early 2000s concerning the use of closed material procedures (CMPs).[66] Early examples include[67] Lord Bingham's judgment

Forsyth (eds), *The Golden Metwand and the Crooked Cork: Essays in Honour of Sir William Wade QC* (Oxford Univerity Press, 1998) Preface.

[59] *West London Mental Health NHS Trust* (n 5) [69].

[60] *R (West Berkshire DC) v Secretary of State for Communities and Local Government* [2016] EWCA Civ 441, [2016] 1 WLR 3923 [60].

[61] *Daniel Johns* (n 13) [45].

[62] *Rowe* (n 55) [106].

[63] *Forest Heath* (n 6) [39].

[64] *AF* (n 8) [43].

[65] *AF* (n 8) [120].

[66] *Chahal v United Kingdom* (1996) 23 EHRR 413; *Al Rawi v Security Service* [2011] UKSC 34, [2012] 1 AC 531; Justice and Security Act 2013. See generally: John Ip, 'The Rise and Spread of the Special Advocate' [2008] *PL* 717; Martin Chamberlain, 'Special Advocates and Procedural Fairness in Closed Proceedings' (2009) 28(3) *Criminal Justice Quarterly* 314; Adrian Zukerman, 'CMP – Denial of Natural Justice: *Al Rawi v Security Service* [2011] UKSC 34' (2011) 30(4) *Criminal Justice Quarterly* 345; Kirsty Hughes, 'The Right to Know the Case Against You' (2012) *CLJ* 21; John Ip, '*Al Rawi, Tariq* and the future of Closed Material Procedures and Special Advocates (2012) 75(4) *MLR* 606; Tim Otty, 'The Slow Creep of Complacency and the Soul of Justice' (2012) 3 *European Human Rights Law Review* 267; Kirsty Hughes, 'Judicial Review and Closed Material Procedure in the Supreme Court' (2013) 72(3) *CLJ* 491; Joseph Chedrawe, 'Blurring the Civil-Criminal Divide for Process Rights: Closed Material Procedures and the Curious Character of Preventative Security Measures' (2013) 24 *King's Law Journal* 1; Eva Nanopoulos, 'European Human Rights Law and the Normalisation of the Closed Material Procedure: Limit or Source?' (2015) 78(6) *MLR* 913.

[67] See also the judgment of Lords Steyn and Bingham in *R (Roberts) v Parole Board* [2005] UKHL 465, [2005] 2 AC 738; *Brown v Stott* [2003] 1 AC 681 (PC).

in *MB*.[68] Most famously, in *A v UK*[69] the Strasbourg Court held the UK's system of preventative detention[70] to be unlawful[71] because it enabled individuals to be detained in circumstances where 'the open material consisted purely of general assertions'.[72] In *AF*[73] the Supreme Court received *A v UK*, some members with considerable reluctance,[74] as having concretised the idea of an irreducible core of process rights. As Lord Hoffmann put it, that individuals 'must be given sufficient information about allegations against him to give effective instructions'[75] was now to be regarded as a 'bottom line, or the core irreducible minimum … [which could] not be shifted'.[76]

Since the high watermark of *AF*, the case law has, however, (ironically) seen the steady erosion of the 'irreducible core',[77] including in the context of CMPs. The most famous (or infamous[78]) example is *Tariq*[79] in which Lord Hope stressed that there is no 'absolute rule that gisting must always be resorted to whatever the circumstances'.[80] More recently, in *Haralambous* the Supreme Court reviewed the 'principles concerning [the] irreducible minimum of disclosure'.[81] Lord Mance, offering the Supreme Court's unanimous view, emphasised again that the basic set of rights discussed in *AF* does not apply in all contexts. As his Lordship put it, 'it cannot be axiomatic … that even the gist of the relevant information must be supplied to any person claiming to be affected by, and wishing to object to'[82] a decision.

To summarise, following the erosion of the idea that procedural review is an exercise in controlling judicial, as opposed to administrative, power post-*Ridge*, scholars and judges have sought a new way of understanding procedural review. The most influential account, which focused on the idea of an 'overarching duty of flexible fairness',[83] achieves fit with the case law, but only at the cost of risking

[68] *Secretary of State for the Home Department v MB* [2007] UKHL 46, [2008] AC 440.
[69] *A v United Kingdom* (2009) 49 EHRR 625.
[70] Anti-Terrorism, Crime and Security Act 2001.
[71] See also *A v Secretary of State for the Home Department* [2004] UKHL 56, [2005] 2 AC 68.
[72] *A* (n 69) [220].
[73] *AF* (n 8).
[74] *AF* (n 8) [70] and [98].
[75] *AF* (n 8) [80].
[76] *AF* (n 8) [81].
[77] A process perhaps expedited by the passage of the Justice and Security Act 2013: Lewis Graham, 'Statutory Secret Trials: The Judicial Approach to CMPs under the Justice and Security Act 2013' (2019) 38(2) *Criminal Justice Quarterly* 189.
[78] Lewis Graham, '*Tariq v UK*: Out with a Whimper? The Final Word on the CMP at the ECtHR' (2019) 25 (1) *European Public Law* 43.
[79] *Tariq v Home Office* [2011] UKSC 35, [2012] 1 AC 452. See also *Tariq v United Kingdom* (Admissibility) (3960/12) (2018) 67 EHRR SE2.
[80] *Tariq v Home Office*, *ibid* [83].
[81] *R (Haralambous) v St Alban's Crown Court* [2018] UKSC 1 [2018] AC 236 [11]. For critique see Daniella Lock, 'A New Chapter in the Normalisation of Closed Material Procedures' (available in *Modern Law Review* early access: https://onlinelibrary.wiley.com/doi/full/10.1111/1468-2230.12484).
[82] *Ibid* [65].
[83] *West London Mental Health NHS Trust* (n 5) [69].

presenting procedural review as an unrestrainedly flexible and 'intuitive'[84] exercise in deciding what is fair. Others, such as attempts or to identify an 'irreducible core'[85] of process rights, have simply not been borne out in the case law.

This analysis gives rise to at least two important questions. First, why is it proving difficult to develop an overarching account of procedural review? Second, do the difficulties in developing such an explanation give rise to concern that procedural review is an inherently unstructured, discretionary exercise in which judges are guided by little more than their own sense of what is 'fair'? The argument of the rest of this chapter is that significant light can be shed on these questions by recognising, what the book has termed, administrative law's complex and varied 'anatomy'.

III. Why is it Proving Difficult to Develop an Overarching Account of Procedural Fairness?

This section focuses on the first question outlined above: why is it proving difficult to develop an overarching account of procedural review? Its core argument is that recognising the complex and varied 'anatomy' of administrative law sheds considerable light on this question. The three core senses in which the legal structures in play in administrative law adjudication are complex and varied, discussed in chapter three, are present in the procedural review case law as much as they are more broadly. Collectively, they suggest a series of reasons why the procedural review case law is not easily explained in general, overarching terms. Subsections A, B and C will discuss each of these senses of complexity and variety, and their importance in the procedural review context, in turn.

A. The Importance of the Legislative Framework

The first sense of complexity and variety inherent in administrative law adjudication was explained in chapter three: the majority of administrative law challenges arise against the background of a specific, and sometimes richly detailed, legislative scheme.[86] These schemes vary considerably in terms of their structure, purposes and detail. A major focus of the courts when adjudicating is on making sense of these schemes and their details therefore play an important shaping role in how the grounds of review are applied.

[84] *Forest Heath* (n 6) [39].

[85] *AF* (n 8).

[86] There are exceptions, such as schemes introduced using prerogative or common law powers: *R (Citizens UK) v Secretary of State for the Home Department* [2018] EWCA Civ 1812, [2018] 4 WLR 123.

Procedural review is no exception to this observation. One aspect of the relationship between legislative frameworks and procedural review is especially worth drawing out: it is now common for primary and secondary legislation, often supplemented by soft law,[87] to make extensive provision for matters of procedure.[88] A considerable proportion of administrative decision-making is now therefore regulated by detailed statutory and policy 'procedural codes'.[89] These codes are tailored to the specific administrative context and, as a result, can vary significantly, in terms of content, from one to the next.

It is useful to illustrate this point by comparing some examples. Consider, first, planning appeals. If an applicant is dissatisfied with a local authority's refusal of planning permission she may appeal to the Secretary of State under the Town and Country Planning Act 1990.[90] This Act makes limited provision for procedural issues, providing only that 'before determining an appeal … the Secretary of State shall, if either the appellant or the local planning authority so wish, give each of them an opportunity of being heard'.[91] The appeal process is, however, substantially fleshed out in Regulations and policy.[92] Broadly, a planning appeal can be determined by a number of different procedures. If the dispute is fairly straightforward, a planning inspector can hold a hearing, the procedure for which is stipulated in the Town and Country Planning (Hearings Procedure) Rules 2000[93] and accompanying guidance.[94] Both the appellant and local planning authority[95] are entitled to take part, as is any party which made representations prior to the initial decision.[96] The hearing 'take[s] the form of a discussion led by the inspector',[97] cross-examination is generally not permitted[98] and contributors are enabled to make representations of any kind they wish.[99] If the issues raised by the appeal are more complex, the planning inspector may hold an inquiry. In this

[87] Greg Weeks, *Soft Law and Public Authorities* (Hart Publishing, 2018).

[88] Carol Harlow and Richard Rawlings, 'Proceduralism and Automation: Challenges to the Values of Administrative Law' in Elizabeth Fisher, Jeff King and Alison Young (eds), *The Foundations and Future of Public Law (in Honour of Paul Craig* (forthcoming in Oxford University Press) (a pre-publication version of the paper is available as *LSE Legal Studies Working Paper No 3/2019*).

[89] Craig (n 10).

[90] Town and Country Planning Act 1990, s78.

[91] *Ibid*, s79(2).

[92] Tribunals and Inquiries Act 1992, s9.

[93] Town and Country Planning (Hearings Procedure) (England) Rules 2000 (SI 2000/1626) ('Hearings Rules 2000').

[94] The Planning Inspectorate, 'Guide to Taking Part in Planning and Listed Buildings Consent Appeals Proceeding by a Hearing – England' (April 2016) (available at: https://assets.publishing.service.gov.uk/government/uploads/system/uploads/attachment_data/file/514291/taking-part_planning-hearing_April_2016.pdf).

[95] Hearings Rules 2000 (n 93), reg 9.

[96] Hearings Rules 2000 (n 93), regulation 9; Town and Country Planning (General Development Procedure) Order 2015 (SI 2015/595), reg 18.

[97] Hearings Rules 2000 (n 93), reg 11(2).

[98] Hearings Rules 2000 (n 93), reg 11(2).

[99] Hearings Rules 2000 (n 93), reg 11(5).

case the applicable rules are contained in the Town and Country Planning Appeals (Determination by Inspectors) (Inquiries Procedure) Rules 2000.[100] A greater array of persons are entitled to take part in the inquiry process.[101] The procedure is also more formal in nature with parties being 'entitled to call evidence'[102] and to 'cross-examine persons giving evidence'[103] subject to the overriding discretion of the inspector.[104]

The planning appeal process can be usefully compared to the procedures prescribed for General Medical Council (GMC) disciplinary cases. This process, contained in the General Medical Council (Registration Appeals Panels Procedure) Rules 2010,[105] differs from the planning appeal procedure in two main ways. In the first place the 'parties'[106] entitled to take part are more restricted. Planning appeals involve at least[107] the appellant, the local planning authority and any third parties who had made representations prior to the original decision. GMC Panel disciplinary hearings, by contrast, are understood as a dispute between two parties only: the appellant and the GMC.[108] Second, proceedings are also more formal in nature. In a planning appeal hearing, cross-examination is generally not permitted. Even in a planning appeal inquiry, cross-examination is subject to the overriding discretion of the inspector. In GMC disciplinary hearings, by contrast, where the Panel hears oral evidence 'witnesses … must first be examined by the party calling them [and then] may be cross-examined by the opposing party'.[109]

These examples illustrate the level of detail in which legislative and policy frameworks can make provision for issues of procedure. Read comparatively, they also highlight some of the considerable differences which apply in different areas of administrative decision-making. These points are of wider importance for the purposes of this chapter. In particular, the existence and variety of procedural codes draws attention to a first reason why it is proving difficult to explain the procedural review case law in general, overarching terms.

As Carol Harlow and Richard Rawlings have written, 'far from the Victorian prototype of the common law supplying "the omission of the legislature" in sparse statutes,[110] [procedural review challenges often involve] judges navigating,

[100] Town and Country Planning (Inquiries Procedure) (England) Rules 2000 (SI 2000/1624) ('Inquiry Rules 2000'); Planning Inspectorate, 'Guide to Taking Part in Planning and Listed Building Consent Appeals Proceeding by an Inquiry – England' (April 2006) (available at: https://assets.publishing.service.gov.uk/government/uploads/system/uploads/attachment_data/file/514292/taking-part_planning-inquiry_April_2016.pdf).

[101] Inquiry Rules 2000 (n 100), rule 11.

[102] Inquiry Rules 2000 (n 100), rule 16(5).

[103] Inquiry Rules 2000 (n 100), rule 16(5).

[104] Inquiry Rules 2000 (n 100), rule 16(5)–(6) and (9).

[105] General Medical Council (Registration Appeals Panels Procedure) Rules Order in Council 2010 (SI 2010/476) ('GMC Registration Appeals Rules 2010').

[106] *Ibid*, rule 2.

[107] Hearings Rules 2000 (n 93), rule 9.

[108] GMC Registration Appeals Rules 2010 (n 105), rules 2 and 6.

[109] GMC Registration Appeals Rules 2010 (n 105), rule 10(2)(d).

[110] *Cooper* n (34).

evaluating and commenting on, whole thickets of legislatively sanctioned administrative procedure'.[111] One consequence of this is that legislative and policy specifics, as opposed to general, overarching principle, play a highly significant role in many procedural review cases. It is perhaps easier to imagine a successful, general account of procedural review in an administrative law landscape where courts fill legislative 'vacuums'[112] by developing their own conception of fair decision-making. The starting-point of procedural review in a good deal of modern adjudication,[113] however, is a highly detailed and particularised procedural code. As these codes vary significantly, courts are beginning from different starting-points when they decide procedural review challenges in different administrative contexts.

B. The Plurality of Values, Interests and Policies Which Administrative Law Protects

The second source of administrative law's complexity concerns its values. As explained in chapter three, administrative law protects and promotes a variety of legal values, interests and policies. This is true in the sense that the origins of administrative law's values are diverse: administrative law seeks to accommodate both the policy goals which underlie legislation and interests 'highly regarded by the common law'.[114] It is also true in terms of administrative law's beneficiaries: administrative law is neither wholly 'public-regarding'[115] nor 'individual-regarding',[116] but seeks to promote the interests of both the public and individuals whose rights and interests are at stake.

This is as true in the procedural review context, as it is across administrative law adjudication more generally. A good illustration is provided by Lord Reed's judgment in *Osborn*[117] where his Lordship explained that:

> … there is no doubt that one of the virtues of procedurally fair decision-making is that it is liable to result in better decisions, by ensuring that the decision-maker receives all relevant information and that it is properly tested.[118]

[111] Harlow and Rawlings (n 88).

[112] Language commonly used in administrative law scholarship: Jeffrey Jowell, 'Of Vires and Vacuums: The Constitutional Context of Judicial Review' [1999] *PL* 448.

[113] This is not to suggest that procedural codes are an exclusively modern creation.

[114] *R v Higher Education Funding Council, ex parte Institute of Dental Surgery* [1994] 1 WLR 242 (DC) 263.

[115] Jason Varuhas, 'The Public Interest Conception of Public Law: Its Procedural Origins and Substantive Implications' in John Bell, Mark Elliott, Jason Varuhas and Philip Murray (eds), *Public Law Adjudication in Common Law Systems: Process and Substance* (Hart Publishing, 2016) 52.

[116] *Ibid.*

[117] *R (Osborn) v Parole Board* [2013] UKSC 61, [2014] AC 1115.

[118] *Ibid*, [67].

'However', his Lordship went on to explain, 'the purpose of a fair hearing is not merely to improve the changes of the tribunal reaching the right decision'.[119] Most importantly,[120] Lord Reed also emphasised 'dignitarian'[121] concerns. According to Lord Reed:

> … justice is intuitively understood to require a procedure which pays due respect to persons whose rights are significantly affected by decisions … Respect entails that such persons ought to be able to participate in the procedure by which the decision is made, provided they have something to say which is relevant to the decision to be taken.[122]

Lord Reed's point is that, when engaging in procedural review, the courts seek to accommodate a broad array of values, purposes and interests including those of the public as a collective and of the individual. This has an important implication for the question being considered here: a further reason why it is proving difficult to develop an overarching account of procedural review is that the case law cannot be explained by reference to a single cluster of normative values.

Scholars attempting to make sense of procedural review have sometimes tried to 'model'[123] the area, by pinpointing a singular normative purpose the case law can be seen as enhancing. In their leading textbook, for instance, Elliott and Varuhas have written that there are two broad understandings of procedural review – the 'instrumental' and 'non-instrumental' views[124] – and that there are areas where 'a choice must … be made about which underlying conception of fairness is paramount'.[125]

Perhaps the most famous example is Denis Galligan's *Due Process and Fair Procedures*.[126] In this work, Galligan has been described as proposing an 'instrumental'[127] account of procedural review because at the heart of Galligan's account is an important idea: all legal procedures have the central aim of promoting the purposes of decision-making in that area. Building on this foundational idea, Galligan offers a distinctive account of administrative procedures. According to this account, because the purpose of much administrative decision-making is the proper application of legal standards to facts, administrative procedures must aim to ensure that decision-makers acquire the information they need in order

[119] *Ibid.*

[120] See further *ibid*, [71] where Lord Reed discusses a 'rule of law' value.

[121] Trevor Allan, 'Procedural Fairness and the Duty of Respect' (1998) 18(3) *OJLS* 497.

[122] *Osborn* (n 117) [68] citing Jeremy Waldron, 'How the Law Protects Dignity' (2012) 71(1) *CLJ* 200.

[123] Jerry Mashaw, 'Administrative Due Process: The Quest for a Dignity Theory' (1981) 61 *Boston University Law Review* 885; Jerry Mashaw, *Due Process in the Administrative State* (Yale University Press, 1985); Thomas W Merrill, 'Jerry Mashaw, The Due Process Revolution and the Limits of Judicial Power' in Nicholas Parrillo (ed), *Administrative Law from the Inside Out: Essays on the Themes in the Work of Jerry L Mashaw* (Cambridge University Press, 2017).

[124] Elliott and Varuhas (n 57) Ch 10.

[125] The authors suggest the main area is in relation to the 'makes no difference' principle: *MB* (n 68); *AF* (n 8).

[126] Denis Galligan, *Due Process and Fair Procedures: A Study of Administrative Procedures* (Clarendon Press, 1997).

[127] Elliott and Varuhas (n 57) Ch 10.

to perform this task properly.[128] Galligan contrasts his account with those which emphasise the importance of ensuring the dignified treatment of the individual in administrative decision-making.[129] Treating individuals with dignity, Galligan argues, is not a separate nor central concern of legal procedures. Rather, individuals are treated with dignity to the extent that their cases are decided in accordance with prevailing legal standards.[130]

Recognising the complex and varied anatomy of administrative law, however, makes clear why the procedural review case law cannot be understood in this way. The case law is not concerned exclusively with, either protecting the rights of individuals nor with promoting the interests of the public. The procedural review case law, in other words, has both 'public-regarding' and 'individual-regarding'[131] elements. Accounts of procedural review which focus on only one, therefore, will fail to capture important aspects of the law.

Thus consider, first, an account of procedural review which emphasises only the importance of protecting the rights and interests of the individual and of ensuring that the individual is treated with dignity. Such an account would capture important aspects of procedural review. It would, for instance, explain why Lord Reed placed emphasis on 'pay[ing] due respect to persons whose rights are significantly affected by decisions' in *Osborn*.[132] It would also help to explain why, as will be discussed below, the common law has established a strong presumption that affected individuals are to be given notice of administrative decisions.[133] At the same time, there are important cases and aspects of procedural review which cannot be explained by emphasising only the importance of protecting the rights and interests of the individual.

Consider, for instance the question of when an individual affected by a decision, can be said to have a right to access the 'gist' of the case against her. If the protection of the individual were the courts only concern in procedural review it might be expected that the courts would insist on this in all decision-making contexts. This, however, is not reflected in the case law. The extent to which an individual is entitled to the gist of the case is also determined by a further layer of considerations: the extent to which providing the gist would promote or undermine the purposes of the background legislative scheme.

In many administrative contexts – indeed, perhaps in the majority – providing affected individuals with the gist of the case is not only consistent with the legislative aims which underlie an administrative scheme, but can positively enhance them. The parole context is a good illustration. The legislative framework which confers the Parole Board's functions demonstrates Parliamentary adherence to at

[128] Galligan (n 126) Ch 1.
[129] Galligan (n 126) Ch 1.
[130] Galligan (n 126) Ch 1.
[131] Varuhas (n 115) 52.
[132] *Osborn* (n 117).
[133] *Bank Mellat (No 2)* (n 11).

least two main aims.[134] In the first place, prisoners are to be released on licence only where the ongoing risk they pose to the public can be safely managed.[135] In the second, the degree of risk is to be assessed by the Parole Board, which is an advisory body, independent of government.[136] Affording the individual whose position is being considered with at least the gist of the case against her will help to enhance both of these aims. Risk can be more accurately assessed if the individual is informed of allegations adverse to them and permitted to respond[137] because it ensures the Board has access to relevant information.[138] Involving the subject also reiterates the Board's independence, by avoiding the impression that it is predisposed to prefer the 'official' statement of events.[139] For these reasons, the case law makes clear that in most cases individuals subject to Parole Board decision-making are entitled to be given, at the very least, the gist of the case against them[140] and are usually entitled to greater procedural protection.[141]

In other contexts, however, the courts have formed the view that requiring the gist of the case to be disclosed to the individual would undermine, rather than enhance, the aims of the relevant scheme and the courts have therefore taken a more restricted approach. Consider the recent Supreme Court decision in *Haralambous*.[142] This case arose against the background of sections 8 and 15 of the Police and Criminal Evidence Act 1984[143] which enables magistrates' courts to authorise the search of premises in order to facilitate criminal investigation. The applicant challenged an order relating to his property. It is a basic principle of the common law, he argued, that individuals affected by decisions are given access to at least the gist of the relevant information and, as a result, magistrates ought not to rely on information which the police would be unwilling to disclose if the decision

[134] Criminal Justice Act 2003, especially ss 239 and 255C; Crime (Sentences) Act 1997 especially s28; Parole Board Rules 2004 (available at: www.justice.gov.uk/downloads/offenders/psipso/pso/pso_4700_lifer_manual_annex_a.doc) (amended by Parole Board (Amendment) Rules 2009 (SI 2009/408) and since repealed by the Parole Board Rules 2011 (SI 2011/2947)).

[135] Crime (Sentences) Act 1997, s28(6): 'the Parole Board shall not give a direction under subsection (5) above … unless … (b) the Board is satisfied that it is no longer necessary for the protection of the public that the prisoner should be confined'.

[136] Criminal Justice and Public Order Act 1994 (which made the Parole Board an 'independent executive Non-Departmental Public Body). See discussion in Nicola Padfield, 'The Parole Board in Transition' (2006) *Criminal Law Review* 2.

[137] As the Supreme Court emphasised, in some contexts oral representations will be necessary to ensure proper testing of the evidence: *Osborn* (n 117) [2].

[138] Endicott (n 27) Ch 4.

[139] *Osborn* (n 117) [2] and [90].

[140] In *Roberts* (n 67) the majority of the House of Lords suggested there may be exceptional cases where gisting is not required. In *Roberts* the Parole Board relied on evidence given by a third party and did not disclose the gist of that evidence in order to preserve their identity. This exception seems to be tightly constrained in practice however (see discussion in Hamish Arnott and Simon Creighton, *Parole Board Hearings: Law and Practice*, 3rd edn (Legal Action Group, 2014) 208–13). It is also unclear whether *Roberts* has been superseded by *AF* (n 8).

[141] *Osborn* (n 117).

[142] *Haralambous* (n 81).

[143] Police and Criminal Evidence Act 1984. See also Criminal Justice and Police Act 2001, s59.

were judicially reviewed. The Supreme Court unanimously rejected this argument. The scheme created by sections 8 and 15 was designed to facilitate police investigations by providing a speedy process for obtaining access to premises.[144] Preventing magistrates from considering non-disclosable information would unacceptably compromise those aims. Such an approach might place pressure on the police to disclose information which would 'reveal … lines or methods of investigation'.[145] Introducing a requirement to separate out disclosable from non-disclosable intelligence would also introduce elements of complexity and delay into proceedings where 'speed is often of the essence'.[146]

What this analysis illustrates is that a purely 'individual-regarding'[147] account of procedural review is insufficient. The courts are not only concerned with guaranteeing the dignified treatment of the individual. The courts are also cautious to ensure that their approach to procedural review does not undermine the purposes of the underlying schemes to which parliament has lent its approval.[148] As such, the extent to which the goals of a legislative scheme would be furthered or compromised by affording generous participation rights significantly shapes the procedural requirements enforced by the courts.

With that said, nor can the procedural review case law be adequately explained purely in terms of 'public-regarding'[149] concerns. In order to illustrate this point, consider a second possible way of thinking about procedural review: a purely 'instrumental'[150] account. According to this way of thinking, the aim of procedural review is not to protect the individual, but to ensure that the procedures used by administrative decision-makers maximise accuracy in decision-making and thereby promote the public interest which underlies the background scheme.[151] Like an individualistic account, this way of thinking would undoubtedly capture important aspects of the procedural review case law. It would help to explain, for instance, the difference between the gisting requirements imposed by the courts in the parole and warrants context just discussed. Such an account would, however, obscure other important aspects of the law.

Consider, for instance, the following important question: why, if the aim of procedural review is to promote accuracy in the application of legal standards, are the processes which courts mandate so limited in scope? As explained in section I, procedural review in English and Welsh administrative law is centrally focused on

[144] *Haralambous* (n 81) [15]; Police and Criminal Evidence Act 1984, s15.
[145] *Haralambous* (n 81) [27].
[146] *Haralambous* (n 81) [27].
[147] Varuhas (n 115) 52.
[148] One exception is in cases where Article 5.4 of the European Convention of Rights is engaged because the decision amounts to a curtailment of an individual's liberty. In such cases, to the extent that legislation is inconsistent with affording the gist of the case to the individual, the legislation will be regarded as incompatible with human rights: *A v UK* (n 69); *AF* (n 8).
[149] Vauhas (n 115) 52.
[150] Elliott and Varuhas (n 57) Ch 10.
[151] Galligan (n 126); Jason Varuhas, 'Judicial Review at the Crossroads' (2015) 74(2) *CLJ* 215.

enabling *individuals and groups to participate* in decision-making. It is, however, far from clear that generous participation opportunities are the most apt processes for maximising accuracy. It is perfectly plausible, for instance, that the accurate application of legal standards would be best realised by introducing a system of internal quality controls whereby randomly selected decisions are subjected to periodic checks.[152] It is clear, however, that as the case law stands, the courts do not see it as their role to mandate processes of this kind. Judicial intervention generally focuses on empowering particularly affected individuals and groups to play a role in decision-making processes.

A further, related, question is why, if procedural review is focused on ensuring that administrative decision-makers access relevant information, procedural review confers participation rights *only on limited subsets of people*. In the parole context, for instance, procedural review focuses on protecting the interests of the person whose right to liberty is actually at stake. The leading cases grapple with questions such as when, in the course of applying for parole, a prisoner is entitled to have *her* case decided by an oral hearing.[153] If the exclusive or central aim of procedural review in the parole context, however, is to promote the 'public-regarding'[154] aims of the parole system, it is not clear why the case law should have this narrow focus. A prisoner, for instance, who has pertinent information about the suitability of his or her cell-mate for release on licence should surely have an equal claim to notice and an opportunity to make representations before the Parole Board as the person who is the subject of the decision. The law, however, is not structured in this way.[155]

To be clear, this is not an argument that the courts ought to take a more expansive approach to the procedures they mandate, such as by introducing obligations to carry out quality checks or affording process rights on third parties in the parole context. The point is that in engaging in procedural review the courts seek to accommodate a variety of legal values, interests and purposes. Both common law presumptions in favour of involving affected individuals and a consideration of legislative purpose play an important role in determining procedural requirements. Relatedly, the law cannot be explained by reference to either 'instrumental'[156] or 'public-regarding'[157] concerns exclusively. This complexity, in

[152] Jerry Mashaw, *Bureaucratic Justice: Managing Social Security Disability Claims* (Yale University Press, 1983); Charles F Sabel and William H Simon, 'The Management Side of Due Process in the Service-Based Welfare State' in Parrillo (ed) (n 123).

[153] *R v Parole Board, ex parte Bradley* [1991] 1 WLR 134 (DC); *R v Parole Board, ex parte Wilson* [1992] QB 740 (CA); *R (West) v Parole Board* [2005] UKHL 1, [2005] 1 WLR 350; *R (Sturnham) v Parole Board* [2013] UKSC 23, [2013] 2 AC 254; *Osborn* (n 117).

[154] Varuhas (n 115) 52.

[155] See further *R (DSD) v Parole Board* [2018] EWHC 694, [2019] QB 285, especially [105]–[115] where the Court doubts the standing of both the Mayor of London and victims of prisoners to challenge release decisions.

[156] Elliott and Varuhas (n 57) Ch 10.

[157] Varuhas (n 115) 52.

turn, suggests an important reason why a general account of the procedural review case law has proven elusive. Commentators have sometimes sought to develop accounts of procedural review by identifying a singular normative value which the law promotes. The plurality of values, interests and purposes in play in administrative law adjudication, however, means that accounts of this kind fail to encapsulate all of the important aspects of the case law.

C. The Array of Legal Relationships in Play in Administrative Law Challenges

The third core sense of complexity and variety in administrative law concerns the legal relationships in play. It has sometimes been suggested that the 'shape' of an administrative law case is fundamentally different to that of a human rights[158] or private law case.[159] In the latter areas, claimants are said to go before the court in order to assert legal rights which they personally hold in relation to the defendant. In administrative law, however, applicants are thought of as relying on duties which are not owed personally to them but to the public as a collectivity.[160] This way of imagining the relationship between the fields is, however, overly simplistic. Administrative law at least[161] concerns legal relationships of different kinds. Again, this observation is applicable in the procedural review context and, again, it suggests a reason why procedural review is not easily explained in terms of general overarching concepts.

There are certainly procedural challenges which cannot be characterised as cases in which the applicants seek to enforce legal duties which are owed to them personally. This is true, for instance, of much of the case law concerning consultation.[162] Consider, for instance, *Moseley*.[163] This case concerned the lawfulness

[158] Jason Varuhas, 'Against Unification' in Mark Elliott, Jason Varuhas and Shona Wilson Stark (eds), *The Unity of Public Law?* (Hart Publishing, 2017).

[159] Nicholas Bamforth, 'Hohfeldian Rights and Public Law' in Matthew Kramer (ed), Rights Wrongs & Responsibilities (Palgrave, 2001); Lord Woolf, 'Public Law – Private Law: Why the Divide? A Personal View' [1986] *PL*.

[160] As Thomas Poole put it, according to this way of thinking 'the individual was marginal to the business of the court, providing a trigger for an action but not necessarily the focal point of legal analysis … the individual's good tended to be sublimated with the common good of protecting the political community from abuses of power': Thomas Poole, 'The Reformation of English Administrative Law' (2009) 68(1) *CLJ* 142, 142–43.

[161] This is not to suggest that human rights and private law neatly fit these descriptions: Joanna Miles, 'Standing in a Multi-Layered Constitution' in Nicholas Bamforth and Peter Leyland (eds), *Public Law in a Multi-Layered Constitution* (Hart Publishing, 2003); Paul Craig, 'Taxonomy and Public Law: A Response' [2019] *PL* 281; *Coventry v Lawrence* [2015] UKSC 50, [2015] 1 WLR 3485.

[162] *R v Brent LBC, ex parte Gunning* (1985) 84 LGR 168 (DC); *R v Devon County Council, ex parte Baker* [1995] 1 All ER 73 (CA); *R (Medway Council) v Secretary of State for Transport, Local Government and the Regions* [2002] EWHC 2516 (Admin), [2003] JPL 583.

[163] *Moseley* (n 12).

of the consultation exercise[164] which preceded the introduction of a new council tax reduction scheme.[165] The applicant argued that the consultation documents unlawfully failed to make clear that a number of possible options for making financial cuts had been discarded. This argument is very difficult to characterise in terms of individual right-duty correlativity. *Moseley* was not a case in which the applicant asserted a personal legal right, entitling *her* to disclosure of the rejected options.[166] The applicant, rather, appeared as a *representative of the public*; her argument was that the local authority was duty-bound to make clear to the public how its decision-making process was proceeding.

It is far from the case, however, that the only legal duties with which procedural review is concerned are obligations owed to the public or subsections of it. On the contrary, *individual* rights clearly play a role in this area in at least two ways. First, section A explained that many procedural review cases now arise against the background of detailed legislative and policy codes. The further point can now be made that is not uncommon for these procedural codes to explicitly confer 'rights' or 'entitlements' on *individuals*.[167] Take, for instance, rule 54 of the Prison Rules:

> **54. *Rights* of prisoners charged**
>
> (1) Where a prisoner is charged with an offence against discipline, *he* shall be informed of the charge as soon as possible and, in any case, before the time when it is inquired into by the governor.[168]

This section expressly purports to lay out a series of 'rights' for individual prisoners. In a similar way consider regulation 7 of the Police (Conduct) Regulations 2012:

> (1) The officer concerned *has the right* to be legally represented, by a relevant lawyer of his choice, at a misconduct hearing or a special case hearing.[169]

Again, the effect of this provision is to create a relationship of *individual* right-duty correlativity between an individual police officer and the decision-maker, entitling the former to legal representation in proceedings before the latter.

Second, and additionally, there is also a clear and consistent tendency on the part of both judges and scholars to speak of the common law as manifesting, at least

[164] Local Government Finance Act 2012, Sch 1A, para 3(1) (inserted by Local Government Finance Act 1992, Sch 4, para 1 and s13A(3)).

[165] Local Government Finance Act 1992, s13A(2) (inserted by Local Government Finance Act 2012, s10(1)).

[166] Local Government Finance Act 2012, Sch 1A, para 3(1): 'before making a scheme, the authority must ... consult *such other persons* as it considers are likely to have an interest in the operation of the scheme' (emphasis added).

[167] Craig (n 10).

[168] Prison Rules 1999 (SI 1999/728), rule 54 (emphasis added).

[169] Police (Conduct) Regulations 2012 (SI 2012/2632), reg 7(1) (emphasis added).

in some contexts, in individual process rights. Consider, for instance, the leading case of *Ridge*.[170] Lord Hodson in this case explained his conclusion as follows:

> I have reached the conclusion … that this appeal should succeed on the ground that *the applicant was entitled to* and did not receive natural justice at the hands of the watch committee.[171]

Lord Hodson here speaks of the common law principle of natural justice as manifesting in a personal legal right, held by Mr Ridge, entitling him to be given an opportunity to participate in decision-making. In a similar way, in the leading case of *Osborn*, Lord Reed expressed his conclusion as follows:

> The board breached its duty of procedural fairness *to the appellant* by failing to offer him an oral hearing.[172]

Many other examples could be given of the tendency to speak of common law principles as manifesting in individualised process rights.[173] There is little point in duplicating them here. The core point is that it is very difficult to characterise procedural review as an area in which courts enforce duties owed to the public at large, as opposed to anyone individual.[174] This is both because legislation and policy frequently purports to confer individualised process rights and because there is a clear and pervasive tendency of regarding the common law as crystallising in personal legal entitlements to participate.

Why is recognising the diversity of legal relationships in play in procedural review important? It suggests a further reason why it has proven difficult to explain the case law in general overarching terms. In seeking an account of procedural review, it may be tempting to begin by posing the question of whether the duty to exercise power in a manner which is procedurally fair is best understood as an obligation which is owed to an individual or to the public as a collectivity.[175] The analysis in this section demonstrates why it is unhelpful to try to explain procedural review in this way. Procedural review cases do not concern a single variety of legal relationship. In some cases, the applicant will rely on a duty to consult

[170] *Ridge* (n 3).

[171] *Ridge* (n 3) 127 (emphasis added).

[172] *Osborn* (n 117) [116] (emphasis added). See also [2]: 'the *right of the prisoner* to request an oral hearing is not correctly characterised as a right of appeal' (emphasis added).

[173] For further examples in the case law, see especially *Attorney General v Ryan* [1980] AC 718 (PC), 727; *R v Secretary of State for the Home Department, ex parte Al Fayed (No 1)* [1998] 1 WLR 763 (CA), 787; *McNicholls v Judicial and Legal Service Commission* [2010] UKPC 6 [42]; *R v Chief Constable of Thames Valley Police ex parte Cotton* [1990] IRLR 344 (CA); *R (Silus Investments) v London Borough of Hounslow* [2015] EWHC 358 (Admin) [69]; *R (Trafford) v Blackpool BC* [2014] EWHC 85 (Admin), [2014] PTSR 989, 79; *Kanda v Malaya* [1962] AC 322 (PC) 337; *Bank Mellat (No 2)* (n 11) [56], [146] and [152]. For further examples from the literature, see especially Kenneth Culp Davis, 'The Requirement of a Trial-Type Hearing' (1956) 70(2) *Harvard Law Review* 193, 199 and 212; De Smith (n 39) 578; Paul Daly, 'Administrative Law: A Values-Based Approach' in Bell, Elliott, Varuhas and Murray (eds) (n 115) 33; Matthew Groves and Greg Weeks, 'The Legitimacy of Expectations about Fairness' in Bell, Elliott, Varuhas and Murray (eds) (n 115) 171.

[174] Woolf (n 159).

[175] Varuhas (n 1) 411–13.

which is aimed at protecting the interests of a broader section of the public.[176] In other contexts, however, individuals will rely on procedural duties which legislation, Regulations or policy, and perhaps the common law, regards as being owed to them personally.

To summarise, the aim of this section has been to demonstrate how recognising the complexity and variety of administrative law's 'anatomy' sheds light on procedural review. It has argued that understanding this anatomy helps to explain why developing a general, overarching account of procedural review has proven difficult. The three core senses of complexity and variety discussed in section III are in play in the procedural review context as much as they are across administrative law adjudication more broadly. Each, in turn, suggests a reason why the procedural review case law is difficult to explain by reference to a 'singular, superior construct'.[177]

In brief outline, those reasons are as follows. First of all, modern procedural review cases now often arise against the backdrop of a detailed procedural code which can vary considerably in detail. These codes provide the starting-points of much adjudication and shape the approach courts take to resolving procedural questions. Also, in engaging in procedural review the courts seek to accommodate a plurality of legal values including common law principle, legislative aims and both 'individual' and 'public-regarding'[178] considerations. The procedural review case law, therefore, cannot be adequately explained by reference to a singular overarching purpose. Lastly, procedural review case law concerns legal relationships of different kinds. As a result, the procedural review case law cannot be understood in terms of a singular duty to exercise power in a manner which is procedurally fair which is owed to the public, or to the individual.

IV. Do the Difficulties in Developing a General Account of Procedural Review Indicate a Lack of Structure in Judicial Reasoning?

As explained above, the analysis in section II gave rise to at least two important questions. The first of these – why it is proving difficult to develop a general, overarching account of procedural review – was considered in the previous section. This section is focused on the second: do the difficulties in explaining procedural review give rise to concern that procedural review is little more than inherently discretionary and legally unstructured in deciding what is 'fair'?

There are different methods which could be used to explore this question. One plausible approach, for instance, might identify a handful of case studies and

[176] *Moseley* (n 12); Local Government Finance Act 2012, Sch 1A, para 3(1).
[177] Elliott (n 2).
[178] Varuhas (n 115) 52.

closely scrutinise the reasoning processes used by judges for evidence of structure (or lack of structure). The drawbacks of this approach, of course, would be that it is not clear how these case studies could be objectively identified and it would be very difficult to know whether they were representative of broader trends. An alternative approach might focus on the leading cases in which appellate courts have offered generalised guidance on how procedural review should be conducted. The difficulty with such an approach, however, is that generalised guidance of this kind is often framed in extremely broad terms. In order to thoroughly assess the degree to which it lends meaningful structure to legal reasoning, one would also need to look at how it has been applied.

In light of these difficulties, this part takes a different approach. Rather than focusing on case studies or the leading case law, it offers an analysis of a larger sample of systematically identified cases. This case law was identified though a free-text search focused on 'procedural fairness'.[179] It was narrowed down to exclude cases which did not concern challenges to administrative decision-making (such as cases brought against private companies or individuals), which used the language of 'procedural fairness' only incidentally and which raised issues concerning bias or the adequacy of reasons. The case sample was also narrowed down to include only cases decided in the UK Supreme Court (27 cases),[180] Privy Council (one case)[181] and English Court of Appeal (Civil Division) (99 cases) within the ten-year period, beginning at the start of 2009 and concluding at the end of 2018. The main reason for focusing on appellate courts only is one of manageability. The free-text search yielded a very large number of results. It seemed preferable to focus on appellate court decisions decided over a longer time-frame than all challenges decided in a shorter time-frame. Furthermore, while no assumption can be made that every case of importance reached the appellate courts, those which did were deemed to have passed the threshold of the second-appeals criteria.[182]

[179] Using Westlaw UK.

[180] *AF* (n 8); *JR17's Application for Judicial Review (NI)* [2010] UKSC 28, [2010] HRLR 27; *Al Rawi* (n 66); *Tariq v Home Office* (n 79); *R (G) v Governors of X School* [2011] UKSC 30, [2012] 1 AC 167; *W (Algeria) v Secretary of State for the Home Department* [2012] UKSC 8, [2012] 2 AC 115; *Pomiechowski v District Court of Legnica* [2012] UKSC 20, [2012] 1 WLR 1604; *Walton v Scottish Ministers* [2012] UKSC 44, [2013] PTSR 51; *Bank Mellat v HM Treasury (No 1)* [2013] UKSC 38, [2014] AC 700; *Bank Mellat (No 2)* (n 11); *R (Reilly) v SoS for Work and Pensions* [2013] UKSC 68, [2014] AC 453; *South Lanarkshire v Scottish Information Commissioner* [2013] UKSC 55, [2013] 1 WLR 2421; *Re Corey's Application for Judicial Review* [2013] UKSC 76, [2014] AC 516; *Osborn* (n 117); *Moseley* (n 12); *VB, CU, CM, EN v Westminster Magistrates' Court* [2014] UKSC 59, [2015] AC 1195; *British Sky Broadcasting* (n 17); *Mandalia v Secretary of State for the Home Department* [2015] UKSC 59, [2015] 1 WLR 4546; *R (Bourgass) v Secretary of State for Justice* [2015] UKSC 54, [2016] AC 384; *Edenred Ltd v HM Treasury* [2015] UKSC 45, [2016] 1 All ER 763; *Lees-Hirons v Secretary of State for Justice* [2016] UKSC 46, [2017] AC 52; *R (Bancoult) v Secretary of State for Foreign and Commonwealth Affairs (No 2)* [2016] UKSC 35, [2017] AC 300; *R (Ingenious Media Holdings) v HMRC* [2016] UKSC 54, [2016] 1 WLR 4164; *Financial Conduct Authority v Macris* [2017] UKSC 19, [2017] 1 WLR 1095; *R (Bancoult) v Secretary of State for Foreign and Commonwealth Affairs (No 3)* [2018] UKSC 3, [2018] 1 WLR 973; *R (Belhaj) v DPP* [2018] UKSC 33, [2019] AC 593; *Haralambous* (n 81).

[181] *R (Hoffmann) v Commissioner of Inquiry* [2012] UKPC 17, [2012] 5 WLUK 668.

[182] Access to Justice Act 1999, s55.

It is likely, therefore, that the sample includes at least some of the most legally difficult and practically important procedural review challenges which the courts have heard in recent years.

The sample considered encompasses 127 cases. This case law is diverse and concerned challenges to decisions in many administrative contexts including, among others:

- age assessments;[183]
- airport regulations;[184]
- anti-social behaviour orders;[185]
- anti-terrorism measures;[186]
- asylum[187] and immigration decisions;[188]
- benefits assessments;[189]
- care proceedings;[190]
- citizenship decisions;[191]
- council tax rule-making;[192]
- defence;[193]
- deportation;[194]
- disclosure;[195]
- education[196] and education complaints;[197]

[183] *R (Z) v Croydon LBC* [2011] EWCA Civ 59, [2011] PTSR 748.

[184] *R (Easyjet) v Civil Aviation Authority* [2009] EWCA Civ 1361.

[185] *Birmingham CC v Jones* [2018] EWCA Civ 1189, [2018] 3 WLR 1695.

[186] *AH v Secretary of State for the Home Department* [2011] EWCA Civ 787; *AM v Secretary of State for the Home Department* [2011] EWCA Civ 710; *BX v Secretary of State for the Home Department* [2010] EWCA Civ 481, [2010] 1 WLR 2463; *Bank Mellat (No 2)* (n 11).

[187] *Citizens UK* (n 86); *R (AM) v Secretary of State for the Home Department* [2018] EWCA Civ 1815; *AM (Afghanistan) v Secretary of State for the Home Department* [2017] EWCA Civ 1123, [2018] 4 WLR 78; *R (TH) v Secretary of State for the Home Department* [2016] EWCA Civ 815; *SH (Afghanistan) v Secretary of State for the Home Department* [2011] EWCA Civ 1284.

[188] *EK* (n 56); *R (E (Russia)) v Secretary of State for the Home Department* [2012] EWCA Civ 357, [2012] 1 WLR 3198.

[189] *Reilly* (n 180); *Sumpter* (n 18).

[190] *R (R) v Children and Family Court Advisory and Support Service* [2012] EWCA Civ 853, [2013] 1 WLR 163.

[191] *R (AHK) v Secretary of State for the Home Department* [2009] EWCA Civ 287, [2009] 1 WLR 2049.

[192] *Moseley* (n 12).

[193] *R (K) v Secretary of State for Defence* [2016] EWCA Civ 1149, [2017] 1 WLR 1671.

[194] *W (Algeria)* (n 180); *R (BB) v Special Immigration and Asylum Commission (No 2)* [2012] EWCA Civ 1499, [2013] 1 WLR 1568; *Abbassi* (n 16); *IR (Sri Lanka) v Secretary of State for the Home Department* [2011] EWCA Civ 704, [2012] 1 WLR 232.

[195] *R (L) v Commissioner of the Metropolitan Police* [2009] UKSC 3, [2010] 1 AC 410.

[196] *R (Durand Academy Trust) v Ofsted* [2018] EWCA Civ 2813.

[197] *Sandler* (n 20).

- energy;[198]
- entry into the UK;[199]
- extradition;[200]
- freedom of information;[201]
- health;[202]
- housing;[203]
- inquiries[204] and investigations;[205]
- legal aid;[206]
- local government structure;[207]
- mental health detention;[208]
- neighbourhood plans;[209]
- ombudsmen;[210]
- parole[211] and prison classification;[212]
- planning[213] and planning enforcement;[214]

198 *R (Drax Power Ltd) v Secretary of State for Energy and Climate Change* [2014] EWCA Civ 1153.

199 *Naidu* (n 20); *R (G1) v Secretary of State for the Home Department* [2012] EWCA Civ 867, [2013] QB 1008; *ZZ v Secretary of State for the Home Department* [2011] EWCA Civ 440.

200 *Westminster Magistrates' Court* (n 180); *Pomiechowski* (n 180).

201 *South Lanarkshire* (n 180); *Browning v Information Commissioner* [2014] EWCA Civ 1050, [2014] 1 WLR 3848.

202 *R (Royal Brompton and Harefield NHS Foundation Trust) v Joint Committee of Primary Care Trust* [2012] EWCA Civ 472; *R (Pharmaceutical Services Negotiating Committee) v Secretary of State for Health* [2018] EWCA Civ 1925; *R (Roche) v Secretary of State for Health* [2015] EWCA Civ 1311, [2016] 4 WLR 46.

203 *Kamara v Southwark LBC* [2018] EWCA Civ 1616, [2019] PTSR 279; *Oduneye v Brent LBC* [2018] EWCA Civ 1595; *R (Milton Keynes Council) v Secretary of State for Communities and Local Government* [2011] EWCA Civ 1575, [2012] JPL 728.

204 *Hoffmann* (n 181).

205 *Federation of Independent Practitioner Organisations v Competition and Markets Authority* [2016] EWCA Civ 777; *Macris* (n 180); *Derrin Brothers* (n 17).

206 *R (S) v Director of Legal Aid Casework* [2016] EWCA Civ 464, [2016] 1 WLR 4733; *R (Howard League for Penal Reform) v Lord Chancellor* [2015] EWCA Civ 819.

207 *Forest Heath* (n 6); *R (Breckland DC) v Electoral Commission Boundary Committee* [2009] EWCA Civ 239, [2009] PTSR 1611.

208 *Lees-Hirons* (n 180); *R (VC) v Secretary of State for the Home Department* [2018] EWCA Civ 57.

209 *Kebbell Developments Ltd v Leeds CC* [2018] EWCA Civ 450.

210 *Miller v Health Service Commissioner for England* [2018] EWCA Civ 144.

211 *Re Corey's Application* (n 180); *Foster* (n 52); *R (Tabbakh) v Staffordshire and West Midlands Probation Trust* [2014] EWCA Civ 827, [2014] 1 WLR 4620.

212 *R (Hassett) v Secretary of State for Justice* [2017] EWCA Civ 331, [2017] 1 WLR 4750; *R (Downs) v Secretary of State for Justice* [2011] EWCA Civ 1422; *McKay* (n 20).

213 *Preston New Road Action Group v Secretary of State for Communities and Local Government* [2018] EWCA Civ 9, [2018] JPL 807; *Secretary of State for Communities and Local Government v Engbers* [2016] EWCA Civ 1183; *Broadview Energy Developments Ltd v SSCLG* [2016] EWCA Civ 562, [2016] JPL 1207.

214 *Secretary of State for Communities and Local Government v Bleaklow Industries* [2009] EWCA Civ 2006, [2009] 1 P & CR 21.

- prison management[215] and discipline;[216]
- procurement;[217]
- professional discipline;[218]
- prosecution;[219]
- roads[220] and transport;[221]
- social care;[222] and
- tax[223] and warrants.[224]

This section offers an analysis of this case law. Its core argument is that a close reading of this case law, with the complex and varied 'anatomy' of administrative law in mind, reveals that, even in the absence of a clear, overarching account of procedural review, there are important sources of structure in play which help to guide legal reasoning. That structure takes two main forms. Subsection A introduces the first, and subsection B the second.

A. 'Procedural Codes'[225] as a Source of Structure

In introducing the first source of structure in judicial reasoning, it is useful to recall again that procedural review challenges commonly arise against the background of detailed legislative and policy frameworks and these schemes often make rigorous provision for issues of procedure. One consequence of this was evident in the case sample analysed: a substantial proportion of procedural challenges now raise fairly narrow questions of statutory or policy construction concerning the meaning of these schemes. Across the sample, the courts tended to decide these cases by attempting to understand the purposes which underlie the relevant frameworks and to resolve the interpretive ambiguity in the manner which would best promote those aims.

It is useful to discuss some examples. These examples can be broadly divided into three categories. In the first category, the procedural code could be found in *primary legislation*. The core question raised by the case was therefore one

[215] *Bourgass* (n 180).
[216] *R (Garland) v Secretary of State for Justice* [2011] EWCA Civ 1335, [2012] 1 WLR 1879.
[217] *Edenred* (n 180).
[218] *G* (n 180)
[219] *Belhaj* (n 180).
[220] *Walton* (n 180).
[221] *R (Robson) v Salford CC* [2015] EWCA Civ 6, [2015] PTSR 1349.
[222] *R (LH) v Shropshire Council* [2014] EWCA Civ 404, [2014] PTSR 1052; *R (Buckinghamshire CC) v Kingston upon Thames RLBC* [2011] EWCA Civ 457, [2012] PTSR 854.
[223] *Ingenious Media Holdings* (n 180); *Rowe* (n 55); *R (Glencore Energy UK Ltd) v HMRC* [2017] EWCA Civ 1716, [2017] 4 WLR 213; *Seabrook* (n 16).
[224] *British Sky Broadcasting* (n 17); *Concordia* (n 17).
[225] Craig (n 10).

about the proper construction of an Act of Parliament. Consider, for instance, *Kebbell*[226] which concerned a challenge to a decision to put to a referendum a proposed 'neighbourhood development order'[227] with different modifications to those recommended by the examiner.[228] The relevant procedural provision was paragraph 13 of Schedule 4B to the Town and Country Planning Act 1990 which provides as follows:

> … if (a) the local planning authority proposes to make a decision which differs from that recommended by the examiner, and (b) the reason for the difference is … as a result of new evidence, or a new fact or a different view taken by the authority as to a particular fact, the authority must notify prescribed persons … and invite representations.[229]

The applicant in *Kebbell* argued for a broad construction of this provision according to which, whenever a council is minded to make modifications to a proposal different to those recommended by the examiner, it will be required to consult 'prescribed persons'.[230] The Court of Appeal rejected this argument. Other provisions in the legislation[231] provided for opportunities for interested parties to participate in the decision-making process at an earlier stage. Against this background, and bearing in mind the restricted language of paragraph 13(b) (which specifies that the duty applies when the disagreement is as a result of 'new evidence, or a new fact or a different view taken by the authority as to a particular fact') the Court thought it was clear that the purpose of this provision was not to 'give parties a second opportunity to advance a case already heard and considered by the examiner'[232] but to permit interested parties to offer comments on new evidence.

A similar, second example is *Breckland*.[233] This case arose against the background of the Local Government and Public Involvement in Health Act 2007 which empowers the Secretary of State to refer a proposal for 'single tier local government'[234] to the Boundary Committee.[235] Section 6(4) provides as follows:

> Before making an alternative proposal … the boundary committee must (a) publish a draft; and (b) take such steps as they consider sufficient to secure that persons who may be interested are informed of (i) the draft proposal and (ii) the period within which representations about it may be made.[236]

The issue in *Breckland* concerned the level of detail in which alternative proposals are required to be published. The Court of Appeal considered that the clear

[226] *Kebbell* (n 209).
[227] Town and Country Planning Act 1990, Sch 4B.
[228] *Ibid*, Sch 4B, para 7.
[229] *Ibid*, Sch 4B, para 13(1).
[230] Neighbourhood Planning (General) Regulations 2012 (SI 2012/637), regulation 17A.
[231] Town and Country Planning Act 1990, Sch 4B, para 9.
[232] *Kebbell* (n 209) [50].
[233] *Breckland* (n 207).
[234] Local Government and Public Involvement in Health Act 2007, s2.
[235] *Ibid*, s5.
[236] *Ibid*, s6(4).

purpose underlying section 6(4) was to enable interested parties, which included the public at large,[237] to understand and offer comments on proposals. Therefore, it was essential that the published documentation set out clearly and accessibly at least 'a summary of the reasons why that change is proposed and … why the proposed change is considered to meet the [relevant legal] criteria'.[238] Unless the documentation did this, the aim of ensuring effective public participation would not be realised.

In a second category of case, procedural provision is made by Regulations, as opposed to Acts of Parliament. In these cases, the courts therefore grapple with questions concerning the proper interpretation of secondary legislation. Consider, for instance, *Garland*.[239] Rule 53(1) of the Prison Rules provides that:

> … where a prisoner is to be charged with an offence against discipline, the charge shall be laid as soon as possible and, save in exceptional circumstances, within 48 hours of the discovery of the offence.[240]

The applicant in *Garland* argued that, although he had been given notice precisely 48 hours after the discovery of the offence, it had not been delivered 'as soon as possible'[241] and that therefore the disciplinary proceedings brought against him were invalid. The Court of Appeal rejected the argument. Tracing the origins of rule 53(1)[242] revealed that its core aim was to 'inject … certainty and reduce the scope for … investigation'[243] into the timeliness of notice. The applicant's proposed construction would undermine this purpose because it would leave open in every case the question of 'whether the charge could possibly have been laid earlier than it was'.[244]

In a similar way, *Makisi*[245] concerned the proper interpretation of the Allocation of Housing and Homelessness (Review Procedures) Regulations 1999 which deal with the process for reviewing applications for housing assistance. Regulation 8(2) provides that:

> … if [a] reviewer considers that there is a deficiency or irregularity in the original decision … but is minded nonetheless to make a decision which is against the interests of the applicant … the reviewer shall notify the applicant … and the applicant … may make representations to the reviewer orally or in writing.[246]

[237] Reflected in the introductory text to the Act.

[238] *Breckland* (n 207), [44].

[239] *Garland* (n 216).

[240] Prison Rules 1999 (SI 1999/728), rule 53(1).

[241] *Ibid*. The applicant sought to draw an analogy with the Civil Procedure Rules 1998, Part 54, rule 5 ('the claim for must be filed (a) promptly; and (b) in any event not later than 3 months'). The Court of Appeal however rejected the analogy: *Garland* (n 216) [10].

[242] Which was introduced in response to *R v Board of Visitors of Dartmoor Prison, ex parte Smith* [1987] QB 106 (CA).

[243] *Garland* (n 216) [12].

[244] *Garland* (n 216) [12].

[245] *Makisi v Birmingham CC* [2011] EWCA Civ 355, [2011] PTSR 1545.

[246] Allocation of Housing and Homelessness (Review Procedures) Regulations 1999 (SI 1999/71), regulation 8(2).

The applicant argued that regulation 8(2) entitled an applicant to make representations in person, and not merely to offer oral representations over the telephone. The Court of Appeal accepted the argument. When regulation 8 was read against the broader legislative framework it was clear that its purpose was to implement section 203 of the Housing Act 1996. This provision empowered the Secretary of State to introduce a procedural code, including by introducing the right to 'an oral hearing',[247] the usual meaning of which entailed making representations in person.

In this first and second category of examples, the relevant procedural code is contained in primary and/or second legislation. The third category of case is different again. These challenges concern the meaning of procedural provisions contained in policy documents. Unlike legislation, policy does not have direct legal force in English and Welsh administrative law. Increasingly,[248] however, it has come to be recognised as having *indirect* legal force. Most importantly, there is now a recognised principle that administrative decision-makers must follow their published policies unless there are good reasons not to.[249] Consequently, courts are increasingly required to grapple with questions concerning the proper interpretation of policy and guidance documents in order to decide whether those provisions have been properly applied,[250] including in the context of procedural review.[251]

Consider, for instance, *Mandalia*.[252] *Mandalia* is a leading case establishing the principle in favour of the consistent application of policy.[253] On another level, however, it also concerned the proper interpretation of a highly particularised policy circular. This circular stipulated that, in processing visa applications, Home Office case workers ought to use a 'flexible process' whereby caseworkers should 'invite … applicants to correct minor errors of omissions'.[254] The document explicitly required caseworkers to alert applicants to bank statements missing from the middle of a series,[255] however there was disagreement about its application in a case where bank statements did not go far back enough in time. The Supreme Court concluded that the purposes of the policy extended to cases of this sort. The policy circular emphasised that its purpose was to ensure flexibility and to give applicants the 'benefit of the doubt'[256] in unclear cases. In all cases where documentation was missing, there would be a possibility that the relevant evidence did

[247] Housing Act 1996, s203.

[248] Aileen McHarg, 'Administrative Discretion, Administrative Rule-Making and Judicial Review' (2017) 70(1) *Current Legal Problems* 267.

[249] *R v Islington LBC ex parte Rixon* [1997] ELR 66 (QB); *R (Lumba) v Secretary of State for the Home Department* [2011] UKSC 12, [2012] 1 AC 245 [26].

[250] Joanna Bell, 'Judicial Review of Executive Action & Common Law Constitutional Rights' in Mark Elliott and Kirsty Hughes, *Common Law Constitutional Rights* (forthcoming in Hart).

[251] *R (Majed) v Camden LBC* [2009] EWCA Civ 1029, [2010] JPL 621.

[252] *Mandalia* (n 180).

[253] *Mandalia* (n 180) [31].

[254] *Mandalia* (n 180) [22].

[255] *Mandalia* (n 180) [26].

[256] *Mandalia* (n 180) [34].

not exist. There was, however, no reason to believe that this was more likely in a case like Mandalia's than in the case of a statement missing from a series.

JR17[257] is similar. Here a school was found to have acted in breach of its own procedural policy on exclusion. Paragraph 4.2.2 of the school's policy specified that pupils could only be suspended on disciplinary grounds and only following that student being given the opportunity to give 'his or her version of events'.[258] The applicant, however, had been excluded without being given this opportunity. The school argued that it had acted lawfully because the applicant had been excluded on precautionary grounds and his case therefore fell outside of the policy. The Supreme Court rejected this argument. The policy was adopted against the background of two reports[259] which emphasised the importance of exhaustively providing for the circumstances in which a pupil could be suspended from school. Promotion of certainty was therefore a central aim underlying the policy and it ought to be interpreted and applied in this light.

The core question posed at the start of this section was whether difficulties in constructing a general, overarching account of procedural review give rise to concern that judicial reasoning in this field lacks structure. What the analysis above highlights is that imagining procedural review as a process by which judges offer an 'essentially an intuitive judgment'[260] on what is fair in a given context does not ring true with many modern procedural review challenges. Acts of Parliament, Regulations and policy documents now commonly put in place extensive procedural codes for administrative decision-making. As a result, judicial reasoning in procedural review cases now often focuses on understanding the underlying purposes of these provisions in order that very particularised ambiguities can be resolved in the manner which would best promote those aims.

Collectively, these cases also illustrate the breadth of techniques the courts use to ascertain the purposes which underlie a procedural code. In *Mandalia*, for instance, the Court looked to the explicit designation of purpose in the policy itself. In *Garland*, the Court considered case law which preceded the introduction of the rule which supplied an indication as to its purpose. In *JR17* the Court focused on a report which the procedural policy reacted to. In *Makisi* the Court had regard to the background legislative framework which conferred power to introduce a procedural code in Regulations. Finally, in *Kebbell* the Court considered that reading the relevant provision against the other procedural stages in the Act of Parliament clarified its purpose. Far from making a free-standing determination of what is 'fair', in much of this case law, the courts were working closely with a detailed procedural code and attempting to understand the purposes its drafters had in mind.

[257] *JR17* (n 180).
[258] *JR17* (n 180) [22].
[259] Known as the 'Taylor' and 'Astin' Reports: *JR17* (n 180) [24]–[27].
[260] *Forest Heath* (n 6) [39].

B. Patterns in How Common Law Interacts with Procedural Codes

The previous subsection focused on the important role legislative and policy codes play in structuring reasoning in procedural review. This discussion, however, should not be taken as indicating that the *common law* no longer plays an important role in procedural review. On the contrary, it is evident from the case sample that common law principles continue to play an important role in *supplementing* the applicable legislative and policy procedural provisions.[261] The second source of structure which could be seen across the cases analysed is a series of clear patterns in how the common law performs this role.

A number of different patterns or themes emerged across the case sample. Unfortunately, space prohibits detailed discussion of them all.[262] By way of illustration, however, it is useful to discuss two especially pervasive examples. The first concerns requirements to notify affected individuals that a decision is to be taken and to invite them to make representations. The second considers the form that opportunities to make representations ought to take.

i. Notice and Invitation to Make Representations

A significant body of cases in the sample considered the following question: say legislation or policy puts in place a procedural code, but that code does not make explicit provision for the individual who is the subject of a decision to be given prior notification and invited to make representations. When, if ever, ought the common law to 'supply the omission of the legislature'[263] by requiring that an opportunity to comment must nonetheless be given?

Before turning to the case law, it is worth noting that a number of different approaches to this question could be, and have been, used by the courts in the past. The Privy Council decision in *Furnell v Whangarei High Schools Board*[264] is an illustration. There, Lord Morris explained that the proper question to be asked in such a case is whether 'the code [is] one that has been carefully and deliberately

[261] See further Matthew Hutchings, 'Fairness: Meeting the Standard: Procedural Fairness in Homelessness Applications' (2007) 10(1) *Journal of Housing Law* 14.

[262] Interesting patterns can be observed, for instance, in how the courts deal with disclosure and consultation issues. Another interesting, though ultimately fairly narrow, pattern was the growth of 'systematic' procedural review: *R (Medical Justice) v Secretary of State for the Home Department* [2011] EWCA Civ 1710; *Tabbakh* (n 211); *S* (n 206); *TH* (n 187); *Howard League* (n 206); *Citizens UK* (n 86).

[263] *Cooper* (n 34).

[264] *Furnell v Whangarei High Schools Board* [1973] AC 660 (PC).

drafted so as to provide procedure which is fair and appropriate?'[265] His Lordship went on to explain that:

> ... it is not lightly to be affirmed that a regulation that has the force of law is unfair when it has been made on the advice of the responsible Minister ... Nor is it the function of the court to redraft this code.[266]

As JM Evans noted, this approach was one of considerable deference to the relevant procedural code.[267] In essence, as long as a code represents 'a careful and deliberate'[268] attempt to provide a suitable procedure, there is no room for the court to supplement it with common law requirements.[269]

Turning now to the modern case law, a distinctive, and rather different, approach to this question appears to have become dominant in recent years and was used across the vast bulk of case law in the sample.[270] According to it, the common law creates a strong presumption that individuals who are the subject of administrative decisions are given notice of that decision and an opportunity to comment. The presumption is capable of being rebutted. However, the courts do not regard the common law starting-point as capable of being lightly set aside and it is certainly not sufficient to point out that the procedural code fails to make explicit provision for notice.[271] In order to decide whether the presumption applies, the courts will closely scrutinise the background legislative framework in order to understand its *purposes*. Where providing notice and an opportunity to comment would not significantly hamper the performance of the administrative decision-maker's statutory task, the courts will regard the administrative decision-maker as being required to do so, even if the procedural code does not explicitly provide for it. Where, however, the challenged body is able to make a convincing argument to the effect that giving notice to the individual would place significant constraints and prevent it from acting so as to further the aims of the statutory scheme, the courts will not insist on notice.

The leading case is *Bank Mellat (No 2)*.[272] The applicant bank challenged an order of Her Majesty's Treasury which prohibited interaction between it and UK financial institutions on the basis of evidence that the bank was providing services

[265] *Ibid*, 679.

[266] *Ibid*.

[267] JM Evans, 'Some Limits to the Scope of Natural Justice' (1973) 36(4) *Modern Law Review* 439. (Although Evans did not use the explicit language of 'deference'.)

[268] *Furnell* (n 264) 679.

[269] See also *Malloch v Aberdeen Corporation* [1971] 1 WLR 1589 (HL) (noted in Jim Farmer, 'Statutory Interpretation and Natural Justice' (1972) 30(1) *CLJ* 12).

[270] One exception was *Neumans LLP v Law Society (Solicitors Regulation Authority)* [2018] EWCA Civ 325, [2018] 3 WLUK 43. The Court of Appeal, however, took itself to be bound by the previous precedent in *Giles v Law Society* (1996) 8 Admin LR 105 (CA).

[271] *Bank Mellat (No 2)* (n 11) [179]: 'a court should be slow to hold that there is no obligation to give the opportunity, when such an obligation is not dispensed with in the relevant statute.'

[272] *Bank Mellat (No 2)* (n 11) [179].

to terrorist organisations.[273] The Treasury, the bank argued, ought to have given advance notice that it was minded to issue the order and invited to make comments on the evidence. The majority of the Supreme Court accepted this argument.[274] In rendering judgment, the majority asserted a strong common law presumption that 'any person who foreseeably would be significantly detrimentally affected by the exercise [of power] should be given [notice and] the opportunity to make representations in advance'.[275] This presumption was treated as being capable of rebuttal. Thus the majority recognised that there could be individual cases where providing notice to an organisation would render the Treasury less effective in safeguarding the public against the threat of terrorism,[276] by allowing the organisation an opportunity to rearrange its affairs. In such cases, the court would not insist on notice. On the facts of Bank Mellat's case itself, however, there was no concern that the bank would be able to behave in this way. The common law starting-point that notice ought to be given had therefore not been displaced.

A number of other cases in the sample are illustrative of the strength of this common law presumption.[277] In *Rowe*[278] the applicant challenged an accelerated payment notice ('APN').[279] The applicable legislation provided a procedural code[280] but it did not include a requirement to provide individuals with an opportunity to comment in advance on whether an APN should be issued. The Court of Appeal nonetheless held that the common law 'supplied the omission of the legislature'.[281] As Arden LJ put it:

> The courts may imply an additional duty [to give notice and an opportunity to comment] even in cases where Parliament has prescribed a procedure for some consultation and written representations … Nonetheless, even in that situation it must be clear that … the implication of the principles of natural justice would not frustrate the purpose of the legislation.[282]

Similarly, in *Miller*[283] an ombudsman was found to have acted unlawfully in failing to give the subject of an investigation early notice and an opportunity to comment on a complaint against her. The common law presumption was held not to have been displaced by the emphasis in the legislation[284] on the 'informal'[285]

[273] Counter-Terrorism Act 2008.
[274] With dissents from Lords Hope, Reed and Carnwath.
[275] *Bank Mellat (No 2)* (n 11) [179].
[276] *Bank Mellat (No 2)* (n 11) [31].
[277] *H v City Council* [2011] EWCA Civ 403; *R (C) v Secretary of State for the Home Department* [2011] EWCA Civ 175.
[278] *Rowe* (n 55).
[279] Finance Act 2014, Part 4, Ch 3.
[280] *Ibid*, ss219–27.
[281] *Cooper* (n 34).
[282] *Rowe* (n 55) [107].
[283] *Miller* (n 210).
[284] Health Service Commissioners Act 1993 (amended by Health Service Commissioners (Amendment) Act 1996; Public Services Ombudsman (Wales) Act 2005).
[285] *Miller* (n 210) [40].

and 'inquisitorial'[286] nature of the ombudsman's function. In *Shoesmith*[287] also, the Court of Appeal concluded that the Secretary of State's decision to suspend the applicant from her position in a local authority was unlawful. She ought to have been given notice and an opportunity to comment, even if the legislative framework did not specifically require this.

In a small subset of cases, the common law presumption in favour of notice was found to have been displaced. In these cases, the court was of the view that supplementing the applicable procedural code with a requirement to give notice would significantly compromise the aims of the background legislative scheme. The most striking examples[288] are *Pathan*[289] and *EK*.[290] In both of these cases the applicants argued that, although the Immigration Rules did not make provision for the eventuality, immigration officers were required to give applicants notice when the certificates offered by their sponsors had been withdrawn. The Court of Appeal in both cases dealt with the question by thinking closely about the underlying purposes of the Immigration Rules.[291] The 'points-based system'[292] to which these rules gave effect, the Court of Appeal opined, demonstrated a clear, and Parliamentary ordained,[293] commitment to 'predictability, administrative simplicity and certainty'[294] 'at the expense of discretion'[295] in the immigration system. Against this background, Sales LJ explained, providing notice in such circumstances would 'result in the public benefits associated with having such a clear and predictable scheme … being placed in jeopardy'[296] and the common law starting-point must therefore be recognised to have been displaced.

Across the 'notice' case law, then, a pattern could be traced in the manner in which common law was used to supplement legislative procedural codes. The courts treated the common law as creating a strong presumption in favour of giving notice to affected individuals. In determining whether this presumption had been displaced, the courts gave careful considerations to the background aims of the legislative scheme. The common law starting-point was treated as displaced only in contexts where there was a strong argument that providing notice would render the decision-maker less adept at realising the purposes underlying it. That the procedural code failed to make provision for notice was regarded as far from determinative.

[286] *Miller* (n 210) [40].
[287] *R (Shoesmith) v Ofsted* [2011] EWCA Civ 642, [2011] PTSR 1459.
[288] See also *Macris* (n 108); *BX* (n 186).
[289] *Pathan v Secretary of State for the Home Department* [2018] EWCA Civ 2103, [2018] 4 WLR 161.
[290] *EK* (n 56).
[291] See also *R (Sayaniya) v Upper Tribunal* [2016] EWCA Civ 85, [2016] 4 WLR 58.
[292] *R (Alvi) v Secretary of State for the Home Department* [2012] UKSC 33, [2012] 1 WLR 2208 [42].
[293] Immigration Act 1971, s3(2).
[294] *Pathan* (n 289) [56] (citing from *Kaur v Secretary of State for the Home Department* [2015] EWCA Civ 13, [2015] Imm AR 526 [41]).
[295] *Pathan* (n 289) [56].
[296] *EK* (n 56) [31].

ii. Representations

A second pattern which could be traced across the case sample addressed the following question: say an individual has been permitted to make representations but is dissatisfied with the manner in which they were permitted to do so. The applicable procedural code is either silent or ambiguous on the question, or else the applicant argues that the answer supplied by a regulatory or policy code is unsatisfactory.[297] When, if ever, will the common law render the decision unlawful on the basis that the way in which the representations were received was insufficient? A number of cases in the sample fit this description. In some, the applicant argued that, although she was permitted to make written representations, the common law entitled her to be given an oral hearing.[298] In others, the applicants argued that they ought to have been able to make representations at an earlier stage in the decision-making process.[299] In others again, the applicant argued that the opportunity they were given to make representations was defective because the live issues were not flagged up to them with sufficient clarity.[300]

The overarching approach which could be seen across the case law in relation to these issues was one of considerable flexibility. Expressed simply, the courts generally approached these questions by asking whether, as a result of the opportunity the applicant was given, she was able to make the relevant points she wished to.[301] If so, the decision-making process was generally regarded as lawful, even if it could in some ways have been improved. If, however, because of the opportunity provided to her, the applicant had not been able to communicate pertinent contributions, the decision-making process was regarded as unlawful.

This general approach had both negative and positive implications. In terms of negative implications, because the duty of the administrative decision-maker is to provide a reasonable opportunity to the individual to get across her points, it was generally insufficient for applicants to point out that the decision-maker could have set out the pertinent issues more clearly.[302] What is essential is that the applicant understood what the live issues were and therefore was able to offer comment on them. Thus in *Hopkins*,[303] the Court of Appeal rejected the applicant's argument that the planning inspector had proceeded unlawfully in basing its decision on considerations not contained in the initial agreed statement of

[297] Of course, if the code is contained in primary legislation the applicant is not able to challenge it directly except on European Union grounds or via the Human Rights Act 1998, ss3–4.

[298] *Osborn* (n 117); *Hassett* (n 212); *Foster* (n 52); *Sandler* (n 20).

[299] *Durand* (n 196).

[300] *Hopkins Developments Ltd v Secretary of State for Communities and Local Government* [2014] EWCA Civ 470, [2014] PTSR 1145; *Borough of Telford & Wrekin v Secretary of State for Communities and Local Government* [2014] EWCA Civ 507.

[301] As long as they bear on the issues at hand: *Perry* (n 20).

[302] *Telford & Wrekin* (n 300); *Derwent Holdings* (n 19).

[303] *Hopkins* (n 300).

common ground.[304] It had become clear during the course of the inquiry that these considerations were contentious and the applicant had been able to make representations in relation to them. A similar negative implication is that there is usually no need to afford applicants with multiple opportunities to make representations on the same subject-matter.[305]

On the flipside, a positive implication of the courts' general position is that there are contexts in which administrative decision-makers must provide assistance to individuals to enable them to understand the issues and to communicate their points. In *AM (Afghanistan)*,[306] for instance, the First-tier Tribunal acted unlawfully in not appointing a litigation friend to assist the applicant, a 15-year-old with learning difficulties, to make representations.[307]

A further implication of the courts' general flexible approach was that there were very few cases in the sample in which applicants successfully argued that, although they had been given an opportunity to communicate their points, the procedure used was nonetheless unlawful. The case of *S1*[308] neatly illustrates the point. Here the applicant argued that he ought to have been permitted to enter the UK in order to appear at a hearing, rather than offering contributions via video-link. According to the applicant, he could have communicated his points more effectively in person and, due to concerns that the video-link to the UK would be intercepted by Pakistani intelligence services, he had felt unable to speak freely.[309] The Court of Appeal rejected the challenge. It had been open to the applicant, the Court reasoned, to travel to different parts of Pakistan or a third country to offer his evidence[310] and he therefore had had an opportunity to make his relevant points in one way or another.

There was, however, a major exception to the courts' general, flexible approach: the parole context. Here, there were circumstances in which it was held to be insufficient for the Parole Board to receive representations in writing, even if the applicant was able to make representations on any subject he wished, where an oral hearing must be arranged. Two considerations in particular appear to have led the courts to treat the Parole Board as bound by a higher standard. First, as discussed above, the Board is charged with performing a distinctive task, namely assessing the level of risk an individual would pose to the public if they were released from prison. Lord Reed in *Osborn*[311] explained that in many cases, such as where accurate risk assessment required consideration of the mental state of the prisoner, receiving oral representations would considerably bolster the Board's ability to

[304] Town and Country Planning Appeals (Determination by Inspectors) (Inquiries Procedure) (England) Rules 2000 (SI 2000/1625), rule 15.
[305] *Drax* (n 198).
[306] *AM* (n 187).
[307] See also *Z* (n 183).
[308] *S1 v Secretary of State for the Home Department* [2016] EWCA Civ 560, [2016] 3 CMLR 37.
[309] *Ibid* [44].
[310] *Ibid* [79].
[311] *Osborn* (n 117).

perform this task. Second, the affected individual's right to liberty is at stake in Parole Board decision-making. Lord Reed considered that the importance of this right meant that greater procedural protection was necessary and that the longer a person was detained beyond their minimum tariff the more appropriate an oral hearing would be.[312]

C. Summary

This section has considered an important question which arose from the analysis in section II: should the difficulties in identifying a concrete 'master idea or principle'[313] lead to concerns that procedural review is an inherently unstructured and discretionary exercise? In order to explore that question it has offered an analysis of 127 cases decided by the appellate courts across a ten-year period. It has argued that a close reading of this case law, with the broader themes of the book in mind, reveals that there are at least two important sources of structure in legal reasoning in the procedural review context.

First, many procedural review cases now arise against the backdrop of extensive procedural codes, contained in legislation and policy. Even at the appellate levels, procedural review challenges therefore commonly raise narrow questions of construction. In many of the cases in the sample, the courts resolved these questions primarily by seeking to extract the underlying purposes of the code and resolving the interpretive ambiguity in the manner which would best promote them. Second, the common law continues to play an important role in supplementing these codes and there are a series of patterns in how it performs this function. In notice cases, for instance, the courts rely on a strong common law presumption that individuals who are the subject of decisions ought to be given notice and an opportunity to make representations. In representation cases, by contrast, the courts generally afford administrative decision-makers considerable latitude in deciding how to receive representations as long as participants are enabled to make relevant points.[314]

Before concluding the chapter, it is important to return to a caveat offered in the introduction. It is no part of the chapter's argument that the courts' approach to procedural review is perfect in every respect. Questions could no doubt be raised concerning the suitability of relying on a strong common law presumption in favour of notice (which some might regard as undue 'judicialisation'[315] of administration,

[312] *Osborn* (n 117) [2].
[313] Smith (n 4) 11.
[314] As explained, Parole Board decisions appear to be exceptional.
[315] Martin Loughlin, 'Procedural Fairness: A Study of the Crisis in Administrative Law Theory' (1978) 28(2) *University of Toronto Law Journal* 215; Peter Cane, *Administrative Law*, 5th edn (Oxford University Press, 2011) 73–75; *West London Mental Health NHS Trust* (n 5) [67]–[68]; *Poshteh v Kensington & Chelsea RLBC* [2017] UKSC 36, [2017] AC 624 [22].

especially in some fields of administration, such as the tax context[316]) and a flexible approach to receiving representations (which others might regard as affording too much latitude to decision-makers to adopt less-than-ideal processes[317]). What this section has taken issue with, rather, is the idea that legal reasoning in this field lacks structure. As Beatson LJ warned, 'there are dangers in concentrating on a flexible notion of overarching fairness'.[318] Emphasising the 'protean'[319] nature of procedural review 'and saying no more'[320] risks obscuring at least two important sources of structure which shape and constrain judicial reasoning on procedural issues.

V. Conclusion

It is useful to conclude the chapter by drawing attention to the relationship between the analysis and the broader themes of the book. Chapter one explained that the book has three major aims. This chapter has been primarily focused on the second: demonstrating the importance of recognising the complex and varied 'anatomy' of administrative law in the specific doctrinal context of procedural review. The core argument of the chapter has been that a greater understanding of administrative law's 'anatomy' sheds useful light on procedural fairness in two main ways.

In the first place, it helps to explain why it is proving so difficult to describe procedural fairness in general, overarching terms. The three core senses in which the legal structures in play, discussed in chapter three, characterise the procedural review case law as much as they do administrative law adjudication more broadly. Each in turn suggests a reason why it is proving difficult to explain procedural review in overarching terms. First, the background legislative and policy frameworks in many administrative contexts now make detailed provision for issues of procedure. These procedural codes can be both dense and highly particularised. Their existence and the variety across them mean that the courts are not approaching procedural review with a blank slate but beginning from different starting-points in different challenges. Second, the variety of legal values, interests and purposes which the courts seek to accommodate means that procedural review cannot be explained by reference to a singular overarching purpose. Procedural review is not purely an exercise in either legislative interpretation nor common law reasoning. Nor is it exclusively 'public' or 'individual-regarding'.[321] It has elements of all of these things. Singular normative accounts of procedural review therefore tend to be unhelpfully reductionist. Third, procedural review case

[316] *Rowe* (n 55) might be an example.
[317] *Hopkins* (n 300) might be an example.
[318] *West London Mental Health NHS Trust* (n 5) [69].
[319] *Moseley* (n 12) [24].
[320] *West London Mental Health NHS Trust* (n 5) [69].
[321] Varuhas (n 115) 52.

law also concerns legal relationships of different kinds. Thinking in terms of a duty of fairness which is owed either to an individual or to the public as a collective therefore obscures the complexity of the case law.

In the second place, recognising the complex and varied anatomy of administrative law also helps to shed light on a further issue: whether these difficulties should give rise to concern that procedural review is little more than an 'intuitive'[322] exercise in deciding what is 'fair'.[323] Section IV argued that this is not necessarily so. A close reading of the modern case law with the complexity of administrative law's anatomy specifically in mind reveals at least two important sources of structure in legal reasoning. First, many procedural challenges now arise against the backdrop of a relatively detailed procedural code. It is not, therefore, uncommon for procedural review cases, even at the appellate level, to concern relatively narrow questions of construction which the courts determine by attempting to resolve in the manner which would best promote the purposes of the background scheme. Second, other cases concern the extent to which the common law supplements these procedural codes. It is possible to see a number of established patterns in the manner in which the common law performs this role.

[322] *Forest Heath* (n 6) [39].
[323] *Re HK* (n 47).

5

Legitimate Expectations

This chapter deals with the second of the book's case studies. The previous chapter showed how recognising the complexity and variety of administrative law's 'anatomy' is important because it sheds new light on procedural review. This chapter argues, similarly, that recognition of this complexity can illuminate the law and literature on legitimate expectations.

The bulk of discussion will be divided into four sections. Section I explains briefly what is meant by a 'legitimate expectations' case. Section II then discusses the evolution of the law and literature on legitimate expectations. The Court of Appeal decision in *Coughlan* in 1999[1] is commonly regarded as having formally concretised the legitimate expectations ground.[2] Following this decision, many attempts have been made across the case law and literature to develop a general account of when and how a decision-maker may go back on a previous assurance. A universally accepted account has, however, proven elusive. A major difficulty has been the frequency with which early case law and literature relied on broad, abstract concepts such as the 'rule of law'[3] and 'abuse of power'[4] as grounds for judicial intervention. These accounts have been much criticised because the vague concepts on which they rely fail to provide meaningful guidance as to how, case-by-case, the courts decide whether a decision-maker has acted unlawfully. Other, 'thicker' accounts, such as the much-discussed 'trust' model,[5] of legitimate expectations have not, however, been meaningfully borne out in the case law. The difficulties incurred in developing a general account of legitimate expectations have contributed to the rise of a popular, but cynical, view of the law on legitimate expectations. According to this view, the law on legitimate expectation is

[1] *R v North & East Devon Health Authority, ex parte Coughlan* [2001] QB 213 (CA).

[2] Kirsty Hughes, '*R v North and East Devon Health Authority* [2001]: *Coughlan* and the Development of Public Law' in Satvinder Juss and Maurice Sunkin (eds), *Landmark Cases in Public Law* (Hart Publishing, 2017).

[3] Soren Schonberg, *Legitimate Expectations in Administrative Law* (Oxford University Press, 2000).

[4] *R (Nadarajah) v Secretary of State for the Home Department* [2005] EWCA Civ 1363 (noted at Mark Elliott, 'Legitimate Expectations: Procedure, Substance, Policy and Proportionality' (2006) 65(2) *CLJ* 254.

[5] Paul Reynolds 'Legitimate Expectations and the Protection of Trust in Public Officials' [2011] *PL* 330.

characterised by a lack of predictability,[6] serves as 'little more than a mechanism for palm-tree justice'[7] and is in need of reform.[8]

At least two important questions are raised by the discussion in section II. First, why is it proving so difficult to develop a workable, general explanation of the law on legitimate expectations? Second, do these difficulties indicate that the law in this area is therefore unpredictable, incoherent and failing to properly restrain judges? Sections III and IV argue that recognition of the complex and varied 'anatomy' of administrative law sheds significant light on these issues.

Section III argues that recognising the complexity and variety of the anatomy of administrative law helps to explain why a general account of legitimate expectations is proving elusive. The three sources of complexity and variety discussed in chapter three characterise the legitimate expectations case law as much they do administrative law adjudication more generally. Each, in turn, suggests a reason why this case law is not easily explained by reference to an overarching theory or framework. First, the legislative framework against which a legitimate expectations challenge arises places meaningful constraints on the extent and manner in which the courts can protect legitimate expectations. The courts, in other words, are not developing the legitimate expectations doctrine against the background of a constant legal landscape, but are deciding challenges which each have their own legislative contours. Second, when adjudicating on legitimate expectations, the courts seek to accommodate a variety of different values, interests and purposes. Intervention on the legitimate expectations ground therefore cannot be characterised as being driven by a singular rationale. Third, legitimate expectations case law concerns legal relationships of different kinds. It cannot be said, therefore, that the legitimate expectations doctrine is either straightforwardly a 'right-conferring'[9] legal standard, nor one which imposes duties owed to the public as a collectivity.[10]

Section IV then turns to the second question of whether the difficulties incurred in developing a workable, general account of legitimate expectations give rise to concern that the law in this area is lacking in predictability, coherence and judicial restraint. In order to explore this question, section IV offers an analysis of 127 recent legitimate expectations challenges heard in across the ten-year period, beginning at the start of 2009 and concluding at the close of 2018. The core argument of section IV is that a close reading of this case law, with the complexity

[6] Jack Watson, 'Clarity and Ambiguity: A New Approach to the Test of Legitimacy in the Law of Legitimate Expectations' (2010) 30(4) *Legal Studies* 633, 633: 'we are very much in the territory of "recognise it when we see it" when it comes to finding legitimate expectations' and that 'we are therefore in a situation where the existence of these expectations is highly uncertain … [which] may lead to arbitrary and inconsistent results'.

[7] *Ibid*, 651; *R v Secretary of State for Education and Employment, ex parte Begbie* [2000] 1 WLR 1115 (CA) 1130.

[8] Rebecca Williams, 'The Multiple Doctrines of Legitimate Expectations' (2016) 132(3) *LQR* 639.

[9] Joanna Bell, 'The Doctrine of Legitimate Expectations: Power-Constraining or Right-Conferring Legal Standard?' [2016] *PL* 437–55.

[10] Lord Woolf, 'Public Law – Private Law: Why the Divide? A Personal View' [1986] *PL* 220.

and variety of administrative law specifically in mind, suggests that there is more structure and predictability in the law than has commonly been assumed.

Section IV, in particular, draws out four broad types of scenario which can be seen to be in play in different combinations in the legitimate expectations case law.[11] Introduced briefly they are:

a) instances where an assurance has been directly communicated to an individual;[12]
b) cases in which an individual challenges a purported failure to properly apply policy to her case;[13]
c) contexts where policy has been changed without making transitional provision for a particular group;[14] and
d) circumstances in which the applicant relies on a statement of intention addressed to the public at large.[15]

Section IV also identifies a series of notable patterns in how the courts approached review across these categories. To give two examples, in category (a) cases the courts have largely focused on the role the individual has played in the administrative decision-maker's *reasoning process*. Whereas in category (c) cases, two factors – detrimental reliance and the degree to which making transitional provisions would undermine the reasons for policy change – appear to play a central role in determining whether judicial intervention is appropriate.

Overall, the analysis across section IV suggests that there seems to be a good deal more predictability, structure and restraint in the modern case law than has sometimes been assumed. The difficulties scholars and judges have incurred in developing a singular, general account of the law on legitimate expectations should not therefore lead too readily to the conclusion that the case law is confused and in significant need of reform.

I. What is a 'Legitimate Expectations' Case?

It is useful to begin by setting out a working explanation of what counts as a 'legitimate expectations' case for the purposes of this chapter. At its simplest, a

[11] Note that the first three categories bear a strong similarity to the three categories of legitimate expectation case discussed in Williams (n 8). Williams' argument, and the degree to which the analysis in this chapter supports her arguments, are discussed in detail below. For an example of a case which combines multiple of these scenarios, see discussion of *R (Patel) v General Medical Council* [2013] EWCA Civ 327, [2013] 1 WLR 2801 below.

[12] *Coughlan* (n 1).

[13] *R (Lumba) v Secretary of State for the Home Department* [2011] UKSC 12, [2012] 1 AC 245 [35]; *Mandalia v Secretary of State for the Home Department* [2015] UKSC 59, [2015] 1 WLR 4546 [29]–[31].

[14] *Patel* (n 11).

[15] *R (Greenpeace) v Secretary of State for Trade and Industry* [2007] EWHC 311 (Admin), [2007] Env LR 29.

legitimate expectations case is one in which the applicant relies on the notion of 'legitimate expectations' in order to challenge an administrative decision-maker's actions. This definition, however, does not reveal very much and so it is useful to draw attention to three generalities which characterise (at least) the bulk of the case law in which applicants rely on the idea of legitimate expectations.

The first is that an administrative decision-maker has, at a previous point, communicated an intention to act in a particular way. Across legitimate expectations case law, there is a great deal of variety in *how* these intentions are communicated. In some cases, for instance, administrative decision-makers directly communicate assurances to individuals, such as by sending letters[16] or making verbal statements in face-to-face meetings[17] or over the phone.[18] In others, administrative decision-makers publish policy statements setting out criteria for how categories of decision are to be taken.[19] In others again, broad assurances are offered to the public, such as in ministerial statements[20] or published White Papers,[21] indicating a commitment to introduce a new policy. There is also considerable diversity in terms of the *content* of the assurances administrative decision-makers communicate. Conventionally, scholarship divides between procedural and substantive assurances.[22] The first are statements that a particular process will be followed in the making of a decision.[23] The second, by contrast, are promises that an identified conclusion on some subject-matter will be reached.[24]

In addition to the fact that an administrative decision-maker has taken, what might be called, an 'initial position', a second important generality across legitimate expectations cases is that an administrative decision-maker later behaves in a way which is alleged[25] to depart from this position. Again, there is a good deal of diversity in how this occurs. In some cases, for instance, an administrative decision-maker rejects an individual's application for a benefit in contravention of a prior assurance that it will be affirmed,[26] or withdraws a benefit despite previous

[16] *Babakandi v Westminster CC* [2011] EWHC 1756 (Admin); *Thomas v Camarthen CC* [2013] EWHC 783 (Admin), [2013] JPL 1266; *R (Hussain) v Secretary of State for the Home Department* [2013] EWHC 3833 (Admin); *R (Taylor) v Secretary of State for the Home Department* [2015] EWHC 3526 (Admin); *R (Dixons) v HMRC* [2018] EWHC 2556 (Admin).

[17] *R (Birks) v Commissioner of Police of the Met* [2014] EWHC 3041 (Admin), [2015] ICR 204.

[18] *R (Mohamed) v HMRC* [2016] EWHC 2455 (Admin).

[19] *R v Secretary of State for the Home Department, ex parte Khan* [1984] 1 WLR 1337 (CA).

[20] *R (Law Society) v Lord Chancellor* [2018] EWHC 2094 (Admin).

[21] *R (Unison) v Secretary of State for Health* [2010] EWHC 2655 (Admin).

[22] Philip Sales, 'Legitimate Expectations' (2006) 11(2) *Judicial Review* 186; Abhijit PG Pandya, 'Legitimate Expectations: Too Deferential an Approach?' (2009) *Judicial Review* 170.

[23] *Attorney General of Hong Kong v Ng Yuen Shiu* [1983] 2 AC 629 (PC).

[24] *Coughlan* (n 1).

[25] The departure is alleged because sometimes the existence or proper meaning of the original assurance is a point of contention. Arguments can therefore arise about whether there has been a departure from the assurance in the first place: *Corkteck v HMRC* [2009] EWHC 785 (Admin); *R (Jorgenson) v Secretary of State for Justice* [2011] EWHC 977 (Admin); *R (Razoq) v Secretary of State for the Home Department* [2014] EWHC 2959 (Admin); *Trail Riders Fellowship v Wiltshire CC* [2018] EWHC 3600 (Admin); *R (Talpada) v SSHD* [2018] EWCA Civ 841; *R (Hewson) v Commissioner of Police of the Met* [2018] EWHC 471 (Admin); *Morrisons Supermarket Plc v Houslow LBC* [2018] EWHC 3426 (Admin).

[26] *R (Kucherov) v Secretary of State for the Home Department* [2014] EWHC 3749 (Admin).

assurances that it would be ongoing.[27] In other cases, an administrative decision-maker makes an individualised decision which is inconsistent with published policy.[28] In others again, an administrative decision-maker makes a generalised policy statement in a way which deviates from an individualised assurance[29] or which amounts to the wholesale displacement of a prior policy.[30] An administrative decision-maker might, furthermore, decide not to introduce a measure despite assuring the public in the past that it intended to.[31] In some unusual cases, an administrative decision-maker might act inconsistently with an assurance offered by another.[32]

A third and final generality is that the applicant appears before the court in order to challenge the departure from the prior assurance. In every legitimate expectations case, therefore, the court must address the same broad question: in deviating from the position previously communicated, has the administrative decision-maker behaved unlawfully? Or, to put it another way, what is the legal effect of a prior assurance (practice, policy, statement of intention, etc) on the administrative decision-maker's choice as to whether, and if so how, to now depart from it?

II. The Development of Legitimate Expectations

With this broad sketch of the problem at the heart of the case law, it is useful next to provide a brief overview of the development of the law and the literature on legitimate expectations.

The courts have long grappled with the question of what the effect of a prior assurance is on an administrative decision.[33] Until relatively recently, however, these questions were analysed through doctrines other than that of legitimate expectations.[34] Throughout the 1960s and 1970s,[35] for instance, an extremely complex body of case law had arisen[36] in which the Court of Appeal[37]

[27] *R (Alansi) v Newham LBC* [2013] EWHC 3722 (Admin).

[28] *Samarkand Film Partnership v HMRC* [2017] EWCA Civ 77.

[29] *R (GSTS Pathology Ltd) v HMfRC* [2013] EWHC 1801 (Admin).

[30] *R (Brooke Energy) v Secretary of State for Business, Energy and Industrial Strategy* [2018] EWHC 2012 (Admin); *R (Dudley MBC) v Secretary of State for Communities and Local Government* [2012] EWHC 1729 (Admin).

[31] *R (Flatley) v Welsh Ministers* [2014] EWHC 2258 (Admin).

[32] *R (BAPIO) v Secretary of State for the Home Department* [2008] UKHL 27; [2008] 1 AC 1003.

[33] *Robertson v Minister of Pensions* [1949] 1 KB 227.

[34] *R (Reprotech (Pebsham) Ltd) v East Sussex CC* [2002] UKHL 8, [2003] 1 WLR 348.

[35] *Wells v Minister of Housing and Local Government* [1967] 2 All ER 1041; *Lever Finance (Ltd) v Westminster Corporation* [1970] 3 All ER 496 (noted in JM Evans, 'Delegation and Estoppel in Administrative Law' (1971) 34(2) *MLR* 335).

[36] Paul Craig, 'Representations by Public Bodies' (1977) *LQR* 398.

[37] Largely led by Lord Denning. See also *Central London Property Trust Ltd v High Trees House Ltd* [1947] KB 140 (HC); *Combe v Combe* [1951] 2 KB 215 (CA); *D & C Builders v Rees* [1965] 2 QB 617 (CA).

was gradually[38] developing the doctrine of estoppel in order to give legal effect to assurances offered by planning officials.[39] The specific language of 'legitimate expectations', by contrast, is relatively new in England and Welsh administrative law.[40] It first began to be used in the 1970s and 1980s across two important clusters of cases. In the first, the courts drew on the language of 'legitimate expectations' in the course of adjudicating on procedural issues.[41] In the second, the appellate courts developed legal limitations specifically in the tax context in order to limit the freedom of tax authorities to change direction in their treatment of individuals.[42]

Across the 1970s and 1980s, therefore, two important developments could be seen to be taking place. First, the courts were increasingly recognising circumstances, primarily in the planning and tax contexts, in which the law would place restrictions on the ability of administrative decision-makers to renege on previous undertakings. Second, the judges were, with growing frequency, drawing on the language of 'legitimate expectations'.[43] These developments led to a series of influential articles being published across the later decades of the twentieth century, arguing for a streamlining of the law. Both Paul Craig[44] and Christopher Forsyth,[45] for instance, argued that the courts ought now to recognise an overriding principle that 'in the absence of … an "overriding public interest" legitimate expectations of some boon or benefit should be fulfilled'.[46]

Craig and Forsyth's arguments took some time to concretise in the case law. The view that legitimate expectations were 'naught but a useful strand of the law

[38] *Southend-on-Sea Corporation v Hodgson (Wickford) Ltd* [1962] 1 QB 416 (DC).

[39] There is a complex legislative story in the background to these cases. Prior to the enactment of the Town and Country Planning Act 1968, s64, local planning authorities did not possess a general power to delegate decision-making functions. In reality, however, planning officers were offering assurances to the effect that particular developments did not require permission to proceed. Estoppel was developed so as to give effect to these statements. The basic idea was that such statements could estop planning authorities from relying on a lack of planning permission as a basis for taking enforcement measures. Following the legislative reforms in 1968, there has been less of a need to rely on estoppel in this context. However, for an example of some of the ideas developed in the estoppel case law continuing to play a role, see *Flanagan & Anor v South Buckinghamshire DC* [2002] EWCA Civ 690, [2002] 1 WLR 2601.

[40] For discussion of origins see: Christopher Forsyth, 'Legitimate Expectations Revisited' (2011) 16(4) *Judicial Review* 429 [5]–[6].

[41] *Schmidt v Secretary of State for Home Affairs* [1969] 2 Ch 149 (CA); *R v Liverpool Corporation, ex parte Liverpool Taxi Fleet Operators Association* [1972] 2 QB 299 (CA); *Ng* (n 23); *Khan* (n 19).

[42] *R v Inland Revenue, ex parte Preston* [1985] AC 835 (HL); *R v Inland Revenue Commissioners, ex parte MFK Underwriting Agents Ltd* [1990] 1 WLR 1545 (CA); *R v Inland Revenue Commissioners, ex parte Unilever Plc* [1996] STC 681 (CA).

[43] The language was also appearing in some discussion of standing issues: *O'Reilly v Mackman* [1983] 2 AC 237 (HL) 275.

[44] Paul Craig, 'Legitimate Expectations: A Conceptual Analysis' (1992) 108(1) *LQR* 79; Paul Craig, 'Substantive Legitimate Expectations in Domestic and Community Law' (1996) 55(2) *CLJ* 289.

[45] Christopher Forsyth, 'The Provenance and Protection of Legitimate Expectations' (1988) 47(2) *CLR* 238.

[46] *Ibid*, 256 quoting from *Khan* (n 19).

on natural justice'[47] held significant sway for many years.[48] Most famously in *Hargreaves*,[49] the Court of Appeal characterised as constitutional 'heresy'[50] any suggestion that the courts could review a decision to change policy direction on any ground other than traditional *Wednesbury* unreasonableness.[51]

Gradually, however, legitimate expectations crystallised as a recognised 'ground of review'. Major steps forward were taken in cases such as *Ruddock*[52] and *Hamble Fisheries*.[53] The *Coughlan* decision[54] in 1999[55] is, however, commonly regarded as the breakthrough moment. *Coughlan* concerned a challenge by a severely disabled woman to a decision to close a residential care facility in contravention of a personal assurance which had been offered to her that she should have a 'home for life'[56] there. The Court of Appeal upheld her challenge and, in doing so, concluded that the 'doctrine of legitimate expectation' had now 'emerged as a distinct application of the concept of abuse of power'.[57] According to Lord Woolf, the law had reached the position where it could now be said that on a generalised basis that:

> … where the court considers that a lawful promise or practice has induced a legitimate expectation … [it] will in a proper case decide whether to frustrate the expectation is so unfair that to take a new and different course will amount to an abuse of power.[58]

The *Coughlan* decision resulted in a significant change of focus in both the case law and the literature. Now that legitimate expectations had been established as a freestanding ground of review, the core question which arose was what, precisely, it required administrative decision-makers to do. Or, to focus on the position of the reviewing court, how judges ought to determine whether an administrative decision-maker had acted unlawfully in changing its position.

[47] *Ibid*, 241.

[48] *R v Secretary of State for Transport, ex parte Richmond-upon-Thames LBC (No 1)* [1994] 1 WLR 74 (QB).

[49] *R v Secretary of State for the Home Department, ex parte Hargreaves* [1997] 1 WLR 906 (CA).

[50] *Ibid*, 921. See further Lord Irvine, 'Judges & Decision-Makers: The Theory & Practice of *Wednesbury* Review' [1996] *PL* 59.

[51] *Hargreaves* (n 49); *Associated Provincial Picture Houses Ltd v Wednesbury Corporation* [1948] 1 KB 223 (CA).

[52] *R v Secretary of State for the Home Department, ex parte Ruddock* [1987] 1 WLR 1482 (QB).

[53] *R v Ministry of Agriculture, Fisheries & Food, ex parte Hamble Fisheries Ltd* [1995] 1 CMLR 533 (QB).

[54] *Coughlan* (n 1).

[55] For comment see Mark Elliott, '*Coughlan*: Substantive Protection of Legitimate Expectations Revisited' (2000) 5(1) *Judicial Review* 27; Paul Craig and Soren Schonberg, 'Substantive Legitimate Expectations after *Coughlan*' [2000] *PL* 564; Karen Steyn, 'Substantive Legitimate Expectations' (2001) 6(4) *Judicial Review* 244.

[56] *Coughlan* (n 1) [1].

[57] *Coughlan* (n 1) [71].

[58] *Coughlan* (n 1) [57].

A vast body of case law[59] and literature[60] has accumulated which grapples with this question. Developing a universally accepted response, has, however, proven extremely difficult and, as will be seen, many remain dissatisfied with both the law and theory. One initial difficulty was that much of the early case law and literature relied on broad and vaguely defined concepts in setting out the courts' role. The Court of Appeal in *Coughlan* itself, for instance, explained that the courts should intervene in a case where disappointing the applicant's expectation would be 'so unfair as to amount to an abuse of power'.[61] Shortly after *Coughlan*, Laws LJ in *Nadarajah*[62] famously recharacterised legitimate expectations as grounded in a concern to promote 'good administration'[63] and proportionate decision-making. Similarly, in one of the first major scholarly contributions on the concept in English and Welsh law, Soren Schonberg proposed a 'rule of law' account of legitimate expectations.[64]

Each of these ways of thinking has been subject to considerable criticism and the difficulties with them need little rehearsing.[65] The major issues can be neatly illustrated by briefly discussing two articles. In the first, Paul Reynolds[66] has argued that, while accounts grounded in ideas of 'fairness' and 'abuse of power' help to capture the '"the moral impetus" of the doctrine',[67] they are incapable of 'adequately explain[ing] and guid[ing] the doctrine'.[68] Because these notions 'sit at such a high level of abstraction',[69] accounts based on them necessarily 'fail to offer practical guidance when actually dealing with a legitimate expectations case'.[70] In the second, Mark Elliott[71] has similarly criticised accounts of legitimate expectations

[59] *Begbie* (n 7); *Nadarajah* (n 4); *R (Bibi) v Newham LBC* [2001] EWCA Civ 607, [2002] 1 WLR 237; *R (Niazi) v Secretary of State for the Home Department* [2008] EWCA Civ 755; *Paponette v Attorney General of Trinidad and Tobago* [2010] UKPC 32, [2012] 1 AC 1 (noted at Alistair Mills, 'Taking a (Taxi) Stand on Legitimate Expectations' (2011) *CLJ* 287); *United Policyholders Group v Attorney General of Trinidad and Tobago* [2016] UKPC 17, [2016] 1 WLR 3383.

[60] At least six books have been published on legitimate expectations: Schonberg (n 3); Robert Thomas, *Legitimate Expectations and Proportionality in Administrative Law* (Bloomsbury, 2000); Richard Moules, *Actions Against Public Official: Legitimate Expectation, Misstatements and Misconduct* (Sweet & Maxwell, 2009); Maya Signon, *Legitimate Expectations Under Article 1 of Protocol No 1 to the European Convention on Human Right* (Intersentia, 2014); Greg Weeks and Matthew Groves, *Legitimate Expectations in the Common Law World* (Hart Publishing, 2017); Alexander Brown, *A Theory of Legitimate Expectations for Public Administration* (Oxford University Press, 2017).

[61] *Coughlan* (n 1) [57].

[62] *Nadarajah* (n 4).

[63] *Nadarajah* (n 4) [68].

[64] Schonberg (n 3) Ch 1.

[65] Joe Tomlinson, 'Do We Need a Theory of Legitimate Expectations?' (26 August 2019. Legal Studies (Forthcoming). Available at SSRN: https://ssrn.com/abstract=3442761).

[66] Reynolds (n 5).

[67] Reynolds (n 5) 332.

[68] Reynolds (n 5) 332.

[69] Reynolds (n 5).332.

[70] Reynolds (n 5) 332.

[71] Reynolds (n 5).

based on 'abuse of power' and proportionality.[72] In the case of abuse of power, the problem is that the term can be used in a number of different ways, and it is difficult to see how any of these uses helpfully illuminates or adds something of value to understanding.[73] A shift to characterising legitimate expectations as an aspect of proportionality review would offer,[74] for Elliott, little by way of improvement. The main issue in this regard is that an account of legitimate expectations which focused purely on proportionality would obscure a number of important aspects of the case law, including the plurality of techniques the courts may use to protect an expectation.[75]

The overarching problem with these early accounts is therefore their reliance on concepts which are extremely 'thin'. This thinness, in turn, inevitably limits the practical utility of the account, rendering them incapable of indicating 'case by case, what is lawful and what is not'.[76] This difficulty has often led scholars to search for 'thicker' explanations of legitimate expectations. As in the procedural review context, however,[77] even the most influential 'thicker' accounts have not been borne out consistently in the case law.

The clearest example of this is the 'trust' account of legitimate expectations. This account has been developed by a number of scholars across a series of articles.[78] At its simplest, the trust account posits that there are circumstances in which individuals vest 'specific trust'[79] in administrative decision-makers on the basis of the assurances they communicate. The legitimate expectations ground is understood as a technique by which the courts identify when specific trust has been vested and decide on the level of protection to afford. The trust account has been the subject of cogent criticism elsewhere.[80] For present purposes the most important point is that it has failed to gain significant traction in the case law. This is so in at least two senses. First, the language of 'trust' has not been drawn on by judges in determining legitimate expectations challenges beyond a few exceptional cases.[81] Second, and more fundamentally, there are also aspects of the legitimate expectations case

[72] Mark Elliott, 'Legitimate Expectations and the Search for Principle: Reflections on *Abdi & Nadarajah*' (2006) 11(4) *Judicial Review* 281.

[73] On Elliott's reading of the case law, for instance, 'abuse of power' has been invoked merely as an 'empty' synonym for unlawfulness; as a conclusory label invoked retrospectively in order to 'confer a reassuring patina of legitimacy on … sometimes bold judicial decisions'; and as an 'acid test of legality' which is essentially 'nebulous' in character and incapable of providing certainty.

[74] *Nadarajah* (4) [68].

[75] Elliott (n 72) [16]–[19]. See also Mark Elliott, 'From Heresy to Orthodoxy: Substantive Legitimate Expectations in the United Kingdom' in Groves and Weeks (n 60) where Elliott doubts that legitimate expectations, and administrative law more broadly, can be explained by reference to 'singular, superior constructs'.

[76] *Nadarajah* (n 4) [67].

[77] See discussion of the 'irreducible core' of process rights in chapter 4; *Secretary of State for the Home Department v AF (No 3)* [2009] UKHL 28, [2010] 2 AC 269.

[78] Forsyth (n 40); Reynolds (n 5); Watson (n 6).

[79] Watson (n 6).

[80] Tomlinson (n 65).

[81] *Mehmood (Legitimate Expectation)* [2014] UKUT 00469 (IAC) [13]–[16].

law which are not capable of being explained by the trust account. One example is the *Greenpeace*[82] decision. Here the Government was held to an assurance in a White Paper that its policy on nuclear power would not be altered without the 'fullest public consultation'.[83] While there are undoubtedly good reasons for judicial intervention in such a case, it would not seem to be an instance in which any identifiable individual invested 'specific trust' in the Government.

The difficulties which have been incurred in developing a general, accepted account of legitimate expectations has given rise to a cynical view of the law.[84] Among other things, legitimate expectations have been described as at risk of becoming 'little more than a smokescreen for an erratic and subjective assortment of judicial ideas',[85] 'an unnecessary envelope capable of being placed around intervention on any ground'[86] and 'a public law panacea for every disaffection or discontentment'.[87] Cameron Stewart has firmly argued against the legitimate expectation ground's introduction in Australia on the basis that 'in inviting judges to weigh up policy considerations, the doctrine … necessarily involves the judge in engaging in a form of policy formulation which invariably results in unpredictable behaviour and results'.[88] He regards the ground as having the 'potential to undermine the judicial role and, through the undermining of legitimacy, damage the rule of law'.[89] Paul Daly, similarly, has described legitimate expectations as a 'cautionary tale'[90] characterised by 'significant confusion'.[91] Daly warns that 'without doctrinal frameworks to guide the works of courts and commentators, the law will only become more confused'.[92]

The major concerns of commentators are aptly summarised in the following passage written by Swati Jhaveri.[93] Jhaveri argues that the Singaporean courts

[82] *Greenpeace* (n 15).

[83] *Greenpeace* (n 15) [9].

[84] Robert Thomas, 'Legitimate Expectations and the Separation of Powers in English and Welsh Administrative Law' in Groves and Weeks (n 60).

[85] Matthew Groves, 'Substantive Legitimate Expectations in Australian Administrative Law' (2008) 32 *Melbourne University Law Review* 470, 487.

[86] Mark Elliott, 'Legitimate Expectations, Consistency, and Abuse of Power: The *Rashid* Case' (2005) 10 *Judicial Review* 281, 283.

[87] *Hassan v Secretary of State for the Home Department* [2013] EWHC 582 (Admin) [45].

[88] Cameron Stewart, 'The Doctrine of Substantive Unfairness and the Review of Substantive Legitimate Expectations' in Matthew Groves and HP Lee (eds), *Australian Administrative Law* (Cambridge University Press, 2007) 282.

[89] *Ibid.*

[90] Paul Daly, 'The Future of Substantive Review in English Administrative Law: *R (Gallaher Group Ltd) v Competition and Markets Authority* [2019] AC 96 (4 March 2019, Administrative Law Matters blog. Available at: www.administrativelawmatters.com/blog/2019/02/26/the-future-of-substantive-review-in-english-administrative-law-r-gallaher-group-ltd-v-competition-and-markets-authority-2019-ac-96/).

[91] *Ibid.*

[92] *Ibid.*

[93] Swati Jhaveri, 'The Doctrine of Substantive Legitimate Expectations: The Significance of *ChiuTeng@Kallang Pte Ltd v Singapore Land Authority*' [2016] *PL* 1.

ought to resist the temptation[94] to borrow and develop the notion of legitimate expectations from English and Welsh law because:

> It is not clear … why administrative law needs to protect substantive legitimate expectations created by administrative decision … Without more elaboration reliance on broad notions of 'moral values', 'fairness' or 'abuse of power' could weaken the utility of the doctrine. There is a need for further guidance to develop over time for judges applying key aspects of the doctrine and for the administration attempting to structure their discretion and make decisions that are consistent with the doctrine.[95]

Related to the growth in cynicism regarding legitimate expectations is a trend which Farah Ahmed and Adam Perry have termed 'doctrinal disaggregation'.[96] As Ahmed and Perry explain, this school of thought responds to a perceived 'danger that the concept of legitimate expectation will collapse into an inchoate justification for judicial intervention'.[97] Scholars who support disaggregation argue that, in light of this, there is a need to begin carving up the case law into discrete categories.[98] Rebecca Williams, for instance, has urged reform of this kind in order to improve 'on the unpredictability of the current law'.[99] She argues that legitimate expectations should no longer be understood as a singular doctrine, but that courts ought to recognise that, operating within the legitimate expectations case law, are 'multiple doctrines'.[100] She identifies three broad categories of issue which these doctrines are said to deal with: the problem of 'almost-contract'[101] cases in which personal assurances are offered to individuals; the need to ensure responsible use of policy[102] and 'consistency'[103] challenges in which applicants argue that published policy ought to be applied to their cases.

Jason Varuhas, similarly, has advanced a case for disaggregation. The case law on legitimate expectations is, according to Varuhas, analogous to a 'partially sculpted block of marble'.[104] Underneath the case law is a 'finely formed doctrine',

[94] *ChiuTeng@Kallang Pte Ltd v Singapore Land Authority* [2013] SGHC 262 (HC(Sing)); *SGB Starkstrom Pte Ltd v Commissioner of Labour* [2016] 3 SLR 598 (CA (Sing)); Kenny Chng, 'An Uncertain Future for Substantive Legitimate Expectations in Singapore: *SGB Starkstrom Pte Ltd v Commissioner of Labour*' [2018] *PL* 192.

[95] Jhaveri (n 93) 4.

[96] Farah Ahmed and Adam Perry, 'The Coherence of the Doctrine of Legitimate Expectations' (2014) 73(1) *CLJ* 61, 62.

[97] *Ibid*, 62 citing Forsyth (n 40).

[98] Richard Clayton, 'Legitimate Expectations, Policy and the Principle of Consistency' (2003) 62 *CLJ* 93; Elliott (n 86); Forsyth (n 40).

[99] Williams (n 8) 655.

[100] Williams (n 8) 655.

[101] Williams (n 8) 640–47.

[102] Williams (n 8) 647–60; *R (Davies & Gaines-Cooper) v Revenue and Customs Commissioners* [2011] UKSC 47, [2011] 1 WLR 2625.

[103] Williams (n 8) 660–62.

[104] Jason Varuhas, 'In Search of a Doctrine: Mapping the Law of Legitimate Expectations' in Groves and Weeks (n 60).

but it is presently 'trapped within an unruly, confused jurisprudence'[105] which needs to be chipped away. Varuhas' suggests that there are four categories of case in which the courts have deployed the language of legitimate expectations which should not be thought of as 'legitimate expectations cases' and which are 'more appropriately analysed by reference to other review doctrines'.[106] When this excess is chipped away, Varuhas argues, it becomes clear that a relatively narrow concern lies at the heart of the legitimate expectations ground: that of promise-keeping.[107] According to Varuhas, the *true* case law on legitimate expectations is driven by the fairly discrete concern of ensuring that administrative decision-makers 'stand by [their] promise[s]'[108] in circumstances where they have 'induce[d] individuals to rely'.[109]

It is useful to conclude this section by offering a brief summary of the analysis. This section has offered a brief overview of the development of the law and literature on legitimate expectations. It has been seen that, following the concretisation of the legitimate expectation ground in *Coughlan*,[110] the main focus in the case law and commentary has been on attempting to understand precisely when and how the law will prevent an administrative decision-maker from going back on an assurance. A universally accepted account has, however, proven elusive and a great deal of dissatisfaction persists. One difficulty has been that early attempts tended to rely on highly abstract notions which provided little guidance as to when, case-by-case, the courts would intervene. Attempts to identify a 'thicker' account, have, however not been borne out consistently in the case law. This has given rise to a popular, but cynical, view of the law on legitimate expectations. According to this view, legitimate expectations is lacking in structure, fails to offer sufficient guidance as to when the courts are likely to intervene, insufficiently constrains judges and is therefore in need of reform. In the course of exploring reform options, scholars have begun to explore the possibility of 'disaggregating' the law on legitimate expectations and explaining the case law by reference to multiple doctrines or other principles of administrative law.

This brief overview of legitimate expectations gives rise to at least two important questions. First, why is it proving so difficult to develop a general explanation of legitimate expectations? Second, do the difficulties incurred in constructing such an account indicate that the law lacks predictability, structure and judicial restraint? The remainder of the chapter shows that significant light can be shed on these questions by the broader themes of the book.

[105] *Ibid.*
[106] *Ibid.*
[107] *Ibid.*
[108] *Ibid.*
[109] *Ibid.* The six-part approach developed by Stuart-Smith J in *R v Jockey Club, ex parte RAM Racecourses Ltd* [1993] 2 All ER 225 is tentatively suggested by Varuhas as a good starting-point for the further development of the doctrine to reflect this.
[110] *Coughlan* (n 1).

III. Why is an Overarching Explanation of Legitimate Expectations Proving Elusive?

This section explores why it has proven difficult to develop an overarching account of the legitimate expectations case law. The broader themes of the book can help to answer this question. The three core senses of complexity and variety to which the book draws attention are in play as much in the legitimate expectations context as in administrative law more generally. Each, in turn, provides a reason why it is not especially surprising that it is proving difficult to explain in general, singular terms when, and how, an administrative decision-maker may depart from a prior assurance.

A. The Importance of the Legislative Framework

The first sense of complexity and variety in administrative law's 'anatomy' concerns the importance of the particular legislative framework in the background of a challenge. It has been emphasised throughout this book that the details of these frameworks matter. The courts pay close attention to the legislative provisions which confer an administrative decision-maker's functions when adjudicating on administrative law issues. Legislative details therefore play an important 'shaping' role in how the grounds of review are applied.

This is as true in the legitimate expectations context as it is in administrative law more broadly. In the legitimate expectations context, the background legislative framework plays a major role in setting outer boundaries on legitimate judicial reasoning. When deciding whether and how to intervene, the courts strive to respect the parameters which the legislative regime puts in place. This can be seen in at least three ways.

First, and most famously, the courts respect the boundaries of the decision-maker's *powers* as laid down in legislation. If, therefore, Parliament has denied the decision-maker the power to deliver the content of an expectation, the courts will not deploy the legitimate expectations ground in a way which requires the decision-maker to do so.[111] This is known as the 'ultra vires' doctrine.[112] The basic rationale is that an administrative decision-maker ought not to be able to extend

[111] For recent examples, see *Rastrum v Secretary of State for Communities and Local Government* [2009] EWCA Civ 1340; *Mosekari v Lewisham LBC* [2014] EWHC 3617 (Admin), [2015] ELR 31.

[112] For critical discussion, see Mark Elliott, 'Unlawful Representations, Legitimate Expectations and Estoppel' (2003) 8(2) *Judicial Review* 71; Yasser Vanderman, 'Ultra Vires Legitimate Expectation: An Argument for Compensation' [2012] *PL* 85.

the ambit of its own powers by generating unlawful expectations.[113] Classic illustrations include *Begbie*[114] and *Rowland*.[115] In the former, assurances offered on the basis of a misinterpretation of statutory powers were held to be incapable of generating legitimate expectations.[116] In the latter, the legitimate expectations ground could not be relied upon to claim private rights to a stretch of river despite these rights being promised;[117] the background legislative scheme required the river to be made available for public use[118] and the Environment Agency did not have the power to alter this.

Second, and similarly, where Parliament has placed the decision-maker under a statutory *duty* which requires it to change direction, the courts are not able to deploy the legitimate expectations ground in a way which prevents the decision-maker from fulfilling the relevant legislative obligation.[119] In *Flasz*,[120] for example, the applicant's legitimate expectation challenge failed because, under the background legislative scheme, the Primary Care Trust was legally obligated to bring GP contracts in line with national minimal standards.[121] Even if the applicants had a legitimate expectation that their contracts would be permanent,[122] therefore, the courts would not treat that expectation as preventing the Trust from making the relevant adjustments. In a similar way, the local authority in *Albert Court Residents' Association*[123] was held not to have violated the legitimate expectations ground in failing to apply its own policy on consultation.[124] The background legislative scheme made clear that the local authority was under a legislative duty to grant the variation unless objections were reached within 28 days[125] and representations had not been achieved within this time limit.

Third and finally, the courts will also not regard an administrative decision-maker as bound by the representations of another where the legislation makes

[113] Sarah Hannett and Lisa Busch, 'Ultra Vires Representations and Illegitimate Expectations' [2005] *PL* 729.

[114] *Begbie* (n 7).

[115] *Rowland v Environment Agency* [2003] EWCA Civ 1885, [2004] 3 WLR 249.

[116] *Begbie* (n 7).

[117] *Rowland* (n 115). In this case Protocol 1, Article 1 to the European Convention on Human Rights did not alter the situation. Although note *Stretch v United Kingdom* (2004) 38 EHRR 12 (discussed in Mark Elliott, 'Legitimate Expectations and Unlawful Representations' (2004) 63(2) *CLJ* 261; David Blundell, 'Ultra Vires Legitimate Expectations' (2005) 10(2) *Judicial Review* 147).

[118] Thames Preservation Act 1885.

[119] See also *R (Sovio Wines Ltd) v Food Standards Agency* [2009] EWHC 382 (Admin).

[120] *Flasz v Havering Primary Care Trust* [2011] EWHC 1487 (Admin).

[121] *Ibid* [36]–[38]; Health Service Act 2006, s92(2); National Health Service (General Medical Services) Regulations 2004 (SI 2004/291), regulation 18; National Health Service (Primary Medical Services) (Miscellaneous Amendments) Regulations 2010 (SI 2010/578).

[122] The Administrative Court also concluded that the representations were insufficiently clear: *Flasz* (n 120) [35].

[123] *R (Albert Court Residents' Association) v Westminster CC* [2011] EWCA Civ 430, [2012] PTSR 604.

[124] *Ibid* [6].

[125] *Ibid* [34]–[36]; Licensing Act 2003, s35.

clear that an assurance is not to have this effect.[126] In *Badger Trust*,[127] for instance, the applicants argued that Natural England ('NE') was prevented by a policy document published by the Department for Environment, Food & Rural Affairs ('DEFRA') from issuing badger-culling licences. This argument was however rejected because, under the background statutory scheme, while formal guidance issued by DEFRA to NE was prima facie binding,[128] less formal policy documents of this kind did not have the same effect. Similarly, in *Cornwall Waste Forum*[129] assurances offered by a planning inspector did not bind the Secretary of State. The background legislative scheme[130] made clear that the authority of the inspectorate was confined to 'holding the inquiry and providing a report'[131] and the Secretary of State could not 'avoid responsibility for the [ultimate] planning decision'[132] which under the statute he had the legal duty to take.

The constraining role which legislation plays on reasoning in legitimate expectations cases is important. It indicates one reason why it is proving difficult to construct a general explanation of how the legitimate expectations ground operates. It is easier to see how a singular account of legitimate expectation could be developed in a legal system in which the courts were developing the doctrine in a legal 'vacuum'.[133] The legal space in which the legitimate expectations doctrine operates is not, however, constant. Every legitimate expectations challenge has its own legislative contours and these contours play an important role in setting parameters on judicial reasoning and the conclusions the courts can reach. Or, as Lord Hodge put it on behalf of the Privy Council in *Rainbow Insurance*, 'the correct approach to legitimate expectation in any particular field of public law depends on the relevant legislation'.[134]

B. The Plurality of Values, Interests and Policies which Administrative Law Protects

The second sense of complexity and variety in administrative law's 'anatomy' concerns the plurality of legal values, interests and policies the courts seek to

[126] Famous cases grappling with this problem include the estoppel cases discussed above and *BAPIO* (n 32).

[127] *R (Badger Trust) v Secretary of State for the Environment, Food & Rural Affairs* [2014] EWCA Civ 1405, [2015] Env LR 12.

[128] *Ibid* [3] and [44]; Natural Environment and Rural Communities Act 2006, ss15–16.

[129] *Cornwall Waste Forum v Secretary of State for Communities and Local Government* [2012] EWCA Civ 379, [2012] Env LR 34.

[130] Conservation of Habitats and Species Regulations 2010 (SI 2010/490), regulation 65.

[131] *Cornwall Waste* (n 129) [36].

[132] *Cornwall Waste* (n 129) [38].

[133] Language commonly used in administrative law scholarship: Jeffrey Jowell, 'Of Vires and Vacuums: The Constitutional Context of Judicial Review' [1999] *PL* 448.

[134] *Rainbow Insurance Company Ltd v The Financial Services Commission and Others (Mauritius)* [2015] UKPC 15 [52].

accommodate. Chapter three stressed that administrative law's values are varied in at least two senses. First, their legal *origins* are diverse in the sense that administrative law is concerned to accommodate both the policy goals underlying legislation and certain interests or principles regarded as especially important by the common law. Second, the *beneficiaries* of administrative law are varied because administrative law is neither wholly 'individual' nor 'public-regarding'.[135]

These observations apply equally in the legitimate expectations context. Thus, in the first place, it is clear that a major concern of the courts is to understand and to promote the public policy aims which underlie the background legislative framework.[136] *Dickinson*[137] and *Rowe*[138] provide neat illustrations. These cases arose against the background of the Finance Act 2014 which introduced a major new scheme on tax evasion investigation.[139] The core aim of the scheme is to remove the 'cashflow advantages'[140] which taxpayers under investigation had previously been able to enjoy. Under the new scheme, tax authorities are empowered, though not duty-bound, to issue 'accelerated payment notices'[141] ('APNs') which require upfront payment of tax alleged to be due. The Court of Appeal, however, regarded the Act as a strong signal from Parliament that the removal of cashflow advantages in tax evasion investigation is of the utmost public importance. It concluded that it would be inappropriate to therefore apply the legitimate expectations ground in a way which prevented the tax authorities from issuing APNs in the applicants' cases, even though they had previously entered into agreements under the old scheme.

A similar example is supplied by *Jackley*.[142] This case arose against the background of the Legal Aid, Sentencing and Punishment of Offenders Act 2012. In passing this Act, Parliament approved the confinement of the Home Detention Curfew programme, under which prisoners were given 'early monitored release from prison for a period prior to the conditional release date',[143] to those who were serving sentences of less than four years.[144] Parliament's approval of this restriction, the Court concluded, meant the legitimate expectations ground should not be applied in a way which would undermine that policy choice.

These cases illustrate the careful consideration courts give to the public policy aims underlying the background legislative scheme. These, however, are evidently

[135] Jason Varuhas, 'The Public Interest Conception of Public Law: Its Procedural Origins and Substantive Implications' in John Bell, Mark Elliott, Jason Varuhas and Philip Murray (eds), *Public Law Adjudication in Common Law Systems: Process and Substance* (Hart Publishing, 2017) 52.

[136] See further *Rainbow Insurance* (n 134); *R (Hossain) v Secretary of State for the Home Department* [2015] EWCA Civ 207.

[137] *Dickinson & Others v HMRC* [2018] EWCA Civ 2798.

[138] *Rowe v HMRC* [2015] EWHC 2293 (Admin).

[139] Finance Act 2014, Part 4, Chapter 3.

[140] *Dickinson* (n 137) [12].

[141] Finance Act 2014, s219.

[142] *R (Jackley) v Secretary of State for Justice* [2015] EWHC 342 (Admin).

[143] *Ibid* [12].

[144] Legal Aid, Sentencing and Punishment of Offenders Act 2012, s246.

not the only normative concerns the courts seek to accommodate. To a large degree, the courts are also concerned in legitimate expectations cases to protect aspects of the *individual's* interests which are regarded as especially important by the common law. Three considerations have been particularly strongly emphasised in judicial reasoning.

First, detrimental reliance. It is commonly said that detrimental reliance is not an essential prerequisite of a legitimate expectations challenge but it is a strong indicator that judicial intervention would be appropriate.[145] As will be seen in section IV, detrimental reliance is especially important in cases where applicants challenge an administrative decision-maker's choice to replace one policy with another. Where the courts intervene in such cases it is usually on the basis that there is a relatively confined group which has irreversibly and materially relied on the original policy.[146] In *Cameron*,[147] for instance, the Court held that while the tax authorities were permitted to alter their approach in deciding when a ship was to be regarded as having left the UK for tax purposes, it had acted unlawfully in introducing its new policy immediately and without affording time to adjust to those who had made arrangements on the basis of the old policy.

Second, the courts are also concerned in some contexts with individual detriment in a broader sense. It was stressed by Schiemann LJ in *Bibi*[148] that in addition to causing *material* harm, withdrawal of an assurance from an individual may also result in 'moral'[149] detriment. Where an assurance is issued by an administrative decision-maker, it will often be reasonable for an individual to rely on that assurance. This reliance will not necessarily take the form of the committal of resources on the basis of the assurance,[150] but may amount to the making of life plans on the assumption that the assurance will be fulfilled. In such circumstances, withdrawing the assurance may therefore amount to a violation of the individual's autonomy[151] and a failure to show respect.[152] In *Bibi*, Schiemann LJ stressed that there may be contexts in which it is appropriate for the court to afford protection against these 'moral harms' in the absence of detrimental reliance.[153]

Third, another concern in some legitimate expectations cases is that of ensuring consistency in the treatment of individuals.[154] This is especially relevant

[145] *R (Bancoult) v Secretary of State for Foreign and Commonwealth Affairs (No 2)* [2009] AC 453 [60]; *Re Finucane's Application for Judicial Review* [2019] UKSC 7, [2019] HRLR 7 [160].

[146] To be clear, this does not mean the courts will always intervene in such cases: *Hamble Fisheries* (n 53). As will be discussed below, the courts also pay close attention to the extent that making transitional provision would undermine the reasons for policy change.

[147] *Cameron v HMRC* [2012] EWHC 1174 (Admin).

[148] *Bibi* (n 59).

[149] *Bibi* (n 59) [55].

[150] Joanna Bell, 'The Privy Council and the Doctrine of Legitimate Expectations Meet Again' (2016) 75(3) *CLJ* 449.

[151] Joseph Raz, *The Morality of Freedom* (Oxford University Press, 1986) chs 14–15.

[152] Joseph Raz, *The Authority of Law*, 2nd edn (Oxford University Press, 2009) Ch 11.

[153] *Bibi* (n 59) [55]; Bell (n 150).

[154] Clayton (n 98).

in circumstances where a decision-maker fails to decide an individual application in line with published policy. In such circumstances, the individual may be concerned that they have been treated less favourably than others in an analogous situation. The Court of Appeal in *Rashid*[155] and *Nadarjah*,[156] famously used legitimate expectations as a ground for providing relief in circumstances of this kind.[157]

Returning to the question of why an overarching explanation of legitimate expectations is proving elusive, the plurality of legal values, interests and policies the courts seek to promote suggests a second reason. Perhaps the most satisfying way of explaining the law on legitimate expectations would be to identify a singular 'meta-value'[158] which the courts can be seen as protecting. Indeed, section II discussed a number of attempts to explain legitimate expectations in this way.[159] The analysis here, however, demonstrates why it is difficult to see how a value could be found. In adjudicating under the legitimate expectations ground, the courts accommodate and protect many different normative considerations. These values are varied in terms of both their origins and the beneficiaries which the law aims to protect. The legitimate expectations ground therefore cannot be neatly characterised as being 'about' protecting a singular value or cluster of values.

C. The Array of Legal Relationships in Play in Administrative Law Challenges

The third and final source of complexity and variety in administrative law concerns the different kinds of legal relationship which can be in play in adjudication. The book has emphasised that it is too simplistic to imagine that a clear legal-structural line can be drawn between administrative law cases, on the one hand, and private law[160] and human rights[161] cases, on the other. Some authors have tried to draw this line. According to them, the hallmark of an administrative law challenge is that an individual appears before the court in order to enforce a legal duty which is owed by the administrative decision-maker to the public as a collectivity.[162] By contrast, claimants in private law and human rights law cases rely on individualised legal

[155] *R (Rashid) v Secretary of State for the Home Department* [2005] EWCA Civ 744, [2005] INLR 744.
[156] *Nadarajah* (n 4).
[157] See discussion below.
[158] Joe Tomlinson, 'The Narrow Approach to Substantive Legitimate Expectations and the Trend of Modern Authority' (2017) 17(1) *Oxford University Commonwealth Law Journal* 75, 81 (citing from Paul Daly, 'A Pluralist Account of Deference and Legitimate Expectations' in Groves and Weeks (n 60)).
[159] For example, the 'trust-based' account: Forsyth (n 40); Watson (n 6).
[160] Nicholas Bamforth, 'Hohfeldian Rights and Public Law' in Matthew Kramer (ed), Rights Wrongs & Responsibilities (Palgrave, 2001).
[161] Jason Varuhas, 'Against Unification' in Mark Elliott and Hanah Wilberg (eds), *The Scope and Intensity of Substantive Review: Traversing Taggart's Rainbow* (Hart Publishing, 2015).
[162] Woolf (n 10).

rights which they claim to personally possess.[163] This way of thinking, however, does not hold up to scrutiny on at least one side of the divide.[164] Administrative law cases take different 'shapes'. Some cases can be aptly characterised as instances where an applicant seeks to enforce a legal duty owed to the public at large or a subsection of it. Others, however, look much more like the private and human rights paradigm of an individual relying on a personal right.

Once again, this sense of complexity and variety is as much in play in the legitimate expectations context as it is in administrative law more broadly, a fact which is not especially surprising when one bears in mind the variety of ways in which an administrative decision-maker might generate an expectation. In the first place, it is certainly true that there are cases in which an applicant argues that the administrative decision-maker has breached a legal duty owed to the *public* as a collectivity. The *Greenpeace* case[165] is a good example. The applicant in this case did not argue that *they*, as a non-governmental organisation, had a personal legal right to be consulted. Rather, they alleged that the *public as a whole* had derived an entitlement, by virtue of the Government's assurance, to express their views before a change in nuclear policy was made.

In other contexts, applicants seek to enforce legal duties which benefit, not the public as a collectivity but, a smaller subsection of it. In *Hamble Fisheries*,[166] for instance, Sedley J emphasised that the applicant's argument amounted to the claim that the Minister ought to have put in place a transitional provision to accommodate, not only *it* but, *all* other fishing companies in its position.[167] The applicant, in other words, appeared as a representative of the subsection of the public to which it belonged.

In the second place, however, and with that said, there are also cases in which the courts regard the legitimate expectations ground as giving rise to legal duties which are owed to *the individual applicant*.[168] The clearest examples of this are cases in which the applicant challenges the failure to apply published policy to individual applications. It is common for the courts to understand challenges of this kind as concerned the personal entitlements of the applicant. As Lord Dyson put it in *Lumba*,[169] '*the individual* has a *basic public law right* to have his or her case considered under whatever policy the executive sees fit to adopt.[170] In a

[163] Wesley Hohfeld, *Fundamental Legal Conceptions as Applied in Judicial Reasoning* (The Law Book Exchange, 2010).

[164] This is not to suggest that the private and human rights side of the divide are simple: Joanna Miles, 'Standing under the Human Rights Act 1998' (2000) 59(1) *CLJ* 133; Joanna Miles, 'Standing in a Multi-Layered Constitution' in Nicholas Bamforth and Peter Leyland (eds), *Public Law in a Multi-Layered Constitution* (Hart Publishing, 2003).

[165] *Greenpeace* (n 15).

[166] *Hamble Fisheries* (n 53).

[167] *Hamble Fisheries* (n 53) [27]–[28].

[168] Bell (n 9).

[169] *Lumba* (n 13).

[170] *Lumba* (n 13) [35] (emphasis added).

similar way, the Supreme Court in *Mandalia*[171] spoke of 'the *applicant's right* to the determination of his application in accordance with policy'.

Another type of case in which it is common to find the courts framing the applicant's challenge in terms of a claim to a personal right are those in which the administrative decision-maker has directly communicated an assurance to the individual.[172] The applicant in *Capital Care*,[173] for instance, argued that in granting a licence to them, the administrative decision-maker had impliedly assured that they would be permitted to sponsor employment visas for two years. The Court of Appeal clearly thought of this argument in terms of the assertion of a personal right to retain the licence. At one point in the judgment, for instance, Laws LJ explains that the 'common law doctrines of estoppel by representation and estoppel by convention':[174]

> … whatever [their] scope … [in relation to] the exercise of public functions … cannot confer any greater *rights on the appellants* than they might enjoy by force of the public law principles of legitimate expectation.[175]

In a similar way in *Alansi*[176] the applicant had been offered a personal assurance that if she were to accept an assured tenancy in the private sector she would retain priority home-seeker status. Throughout his judgment, Stuart-Smith J spoke throughout of the applicant asserting that she held 'a substantive right'[177] to the content of the assurance.

The plurality of legal relationships which arise across legitimate expectations cases is a third reason why a clear, general explanation of the ground is proving elusive. A commentator seeking an account of legitimate expectations might be tempted to proceed by asking whether the doctrine is either a legal standard which either creates legal duties owed to the public at large or obligations, or confers personal rights on individuals.[178] The plurality of legal relationships in play in the case law, however, shows that the ground can, in different contexts, give rise to both kinds of relationship.

It is useful to conclude this section by returning to the key question raised at the start: why have scholars struggled to develop a universally accepted explanation of the legitimate expectations case law? This section has demonstrated the considerable light which can be shed on this issue by the broader arguments of

[171] *Mandalia* (n 13).

[172] For a further example, see *R v Devon County Council, ex parte Baker* [1995] 1 All ER 73 (CA), 88 discussed in Bell (n 9).

[173] *R (Capital Care Services UK Ltd) v Secretary of State for the Home Department* [2012] EWCA Civ 1151.

[174] *Ibid* [15]. On the relationship between legitimate expectations and estoppel, see more broadly *Reprotech* (n 34); John Cartwright, 'Protecting Legitimate Expectations and Estoppel in English Law' (2006) 10(3) *Electronic Journal of Comparative Law*.

[175] *Capital Care* (n 173) (emphasis added).

[176] *Alansi* (n 27).

[177] *Alansi* (n 27), see especially [26], [28] and [32].

[178] Jason Varuhas, 'The Reformation of English Administrative Law? "Rights", Rhetoric and Reality' (2013) 72 *CLJ* 369.

the book. The three sources of legal complexity and variety to which the book draws attention are in play in the legitimate expectations context as much as they are across administrative law more broadly. Each in turn suggests a reason why the legitimate expectations case law is not easily explained by reference to an overarching framework.

First, the detail of the legislative framework in the background of a legitimate expectations case places meaningful limitations on the extent and manner in which the courts can protect expectations. The courts are not therefore developing the law on legitimate expectations in a legislative vacuum, but are deciding cases which are each characterised by their own legislative contours. Second, the courts seek to accommodate a plurality of values, interests and policies when adjudicating on legitimate expectations issues. It is not therefore possible to characterise legitimate expectations as being concerned with one overarching 'meta-value'.[179] Third, legitimate expectations challenges concern legal relationships of different kinds. In some, the applicant seeks to uphold a duty which benefits the public as a collectivity or a subsection of it. In others, however, the courts clearly think of the applicant as relying on a personal legal right to be treated in a particular way. One consequence of this is that legitimate expectations cannot be aptly characterised either as a ground which gives rise to 'public-regarding'[180] legal duties, or which confers personal legal rights on the individual, in all cases.

IV. Is the Law Characterised by Unpredictability, Incoherence and Lack of Judicial Restraint?

Section II, after overviewing the development of the law and literature on legitimate expectations, set out two important questions. The first – why is it proving difficult to develop a generally accepted, overarching account of legitimate expectations? – was discussed in the previous part. This section turns to the second: do the difficulties in constructing a general account of legitimate expectations mean that the law on legitimate expectations is unpredictable, places too little restraint on judges and is in need of reform? This section explores that question.

As discussed in the previous chapter in the context of procedural review, it is possible to take a number of different approaches to addressing a question of this kind. One possibility, for instance, would be to look at the leading cases in order to ascertain the degree of guidance they afford to lower courts. Such an approach, however, seems particularly inapt in the legitimate expectations contexts where there is relatively little case law at the appellate levels.[181] Another would be to

[179] Tomlinson (n 158).

[180] Varuhas (n 135) 52.

[181] The Supreme Court has engaged with legitimate expectations relatively infrequently: *Bancoult* (n 145); *BAPIO* (n 32); *Davies* (n 102); *Finucane* (n 145) are a few rare examples.

make use of a handful of specific, representative case studies in order to examine closely the degree to which legal reasoning in them was restrained by a meaningful framework. Again, this approach has significant drawbacks in the legitimate expectations context. As section I discussed, there is considerable variety across the facts in legitimate expectations cases and it would be very difficult, therefore, to identify representative case law.

As a result, this section takes a different approach. Rather than focusing only on the leading case law, or a few representative cases, it looks at a sample of systematically identified case law. The analysis in this section, more particularly, is based primarily on a close reading of a body of recent challenges decided in the ten-year period, beginning at the start of 2009 and concluding at the end of 2018. This case law was identified by using a key-word search focusing on 'legitimate expectations'[182] and the results were narrowed to include only decisions by the English and Welsh Administrative Court and Court of Appeal, UK Supreme Court and Privy Council. If lower-instance decisions from which an appeal has taken place are discounted, the search yielded 123 cases. Of these, 97 were decided in the Administrative Court, 21 in the Court of Appeal, one in the Supreme Court[183] and four in the Privy Council.[184] The cases in this sample concerned many branches of administration including:

- agriculture;[185]
- airports;[186]
- care;[187]
- civil service employment;[188]
- conservation;[189]
- education;[190]
- elections;[191]
- energy;[192]
- entry;[193]

[182] Using Westlaw.
[183] *Davies* (n 102).
[184] *Paponette* (n 59); *Rainbow Insurance* (n 134); *United Policyholders* (n 59); *Barrow v AG of Saint Lucia* [2016] UKPC 38.
[185] *R (Peter Strawson) v DEFRA* [2010] EWHC 3286 (Admin).
[186] *Barbone v Secretary of State for Transport* [2009] EWHC 463 (Admin).
[187] *R (Davis) v West Sussex CC* [2012] EWHC 2152 (Admin); *R (Karia) v Leicester CC* [2014] EWHC 3105 (Admin).
[188] *R (FDA) v Minister for the Cabinet Office* [2018] EWHC 2746 (Admin).
[189] *Trillium Prime Property Ltd v Tower Hamlets LBC* [2011] EWHC 146 (Admin).
[190] *R (Grimsby Institute of Further and Higher Education) v Chief Executive of Skills Funding* [2010] EWHC 2134 (Admin).
[191] *R (Wilson) v Dover DC* [2016] EWHC 2556 (Admin).
[192] *Brooke Energy* (n 30); *R (Energie EST) v Secretary of State for Energy and Climate Change* [2013] EWHC 3026 (Admin).
[193] *R (Naik) v Secretary of State for the Home Department* [2011] EWCA Civ 1546.

- environment;[194]
- finance;[195]
- fishing;[196]
- health[197] and hospitals;[198]
- housing;[199]
- inquiries;[200]
- legal aid;[201]
- libraries;[202]
- licensing,[203]
- local authority funding,[204]
- parole,[205]
- pensions,[206]
- police,[207]
- procurement,[208]
- professional discipline and regulation,[209]
- roads[210] and universities.[211]

[194] *Badger Trust* (n 127).
[195] *United Policyholders* (n 59).
[196] *UK Association of Fish Producer Organisations v DEFRA* [2013] EWHC 1959 (Admin).
[197] *Unison* (n 21).
[198] *R (Buckingham) v NHS Corby* [2018] EWHC 2080 (Admin); *Flatley* (n 31); *R (Enfield LBC) v Barnet Clinical Commissioning Group* [2013] EWHC 3496 (Admin); *R (Royal Brompton & Harefield NHS Foundation Trust) v JC of PCTs* [2012] EWCA Civ 472.
[199] *Babakandi* (n 16) *Obiorah v Lewisham LBC* [2013] EWCA Civ 325, [2013] HLR 35.
[200] *R (Jefferies) v Secretary of State for the Home Department* [2018] EWHC 3239 (Admin).
[201] *Law Society* (n 20); *R (Whitston) v Secretary of State for Justice* [2014] EWHC 3044 (Admin).
[202] *R (Page) v Darlington BC* [2018] EWHC 1818 (Admin).
[203] *R (Assisted Reproduction and Gynaecology Centre) v Human Fertilisation and Embryology Authority* [2013] EWHC 3087 (Admin); *Wilcock v Lancaster CC* [2013] EWHC 1231 (Admin), [2013] LLR 607; *R (Central College of London) v Secretary of State for the Home Department* [2012] EWHC 1273 (Admin).
[204] *Dudley MBC* (n 30); *R (Cheshire East Borough Council) v DEFRA* [2011] EWHC 1975 (Admin); *R (Luton) v Secretary of State for Education* [2011] EWHC 217 (Admin).
[205] *Jorgenson* (n 25); *R (McShane) v Secretary of State for Justice* [2018] EWHC 2049 (Admin).
[206] *R (Staff Side of the Police Negotiating Board) v Secretary of State for Work and Pensions* [2011] EWHC 3175 (Admin).
[207] *Hewson* (n 25); *Birks* (n 17); *R (Simpson) v CC of GMP* [2013] EWHC 1858 (Admin).
[208] *R (London Secure Services) v Youth Justice Board* [2009] EWHC 2347 (Admin); *R (Enfield LBC) v Abellio* [2016] EWCA Civ 480.
[209] *British Dental Association v General Dental Council* [2014] EWHC 4311 (Admin); *R (Sagar) v NHS Health Education Yorkshire and Humberside* [2014] EWHC 3696 (Admin); *R (B) v Nursing & Midwifery Council* [2012] EWHC 1264 (Admin).
[210] *Trail Riders* (n 25).
[211] *R (Hassan) v Coventry University* [2016] EWHC 654 (Admin).

The administrative contexts in relation to which the greater number of challenges arose were immigration/asylum (27 cases; 22 per cent of the sample), tax (19 cases; 15.4 per cent of the sample) and planning (16 cases; 13 per cent of the sample).

The aim in analysing this case law was to explore whether it is fair to say that the legitimate expectations ground is characterised by incoherence and unpredictability. Or whether, to the contrary, it is possible to see discernible patterns running through the case law in terms of how the courts responded to challenges. In exploring this question, a two-stage process proved to be illuminating. In the first stage, the case law was allocated to categories depending on the *kind of legal relationship* which subsisted between the applicant and the decision-maker.[212] Four main scenarios emerged.[213] Briefly stated these were: (a) instances where an individual had been offered a directly communicated assurance that they would be treated in a particular way; (b) cases where the applicant challenged the application of policy to the individual circumstances of her case; (c) contexts in which the applicant argued that transitional arrangements should have been made for a group to which she belonged; and (d) challenges in which the applicant relied on a statement of intention addressed to the public at large.[214] Second, once identified, the case law within each category was then analysed in order to ascertain whether patterns could be traced in how the courts approached review.

The overarching argument of this section is that a close reading of this case law, with the complex and varied anatomy of administrative law in mind, suggests that there is a good deal more structure, predictability and restraint in the judicial approach to legitimate expectations than has sometimes been imagined. Across each of the four scenarios it was possible to observe some relatively clear patterns in judicial reasoning. Subsections A–D discuss each of the four scenarios in turn. Subsection E summarises by returning to the question of whether the law lacks predictability, structure and judicial restraint and subsection F then discusses two important points of clarification.

A. First Scenario: Assurance Directly Communicated to Individual

The first scenario which occurred commonly in the case law was that in which an administrative decision-maker had communicated directly with an individual by offering an assurance to the effect that they would be treated in a particular

[212] The third sense of complexity and variety to which the book draws attention.

[213] The idea that legitimate expectations cases fit different fact patterns is not new: Craig, 'A Conceptual Analysis' (n 44) 83–85; Williams (n 8). Note also that the schema outlined below is not exhaustive. One small cluster of cases not discussed, for instance, are those in which local authorities challenged a withdrawal of funding on the basis of a legitimate expectation of compensation: *Luton* (n 204); *R (Cheshire East Borough Council) v DEFRA* [2011] EWHC 1975 (Admin); *Dudley MBC* (n 30).

[214] This is not to suggest that all cases fit into only one category: see discussion in subsection F below.

manner. Direct communication took a number of forms. Commonly it took the form of a letter,[215] an email[216] or a verbal assurance offered over the telephone[217] or in person.[218] More formally, and especially in the tax context, it also sometimes took the form of a written agreement[219] or provisional ruling.[220] In some cases applicants argued that a practice or continued course of conduct constituted implied communication.[221] The case law has, however, made clear that a practice must be particularly consistent and long-standing in order to count as implied communication.[222]

Across the sample, assurances of this kind were required to meet a high standard of clarity in order to be recognised as having legal effects. The courts applied the *MFK* requirement that the assurance be 'clear, unambiguous and devoid of relevant qualification'[223] with rigour. As a result, there were many instances of challenges being rejected on the basis that a 'legitimate expectation' had not been generated.[224] The courts repeatedly emphasised that it is not enough that, as a result of their interactions with the decision-maker, the recipient *in fact expected* that she would be treated in some manner.[225] The decision-maker must be shown to have issued a sufficiently clear assurance to the effect that that treatment *would* be conferred.[226]

If the assurance met the clarity requirement, how did the courts review the decision to depart from it? The main pattern which could be seen was that the courts would closely scrutinise the reasoning which informed the administrative decision-maker's conclusion in order to ensure that particular and meaningful consideration was given to both the fact that the assurance has been given to the possibilities for accommodating it. The courts paid attention to three main things in particular.

[215] *Jackley* (n 142).

[216] *R (Veolia Landfill Ltd) v HMRC* [2016] EWHC 1880 (Admin); *R (Youssef) v SSHD* [2015] EWHC 1600 (Admin); *Morrisons* (n 25).

[217] *Mohamed* (n 18).

[218] *Birks* (n 17).

[219] *Dickinson* (n 137).

[220] *R (Biffa Waster Services Ltd) v HMRC* [2016] EWHC 1444 (Admin), [2017] Env LR 10.

[221] *Mosekari* (n 111).

[222] *Naik* (n 193); *Flattery v Secretary of State for Communities and Local Government* [2010] EWHC 2868 (Admin); Mark Elliott and Jason Varuhas, *Administrative Law*, 5th edn (Oxford University Press, 2017) Ch 6.

[223] *MFK* (n 42).

[224] *Karia* (n 187); Jackley (n 142); *Dixons* (n 16); *Royal Brompton* (n 198); *Babakandi* (n 16); *R (Huntingwood Trading Ltd) v HMRC* [2009] EWHC 290 (Admin); *R (St John's School) v Hillingdon LBC* [2011] EWHC 3261 (Admin), [2012] JPL 693; *Keevil v Secretary of State for Communities and Local Government* [2012] EWHC 322 (Admin); *Ansar v Secretary of State for Home Department* [2014] EWHC 4361 (Admin); *R (Prudential Assurance Co Ltd) v HMRC* [2017] EWHC 1484 (Admin).

[225] *R (Lewisham LBC) v AQA* [2013] EWHC 211 (Admin); *Energie EST* (n 192).

[226] Sometimes the live issue is whether the alleged assurance was in fact issued and, if so, what its precise content was. This is especially so in cases of alleged verbal assurances: *Corkteck* (n 25).

First, the courts scrutinised the decision-maker's evidence closely to ensure that the fact that the assurance was given had been recognised and factored into the decision-making process.[227] Where it became clear that a decision has been taken abruptly and without recognition of the fact that it was in breach of a prior assurance, the courts regarded the decision-maker as having violated the applicant's legitimate expectations. A good example[228] is the *Assisted Reproduction and Gynaecology Centre* case.[229] Here the regulatory authority imposed a condition into the applicant's licence to run a fertility clinic in contravention of a previous assurance that no changes would be made until after the conclusion of an ongoing appeal. The Court held the authority had acted unlawfully because there was 'no evidence that [the deciding official] took into account the previous representations or conduct of his own authority'.[230]

Second, the courts also required the decision-maker to explain in detail the reasons which underlay its decision to change direction and why it had formed the view that fulfilling the assurance to the applicant would be inconsistent with these reasons. Only if the administrative decision-maker could offer a convincing explanation as to why fulfilling the assurance would significantly undermine its aims in changing policy direction would the court conclude that it has acted lawfully.

Compare, for instance, *Alansi*[231] with *Patel*.[232] In the former the local authority convinced the Court that fulfilling the content of the assurance offered to the applicant, and a number of others who had received identical assurances, would significantly undermine the new housing priority scheme it had brought in. The aim of the scheme was to provide a fairer way of ranking priority, and treating the assurances as binding would elevate the applicant and others, who were securely housed, above groups which were not, thereby undermining the hierarchy the authority had introduced. In the latter, by contrast, the Court of Appeal was unconvinced that making good the assurance to the applicant would significantly undermine the General Medical Council's ('GMC') new policy. The GMC had decided that primary medical degrees with a significant long-distance learning element should no longer render a doctor eligible to practice in the UK. The policy had been adopted as a response to findings that a number of institutions in the UK claimed false connections with educational institutions abroad. Rather than undertaking an investigation in each individual case, the GMC had introduced a blanket minimum face-to-face learning element as a proxy requirement. Against this background, the Court of Appeal considered that making good the specific assurance to the applicant that his overseas qualification would render him able to practice in the UK would not undermine the GMC's reasons for changing policy.

[227] *Bibi* (n 59).
[228] See also *Birks* (n 17).
[229] *Assisted Reproduction and Gynaecology Centre* (n 203).
[230] *Assisted Reproduction and Gynaecology Centre* (n 203) [90].
[231] *Alansi* (n 27).
[232] *Patel* (n 11).

There was no suggestion in the case of the applicant that his qualification had been obtained from an institution claiming false connections[233] and the GMC would be able to apply the policy to future cases.

Third and finally, the courts also required administrative decision-makers to demonstrate that consideration has been given to any 'midway' options open to it which would have cushioned the blow of policy change to the applicant. Again, if the decision-maker had elected not to make use of any such options, it had to offer good reasons for not doing so.[234] *Coughlan*[235] itself is a neat illustration of this point. Part of the reason why the local health authority had acted unlawfully in this case was that it had not demonstrated consideration of alternative means of housing the applicant on a permanent basis in order to go some way to delivering its promise of a 'home for life'.[236] Similarly, in *Bibi*[237] the Court of Appeal referred the decision not to house the applicant's family on a permanent basis in contravention of a previous assurance back to the local authority. In doing so, Schiemann LJ emphasised the necessity of considering whether 'if it consider[ed] it inappropriate'[238] to fulfil the assurance in its entirety 'it should adopt any other way of helping the applicants to obtain secure housing whether by cash or other aid or by amending the allocation scheme'.[239]

To summarise, in cases where an administrative decision-maker had directly communicated a clear assurance to an individual to the effect that they would be treated in a particular way, the main pattern which could be observed in the case sample analysed was close judicial scrutiny of the decision-maker's reasoning process. The court, in particular, paid close attention to three things: (i) whether specific consideration had been given to the fact the assurance was given; (ii) whether the decision-maker had offered convincing reasons for concluding that fulfilling the assurance would significantly undermine its reasons for changing position; and (iii) whether the decision-maker had given thought to any 'midway' options which would serve to cushion the blow to the individual and had good reasons for concluding they should not be implemented.

B. Second Scenario: Alleged Failure to Apply Policy

The second type of scenario involved instances where the applicant challenged an alleged failure to apply published policy to a decision relating to her in particular.

[233] *Patel* (n 11).
[234] *F&I Services Ltd v Commissioners of Customs and Excise* [2001] EWCA Civ 762 [72]; *Grimsby* (n 190).
[235] *Coughlan* (n 1).
[236] *Coughlan* (n 1) [89].
[237] *Bibi* (n 59).
[238] *Bibi* (n 59) [58].
[239] *Bibi* (n 59) [58].

The overarching approach in play in such cases is now well recognised. As explained above, the Court of Appeal in *Rashid*[240] and *Nadarajah*[241] expanded the legitimate expectations ground in order to afford relief in such cases. This expansion of legitimate expectations has been subject to considerable criticism.[242] It is unduly 'strained',[243] it has been said, to invoke the language of 'expectation' in such cases, especially in contexts where the applicant does not know of the policy. On the basis of these criticisms, the Supreme Court in *Lumba*[244] and *Mandalia*[245] characterised judicial intervention in such cases as being grounded in a 'free-standing'[246] principle, 'related to the doctrine of legitimate expectations',[247] which requires that 'a decision-maker must follow his published policy … unless there are good reasons for not doing so'.[248]

There was nothing in the case law sample analysed which cast doubt on this basic principle. One minor complication was some inconsistency in terms of how challenges were framed. In some contexts, applicants relied on the idea that inconsistent application of policy is now a freestanding ground of review and framed their challenge accordingly.[249] In many cases, however, challenges continued to be framed in terms of a legitimate expectation to have policy applied.[250]

Where more significant legal complexity was present in such cases it tended to take one of two forms. First, and most commonly, these cases often raised questions about the proper *construction* of policy. The individual's 'right',[251] after all, is to have the administrative decision-maker's policy *properly* applied to the facts of her case. There were, unsurprisingly, numerous cases where the applicant and the decision-maker offered opposing interpretations of a policy and therefore disagreed on whether the content of this right had been delivered.[252] *Mandalia*[253] itself is a good example. The applicant in this case argued that an official in the Home

[240] *Rashid* (n 155).
[241] *Nadarajah* (n 4).
[242] Clayton (n 98).
[243] *Mandalia* (n 13), [29].
[244] *Lumba* (n 13).
[245] *Mandalia* (n 13).
[246] *Mandalia* (n 13) [29].
[247] *Mandalia* (n 13) [29].
[248] *Lumba* (n 13) [35].
[249] *R (Project Management Institute) v Minister for the Cabinet Office* [2016] EWCA Civ 21; [2016] 1 WLR 1737 [41].
[250] *Ibid* [40]; *R (Project Management Institute) v Minister for the Cabinet Office* [2014] EWHC 2438 (Admin).
[251] *Mandalia* (n 13) [29].
[252] *R (Majed) v Camden LBC* [2009] EWCA Civ 1029, [2010] JPL 621; *Davies* (n 102); *R (Bampton) v HMRC* [2012] EWCA Civ 1744; *Hassan* (n 87); *R (Das)v SSHD* [2013] EWHC 682 (Admin); *R (Okurut) v Secretary of State for the Home Department* [2014] EWHC 258 (Admin); *R (Carrasco) v Secretary of State for the Home Department* [2014] EWHC 3071 (Admin); *Sagar* (n 209); *Hossain* (n 136); *R (Gerber) v Wiltshire CC* [2016] EWCA Civ 84, [2016] 1 WLR 2593; *Samarkand* (n 28); *R (Liverpool CC) v Secretary of State for Health* [2017] EWHC 986 (Admin), [2017] PTSR 1564.
[253] *Mandalia* (n 13).

Department had departed from published policy which required her to alert the applicant to a minor error in her visa application and to afford her the opportunity to correct it. The Home Department, by contrast, took an opposing view of the proper meaning of its own policy. The central legal question raised by *Mandalia* was therefore a narrow interpretive question concerning the meaning of the Home Office's error-correction policy.

Second, there were numerous cases which raised questions about *which version* of an administrative decision-maker's policy the applicant's case was to be decided under.[254] A significant body of case law, for instance, arose as a result of the Home Office's 'legacy' programme. This programme aimed to clear a backlog of asylum applications[255] by creating a speedier decision-making system for individuals who had applied for asylum a number of years ago and had neither been granted asylum nor deported. Significantly, it tended to grant leave to remain on generous terms.[256] Importantly, however, the Home Office's published policy was never changed to reflect this policy. When the legacy programme was abolished, the question arose whether individuals who fell within its remit had acquired a legal right to have their cases decided under the scheme. The Court held that they did not. The individuals' rights were to have their case decided in accordance with *promulgated* policy. The Home Department had acted in accordance with this right and the more generous internal legacy programme had not altered this.

The emphasis on the importance of *promulgated* policy could also be seen to be in play, albeit in a different way, in *Save Britain's Heritage*.[257] The Secretary of State for Communities and Local Government had published a policy to the effect that a statement of reasons would be offered where a request for a planning decision to be 'called-in'[258] was rejected.[259] The Secretary of State later announced in Parliament that a new, and more restrictive, policy to call-in decisions would be implemented to reflect the Government's decision to better localise decision-making.[260] Importantly, however, the original policy relating to reason-giving was never formerly withdrawn. Because of this, the Court of Appeal concluded,[261] applicants

[254] For a classic example see *Lumba* (n 13).

[255] *R (Geraldo) v Secretary of State for the Home Department* [2013] EWHC 2703 (Admin); *R (Mohammed) v Secretary of State for the Home Department* [2014] EWHC 98 (Admin); *R (Jaku) v Secretary of State for the Home Department* [2014] EWHC 605 (Admin); *R (Mayanja) v Secretary of State for the Home Department* [2014] EWHC 2672 (Admin); *R (Shah) v Secretary of State for the Home Department* [2014] EWHC 3337 (Admin); *R (Ortiz) v Secretary of State for the Home Department* [2014] EWHC 4226 (Admin); *R (Kabashi) v Secretary of State for the Home Department* [2014] EWHC 3424 (Admin).

[256] See discussion in *R (Canameti) v SSHD* [2014] EWHC 2270 (Admin).

[257] *R (Save Britain's Heritage) v Secretary of State for Communities and Local Government* [2018] EWCA Civ 2137.

[258] Town and Country Planning Act 1990, s77.

[259] *Save Britain's Heritage* (n 257) [7]–[8].

[260] Localism Act 2011.

[261] Reversing *R (Save Britain's Heritage) v Secretary of State for Communities and Local Government* [2017] EWHC 3059 (Admin).

remained entitled under the legitimate expectations ground to have the promulgated policy to be applied to their requests.[262]

To summarise, the second common scenario in play across the case law was one in which applicants argued they were entitled to have a policy applied to their case. The basic legal principle in such cases was clear: administrative decision-makers are generally required to apply promulgated policy to the scenario before them. Where legal disputes arise, therefore, they usually concerned narrow questions of interpretation or questions concerning the proper version of a policy to be applied, rather than arguments about the overarching principles in play.

C. Third Scenario: Change of Policy without Transitional Provision for a Group

A third scenario was that in which the administrative decision-maker had changed policy direction without making transitional provisions for a group to which the applicant belonged. In these cases the applicant argued that the administrative decision-maker had acted unlawfully in either omitting to make transitional provisions at all[263] or by failing to extend the provisions to her group.[264]

Again, clear patterns could be seen in how the courts approached review in these cases. The courts, in particular, paid close attention to two main considerations.

The first was detrimental reliance. Applicants were unable to convince the courts to require an administrative decision-maker to make transitional provision for a group unless that group had materially changed its position on the basis of the original policy. A striking example of this is *Hely Hutchinson*.[265] This case concerned a challenge to a change by Her Majesty's Revenue & Customs ('HMRC') of its 2003 policy on capital gains tax. Transitional provisions were put in place under which the 2003 policy would be applied to any taxpayer who could demonstrate detrimental reliance on it.[266] The applicant, however, argued that these transitional provisions were not generous enough; there was a group of some 600[267] taxpayers who had made applications in the late 1990s whose claims were ongoing and who had legitimately expected that the 2003 policy would be applied to their cases and the transitional provisions should be extended to them. The Court of Appeal rejected this argument. Central to the Court's reasoning was that, because the applications of these taxpayers had been made prior to the introduction of the 2003 policy, they could not be said to have altered their position on the basis of it.[268]

[262] *Save Britain's Heritage* (n 257) [51].
[263] *Patel* (n 11); *Simpson* (n 207).
[264] *Hamble Fisheries* (n 53); *Grimsby* (n 190).
[265] *R (Hely Hutchinson) v HMRC* [2017] EWCA Civ 1075, [2018] 1 WLR 1682.
[266] *Ibid* [17].
[267] *Ibid* [18].
[268] *Ibid* [92]–[93].

In order to trigger a duty to make transitional provisions, it seems detrimental reliance also must be irreversible. In *Niazi*,[269] for instance, the applicant argued that it was unlawful to change the policy on the payment of legal fees in relation to miscarriage of justice applications without making a transitional provision for firms which had already entered into retainer agreements. Laws LJ rejected this argument. One major basis for doing so was that it remained open to the firms to withdraw from these arrangements.[270] Although the firms had relied on the policy statement, therefore, they retained the ability to undo any detriment which might result from it.

It also seems that, in order to convince the courts that transitional provisions must be put in place to protect groups, it is insufficient to point out that, in reliance on the prior policy, that group had taken a course of conduct which they were legally required to in any event. In *Abbassi*,[271] for instance, the applicant was not able to argue that the transitional provisions should have extended to his family because, in reliance on the decision-maker's 'seven-year child concession'[272] policy, the family had made themselves known to the Government rather than '[lying] low until their children had been [in the UK] for seven years'.[273]

In addition to detrimental reliance, the second consideration which was of particular importance in determining whether transitional provisions were required was the degree to which making transitional provisions for the relevant group would undermine the reasons for changing policy direction. Broadly, if making a transitional provision to accommodate a group which had detrimentally relied on the original policy, would not have substantially undermined the rationale for change the courts regarded the administrative decision-maker as required to make that provision. *HSMP Forum*,[274] for instance, concerned a decision to increase the minimum number of years a person must have been present in the UK before they would qualify for indefinite leave to remain ('ILR') under the highly-skilled migrants programme[275] from four to five. The reasons for the change were that the Government wished to align its approach to granting ILR with the five-year minimum used in other areas. This rationale, the Court concluded, would not be significantly undermined by the introduction of a transitional provision for the 'specific, well-defined group of people'[276] presently residing in the UK who had entered under the original programme. The numbers of persons who would be granted ILR after four years would be small[277] and the Home Office was not being prevented from applying the five-year minimum policy in future cases.

[269] *Niazi* (n 59).
[270] *Niazi* (n 59) [18].
[271] *Abbassi v Secretary of State for the Home Department* [2011] EWCA Civ 814.
[272] *Ibid* [1].
[273] *Ibid* [43].
[274] *R (HSMP Forum) v Secretary of State for the Home Department* [2009] EWHC 711 (Admin).
[275] *Ibid* [13].
[276] *Ibid* [71].
[277] *Ibid.*

By contrast, in instances where the administrative decision-maker could offer a convincing explanation as to why making a transitional provision for the relevant group would substantially compromise the rationale underlying policy change, the courts did not require the making of such provisions.[278] A good example is *Walapu*.[279] The applicant argued that in changing its approach to the investigation of tax evasion, HMRC ought to have operated a transitional approach by which it continued to apply the old policy to those who were members of suspected evasion schemes set up before the new APN scheme came into force.[280] The Court rejected this argument. Were HMRC to operate in this way the old scheme would have been applied in some 65,000 investigations[281] and the effect would be to significantly undermine Parliament's policy choice to deny taxpayers suspected of evasion of the 'cashflow advantages'[282] of the old scheme.

To summarise, there was a significant body of challenges in the case law analysed in which applicants argued that transitional provisions should have been put in place for groups to which they belonged. The courts did not accept these arguments lightly. Two considerations in particular were of overarching importance. First, detrimental reliance: the courts only required the making of transitional provisions for groups that they had materially and irreversibly changed their position in reliance on the original policy. Second, the degree to which putting in place a pipeline provision would undermine the rationale for policy change. In particular, even in contexts where a group had detrimentally relied, the courts would not require provision to be made for their cases if to do so would substantially undermine the reasons for policy change.

D. Fourth Scenario: Public Statement of Intention

The final scenario concerned statements of intention addressed to the public at large. This scenario is different from the three considered above. In the first scenario an administrative decision-maker directly communicated with an individual and offered an assurance that they would be treated in a particular way. In the second and third, an administrative decision-maker published and implemented a policy which they then failed to apply to the case of an individual (scenario two) or revoked wholesale (scenario three). The fourth scenario, by contrast, concerned statements addressed to the public at large about a policy which an administrative decision-maker intended to implement in the future. In cases in this category, the administrative decision-maker went back on the statement and the applicant argued that they ought to be held to their word. Good examples include: *Jefferies*[283]

[278] *Hamble Fisheries* (n 53).
[279] *Walapu v HMRC* [2016] EWHC 658 (Admin).
[280] Finance Act 2014, Part 4, Chapter 3.
[281] *Walapu* (n 279) [54].
[282] *Dickinson* (n 137), [12].
[283] *Jefferies* (n 200).

in which the Government had publicly announced that the Leveson Inquiry into press standards would proceed to a second stage; *United Policyholders*[284] in which the Government of Trinidad and Tobago had publicised an intention to make good on the financial commitments of an insurance company negatively impacted by the financial crisis and *Solar Century*[285] in which the Government stated publicly that a renewable obligations scheme would remain in place until a particular date. The more recent decision in *Finucane*,[286] which concerned a governmental statement that a public inquiry into the death of a solicitor in Northern Ireland would take place, also falls within this category.

The overarching theme across these cases was that it was very rarely that the courts regarded statements of this kind as having any kind of legal effect. In none of the cases in the sample did the court conclude that an administrative decision-maker was bound by a statement of intention that it would follow a particular *substantive* policy. In each of *Jefferies*, *United Policyholders*, *Solar Century* and *Finucane*, for instance, the administrative decision-maker was held to have acted lawfully in changing its position. In most of the cases the statement of intention was held not be sufficiently clear to communicate the Government's absolute commitment to a particular course of conduct.[287] In those in which the court was prepared to assume that a legitimate expectation had been generated,[288] however, emphasis was placed on the importance of permitting government to change policy direction where it had formed the view that its previous statement of intention was no longer sustainable.[289]

The small cluster of cases in which public statements of intention *were* found to have legal effect involved assurances that a change in policy would not take place until a particular process of consultation had been followed. The classic case is *Greenpeace*.[290] As discussed above, the Government in this case was found to have acted unlawfully when it went back on a statement that nuclear policy would not be altered without the 'fullest public consultation'.[291] In a similar way, in both *Buckingham*[292] and *British Dental Association*,[293] administrative decision-makers acted unlawfully when they failed to follow through on statements to the effect that major changes would only be made to their policy position following a transparent public consultation exercise.

[284] *United Policyholders* (n 59).
[285] *Solar Century Holdings Ltd v SoS for Energy & Climate Change* [2016] EWCA Civ 117.
[286] *Finucane* (n 145).
[287] *Badger Trust* (n 127); *Whitston* (n 201); *Flatley* (n 31); *Unison* (n 21); *R (Godfrey) v Southwark LBC* [2012] EWCA Civ 500; *R (Association of British Insurers) v Lord Chancellor* [2017] EWHC 106 (Admin).
[288] *United Policyholders* (n 59); *Barbone* (n 186).
[289] A further difficulty in some cases was that the public assurance related to proceedings in Parliament: *Wheeler v Office of PM* [2014] EWHC 3815 (Admin), [2015] 1 CMLR 46.
[290] *Greenpeace* (n 15).
[291] *Greenpeace* (n 15) [9].
[292] *Buckingham* (n 198).
[293] *British Dental Association* (n 209).

E. Does the Law Lack Predictability, Structure and Restraint?

At this juncture it is useful to return to, and offer some reflections on, the core question of this section: do the difficulties in developing a general account of legitimate expectations naturally suggest that the case law is unsatisfactory and that there is a significant need for reform? Section II explained that this is a popular view. The analysis in subsections A–D, however, suggests that the picture is much more nuanced.

Take, first, the common critique that the law on legitimate expectations lacks structure and predictability. This is often taken to flow from the difficulties in developing a general account of legitimate expectations. The idea is that, because there is not a singular 'meta-value'[294] or idea which guides legitimate expectations, there is a risk that judges are acting on different understandings of the doctrine. The consequence is that it is very difficult to know how a particular court will approach review or what the outcome of a challenge is likely to be.

The analysis in subsections A–D, however, suggests that this concern may be overstated. A close reading of the modern legitimate expectations case law suggests that there is more structure and predictability in the law than this critique assumes. It is possible to see within the case law four major scenarios. In the context of each, clear and consistent patterns can be seen in how the courts approached review. Those scenarios and patterns are summarised in Table 1.

Table 1 Scenarios as to How Courts Approach Review

Scenario	Approach to Review
Assurance is directly communicated to an individual	Close scrutiny of reasoning to ensure: (i) the assurance was factored in; (ii) there are good reasons for concluding that fulfilling the assurance would undermine the rationale for policy change; (iii) 'midway' options have been considered
Promulgated policy is not applied to an individual's case	Administrative decision-maker must generally apply promulgated policy unless there is a good reason not to
Policy is changed without making transitional provision for a group	Transitional provisions must be made if: (i) group has demonstrably and irreversibly detrimentally relied; and (ii) making provision would not significantly undermine the rationale for policy change
Public statement of intention is not implemented	Government not usually held to public statements of intention except outside of cases where the assurance is of consultation before policy change

Consider also the idea that the law on legitimate expectations facilitates judicial over-intervention. This is an influential critique. As explained above, numerous

[294] Tomlinson (n 158).

commentators have expressed concern that 'there is so much uncertainty that there is a real danger that the concept of legitimate expectations will collapse into an inchoate justification for judicial intervention'.[295]

The analysis in this section throws some cold water on this critique in at least two senses. First, and specifically, the doctrinal patterns which have been drawn out of each of the four scenarios suggest that judicial review is more restrained in these contexts than this criticism assumes. In 'directly communicated assurance' or 'scenario one' cases, for instance, the major focus of the courts was on ensuring that the reasoning of the decision-maker demonstrated sufficient engagement with the fact that a promise had been issued, rather than on the question of whether the assurance should or should not 'bind'. Where, furthermore, the administrative decision-maker was able to demonstrate convincingly that fulfilling the assurance would undermine its reasons for policy change, the courts did not insist on its enforcement.[296] Similarly, in 'change of policy' or 'scenario three' cases, it was only in unusual circumstances that the courts required a decision-maker to make transitional provision for a group.[297] Specifically, challenges were only successful where the relevant group had detrimentally and irreversibly relied on the original policy and accommodating them would not significantly undermine the rationale for changing direction.

If commentators are imagining, in other words, that the courts have been routinely preventing administrative decision-makers from altering policy direction by insisting that they comply with prior assurances or policy commitments, their concerns may be over-exaggerated. The patterns drawn out in this part suggest that the courts are highly wary about preventing, or undermining the reasons for, policy change. Their main concern has been to ensure that change is *managed* in a way which gives due consideration to expectations.

Second, and more generally, the case sample analysed also evidenced judicial restraint in another way. In recent years, Robert Thomas[298] and Joe Tomlinson[299] have both raised the question of whether critics of legitimate expectations overestimate the quantum of cases in which applicants have successfully relied on the ground. Tomlinson, for instance, has written that:

> … if one were to venture an observation … it would be that it is fairly difficult to find cases where the courts have actually directed the public authority to uphold the expectation. In fact, it is highly likely that there are, collectively, more monographs, journal articles and book chapters considering the potential perils of the doctrine of substantive expectations than there are cases where a public authority has been directed to act in line with its earlier representation.[300]

[295] Forsyth (n 40) 429–30.
[296] *Alansi* (n 27).
[297] *Hely Hutchinson* (n 265).
[298] Thomas (n 84).
[299] Tomlinson (n 158).
[300] Tomlinson (n 158) 81.

As both Thomas and Tomlinson have observed, it is difficult to trace precisely what proportion of legitimate expectations challenges have succeeded and no claim to that effect is made here. It is interesting to note, however, that the research underlying this part of the chapter generally supports Tomlinson's intuition. Of the 123 challenges considered, the applicant succeeded in only 22, giving a relatively low[301] success rate of just 17.9 per cent.[302] The case sample analysed for the purposes of this section, in other words, suggests that it is in reality rather difficult for applicants to successfully challenge administrative conduct on the basis of the legitimate expectations ground.

F. Two Clarifications

Before concluding, it is useful, finally, to offer two important clarifications about the analysis in this section.

First, the analysis above should not be taken to suggest that all legitimate expectations cases neatly map onto only one of the four scenarios outlined above. It is perfectly possible that a case will straddle multiple categories. This was true of some of the cases analysed. *Davis*,[303] for instance, contained elements of both scenarios one and two. Here the applicant successfully challenged the procedure used in the course of a case conference on the basis that both the administrative decision-maker had failed to act on assurances directly offered to the applicant and that there had been a failure to comply with published policy. *Patel*[304] straddled both scenarios one and three. In this case the applicant relied on assurances which had been directly communicated to him and also argued more broadly that transitional provisions should have been introduced in the GMC's new policy for a group to which he belonged. *UK Association of Fish Producer Organisations*[305] was characterised by elements of scenarios three and four. Here the applicants both argued that transitional provisions should have been put in place in DEFRA's new fishing quota allocation policy to cushion the blow of change to fishing companies and that public statements of intention to the effect that the old policy would remain in force should prevent the taking of a new course.

[301] By comparison quantitative research found applicant success rate in judicial review challenges across 2010–2012 to be 44%: Varda Bondy, Lucinda Platt and Maurice Sunkin, 'The Value and Effects of Judicial Review: The Nature of Claims, their Outcomes and Consequences' (Public Law Project, 2015) 24.

[302] The precise nature of the breach and the courts' remedial response varied considerably across this case law. The variations included affording substantive enforcement of a substantive expectation (for instance *Patel* (n 11)); procedural protection of a procedural expectation (for instance *Davis* (n 187)); procedural protection of a substantive expectation (for instance *Luton* (n 204)); reversion of the decision back to the decision-maker for reconsideration (for instance *Assisted Reproduction and Gynaecology Centre* (n 203)) and a declaration of breach of legitimate expectation (for instance *Majed* (n 252)).

[303] *Davis* (n 187).

[304] *Patel* (n 11).

[305] *UK Association of Fish Producer Organisations* (n 196).

The second issue to be addressed is the extent to which the above analysis is an argument for 'doctrinal disaggregation'.[306] As explained above, Perry and Ahmed have noted an increasing trend in the literature towards making arguments for the disaggregation of the law on legitimate expectations. Rebecca Williams, for instance, has argued for the recognition of 'multiple doctrines'[307] in the legitimate expectations case law. Jason Varuhas, similarly, has made a case for 'chipping away'[308] broad swathes of case law which are not properly categorised under the legitimate expectations head. When this is done, Varuhas argues, legitimate expectations can be understood as a very narrow doctrine, applicable in only a few circumstances, and concerned centrally with promise-keeping.

To what extent is this chapter making an argument in line with those of Williams and Varuhas and in favour of 'doctrinal disaggregation'? There are certainly very clear similarities. In particular, the first three categories of case outlined above correspond fairly closely with those proposed by Williams. What this part has shown is that, within the legitimate expectations case law, it is possible to see different scenarios in play. These scenarios can be usefully disentangled because it is possible to note clear and helpful patterns in how the courts have responded to them. What might be termed 'internal' disaggregation of legitimate expectations is therefore highly illuminating.

With that said, three further points should be noted concerning differences between the argument developed here and those of Williams and Varuhas. The first is that, as explained above, Williams and Varuhas develop arguments which are largely reactionary to what they perceive as a significant problem in the legitimate expectations case law. Their arguments are, therefore, presented as options for *reform* rather than explanations of what the courts are already doing. As Williams has put it, in her view, there is a need for a change in thinking in order to improve 'on the unpredictability of the current law'.[309] The argument in this chapter has been different in nature. Rather than presenting an agenda for reform, section IV looked closely at a body of recent legitimate expectations case law in order to examine whether judicial reasoning is characterised by fluidity and a lack of restraint. Its argument has been that a careful reading of this case law, with the complex and varied anatomy of administrative law specifically in mind, suggests that there is more structure, predictability and judicial restraint in this field than has sometimes been assumed. To put all of this another way, this section has argued that disaggregation is useful, not because it supplies an attractive option for reform, but because it helps us to develop a better understanding of *what is actually happening* in the case law.

Second, this part is consistent with the idea of doctrinal disaggregation only to an extent. To use the language above, it presents a case for 'internal' disaggregation.

[306] Ahmed and Perry (n 96) 62.
[307] Williams (n 8).
[308] Varuhas (n 104).
[309] Williams (n 8) 655.

That is, the carving out of categories *within* legitimate expectations in order to improve understanding. Others, especially Varuhas, have gone further. There are, according to Varuhas, broad swathes of case law which use the language of 'legitimate expectations' which are actually better analysed under other heads of review. This can be thought of as an argument for 'external' disaggregation. The call is for the foisting of certain categories of case into the remit of other administrative law doctrines.

The difficulties with this stronger form of disaggregation can be most usefully illuminated by discussing a specific example. One of the most important categories of case which Varuhas suggests are best analysed, not as legitimate expectations cases, but under grounds of review, are those in which an administrative decision-maker has replaced an existing policy with a new one. Such cases, Varuhas argues, ought to be recognised, not as legitimate expectations but, as *rationality* cases. The overarching question in cases of this kind is therefore whether the 'new policy itself, transitional provisions within the new policy or … the omission to make transitional arrangements'[310] were irrational.

There are at least two potential drawbacks to this argument. First, the argument that change-of-policy cases are improperly characterised as legitimate expectations challenges is difficult. Many of the best-known cases in which the courts have developed the legitimate expectations ground fit this fact pattern.[311] In recent years, the courts have been faced with a significant body of change-of-policy cases, all of which have been argued and decided under the legitimate expectations head.[312] It is difficult to see why factual contexts in which administrative decision-makers offer promises to individuals have any greater claim to be termed true 'legitimate expectations cases' than those in which a decision-maker replaces one policy with another. The presupposition seems to be that, because *Coughlan* entailed a promise to an individual,[313] then a promise must be regarded as the hallmark of a legitimate expectations case. The line of reasoning is, however, not especially convincing.[314]

The second, and more important, problem with Varuhas' argument is that explaining change-of-policy challenges as cases in which the courts decide whether transition was managed in a way which was 'rational' is simply not very illuminating. This characterisation of the case law tells us very little about how, precisely, administrative decision-makers must manage policy change in order to

[310] Varuhas (n 104).

[311] Including *Hamble Fisheries* (n 53); *Begbie* (n 7); *Niazi* (n 59); *BAPIO* (n 32).

[312] See discussion in subsection C above.

[313] *Coughlan* (n 1).

[314] For one, while *Coughlan* was decided in the Court of Appeal, there is at least one House of Lords decision (*BAPIO* (n 32)) in which the Court spoke of a change-of-policy case as giving rise to a legitimate expectations issue. For another, *Coughlan* has probably proven itself to be the most controversial legitimate expectations case on its facts (Elliott (n 75)). It is difficult to see therefore why it has any greater claim to be regarded as the 'paradigm' legitimate expectations case than other cases which have arguably offered more in terms of developing the law.

act lawfully. As has been seen in this section, there is a good deal of legal structure and predictability in this case law. This structure is, however, unhelpfully obscured by an account which characterises the courts as simply asking themselves whether the manner of change was 'rational'.

The broader lesson to be learnt here, therefore, is that there is reason to treat calls for 'external' doctrinal disaggregation with caution. Removing categories of case from the ambit of legitimate expectations might leave a narrow range of issues, thereby making it simpler to generate a singular account of the doctrine. The cost of doing this, however, might be that large clusters of case law are ignored by the account or explained through broad concepts such as 'rationality'.

Third and finally, it is also a striking feature of both Williams' and Varuhas' arguments that, in the process of disaggregation they draw close analogies between private law doctrines of contract and estoppel and, what were termed above 'scenario 1' or 'directly communicated assurance' cases.[315] Williams, for instance, characterises cases of this kind as 'almost contract'[316] cases and suggests that, in the process of disaggregation, public lawyers should look to private law for ideas as to how to develop an appropriate approach to these challenges. There is, of course, an element of truth in the comparisons between scenario one cases and the law on contract and estoppel. The direct communication of an assurance or promise is, for instance, a common feature of all. There is, however, reason to be cautious about assuming too close an analogy.

The main problem in the case of analogies with contract is that 'bindingness' in contract law is an all-or-nothing concept.[317] Either a promise forms part of a valid contract, in which case the party is bound to comply with its precise terms,[318] or it is invalid and has no binding effect.[319] As subsection A explained above, however, the courts' approach to scenario one cases in the sample considered did not have this binary quality. The courts did not ask whether the assurance was bound or not but focused, rather, on the quality of the decision-maker's reasoning process. The concern was to ensure both that the decision to disappoint the assurance was not a knee-jerk reaction taken in ignorance of it and that possibility for accommodating the applicant's case had been conscientiously explored. Relatedly, even in instances where the administrative decision-maker was permitted to go back

[315] See also Lord Carnwath's judgment in *United Policyholders* (n 59) (subsequently refined in *Finucane* (n 145)).

[316] Williams (n 8) 640.

[317] Certain forms of estoppel, especially proprietary estoppel where the focus is on 'satisfying the equity', do not have this character: *Jennings v Rice* [2002] EWCA Civ 159. The difficulty with analogies between assurance cases and estoppel however is that detrimental reliance plays a more significant role in the latter.

[318] Breach of this obligation usually results in an order to pay the full worth of the promise in compensation. Specific performance is a less common remedy: *Co-operative Insurance v Argyll Stores* [1997] 3 All ER 297 (HL).

[319] For instance, because the term amounts to a penalty clause (*ParkingEye Ltd v Beavis* [2015] UKSC 67) or violates Consumer Rights Act 2015 (see especially s62(2) which provides that unfair terms in consumer contracts are 'not binding on the consumer').

on its assurance, it is not because the assurance was not 'binding' and therefore has no legal effect whatsoever. On the contrary, the individual was still regarded as entitled to have careful consideration given to whether there were measures which would cushion the effects of the change to her. It is important not to overlook the nuanced approach the courts seem to be making use of in responding to assurance cases,[320] and to assume that private law techniques are the most appropriate guide to structuring the law.

In the case of analogies with estoppel the problem is that in order to establish many forms of estoppel it is often necessary to demonstrate detrimental reliance. On the legitimate expectations side, by contrast, detrimental reliance is a central focus in policy cases which fall within 'scenario three', discussed above. Here, as explained above, the courts have found a failure to make transitional provisions to cushion the blow of policy change to a group only where that group has detrimentally relied. In 'directly communicated assurance' or 'scenario one' cases, however, detrimental reliance played a less central role. Here the focus appears to be on ensuring that the interests of the individual recipient of an assurance are conscientiously taken into consideration in the course of the decision-making process.

V. Conclusion

The analysis in this chapter has been detailed and rich. Rather than attempting to summarise all of its arguments, it is useful to conclude by offering some reflections on the relationship between this chapter and the broader aims of the book.

As explained in the introductory chapter, this book has three main aims. First, the book aims to develop a further understanding of the 'anatomy' of administrative law and, in particular, to draw attention to three core senses in which the legal structures in play are both complex and varied. Summarised briefly they are: (a) the importance of legislative detail; (b) the plurality of values, interests and purposes the courts seek to accommodate; and (c) the variety of legal relationships which may be in play each provide reasons why legitimate expectations is not easily amenable to monistic analysis. This chapter is important because it provides a further illustration of these points. Thus section II explained that the three core senses of complexity and variety characterise the legitimate expectations case law as much as they do administrative law adjudication more broadly.

Second, the book also seeks to illustrate the important light which can be shed on specific doctrinal issues by recognising the complexity of administrative law's 'anatomy'. This chapter provides a neat case study. It has explained how the three core senses of complexity and variety in administrative law adjudication explain why it is proving difficult to explain legitimate expectations in broad, overarching

[320] Not least because it might afford a degree of protection to recipients of ultra vires assurances: *Rowland* (n 115).

terms. Section III also showed how a close reading of recent legitimate expectations case law, with the complex and varied anatomy of administrative law specifically in mind, calls attention to a series of patterns which characterise the modern legitimate expectations case law. These patterns suggest that there is good deal more predictability, structure and judicial restraint in this field than has sometimes been assumed.

Third and finally, the book also seeks to raise an important but underexplored question: is it plausible or useful to seek to explain administrative law doctrine in 'monistic' terms? That is, by identifying an overarching 'master idea or principle'[321] which guides the law? This chapter begins to indicate why there is reason for cynicism. The complexity and variety of the legal structures in play in the legitimate expectations case law mean that scholars have struggled to explain the ground in terms of a singular guiding 'meta-value'[322] or 'superior construct'.[323] It is possible that these struggles offer lessons about the plausibility of monistic analysis across administrative law more widely.

[321] Stephen Smith, *Contract Theory* (Oxford University Press, 2004) 11.
[322] Tomlinson (n 158).
[323] Elliott (n 75).

6

Standing

This chapter deals with the last of the book's case studies. The previous chapters showed how recognising the complexity and variety of administrative law's 'anatomy' sheds important light on both procedural review and legitimate expectations. This chapter makes a similar argument in the context of standing.

The discussion is divided into three main sections. Section I explores the evolution of standing in English and Welsh administrative law, focusing on four main stages:

i. pre-1977 case law;
ii. the Law Commission and the procedural reforms of the late 1970s;[1]
iii. the House of Lords' decision in *Fleet Street Casuals*;[2] and
iv. post-*Fleet Street Casuals* developments.

In exploring this history, the core point section I will stress is that the evolution of standing in English and Welsh administrative law has been beset by a tension between two sets of considerations. On the one hand, judges and scholars have sometimes sought to offer general propositions about how issues of standing are resolved by the courts. There is, for instance, a common way of thinking, according to which, prior to 1977,[3] the courts made use of a predominantly 'rights-based approach' to standing. More recently, it is also common to find broad propositions such as that, post-*Fleet Street Casuals*, the courts have developed a 'liberal'[4] test of standing, fundamentally different in nature from the 'rights-based standing rules'[5] of private law[6] and human rights law.[7] On the other hand, however, the case law, including leading recent case law, resists explanation in such terms. At none of the core stages, in other words, have the courts made use of a singular approach to standing.

[1] Rules of the Supreme Court (Amendment No 3) (SI 1977/1955).

[2] *R v Inland Revenue Commissioners, ex parte National Federation of Self-Employed* [1982] AC 617 (HL).

[3] See for instance Mark Elliott and Jason Varuhas, *Administrative Law*, 5th edn (Oxford University Press, 2016) Ch 14.

[4] See, eg, John McGarry, 'The Importance of an Expansive Test of Standing' (2014) 19(1) *Judicial Review* 60.

[5] Jason Varuhas, 'Against Unification' in Mark Elliott and Hanna Wilberg, *The Intensity and Scope of Substantive Review: Traversing Taggart's Rainbow* (Hart Publishing, 2015) 101.

[6] See, eg, *Brushmoor UK Ltd v BP Raffinaderij Rotterdam BV*, 24 February 2014 (QB) (unreported).

[7] See especially Human Rights Act 1998, s7; Joanna Miles, 'Standing under the Human Rights Act 1998' (2000) 59(1) *CLJ* 133.

The analysis in section I gives rise to at least two important questions. First, why has a singular interpretation of the sufficient interest test not emerged in English and Welsh administrative law? Second, if the courts are not using a fixed and uniform approach to decide standing issues, how do they determine whether an applicant has standing to being a challenge?

Sections II and III argue that considerable light can be shed on these questions by the broader themes of the book.

Section II argues that it is not especially surprising that a clear and uniform approach has not emerged. As with procedural review and legitimate expectations, the three senses of complexity and variety inherent in administrative law's anatomy are in play in the standing case law. Each in turn suggests a reason why a singular interpretation of 'sufficient interest' has proven elusive.

Section III then begins to grapple with the important question of how the courts determine questions about standing if they are not guided by a clear, overarching test. Answering this question in categorical terms is very difficult for a number of reasons. Section III will nonetheless draw attention to three important but often overlooked aspects of the standing jurisprudence. First, it is important to recognise that there is not one singular 'test' of standing in English administrative law. The courts, rather, make use of different approaches depending on the nature of the legal argument(s) the applicant seeks to make. Second, contrary to some of the commentary, there are contexts in which courts might be described as making use of a 'rights-based' approach, analogous to that used in private law and human rights law. To be clear, the courts do not and should not insist in every case that the applicant has a right or especially important interest at stake. The case law suggests, however, that there are categories of administrative law challenge where standing may be confined to the individual who holds the right correlative to the duty relied on in legal argument. Third and finally, it does not logically follow from the conclusion that an applicant has standing to challenge a decision on one legal ground that she has standing to rely on all. Collectively, these aspects of the courts' approach to standing can be encapsulated in the idea that standing, in English and Welsh administrative law, is 'ground-dependent'.

I. The Evolution of Standing

The first task of this chapter is to explore the evolution of the law of standing in English and Welsh administrative law. The discussion can be usefully divided into four parts:

i) pre-1977 case law;
ii) the recommendations of the Law Commission and the procedural reforms in late 1970s;[8]

[8] Rules of the Supreme Court (Amendment No 3) (SI 1977/ 1955).

iii) the House of Lords' decision in *Fleet Street Casuals*;[9] and
iv) post-*Fleet Street Casuals* developments.

This section will explore each stage in turn. The main argument developed across this section is that the evolution of standing in English and Welsh administrative law has been beset by a tension. On the one hand, judges and scholars have sometimes sought to explain the law on standing by reference to general propositions. On the other, the case law continues to resist explanation in this way. The courts, in other words, have generally maintained that different approaches to standing are appropriate in different contexts.

A. Pre-1977

The first stage in the development of standing concerns the pre-1977 case law. As explained in chapter two, there was, at this time, no purpose-built procedural route by which challenges to administrative decisions could proceed. As a result, barristers[10] had creatively repurposed procedural routes which had originated for other purposes. By the late 1970s, therefore, administrative law challenges were commonly brought as an application or claim for one, or a combination, of five remedies: the three prerogative writs[11] – certiorari, mandamus and prohibition – or the private law remedies of the declaration and injunction. These procedural routes had, however, originated for the purpose of providing relief in cases which had specific sets of features. When applicants sought to use them in new contexts, difficult questions about standing often arose.[12]

On the question of how these questions were dealt with,[13] it is helpful to begin with the following passage from Mark Elliott and Jason Varuhas' leading textbook:

> Up until at least the late 1970s three features characterised the law on standing. First, different rules of standing applied to different remedies. Second, judicial review generally and the law of standing specifically more closely adhered to the rights-based or private law model of review rather than to the public interest model. Third, the law on standing was characterised by inconsistency.[14]

[9] *Fleet Street Casuals* (n 2).

[10] Stephen Sedley, *Lions under the Throne: Essays on the History of English Public Law* (Cambridge University Press, 2015) Ch 1.

[11] Stanley De Smith, 'The Prerogative Writs' (1951) 11(1) *CLJ* 40; Edith Henderson, *Foundations of English Administrative Law: Certiorari and Mandamus in the Seventeenth Century* (Harvard University Press, 2013); Paul Craig, *UK, EU and Global Administrative Law: Foundations and Challenges* (Cambridge University Press, 2015) Ch 1.

[12] Note that not all of the complications arose as issues of standing: Philip Murray, 'Process, Substance and the History of Error of Law Review' in John Bell, Mark Elliott, Jason Varuhas and Philip Murray (eds), *Public Law Adjudication in Common Law Systems: Process and Substance* (Hart Publishing, 2016).

[13] Stanley De Smith, *Judicial Review of Administrative Action* (Stevens, 1951); Paul Craig, *Administrative Law*, 8th edn (Sweet & Maxwell, 2016) Ch 25.

[14] Elliott and Varuhas (n 3) 548.

This passage is interesting because it embodies the tension this section draws attention to. On the one hand, the second proposition – that 'the law of standing … generally … adhered to a rights-based or private law model of review' – seeks to explain the case law on standing by reference to a general, overarching conception of standing. The idea being posited is that it is possible to carve out two broad ways of thinking about the nature of administrative law and how issues of standing should be approached within it. According to the first which is termed the 'rights-based model':

> … the principal concern of judicial review is to ensure protection of and grant remedies for invasion of the individuals' personal rights and interests. Within this model standing would be limited to the holders of those legal entitlements and interests which are the object of the law's protection.[15]

This model of administrative law, in other words, views administrative law as concerned with identifying and protecting fundamental individual interests. It therefore regards standing as confined to those individuals who are able to show that an administrative decision has infringed such an interest.[16]

By contrast, according to the second view:

> … the principal function of judicial review is to ensure that administrators exercise their powers properly in accordance with … the public purposes for which parliament has conferred those powers … On this account, a rights-based test [of standing] would … unduly constrain the courts' ability to intervene where an authority had clearly acted unlawfully and deviated from public goals.[17]

Elliott and Varuhas suggest that the law on standing prior to 1977 'more closely adhered to' the first way of thinking. On this understanding, prior to 1977, the judiciary tended to understand administrative law as a mechanism for protecting the individual and shaped their approach to standing accordingly. This is in accordance with Varuhas' suggestion elsewhere that there was, at this time, an 'old'[18] vision of administrative law in operation 'which ha[d] individual rights and interests at its heart'.[19]

While their second proposition seeks to explain the pre-1977 standing case law by reference to a *general* understanding of administrative law and standing, Elliott and Varuhas' first and third propositions point to a somewhat different idea: there was not, in practice, a singular test of standing in operation at this time. Rather distinct bodies of precedents had grown up around each of the main remedies. These bodies of precedents were, furthermore, often very complex. An example of this was discussed in chapter two. The application for mandamus expanded across

[15] Elliott and Varuhas (n 3) 546.

[16] Louis L Jaffe, 'Standing to Secure Judicial Review: Private Actions' (1961) 75(2) *Harvard Law Review* 255; Gerald Frug, 'The Ideology of Bureaucracy' (1983–1984) 97 *Harvard Law Review* 1276.

[17] Elliott and Varuhas (n 3) 546.

[18] Jason Varuhas, 'Judicial Review at the Crossroads' (2015) 74(2) *CLJ* 215, 215.

[19] *Ibid.*

the seventeenth century in order to provide relief to individuals who had been removed from office and denied statuses.[20] When, from at least the late 1800s,[21] applicants sought mandamus to enforce statutory duties benefitting collective interests, a difficult question arose: to what extent was mandamus available for applicants who could claim no personal right to have a legal duty performed? The case law on mandamus illustrates the difficulties the court had in developing a coherent answer to this question.[22]

The consequence of all of this is that Elliott and Varuhas' three propositions do not sit particularly comfortably with each other. The complexity in, and variety of approaches to standing across, the pre-1977 case law make it difficult to accept, at least without very heavy qualification, the statement that 'the law of standing … generally … adhered to a rights-based or private law model of review'. There are at least two particular issues with this suggestion.

First, while there are certainly early cases which can be quite naturally analysed as instances where the courts made use of a 'rights-based' approach to standing, it is also not difficult to find well-known challenges where the courts made use of much broader approaches. A clear example of a case of the first sort is *Lewisham Union Guardians*[23] which was discussed at length in chapter two. In *Lewisham Union Guardians*, the Divisional Court refused to consider compelling the guardians of the poor to take steps to safeguard the public against the spread of infectious disease.[24] The reason given by the Court was that an 'applicant, in order to entitle himself to a mandamus, must first of all shew that he has a legal specific right to ask for the interference of the court'.[25] The Court went on to explain that, in its view, it:

> … would be far exceeding its proper functions if it were to assume jurisdiction to enforce the performance by public bodies of all their statutory duties without requiring clear evidence that the person who sought its interference *had a legal right to insist upon such performance*.[26]

Mandamus, in other words, was treated as confined to contexts in which the duty alleged to have been breached correlated with a right held by the individual. Chapter two also discussed the difficulties with confining mandamus in this way. The effect of doing so was to render statutory duties enacted to benefit collective, as opposed to individual, interests very difficult if not impossible to enforce.

[20] De Smith (n 13) 55; *Bagg's Case* (1615) 11 Co Rep 93b.

[21] *R v Guardians of the Lewisham Union* [1897] 1 QB 498 (DC).

[22] *Ibid*; *R v Russell ex parte Beaverbrook Newspapers Ltd* [1969] 1 QB 342 (DC); *R v Commissioners of Customs & Excise, ex parte Cook* [1970] 1 WLR 450 (QB); *R v Hereford Corporation, ex parte Harrower* [1970] 1 WLR 1424 (QBD).

[23] *Lewisham Union Guardians* (n 21).

[24] Vaccination Act 1871.

[25] *Lewisham Union Guardians* (n 21) 500.

[26] *Lewisham Union Guardians* (n 21) (emphasis added).

Not every issue of standing was resolved so restrictively prior to 1977, however. Consider, for instance, *Blackburn*.[27] Mr Blackburn sought a prohibition to prevent a licensing authority from permitting an indecent film to be shown in a local cinema on the basis of a breach of the Obscene Publications Act.[28] On the question of whether the applicant had standing, Lord Denning opined as follows:

> It was suggested that Mr Blackburn has no sufficient interest … On this point I would ask: who then can bring proceedings when a public authority is guilty of misuse of power? Mr Blackburn is a citizen … His wife is a ratepayer. He has children who may be harmed by the exhibition of pornographic films. If he has no sufficient interest, no other citizen has.[29]

Lord Denning's suggestion here is that the Obscene Publications Act sought to advance the 'public-regarding'[30] aim of preventing obscene publications. That is, its aim was not to benefit any identifiable individual, but to safeguard the public more broadly. It was important, Lord Denning explained, that the courts' approach to standing in prohibition challenges should not 'unduly constrain'[31] it from protecting the public's interests in that context. It would, therefore, have been improper to deny Mr Blackburn standing on the basis that he did not hold a personal legal right entitling him to fulfilment of the relevant duty.

Second, and more broadly, there are difficulties with analysing the pre-1977 standing case law in terms of normative 'models' of standing. This form of analysis frames the complexities which existed at this time in terms of competing normative visions of the nature of administrative law. That is, it understands different views expressed in *Lewisham Union Guardians*[32] and *Blackburn*[33] as the result of different judges' proceedings from different understandings of the purpose of administrative law. To think in this way, however, overlooks an important point emphasised in chapter two: much of the complexity which pervaded the case law at this time was procedural in nature. Before 1977, issues of administrative law arose as claims for a series of different remedies, each of which had their own rich and complex history. The reality, accordingly, was that differences in the case law can, at best, be only partly explained as the product of differing visions of administrative law. The complications surrounding standing were also the result of applicants bringing different kinds of claim, each of which was surrounded by its own history and body of precedents.[34]

[27] *R v Greater London Council, ex parte Blackburn* [1976] 1 WLR 550 (CA).

[28] Obscene Publications Act 1959, s1(1).

[29] *Blackburn* (n 27) 558. See also *Attorney General (McWhirter) v Independent Broadcasting Authority* [1973] QB 629 (CA).

[30] Varuhas (n 5) 52.

[31] Elliott and Varuhas (n 3) 546.

[32] *Lewisham Union Guardians* (n 21).

[33] *Blackburn* (n 27).

[34] The 'difference', for example, between the courts' response in a case such as *Lewisham Union Guardians* (n 21) and a case such as *Blackburn* (n 33) was likely to a large degree due to the fact that these cases were brought as applications or claims for different remedies; in the former case, a mandamus, in the latter, a prohibition.

B. The Law Commission Report and the 1977 Procedural Reforms

The second stage standing's development concerns the procedural reforms of the 1970s. In response to the issues discussed in the previous subsection, the Law Commission published an influential report on procedure and remedies in administrative law in 1976.[35] This report recommended substantial change. At the core of the Commission's recommendations was the creation of a unified process termed the 'application for judicial review'[36] ('AJR'). Through this process, an applicant would be able to claim any one, or a combination of certiorari, mandamus, prohibition, declaration and injunction. The AJR procedure, as recommended by the Law Commission, would have two stages:

a) the applicant would apply to the High Court for permission;[37]
b) if permission were granted, there would then be a substantive hearing.

Most interesting, for present purposes, are the Law Commission's recommendations on standing. Here, the Law Commission recommended a change of approach. The Law Commission, in particular, argued that, regardless of the remedy which the applicant sought to claim, standing issues should be framed in terms of a singular question: whether the applicant had 'such interest as the Court considered sufficient in the matter to which the application relates'.[38] It might be tempting to understand this recommendation as an attempt to put in place a general formulation which would be applied uniformly in all cases. This was not, however, the basis of the Law Commission's recommendation. Here, it is worth citing the Law Commission's reasoning in full:

> The predominant view expressed in the consultation on our Working Paper … was that any attempt to define in precise terms the nature of the standing requirement would run the risk of imposing an undesirable rigidity … We appreciate this danger, and think that what is needed is a formula which allows for further development of the requirement of standing by the court having regard to the relief which is sought.[39]

This passage illustrates that the Law Commission's endorsement of the 'sufficient interest' formulation was based on a concern to ensure, not uniformity, but flexibility and adaptability. The Law Commission was of the view that it would be inappropriate to try to define in the abstract a precise standing criterion which should apply in every case. The perceived of the 'sufficient interest' test lay in the fact that it was *vague* and would therefore delegate to the judiciary the task of continuing to develop the law on standing. Relatedly, the Law Commission

[35] Law Commission, 'Report on Remedies in Administrative Law' (Law Comm No 73, 1976).
[36] *Ibid* [43]–[44].
[37] *Ibid* [46].
[38] *Ibid* [48].
[39] *Ibid* [48].

made no assumption that the courts would use this remit to introduce a singular approach to standing. On the contrary, the Law Commission clearly envisaged that the courts would continue to 'have regard' to the precise form of relief sought in determining the appropriate approach to standing in a given case.

To put all of this another way, the Law Commission's report itself is an illustration of the tension between generality and variability in the development of standing. On the one hand, the Law Commission recommended simplifying the law with a general sufficiency of interest test. On the other, it clearly envisaged that that test would function differently in different cases.

The Law Commission's recommendations proved to be influential. The AJR procedure was introduced in 1977 through an amendment to the Supreme Court Rules.[40] This was later incorporated into primary legislation in 1981.[41] In introducing these reforms, Parliament accepted in full the Law Commission's recommendations on standing. The applicable legislation therefore now provides that 'the court shall not grant leave to make such an application unless it considers that the applicant has a sufficient interest in the matter to which the application relates'.[42]

C. The *Fleet Street Casuals* Case

The third major stage in the development of standing concerns the decision in *Fleet Street Casuals*.[43] This case saw the House of Lords grapple with the 'sufficient interest' test for the first time. It is a deeply interesting case because it illustrates again, and in a very clear way, the tension to which this section draws attention between generality and variability in the law on standing.

Fleet Street Casuals concerned a challenge by a representative organisation[44] to a decision by the tax authorities to grant an 'amnesty'[45] to a group of casual workers. The effect of the amnesty was to exempt these workers from paying tax relating to previous years in exchange for a commitment to follow a particular tax declaration procedure in the future. The applicant sought a declaration to the effect that the granting of this amnesty was unlawful[46] and a mandamus compelling the proper collection of tax.

The judgments of the House of Lords in the case reflect important differences in their understanding and application of the new sufficient interest test. Their Lordships, in particular, can be divided into three groups.

[40] Rules of the Supreme Court (Amendment No 3) (SI 1977/1955).

[41] Senior Court Act 1981.

[42] *Ibid*, s31(3).

[43] *Fleet Street Casuals* (n 2).

[44] Dominic de Cogan, '*CIR v National Federation of Self-Employed and Small Businesses* 1981: All Grievances Converging on Tax Law' in John Snape and Dominic de Cogan (eds), *Landmark Cases in Revenue Law* (Hart Publishing, 2019).

[45] *Fleet Street Casuals* (n 2) 629.

[46] *Fleet Street Casuals* (n 2) 629.

In the first group was the majority – Lords Wilberforce, Fraser and Roskill. A number of broad themes run through their Lordships' judgments. The first is that these judges emphasised that the purpose of the sufficient interest test was *not* to introduce a singular approach to standing, which would be applied identically in every case. The courts' approach to standing, rather, was to be shaped by the argument the applicant sought to make. Different approaches to standing, in other words, would be appropriate in different types of challenge. Thus Lord Wilberforce explained that:

> The fact that the same words are used [in the sufficient interest test] to cover all the forms of remedy allowed by the rule does not mean that the test is the same in all cases ... The interest of a person seeking to compel an authority to carry out a duty [therefore] is different from that of a person complaining that a judicial or administrative body has, to his detriment, exceeded its powers.[47]

A further important theme was the idea that, where an applicant sought to argue that an administrative decision-maker had failed to comply with duties conferred on it by legislation, it was important to consider closely the precise detail and underlying purposes of the statute.[48] It was important in the majority's view that the courts' approach to standing, at the very least, did not undermine the aims and structure of the legislation.

Lastly, their Lordships were of the view that, when one undertook this exercise in the context of the legislative background[49] to the *Fleet Street Casuals* case it became clear that the applicants seeking to challenge decisions concerning the treatment of others by the tax authorities they would often lack a sufficient interest to do so. A number of the features of the background legislative scheme led the majority to this view.[50] In the first place, the tax framework, did not make explicit provision for taxpayers to challenge the lawfulness of decisions made by the administrators responsible for implementing the scheme. In this way it was fundamentally different from the rate framework.[51] In the second place, in their Lordships' view, the legislation also made clear that the duties contained therein were owed *to the Crown*, rather than to members of the public. Finally, and most importantly, the legislation made explicit provision for the absolute confidentiality of the affairs of an individual taxpayer. The recognition of an ability, on the part of a third party taxpayer, to challenge the lawfulness of the level of tax paid by another, was thought to undermine the centrality of confidentiality.

The second opinion expressed in the *Fleet Street Casuals* case was that of Lord Scarman. Though his Lordship would have ultimately recognised the standing of the federation had he been convinced that their grounds were arguable, his

[47] *Fleet Street Casuals* (n 2) 631.
[48] *Fleet Street Casuals* (n 2) 646.
[49] Inland Revenue Act 1890; Taxes Management Act 1970.
[50] *Fleet Street Casuals* (n 2) 633.
[51] General Rate Act 1967.

judgment bore a great deal of similarity to the view of the majority. Lord Scarman accepted many of the themes which characterised the majority's judgments, including the importance of paying close attention to the particular legislative scheme where applicants based their legal challenges centrally on it.[52] Where his Lordship differed from the majority was in interpreting the tax regime and extracting its implications for standing. On this point, Lord Scarman rejected Lord Wilberforce's characterisation of the tax authorities' duties as being owed to the Crown. More fundamentally, Lord Scarman also concluded that the legislative scheme, when read in light of the common law, included a 'legal duty owed by the revenue *to the general body of the taxpayers* to treat taxpayers fairly'.[53] The federation, as a body representing the interests of taxpayers, was regarded by Lord Scarman as having standing to challenge alleged breaches of this duty.

The third and final opinion expressed in *Fleet Street Casuals* was that of Lord Diplock. In an oft-cited passage his Lordship opined that:

> It would, in my view, be a grave lacuna in our system of public law if a pressure group, like the federation, or even a single public-spirited taxpayer, were prevented by outdated technical rules of locus standi from bringing the matter to the attention of the court to vindicate the rule of law and get the unlawful conduct stopped.[54]

Lord Diplock's judgment represents a approach to that taken by the rest of their Lordships. The main difference is that, whereas the other judges focused on determining what constituted a sufficient interest in the *tax administration* context, Lord Diplock sought a more generalised conception of standing.[55] According to Lord Diplock, the court's approach to standing should proceed from a general recognition of the importance of 'vindicat[ing] the rule of law'. In light of this, 'pressure groups' and 'public-spirited taxpayers'[56] ought to be granted easy access to the courts in administrative law challenges, and the central question ought in all cases to be whether they are able to advance arguable challenges. As Mark Elliott and Jason Varuhas put it, Lord Diplock's judgment therefore envisaged a general 'public interest model of standing'.[57]

D. Post-*Fleet Street Casuals*

The final stage in the development of standing concerns the case law and the literature which has followed from their Lordships' judgment in *Fleet Street Casuals*. Again the post-*Fleet Street Casuals* developments illustrate the tension between

[52] *Fleet Street Casuals* (n 2) 648–49.
[53] *Fleet Street Casuals* (n 2) 651 (emphasis added).
[54] *Fleet Street Casuals* (n 2) 644.
[55] On Lord Diplock's influence in the evolution of administrative law, see Richard Wilberforce, 'Lord Diplock and Administrative Law' [1986] *PL* 6.
[56] *Fleet Street Casuals* (n 2) 644.
[57] Elliott and Varuhas (n 3) 533.

generality and variability which is visible in earlier stages. Two main developments are worth explicit consideration.

The first has been discussed at some length in chapter two and so can be outlined briefly here. One of the earliest cases decided following the *Fleet Street Casuals* decision was *Rose Theatre*.[58] As explained in chapter two, Schiemann J read the majority in *Fleet Street Casuals* as purporting to lay down a *general test* of standing. In particular, he read their Lordships as having decided that the task of the court in all cases was to look to 'the statute under which the decision was taken … and decide whether that statute gives that individual expressly or impliedly a greater right or expectation than any other citizen of this country to have the decision taken lawfully'.[59] This was an unfortunate decision. Part of the issue was that it overlooked that, in determining *Fleet Street Casuals*, the majority of the House of Lords had not sought to articulate a general approach. They had, rather, sought to determine what should count as a sufficient interest in the *tax administration context*, bearing in mind the details of the legislative framework. Another was that, had Schiemann J's approach been embraced on a generalised basis, it would have had the unfortunate consequence of rendering statutory duties, enacted to protect broader collective interests as opposed to those of any one individual, effectively unenforceable. To return to *Lewisham Union Guardians*,[60] all citizens had an interest in the containment of infectious diseases. None, however, could be said to have a 'greater right or expectation than any other citizen' to have the guardians of the poor to take steps to ensure this. This consideration in particular led Sedley J to cast doubt on Schiemann J's judgment in *Dixon*.[61]

A second development worth considering concerns an important cluster of cases decided across the 1980s and 1990s. Very broadly, in these cases a representative organisation[62] or 'public-spirited'[63] individual[64] challenged an administrative decision on the basis that it undermined a collective interest protected by a legislative scheme. As chapter two described, the courts have developed the idea of 'representative' or 'public interest standing'[65] in order to facilitate review in these cases. A well-known example is the *World Development Movement* case.[66]

[58] *R v Secretary of State for the Environment, ex parte Rose Theatre* [1990] 1 QB 504 (QB).

[59] *Ibid.*

[60] *Lewisham Union Guardians* (n 21).

[61] *R v Somerset Country Council, ex parte Dixon* [1998] Env LR 111 (QB).

[62] *R v Inspectorate of Pollution ex parte Greenpeace (No 2)* [1994] 2 CMLR 548 (QB).

[63] *Fleet Street Casuals* (n 2) 644.

[64] *R v HM Treasury, ex parte Smedley* [1984] QB 657 (CA); *R v Secretary of State for Foreign and Commonwealth Affairs, ex parte Rees-Mogg* [1994] QB 522 (QB); *R v Somerset Country Council, ex parte Dixon* [1998] Env LR 111 (QB); *Walton v Scottish Ministers* [2012] UKSC 44, [2013] PTSR 51.

[65] Peter Cane, 'Standing up for the Public' [1995] *PL* 276; David Feldman, 'Public Interest Litigation and Constitutional Theory in Comparative Perspective' (1992) 55 *MLR* 44; Tom Mullen, 'Public Interest Litigation in Scotland' (2015) *Juridical Review* 363.

[66] *R v Secretary of State for Foreign and Commonwealth Affairs, ex parte World Development Movement* [1995] 1 WLR 386 (QB).

The applicant non-governmental organisation challenged a financial grant relating to an 'economically unsound'[67] project, on the basis that it was contrary to the aim of the Overseas Development and Co-operation Act 1980[68] of ensuring effective distribution of the foreign aid fund. The Divisional Court accepted that the applicant organisation had standing to make this challenge: factors such as 'the importance of vindicating the rule of law'[69] and 'the prominent role of these applicants in giving advice, guidance and assistance with regard to aid'[70] meant that the organisation should be recognised as having standing to safeguard the public's collective interest.[71]

These cases have sometimes been received, or at least spoken about, as laying down a new and general approach to standing. One prevalent idea, for instance, is that cases such as *World Development Movement* have concretised a general 'liberal' test of standing. Elliott and Varuhas, for instance, have spoken of Lord Diplock's broader and general approach in *Fleet Street Casuals* as having 'won out'[72] over the more contextualised approach of the other judges.

John McGarry has also observed that:[73]

> It is [the] perceived need to hold the Government to account that underlies the courts' development of the *current liberal approach* to the question of standing. The ruling of the House of Lords in *Fleet Street Casuals* may be seen as the beginning of that approach.[74]

In a similar way, SH Bailey has said of the Supreme Court's judgment in *Walton*[75] that the:

> … observations [of their Lordships] … are generally consistent with the *flexible, and relatively liberal,* approach to standing to be found in the cases on standing [in England and Wales].[76]

Another prevalent idea is that, post-*Fleet Street Casuals* the courts have rejected the 'rights-based standing rules'[77] of private law[78] and human rights law[79] for one which focuses on *public* interests. The idea is as follows: in both private law and human rights law the courts can aptly be said to make use of a

[67] *Ibid* 402.
[68] Overseas Development and Co-operation Act 1980 (since repealed by International Development Act 2002).
[69] *World Development Movement* (n 66) 395.
[70] *World Development Movement* (n 66) 395.
[71] See also *Greenpeace* (n 62); *R v Poole BC, ex parte Beebee* [1991] JPL 642 (QB).
[72] *Fleet Street Casuals* (n 2) 644.
[73] McGarry (n 4).
[74] McGarry (n 4) [13] (emphasis added).
[75] *Walton v Scottish Ministers* [2012] UKSC 44, [2013] PTSR 51.
[76] SH Bailey, 'Reflections on Standing for Judicial Review in Procurement Cases' (2015) 4 *Public Procurement Law Review*122, 128 (emphasis added).
[77] Varuhas (n 5) 101.
[78] See, eg, *Brushmoor* (n 6).
[79] See especially Human Rights Act 1998, s7.

'rights-based approach'.[80] This approach involves confining the ability to rely on a legal duty in legal proceedings to the individual who holds *the right which is correlative* to that duty. In the event that any person other than the right-holder seeks to rely on the duty, her claim generally fails for want of locus standi.

Two examples will suffice to illustrate.[81] Take, first, *Brushmoor*[82] which concerned a confidentiality agreement. Sometime after entering the agreement, the claimant assigned its rights to a third party. When the claimant became concerned that the defendant had acted in breach of its duties, the question arose whether it had standing to rely on them. The Court's answer was that it did not: from the point at which the claimant's rights were assigned to the third party, the rights which were correlative to the defendant's duties were vested in that third party. Accordingly, the third party, and the third party alone, had standing to enforce the duties.[83] By way of a second illustration, consider the Human Rights Act 1998. Under section 7,[84] standing to argue that a body exercising a 'public function'[85] has acted in breach of its legal duty to abide by Convention rights[86] is limited to the 'victim' of the alleged breach. As Joanna Miles has explained,[87] the effect of this provision is to create a relationship of 'privity' between public bodies and individuals. Challenges to conduct which breach duties under the Human Rights Act 1998 is thereby limited to right-holders.[88]

According to the influential view under consideration, Lord Diplock's judgment in *Fleet Street Casuals* encouraged the court to develop a fundamentally different approach to standing in administrative law. This approach focuses on promoting the interests of the public rather than protecting individual rights. Take for instance, the following passage written by Jason Varuhas:

> The courts have recognised that the exercise of the court's supervisory jurisdiction necessarily requires a different approach to standing from the rights-based approach in other fields … [administrative law] protects something we all have a legitimate interest in: the proper exercise of public power in the public interest. It is true that individual detriment is a factor that goes to standing. But it is in the nature of an indicator of

[80] Varuhas (n 5) 52.

[81] For further examples see *Kirkpatrick v Snoozebox Ltd* [2014] BCC 477 (QB); *Meadows Insurance Co Ltd & Insurance Corporation of Ireland v International Commercial Bank* [1989] 2 Lloyd's Rep 298 (CA).

[82] *Brushmoor* (n 6).

[83] *Brushmoor* (n 6) [20].

[84] Human Rights Act 1998, s7.

[85] *Ibid*, s6; *Aston Cantlow Parochial Church Council v Wallbank* [2003] UKHL 37; *YL v Birmingham CC* [2007] UKHL 27, [2008] 1 AC 95; Dawn Oliver, 'Functions of a Public Nature under the Human Rights Act' [2004] *PL* 329; Maurice Sunkin, 'Pushing Forward the Frontiers of Human Rights Protection: The Meaning of Public Authority Under the Human Rights Act' [2004] *PL* 643.

[86] Convention for the Protection of Human Rights and Fundamental Freedoms (European Convention on Human Rights, as amended) as incorporated into the Human Rights Act 1998 by Sch 1.

[87] Miles (n 7); Joanna Miles, 'Standing in a Multi-Layered Constitution' in Nicholas Bamforth and Peter Leyland (eds), *Public Law in a Multi-Layered Constitution* (Hart Publishing, 2003).

[88] For a controversial recent example, see *Northern Ireland Human Rights Commission's Application for Judicial Review* [2018] UKSC 27; Jane M Rooney, 'Standing and the Northern Ireland Human Rights Commission' (2019) 82(3) *MLR* 525.

> the genuineness of the applicant's claim. That is, it tells against the application being 'prompted by an ill-motive' or the applicant being a 'mere busybody or a troublemaker' such that standing should be denied for abuse of process.[89]

The idea being expressed in this passage is that, post-*Fleet Street Casuals*, administrative law has come to be understood as promoting a distinct set of normative concerns from those which arise in private law[90] and human rights law.[91] Its concern, in particular, is seen as the promotion of public as opposed to individual interests. As a result of this, courts make use of a broader approach to standing. This involves rejecting the 'rights-based standing rules'[92] which prevail in other areas and focusing on motive. In particular, issues of standing in administrative law are resolved by considering whether the applicant has initiated legal proceedings as a result of a 'sincere'[93] or 'genuine concern'[94] that the public authority had acted unlawfully, or for some other 'ill motive'.[95]

These examples illustrate an important point. They demonstrate a common way of thinking about the *World Development Movement* line of cases. According to it, those precedents have concretised a new and general approach to standing. This approach has been described in different ways. It is sometimes referred to as 'liberal'. Others have characterised it as a rejection of a rights-based approach in favour of one which focuses on promoting the public interest. Regardless of these differences, the important point is it is common to find reference to the idea that the post-*Fleet Street Casuals* case law has established a broad approach to standing.

Propositions such as these, however, are not borne out consistently across the case law. Three complexities in particular should be discussed.

The first is that courts, including those at the highest levels, have emphasised explicitly that what counts as a 'sufficient interest' alters depending on legislative and administrative context. The courts, that is, continue to resist the idea that there is a *singular approach* to standing which applies in all challenges. This notion can be seen most clearly in the judgments of the two modern leading Supreme Court cases on standing: *AXA*[96] and *Walton*.[97] In the former, Lord Reed explained that:

> A requirement that the applicant demonstrate an interest in the matter complained of *will not … operate satisfactorily if it is applied in the same way in all contexts.* In some contexts, *it is appropriate to require an applicant for judicial review to demonstrate that*

[89] Varuhas (n 5) 101.
[90] Varuhas (n 18).
[91] Varuhas (n 5).
[92] Varuhas (n 5) 101–102; Varuhas (n 18) 57–60.
[93] *Rees-Mogg* (n 64).
[94] *R (Feakins) v Secretary of State for the Environment, Food and Rural Affairs* [2003] EWCA Civ 1546, [2004] 1 WLR 1761 [23].
[95] *Ibid*; *Morbaine Ltd v First Secretary of State* [2004] EWHC 1708 (Admin), [2005] JPL 377 [15].
[96] *AXA General Insurance Ltd v HM Advocate* [2011] UKSC 46, [2012] 1 AC 868.
[97] *Walton* (n 64) [92]–[94].

> *he has a particular interest in the matter complained of*: the type of interest which is relevant, and therefore required in order to have standing, will depend upon the particular context. In other situations, such as where the excess or misuse of power affects the public generally, insistence upon a particular interest could prevent the matter being brought before the court and that in turn might disable the court from performing its function to protect the rule of law.[98]

Lord Reed explains here that what is recognised as a sufficient interest alters depending on the context. In certain kinds of administrative law challenge, such as those where an alleged 'excess or misuse of power affected the public generally',[99] it may be proper to make use of a liberal approach which recognises the standing of any properly motivated individual or organisation able to make an arguable case. In other contexts, however, Lord Reed suggests a more restrictive approach may be appropriate. In such cases, the court might insist that the applicant show 'a particular interest in the matter complained of'.[100]

This leads on to a second important point: there are significant examples of modern case law in which the courts have taken an approach to standing which is not easily described as 'liberal'. A good example is *DSD*.[101] The Mayor of London sought to challenge the decision of the Parole Board to release a convicted sex offender on licence. The Administrative Court concluded that he lacked standing to bring the challenge.[102] The Court explained that:

> The Mayor is, of course entitled to comment on Parole Board decisions, and any concerns he might express would attract public attention, but, in our view, he is no different position from any other politician, or indeed, any member of the public … *There are situations where the court adopts a very liberal approach to the issue of standing, but this is not one of them.*[103]

The third and final point is that the idea that the courts have repudiated the 'rights-based approach'[104] to standing in favour of one which focuses on the public interest reflects only a partial truth. On the one hand, it is certainly the case that the courts clearly do not insist, in every case, that the applicant demonstrates that she has a personal legal right to have the requisite legal duty performed.[105] On the other however, this does not rule out the possibility that there are categories of case in which standing to rely on a legal duty *is* confined to a single individual. This point will be discussed in detail in section III. For present purposes, however, it suffices to point to the following passage written by Sarah Nason:

> Whilst many Administrative Court applications for judicial review fit within these constitutional categories, still a large proportion (perhaps as many as half) of all

[98] *AXA* (n 96) [170] (emphasis added).
[99] *AXA* (n 96) [170].
[100] *AXA* (n 96) [170].
[101] *R (DSD) v Parole Board* [2018] EWHC 694 (Admin), [2018] 3 WLR 829.
[102] The Court also went on to doubt the standing of victims of offenders.
[103] *DSD* (n 101) [109]–[110] (emphasis added).
[104] Varuhas (n 5) 101.
[105] *Rose Theatre* (n 58); *Dixon* (n 61).

> claims are own fact (individual grievance) claims that do not turn out to have wider consequences for the development of legal principles, human rights or administrative practice.[106]

What Nason is drawing attention to here is a disparity between the influential idea that administrative law is concerned with promoting the interests of the public and the day-to-day realities of Administrative Court adjudication. A considerable proportion of applications for judicial review, Nason points out, are claims brought by individuals seeking to challenge particularised decisions, such as in the social security and housing contexts. It is important, in other words, not to assume that 'public interest' cases, such as *World Development Movement*, are reflective of all, or even the bulk, of administrative law adjudication.

By way of concluding this section it is helpful to offer a brief summary of its main points. This section has explored the development of standing, beginning with the pre-1977 position. It has argued that the law and literature on standing has been beset with a tension. On the one hand, scholars and judges have sometimes sought to explain standing in terms of a singular overarching test or approach. On the other, the case law makes use of different approaches. Most visibly, the Supreme Court has argued explicitly that 'a requirement that the applicant demonstrate an interest in the matter complained of *will not … operate satisfactorily if it is applied in the same way in all contexts*'.[107]

This analysis gives rise to at least two questions. First, why has a singular approach to standing not emerged in English and Welsh administrative law? Second, if the courts are not determining questions about standing by reference to a singular overarching test, how are they deciding whether applicants have a sufficient interest? The remainder of this chapter argues that significant light is shed on these questions by the broader themes of this book.

II. Why has a Singular Approach to Standing not Emerged?

This section considers the first of these questions: why has a singular approach to standing not emerged in English law? This is an important question. It might appear to some that the procedural reforms presented the courts with an opportunity to simplify the law by attributing a singular meaning to 'sufficient interest'. The Supreme Court's suggestion that what constitutes a sufficient interest varies from context to context might be thought of as a failure to embrace that opportunity. The core argument of this section, however, is that recognising the complexity and variety of administrative law's 'anatomy' sheds considerable light on this question.

[106] Sarah Nason, *Reconstructing Judicial Review* (Hart Publishing, 2017) 111.
[107] *AXA* (n 96) [170] (emphasis added).

The three core senses of complexity and variety to which the book draws attention are in play in the standing context as much as they are across administrative law adjudication more broadly. Each in turn suggests a reason why 'sufficient interest' bears different forms in different contexts

A. The Importance of the Legislative Framework

The first core sense of complexity and variety inherent in administrative law's 'anatomy' concerns the importance of background legislative frameworks. As chapter three emphasised, the bulk of administrative law adjudication arises against the background of a particular, and often highly detailed, legislative scheme. These schemes interact closely with administrative law doctrine and play an important shaping role in how the grounds of review are applied. This applies not only to grounds of review, but in relation to issues of standing. Questions of standing do not arise in a legal vacuum. Rather, they usually arise against the background of a detailed statutory scheme. In determining standing questions, the courts consider closely the details and underlying aims of these schemes and are careful to ensure that their approach is consistent with it. 'Sufficient interest' is therefore a concept which takes its colour, at least in part, from legislative context.

This chapter has already discussed an important example of this.[108] As explained above, four of the five judges in *Fleet Street Casuals*[109] set about determining whether the applicant federation had standing by examining the detail of the legislative scheme. Three of the four ultimately concluded that a broad approach to standing would be inconsistent with the legislation's emphasis on the importance of confidentiality between the taxpayer and the revenue. It has sometimes been suggested that Lord Diplock's more generalist approach 'won out' over that of the majority. To think in this way, however is to fail to notice the important role that the detail of the legislative framework continues to play in the resolution of standing issues in the decades following *Fleet Street Casuals*.

Three examples will suffice to illustrate, although many more could be offered.[110] Consider first *Williams*.[111] This case concerned a challenge to a local authority decision to reorganise the provision of library services in its area.

[108] See further *DSD* (n 101).

[109] *Fleet Street Casuals* (n 2).

[110] *R (Hussein) v Secretary of State for Defence* [2014] EWCA Civ 1087; *Al Bazzouni v Prime Minister* [2012] 1 WLR 1389; *Gibraltar Betting & Gaming Association Ltd v Secretary of State for Culture, Media and Sport* [2014] EWHC 3236 (Admin), [2015] 1 CMLR 28; *R v Secretary of State for Employment, ex parte Seymour-Smith (No 1)* [1996] All ER 1 (CA). On the relationship between standing and the public procurement regime, see: *R (Chandler) v Secretary of State for Children, Schools and Families* [2009] EWCA 1011, [2010] PTSR 749; *Wylde v Waverley BC* [2017] EWHC 466 (Admin); Bailey (n 76); Eleanor Aspey, 'The Search for the True Public Law Element: Judicial Review of Procurement Decisions' [2016] *PL* 35.

[111] *R (Williams) v Surrey CC* [2012] EWHC 867 (QB).

The local authority determined to close 52 branch libraries and replace them with a 'Community Partnership Model'.[112] The applicant in the case was an individual who resided outside of the area.[113] She sought to challenge the local authority's library policy on the basis of a failure to comply with the Public Sector Equality Duty contained in section 149 of the Equality Act.[114] This provision places authorities under a duty to have due regard to the 'need to eliminate discrimination … [and] advance equality of opportunity between persons'.[115] On the question of whether the applicant had standing to bring this challenge, the Administrative Court reasoned as follows:

> It is true that the statutory duties imposed by the libraries legislation are expressly stated to be owed to those living … within the area of the local authority … but the Equality Act duties *are not subject to any such restriction* … the duties owed under the Equality Act *are owed to a much wider range of persons and interest groups* … [and the Act] is expressly intended to further equality and the equality of opportunity across *the community as a whole.*[116]

Williams, in other words, had standing to rely on the relevant provision in the Equality Act because the aim of that section was to confer a benefit on 'the community as a whole',[117] namely by requiring public authorities to undertake a rigorous assessment of equality issues prior to enacting major changes in policy. To deny Williams standing in a case where she, unlike many others, had the 'financial means'[118] to bring a challenge, would undermine this collective interest. It is noteworthy, however, that had Williams' challenge been based on the 'libraries legislation'[119] rather than the Equality Act, the courts' answer to the question of whether she had standing may have been different: this legislation 'expressly stated'[120] that the duties contained therein were 'owed to those living … within the local authority'.[121] As Williams was not a member of this group, the courts' view was seemingly that she would have lacked standing to rely on these duties.

One thing which is noteworthy about this decision is that scrutiny of the detail of the Equality Act ultimately led the court to conclude that a 'liberal' approach to standing was a proper one: a 'public-spirited'[122] citizen, seeking to represent the interests of the public, ought to be permitted to make a challenge under the equality public sector equality duty. It is, however, important to recognise that

[112] *Ibid* [1].
[113] *R (Williams) v Surrey CC* [2012] EWHC 516 (Admin) [14].
[114] Equality Act 2010, s149.
[115] *Ibid*, s149(1).
[116] *Williams* (n 111) [12]–[13] (emphasis added).
[117] *Williams* (n 111) [12]–[13].
[118] *Williams* (n 111) [14].
[119] See,eg, Public Libraries and Museums Act 1964.
[120] *Williams* (n 111) [12].
[121] *Williams* (n 121) [12].
[122] *Fleet Street Casuals* (n 2) 644.

the background legislative scheme does not always shape the courts' approach to standing in this way.

Thus consider, by way of a second example, *Millard & Connolly*.[123] This case centred on the Housing Benefit (General) Regulations 1987,[124] a piece of secondary legislation regulating payment of housing benefit by local authorities. The most important part of these Regulations for present purposes is Part XI. This part lays down a set of procedural duties to be followed by a housing authority in the course of assessing how much housing benefit to pay to an individual.[125] These duties included an obligation to review the quantum of housing benefit if requested to do so. Most importantly, for present purposes, the Regulations stipulated that only a limited subset of individuals were entitled to request a review: namely, those who were 'affected'[126] by the determinations of the local housing authority. There is some important discussion in *Millard & Connolly* on the question of who counts as an 'affected' individual.[127] The answer given by the Court, very briefly, was that in the vast majority of cases the only 'affected' person would be the *recipient* of housing benefit. That is, the *individual* who met the eligibility criteria and to whom the benefit was due.

In *Millard & Connolly* the applicants sought judicial review in order to challenge an allegedly unlawful refusal by Birmingham City Council to review the quantum of housing benefit being paid to an individual. Importantly, however, neither Millard nor Connolly, the applicants in the case, were the recipients of housing benefit. They were, rather, the *private landlords* of the relevant recipient. They had a material interest in the decision not to review the quantum in the sense that this decision bore on the rent they received from their tenants. The important question nonetheless arose of whether the applicants had standing to rely on the housing authority's legal duties under the Regulations? The Court's answer was as follows:

> The landlord here has no sufficient interest … To permit him to mount such a challenge in all the circumstances would be to defeat the statutory scheme … The applicants were not entitled to review of the quantum of housing benefit which they sought. Only the tenant had the right to such a review.[128]

The detail of the statutory scheme, in other words, and in particular the explicit designation in the Housing Regulations of *recipients*, or affected persons, as the only persons entitled to request a review of quantum, meant the landlords lacked a 'sufficient interest' to make their challenge. To read 'sufficient interest'

[123] *R v Birmingham CC, ex parte Millard & Connolly* (1994) 26 HLR 551 (QB).
[124] Housing Benefit (General) Regulations 1987 (SI 1987/1971) (since repealed by the Housing Benefit and Council Tax Benefit (Consequential Provisions) Regulations 2006 (SI 2006/217)).
[125] *Ibid*, regs 77–81.
[126] *Ibid*, reg 77. Defined by reg 2.
[127] *Millard & Connolly* (n 123) 562.
[128] *Millard & Connolly* (n 123) 559.

more generously in this context was thought to undermine the explicit decision in the applicable Regulations to deny landlords the option of requesting a review of quantum.

The chapter will return to *Millard & Connolly* shortly. For now, however, the important point is that it is a clear illustration of two main things. On the one hand it highlights the role that background legislation continues to play in shaping the approach courts take to determining issues of standing. On the other, it demonstrates the way in which the background legislative framework has sometimes led courts to conclude that only the *beneficiary* of a legal duty has standing to enforce it. The third example, the case of *Bateman*,[129] is similar.[130] This case concerned the Civil Legal Aid (General) Regulations 1989.[131] These Regulations created procedures to be followed when determining the amount of tax to be paid by a solicitor in relation to a client's bill. Of most importance is regulation 114 which provided as follows:

> Where the assisted person or his solicitor, as the case may be, is dissatisfied with the decision of the taxing officer … *the solicitor* shall apply to the board for authority to have the taxation reviewed.[132]

The most important point to note about this regulation is that it requires a request for review to be submitted by the solicitor herself. Thus, as Nolan LJ explained:

> The first thing to observe about these regulations is that [a client] … has no right to take part in it … The only person who is entitled to make representations and to be heard is the solicitor.[133]

The applicant in *Bateman*, however, *was* a client and not a solicitor. As in *Millard & Connolly*, the important question accordingly arose as to whether Bateman had standing to seek relief to enforce those duties. The Court's answer was as follows:

> The crucial feature of the present case is that the *principal, if not the only party directly affected by the refusal of authority* is the firm [of solicitors] … [The central question is whether] Bateman has a sufficient interest in [the application's] subject matter … the inevitable answer to the question, in my judgment, is 'No'.[134]

The aims and wording of the Regulations, in other words, shaped what counted as a 'sufficient interest' in the context. Only the solicitor was permitted to request a review and to make representations. Accordingly, only the solicitor had a 'sufficient interest' to seek judicial review of a refusal to conduct a review.

[129] *R (Bateman) v Legal Aid Board* [1992] 1 WLR 711 (QB).
[130] See also *R (WB) v Leeds Organisation Committee* [2002] EWHC 1927 (Admin), [2003] ELR 67.
[131] Civil Legal Aid (General) Regulations 1989 (SI 1989/339) (since repealed by Civil Legal Aid (General) (Amendment) Regulations 2000 (SI 2000/451)).
[132] *Ibid*, reg 114 (emphasis added).
[133] *Bateman* (n 129) 716.
[134] *Bateman* (n 129) 717 (emphasis added).

To summarise, the first sense of complexity and variety to which this book draws attention – the importance of legislative frameworks – is in play in the standing case law as much as it is more broadly. The cases discussed in this section are illustrations. In each, the Court looked closely at the details of the background scheme and sought to ensure that their approach to standing was consistent with it. This, in turn, suggests a first significant reason why a uniform approach to standing has not emerged. Sufficiency of interest is not a freestanding legal concept which courts apply in a legislative vacuum. What is and is not a sufficient interest depends to a significant degree on the legislative context in which a challenge is brought.

B. The Plurality of Values, Interests and Policies Which Administrative Law Protects

The second core sense of complexity and variety to which the book draws attention concerns the plurality of legal values, interests and policies which the courts seek to accommodate when adjudicating. These values vary in terms of their *origin*; judges pay close attention both to the aims which underlie the background legislative framework and to values 'highly regarded'[135] by the common law. The *beneficiaries* of administrative law doctrine also vary. In some cases, the primary focus of doctrine is on promoting the interests of the public. In others, a core concern is ensuring the fair treatment of the individual.[136]

The normative plurality of administrative law has important consequences in the standing context. When adjudicating on standing issues the courts will consider the values, interests and purposes the law seeks to protect in a given area. These values, in turn, play an important shaping role in how the sufficient interest test is applied. Three examples will suffice to illustrate this point.

Consider again, first, *World Development Movement*.[137] The applicant in this case sought to argue that the administrative decision-maker had acted contrary to the Overseas Development and Cooperation Act by making a grant from the foreign aid fund in order to fund an 'economically unsound'[138] project. As explained above, the Court concluded that the applicant had a sufficient interest to make this challenge. This conclusion can be understood by reference to the nature of the values and interests the background legislative scheme sought to promote. This was not a case in which the background legislative scheme conferred benefits or protections on individuals. The legislation, more broadly, put in place a decision-making scheme through which the foreign aid fund would be distributed.

[135] *R v Higher Education Funding Council, ex parte Institute of Dental Surgery* [1994] 1 WLR 242 (DC), 263.

[136] *Bank Mellat v HM Treasury* [2014] UKSC 39, [2014] AC 700.

[137] *World Development Movement* (n 66). See also *Greenpeace* (n 62).

[138] *World Development Movement* (n 66) 402.

At the heart of the applicant's challenge was the idea that the Secretary of State was undermining the public's interests in having the fund distributed effectively. The Court regarded the non-governmental organisation as being, in light of its expertise, well-placed to make that argument.

In some contexts, however, the background legislative framework may protect values and interests of another kind. Thus consider again, *Millard & Connolly*.[139] The applicant landlords sought to compel the local housing authority to review the quantum of housing benefit[140] owed to their tenants. In considering whether the applicants had standing, the Court paid close attention to the interests which the background legislative framework sought to promote. Part XI of the Housing Benefit (General) Regulations was fundamentally different in nature from the framework in the background of *World Development Movement*. Its purpose was not to promote a collective public interest but to confer a series of procedural protections on a vulnerable group of individuals, namely recipients of housing benefit. There may, furthermore, have been good practical reasons for not extending these protections to landlords. Local authority housing resources are scarce. It is possible that the procedural protections were confined to recipients in order to ensure that resources were directed to those most in need. Empowering a landlord to request a review would also enable her to require the decision-maker to consider the personal details of the recipient. This may be problematic in cases where the recipient has not consented to the request. Considerations such as these help to explain the Court's conclusion that the landlords lacked standing in this case. As the Court put it, to enable landlords to make a challenge of this kind would 'defeat the statutory scheme'[141] by enabling the applicants to rely on provisions which were designed to protect the interests of others and not theirs.

In the first two examples, the courts' approach to standing was shaped by the values, interests and purposes protected by the background legislative scheme. There are also instances where the courts' approach to standing is shaped by the aims which underlie common law principle. Consider an important cluster of cases discussed in chapter four. They can be called, for present purposes, 'notice cases'.[142] In these cases, applicants challenge individualised decisions; that is decisions about them and which adversely affected their interests, on the basis that they ought to have been given notice. Many of the best known procedural review cases fit this pattern. For instance *Cooper*[143] concerned a decision to demolish the applicant's property; in *Ridge*[144] the applicant had been removed

[139] *Millard & Connolly* (n 123).
[140] Housing Benefit (General) Regulations 1987 (SI 1987/1971).
[141] *Millard & Connolly* (n 123) 559.
[142] *Bank Mellat* (n 136); *R (Rowe) v Revenue and Customs Commissioners* [2017] EWCA Civ 2105, [2018] 1 WLR 3039.
[143] *Cooper v Wandsworth Board of Works* (1863) 143 ER 414.
[144] *Ridge v Baldwin* [1964] AC 40 (HL).

from office; and *Osborn*[145] concerned a decision to deny the applicants parole. The decisions in all of these cases were challenged on the basis that the common law conferred on the applicant a presumptive right to be given notice.

In at least the vast bulk of notice cases, the challenge is brought by the individual subject of the decision. Imagine, however, a case where the applicant is a third party. Perhaps they are in some way affected by the decision (for instance because they are a family member of the individual affected) or act from a sense of moral outrage. Would a third party be regarded by the courts as having a 'sufficient interest' to bring the challenge? The case law suggests no. Consider the following passage from *Durayappah*:[146]

> If in *Ridge v Baldwin* the appellant Ridge, who had been wrongly dismissed because he was not given the opportunity of presenting this defence, had preferred to abandon the point and accept the view that he has been properly dismissed, their Lordships can see no reason why any other person … should have any right to contend that Mr Ridge was still the Chief Constable of Brighton. … If a person in the position of Mr Ridge had not felt sufficiently aggrieved to take any action by reason of the failure to afford him his strict right to put forward a defence … no one else should have any right to complain.[147]

The idea expressed by their Lordships in this passage is that in notice challenges, only the individual who is the subject of the challenged decision will have standing to argue that their presumptive right to notice has been breached. Although *Duryappah* was decided prior to the 1977 procedural reforms, there is reason to think it is still good law.[148] At least one leading textbook[149] continues to speak of the case as having this effect. Wade and Forsyth write, for instance, that:

> It seems plain that denial of a fair hearing is a wrong which is personal to the party aggrieved. If he waives the objection and does not complain, it is not the business of other people to do so, for against them there is nothing wrong with the decision.[150]

There also does not appear to be a case in which a third party has been permitted to challenge an individualised decision[151] concerning another on the basis of a failure to give notice in their own right.[152]

[145] *R (Osborn) v Parole Board* [2013] UKSC 61, [2014] AC 1115.
[146] *Durayappah v Fernando* [1967] 2 AC 337 (PC).
[147] *Ibid*, 352–53 citing *Ridge* (n 144).
[148] Note that although *R (Grierson) v OFCOM* [2005] EWHC 1899 (Admin), Official Transcript overruled *Durayappah* (n 146), the Court did not cast doubt on the discussion of standing.
[149] William Wade and Christopher Forsyth, *Administrative Law*, 11th edn (Oxford University Press, 2015).
[150] *Ibid*, 427.
[151] See the discussion of systematic review cases below.
[152] A possible exception is *Police Superintendents Association of England & Wales v Chief Constable of Bedfordshire* [2013] EWHC 2173 (Admin), Official Transcript. It is clear, however, that the applicant organisation in this case was acting in a representative capacity in relation to the individuals who sought to complain. See the discussion below.

Such a view, furthermore, can be understood by reference to the values which the common law seeks to promote in such cases. Chapter four emphasised that the courts seek to accommodate a number of values, interests and purpose when adjudicating on procedural review cases. In notice cases, one important value which has been strongly emphasised by courts is the protection of the *individual* against undignified treatment.[153] It is at least arguable that recognising the standing of a third party in such a case would undermine, rather than facilitate, that purpose. The individual subject of the decision might have good, personal reasons for not challenging the decision. To recognise the standing of a third party would permit that other to undermine their choice.

There are, furthermore, other normative consideration pointing against recognising standing in such a case. One is privacy.[154] The hearing of a challenge to an individualised dismissal[155] or parole decision[156] entails the courts considering in close detail personal information concerning the individual. There are significant difficulties with the suggestion that a third party should be permitted to request the courts to do this when the individual who is the subject of the decision has elected not to initiate legal proceedings in their own name or consented to another doing it on her behalf. A further, and final, set of considerations concerns consistency across the law. Put briefly, were a challenge to a failure to supply notice in relation to a dismissal or parole decision to be framed in human rights terms,[157] or as a claim for breach of contract,[158] standing would be confined to the individual subject of the decision whose rights are alleged to have been breached.[159] It is not obvious why a fundamentally different approach to standing ought to be used because the challenge is framed in administrative law terms.

To summarise, this section has emphasised a second sense of variety and complexity in play in the standing case law: the courts seek to accommodate a variety of values, interests and purposes. This complexity suggests a further reason why a uniform test of standing has not emerged in administrative law. In making administrative law challenges, applicants will rely on a broad variety of legislative frameworks and common law principles. There is not, however, a singular set of normative values which these legal standards promote. Legislation, for instance, is enacted to protect different clusters of interests. Some focus on promoting collective goods and others on conferring benefits or protections on individuals. Common law principle too is illuminated by different values. In determining

[153] *Osborn* (n 145) [68].

[154] See Elizabeth Fisher and Jeremy Kirk, 'Still Standing: An Argument for Open Standing in Australia and England' [1997] *Australian Law Journal* 370, 384.

[155] *Ridge* (n 144).

[156] *Osborn* (n 145).

[157] See especially Convention for the Protection of Human Rights and Fundamental Freedoms (European Convention on Human Rights, as amended) Art 6.

[158] Because, for instance, the right to be heard was contained in the employment contract.

[159] See especially Human Rights Act 1998, s7 and *Brushmoor* (n 6).

issues of standing, the courts have close regard to the values, interests and purposes that the applicable legal standards promote. Their approach to standing in a given case is shaped by what they take the purpose of the law in a particular case to be.

C. The Array of Legal Relationships in Play in Administrative Law Challenges

The third and final sense of complexity and variety in administrative law concerns the legal relationships in play. As explained in chapter three, scholars have sometimes sought to draw a distinction between administrative law, on the one hand, and other fields such as human rights and private law, on the other. On this view, while human rights and private law concerns on the basis that while the latter concern legal duties owed to individuals, administrative law concerns legal obligations owed to the public as a collectivity.[160] This book has argued throughout, however, that this view is too simplistic. Administrative law challenges concern legal relationships of different kinds. As previous chapters have illustrated, there are categories of administrative law case which are aptly characterised as challenges in which individuals rely on legal duties alleged to be owed to them personally.

This has important implications for standing. The discussion above drew attention to an influential way of thinking about standing. According to it, because legal duties in administrative law are owed the public and not individuals, it is improper to make use of a 'rights-based'[161] approach. Rather, the very nature of administrative law doctrine requires a broader conception of standing.[162] *World Development Movement*,[163] discussed above, is a clear example.

There are, however, administrative law challenges where the courts have treated the legal duty in play as being owed to an individual.

Consider again, by way of illustration, *Bateman*.[164] As explained above, the regulatory framework at the background of this case purported to confer a series of procedural rights on *solicitors*. The legal duty the applicant sought to rely on in this case was therefore different in nature to that in *World Development Movement*: it was a duty explicitly stated to be owed to a particular individual. This in turn shaped how the Court approached the question of standing. As explained above,

[160] Lord Woolf, 'Public Law – Private Law: Why the Divide? A Personal View' [1986] *PL* 220; Nicholas Bamforth, 'Hohfeldian Rights and Public Law' in Kramer M, *Rights Wrongs & Responsibilities* (Palgrave, 2001) 11.

[161] Varuhas (n 5) 101.

[162] Elliott and Varuhas (n 3) Ch 14; Farah Ahmed and Adam Perry, 'Standing and Civic Virtue' (2018) 134 *LQR* 239.

[163] *World Development Movement* (n 66).

[164] *Bateman* (n 129).

the applicant here was found to lack standing because she, as a client, was not the holder of the right she sought to enforce.

A further, similar, example is *Ruddock*.[165] This case concerned a policy, adopted by the Home Secretary, which laid down the criteria which would be applied in the course of taking decisions about whether the telephone of an individual should be tapped. When the Home Secretary took the decision to tap the telephone of a Mr Cox, judicial review proceedings were initiated on the basis of a contravention of the published policy. As noted in chapter five, the courts have tended to view the legal relationship at stake in cases of this kind in a particular way.[166] Judges have, in particular, tended to speak of the affected individual as holding a *personal legal right* to have the terms of the published policy applied to the individual circumstances of her case.

This way of thinking about the legal relationship in issue, in turn, was reflected in the Court's discussion of standing in *Ruddock*. This issue arose because the applicants in *Ruddock* included not only Mr Cox, but two correspondents of Mr Cox whose calls had been intercepted. On the question of whether these applicants had standing to bring the challenge, Taylor J concluded as follows:

> If a warrant was signed unlawfully, the unlawfulness would be due to Mr Cox as an individual falling outside the guidelines or criteria justifying such a warrant. Whether or not Mr Cox so fell must be an issue arising upon his application and his alone.[167]

One way of understanding this case, in other words, is that because the legal argument advanced by the applicants required the court to conduct an inquiry into whether Mr Cox's personal right to have published policy applied to his case, only Cox had a sufficient interest to make that argument. Had, Mr Cox not appeared as an applicant in *Ruddock*, Taylor J would have dismissed the case for want of standing.

It is helpful, by way of concluding this part of the chapter, to offer a brief summary of the arguments developed herein. The main aim of this section has been to explore an important question raised in section I: why has a singular interpretation of the sufficient interest test not emerged in administrative law? Its core argument has been that significant light is shed on this question by the complex and varied anatomy of administrative law. The three core senses of complexity and variety to which the book draws attention are in play in the standing context as much as they are in administrative law case law more broadly. Each in turn suggests a series of reasons why 'sufficient interest' is a legal concept which is shaped by context.

First, issues of standing arise in the context of an array of different legislative schemes. The detail of these schemes plays an important role in how the

[165] *R v Secretary of State for the Home Department, ex parte Ruddock* [1987] 1 WLR 1482 (QB).

[166] *R (Lumba) v Secretary of State for the Home Department* [2011] UKSC 12, [2012] 1 AC 245; *Mandalia v Secretary of State for the Home Department* [2015] UKSC 59, [2015] 1 WLR 4546.

[167] *Ruddock* (n 165) 1485.

courts determine whether an applicant has standing. Sufficiency of interest, in other words, is a concept which takes its colours significantly from the legislative context in which a challenge arises. Second, when adjudicating on administrative law issues the courts seek to accommodate a variety of values, interests and purposes. This is equally true in the standing context. The legal standards on which applicants rely protect different kinds of values and interests. The courts pay close attention to the aims of the law in a given area and shape their approach to standing by reference to them. Third, and similarly, administrative law adjudication is concerned with a variety of different kinds of legal relationship. It is therefore too simplistic to say that, because administrative law duties are owed to the public at large, the courts must reject a 'rights-based'[168] approach in favour of one which focuses on the public interest. The meaning of the sufficient interest test, in other words, cannot be settled by identifying *the* type of legal relationship with which administrative law is concerned.

III. How do the Courts Determine Whether an Applicant has a Sufficient Interest?

Section I of this chapter, after exploring the development of standing, posed two important questions. The first was why a uniform approach to standing has not emerged in English and Welsh administrative law. This question was explored in the previous section. Its core argument was that a better understanding of the complex and varied 'anatomy' of administrative law suggests a series of reasons why a generalised approach to standing has not developed. This section is concerned with a second important question: if the courts are not determining standing issues by reference to a singular, overarching approach, how do they determine whether an applicant has a 'sufficient interest in the matter to which the application relates'?[169]

Answering this question in categorical terms is very difficult. Indeed comprehensive scholarly research on standing more broadly is very challenging. This is so for at least three reasons.

First, much judicial consideration on the issue of standing takes place at the 'permission'[170] stage of an application for judicial review. It is unclear what proportion of permission decisions are reported[171] or included in databases but

[168] Varuhas (n 5) 101.

[169] Senior Courts Act 198, s31(3).

[170] Civil Procedure Rules 1998, Part 54, rule 4.

[171] It is very difficult to find accurate data on the number of permission decisions which are reported. However, for a very insightful empirical discussion of the judicial review process, see Varda Bondy and Maurice Sunkin, 'The Dynamics of Judicial Review Litigation: The Resolution of Public Law Challenges Before Final Hearing' (Public Law Project, 2009).

there is a strong possibility that much discussion of standing is simply not accessible. Second, there is reason to think that counsel sometimes will not raise issues of standing even when there is an arguable case that the applicant lacks a sufficient interest to make a challenge. Certainly, there are well-known cases in which courts have raised questions of standing unprompted by barristers.[172] There are numerous considerations which can explain this. One is that it might be in the interests of the administrative decision-maker that a legal question is resolved.[173] Another is that, as others have suggested, the points counsel take can be a matter of 'fashion'.[174] It may be that arguments concerning standing have tended to be viewed as unduly technical. Third, it is also probable that the barristers actively seek to ensure that the applicant in whose name an application is brought is one whose standing is uncontentious.[175] Behind-the-scenes 'shuffling' of this kind would serve to prevent 'borderline' cases of standing from very often finding their way before a court.

The collective effect of these factors is that, compared to other areas of doctrinal administrative law, there is a relative dearth of reported case law which engages explicitly with questions about standing. Because of this, the aim of this section must be relatively modest. The hope is not to answer categorically the question of how the courts, in the absence of an overarching approach to standing, decide whether an applicant has a sufficient interest. The discussion below, rather, will draw attention to three important but overlooked aspects of the law on standing which emerge from the case law which is available.

Subsections A, B and C will discuss each in turn. Section D will then explain how these three features of standing can be encapsulated in the idea that standing in English and Welsh administrative law is 'ground-dependent' in nature.

A. The Courts Make Use of Different Approaches to Standing in Relation to Different Legal Arguments

The first important point runs throughout much of the discussion above. It is, however, worth stressing again here because, as the analysis in section I illustrates, it is commonly overlooked: the 'sufficient interest' test has not been treated as

[172] *Walton* (n 75); *R (Project Management Institute) v Minister for the Cabinet Office* [2014] EWHC 2438 (Admin).

[173] *DSD* (n 101).

[174] Konrad Schiemann, 'Locus Standi' [1990] *PL* 342. See also David Feldman, '*Anisminic Ltd v Foreign Compensation Commission* [1968]: In Perspective' in Maurice Sunkin and Satvinder Juss (eds), *Landmark Cases in Public Law* (Hart Publishing, 2017).

[175] *R v Secretary of State for Employment, ex parte Equal Opportunities Commission* [1994] 2 WLR 409 (HL). For examples of the courts speaking about reshuffling of this kind (albeit for the purpose of obtaining legal aid rather than avoiding a locus standi challenge), see also *WB* (n 130); *R (Edwards) v Environment Agency & Another* [2013] UKSC 78, [2014] 1 WLR 55.

laying down a uniform 'test' of standing. It is not, for example, the case that the courts in every instance have determined whether the applicant has standing to bring the relevant challenge by inquiring into her motive for doing so.[176] Nor have they uniformly adopted a 'rights-based approach'. The courts, rather, have made use of different approaches in different contexts.

Thus, on the one hand, there are certainly cases such as *World Development Movement*[177] and *Greenpeace*[178] in which the courts have made use of what can aptly be called a 'liberal' approach. As explained, in these cases, the courts have proceeded from a recognition of a generalised public interest in having the relevant legal duty enforced. On this basis, they have recognised the applicant as having a 'sufficient interest' to represent that strand of the public interest. This line of reasoning, however, has not been used in every case. In particular, in relation to other kinds of legal duty, especially legal duties which have been created primarily to provide legal benefits or protection to individuals, the courts have approached issues of standing rather differently. Thus, for instance, in both *Millard & Connolly*[179] and *Durayappah*,[180] discussed above, the courts regarded standing as being confined to the individual beneficiaries of the legal duties alleged to have been breached.

Two further points, which emerge from the discussion above, ought to be noted before moving on. The first is that, as section II emphasises, there are at least three closely related considerations which the courts take into account in determining the proper approach to standing to take in a given case. The detail of the legislative scheme which sits in the background of the challenge; the normative values and interests which the legal standards relied on promote and the legal relationships in issue in the case are all important considerations.

The second is that, while it may look at first sight as if the courts' variation of their approach to standing is inconsistent with Parliament's intention in enacting the 'sufficient interest' test, it is in fact concordant with the pre-legislative history.[181] As emphasised above, Parliament enacted the sufficient interest test on the recommendation of the Law Commission. The Commission favoured the test precisely because its vague phrasing would effectively delegate to the judiciary the task of developing the law on standing. Importantly, the Law Commission envisaged that the courts would do this 'having regard to the relief which is sought'.[182] That is, that the courts would consider the precise nature of the argument which the applicant sought to make in settling on an approach to standing in a given case.

[176] *Dixon* (n 61).
[177] *World Development Movement* (n 66).
[178] *Greenpeace* (n 62).
[179] *Millard & Connolly* (n 123).
[180] *Durayappah* (n 146).
[181] Senior Courts Act 1981, s31(3).
[182] Law Commission, 'Report on Remedies in Administrative Law' (Law Comm No 73, 1976) [48].

B. The Courts May Use a 'Rights-Based Approach' in Some Cases

The second important feature of the case law which can be drawn out from the discussion above concerns the place of a 'rights-based approach' in administrative law. As stressed throughout this chapter, the courts have, for very good reason, rejected the possibility of making use of a rights-based approach to standing on a generalised basis.[183] It is, in other words, not the case that an applicant must show in every instance that she has a personal legal right or protected interest at stake. Nor *should* the courts make use of such an approach. As the discussion above and in chapter two regarding *Lewisham Union Guardians* emphasised,[184] the generalised use of such an approach would have unfortunate consequences. In particular, it would limit the courts' ability to hold decision-makers to statutory duties enacted to protect collective interests.

That said, the influential view that the courts' approach to standing in administrative law is fundamentally different to the 'rights-based standing rules'[185] which are used in private law[186] and human rights law[187] goes too far. There is reason to believe that there are categories of legal administrative law challenge in which the courts would treat standing as being confined to the individual beneficiary of a duty. Four examples have emerged throughout the course of argument in this book. It is helpful to briefly discuss each in turn.

First, as has been emphasised in this and previous chapters,[188] it is not uncommon for legislation to place public authorities under legal duties and to explicitly designate those legal duties as owed to an individual right-holder. Furthermore, as discussed above, there might be good normative and practical reasons for doing so. Where this is the case, *Millard & Connolly*[189] and *Bateman*[190] both illustrate that the courts may treat standing as being confined to the *individual* designated by the statute as the holder of the right. As the court emphasized in *Millard & Connolly*, to hold otherwise may 'defeat' the aims and structure of the statutory scheme'.[191]

A second cluster of cases were termed above as 'notice cases'. In these cases, a particularised decision concerning the proper treatment of an individual is challenged on the basis that she ought to have been given notice. As explained

[183] See especially Sedley J's discussion of *Rose Theatre* (n 58) in *Dixon* (n 61).
[184] *Lewisham Union Guardians* (n 21).
[185] Vauhras (n 5) 101,
[186] See for example *Brushmoor* (n 6).
[187] See especially Human Rights Act 1998, s7.
[188] See especially the discussion of *R (Conville) v Richmond-upon-Thames LBC* [2006] EWCA Civ 718, [2006] 1 WLR 2808 in chapter 3.
[189] *Millard & Connolly* (n 123).
[190] *Bateman* (n 129).
[191] *Millard & Connolly* (n 129) 559.

above, there is reason to think that in such cases standing would be confined to the individual alleged to have the right to have been given notice (or perhaps a person acting in a representative capacity). The Privy Council in *Durayappah*[192] was certainly of this view. A series of normative considerations, including the importance of protecting the dignity and privacy of the individual and consistency, also point against recognising the standing of third parties to challenge such decisions.

To be clear, this is not to say that an individual whose rights to notice have been breached should not be able to authorise another, such as a professional organisation,[193] to represent her interests. It is also important to recognise a distinction between a paticularised notice case and a 'systematic'[194] challenge to decision-making arrangements or policies on the basis that they create an unacceptable risk that the process rights of individuals will be breached. Systematic challenges are different in nature to the cases considered here. They entail a challenge to a decision-making structure rather than to an individualised decision. The core point for present purposes is that there is reason to think that the option of challenging a *particularised decision* for *failure to give notice* is one available to the affected individual alone.

A third important cluster of cases are those in which an administrative decision-maker is argued to have improperly applied published policy to the facts of an individual's case. Chapter five emphasised that the courts have commonly spoken of this duty as corresponding to a personal legal right on the part of the individual to have policy applied.[195] Relatedly, in *Ruddock*,[196] the Court concluded that a challenge to phone-tapping on the basis of misapplication of policy could only be brought by the subject of the warrant.

It is however important to flag up a complication: much seems to turn on the nature and aims of the policy in question. In many administrative contexts, published policy sets out the terms in which an individual's application for a benefit will be assessed. In these contexts, *Ruddock* suggests that standing is confined to the affected individual. In other contexts, however, policy may seek to protect a broader array of interests and this can have implications for standing. *Project Management Institute*[197] is a good example. This case was discussed in detail in chapter three. It arose against the backdrop of the Royal Charter framework. The framework has a dual function. In the first place it sets out the criteria on which Royal Charter applications are determined. In the second it

[192] *Durayappah* (n 146).
[193] *Police Superintendents Association* (n 152).
[194] *R (Medical Justice) v Secretary of State for the Home Department* [2011] EWCA Civ 1710; *R (Tabbakh) v Staffordshire and West Midlands Probation Trust* [2014] EWCA Civ 827, [2014] 1 WLR 4620; *R (S) v Director of Legal Aid Casework* [2016] EWCA Civ 464, [2016] 1 WLR 4733; *R (Howard League for Penal Reform) v Lord Chancellor* [2015] EWCA Civ 819.
[195] *Lumba* (n 166); *Mandalia* (n 166).
[196] *Ruddock* (n 165).
[197] *Project Management Institute* (n 172).

also confers a series of protections for economic competitors. These include requirements to 'take soundings'[198] and a presumption against granting Charter companies with a significant overlap of economic interest with others.[199] In light of this, the Court of Appeal[200] concluded that economic rivals should have standing to challenge Royal Charter decisions on the basis of improper application of policy.

Overall, then, in challenges concerning proper application of policy, much turns on the nature and content of the policy in question. Where policy stipulates the conditions on which an individual's application for a benefit or burden will be determined, standing to challenge a breach of the policy may be confined to individual applicants. Where, however, the same policy also creates explicit forms of protection for other parties, those parties may also have a sufficient interest to seek judicial review.

A fourth and final category of case worthy of mention here relates to a discussion in earlier chapters. Chapter five discussed legitimate expectations. Section IV of that chapter drew attention to four different kinds of case with which the courts have been faced in recent years. The first can be termed the 'individual assurance' case. Here, an administrative decision-maker offers an individual an assurance, perhaps by letter,[201] email,[202] verbally[203] or via a more formal form of communication,[204] that they will be treated in a particular way only to later depart from that assurance. As chapter five explained, in cases of this kind the courts look closely at the reasoning process the administrative decision-maker went through in deciding whether to depart from the assurance. They will require the administrative decision-maker to demonstrate that the assurance was conscientiously factored into the decision-making process,[205] that there were good reasons for concluding that upholding the assurance would undermine the reasons for policy change[206] and that any 'mid-way'[207] options for cushioning the blow were considered.

There does not seem to have been an instance in which an 'individual assurance' case has been challenged by any person or organisation other than the

[198] *Project Management Institute* (n 172).[9].

[199] *Project Management Institute* (n 172).[9].

[200] Reversing *R (Project Management Institute) v Minister for the Cabinet Office* [2014] EWHC 2438 (Admin).

[201] *Babakandi v Westminster CC* [2011] EWHC 1756 (Admin); *Thomas v Camarthen CC* [2013] EWHC 783 (Admin), [2013] JPL 1266; *R (Hussain) v Secretary of State for the Home Department* [2013] EWHC 3833 (Admin); *R (Taylor) v Secretary of State for the Home Department* [2015] EWHC 3526 (Admin); *R (Dixons) v HMRC* [2018] EWHC 2556 (Admin).

[202] *R (Veolia Landfill Ltd) v HMRC* [2016] EWHC 1880 (Admin); *R (Youssef) v Secretary of State for the Home Department* [2015] EWHC 1600 (Admin).

[203] *R (Birks) v Commissioner of Police of the Met* [2014] EWHC 3041 (Admin), [2015] ICR 204.

[204] *R (Biffa Waster Services Ltd) v HMRC* [2016] EWHC 1444 (Admin), [2017] Env LR 10.

[205] *R (Bibi) v Newham LBC* [2001] EWCA Civ 607, [2002] 1 WLR 237.

[206] *R (Alansi) v Newham LBC* [2013] EWHC 3722 (Admin).

[207] *R v North & East Devon Health Authority, ex parte Coughlan* [2001] QB 213 (CA).

individual who was offered the assurance. This may not be a coincidence. It is at least possible that the absence of a case of this kind reflects a shared background understanding to the effect that this stranger lacks a 'sufficient interest in the matter'[208] to which her application relates.

There are, furthermore, good normative reasons to think that standing, in such cases, ought to be confined to the recipient of the assurance.

It is helpful to illustrate with an example. Consider the well-known decision in *Coughlan*.[209] Imagine that, as happened in *Coughlan*,[210] a promise is issued to Miss Coughlan that, if she relocates to a facility known as Mardon House, she will have a 'home for life'[211] there. Now imagine that, at a later point in time, another resident ('Miss A') is moved into the same facility. Importantly, she receives no equivalent promise. When the decision is taken to close Mardon House, Miss Coughlan does not initiate legal proceedings. Perhaps, for instance, she is content with alternative residential arrangements which have been made for her.[212] Miss A, however, is much less accepting. She initiates judicial review proceedings and, in doing so, seeks to rely on the legitimate expectation ground. Her argument, more particularly, is that in offering an assurance to Miss Coughlan the local health authority had given rise to a legitimate expectation which now prevents it from closing Mardon House.

In this context, the important question would arise: does Miss A have a 'sufficient interest'[213] to make this challenge? There are at least three normative considerations which would tend to point against recognising Miss A's standing. First, judicial reasoning in 'individual assurance' cases of this kind focuses centrally on ensuring that the individual recipient of an assurance is fairly factored into the administrative decision-making process. A major concern is surely to ensure that the individual's autonomy is respected. As Schiemann LJ explained in *Bibi*,[214] individual recipients of assurances will often make life plans on the assumption that the administrative decision-maker will comply with them. Departure can therefore result in a form of 'moral detriment'[215] whereby the administrative decision-maker undermines those choices. This focus on the interests and autonomy of the individual is, however, difficult to square with recognising the standing of Miss A. If a major concern of the law in these cases is protection of the interests and autonomy of the individual, then arguably the decision as to whether to challenge a departure from an assurance should lie with her and her alone. Second, and relatedly, the hearing of Miss A's case would involve a

[208] Senior Courts Act 1981, s31(3).
[209] *Coughlan* (n 207) [89].
[210] *Coughlan* (n 207) [89].
[211] *Coughlan* (n 207) [1].
[212] *Coughlan* (n 207) [1].
[213] Senior Courts Act 1981, s31(3).
[214] *Bibi* (n 205).
[215] *Bibi* (n 205) [55].

substantial invasion of Miss Coughlan's privacy. Such an invasion, in the absence of Miss Coughlan's consent, is surely difficult to justify.[216] Third, recognition of Miss A's standing also gives rise to inconsistences in the law; were the legal challenge to be brought in the realm of contract law[217] or human rights law[218] it is clear that standing would be confined to Miss Coughlan.

To summarise, what the discussion in this section has shown is that, contrary to some popular thinking, there are clusters of cases in which the courts may deploy 'rights-based standing rules'[219] similar to those used in private and human rights law. The courts have, for good reason, rejected a *generalised* approach to standing requiring the applicant to show that she has a personal legal right or interest at stake. There are, however, categories of case where the courts either do, or there is good reason to think the court would, regard standing as being confined to the individual who holds a right correlative to the legal duty relied on. Four categories of challenge have been discussed here: cases in which applicants rely on statutory duties designated as being owed to identified individuals; 'notice cases' in which a particularised decision is challenged on the basis that the affected individual should have been able to participate; certain cases in which administrative decision-making is challenged for failure to properly apply policy; and legitimate expectations cases in which an assurance has been directly communicated to an individual.

C. Standing to Rely on One Ground May not Entail Standing to Rely on All

A third and final overlooked aspect of the courts' approach to standing flows from the previous point: it is a perfectly logical possibility that an applicant who has been found to have standing to challenge a decision on one ground may lack standing to challenge the same decision on another.

This is a possibility which is best illustrated through an example. Consider, again, an imaginary twist on the facts of *Coughlan* set out above. Imagine this time, however, that Miss A seeks to rely on two legal grounds. First, she seeks to argue, as above, that the closure decision amounted to an unlawful breach of Miss Coughlan's legitimate expectation. Second, she also seeks to argue that the local health authority had failed to properly comply with a statutory duty to consult the residents of Mardon House, of which she was one.[220] In these circumstances,

[216] Elizabeth Fisher and Jeremy Kirk, 'Still Standing: An Argument for Open Standing in Australia and England' [1997] *Australian Law Journal* 370, 384.

[217] Because, for example, the promise of a home for life was contained in a contractual agreement.

[218] See especially Convention for the Protection of Human Rights and Fundamental Freedoms (European Convention on Human Rights, as amended), Art 1 of Protocol 1.

[219] Varuhas (n 5) 101.

[220] See especially *R v Devon County Council, ex parte Baker* [1995] 1 All ER 73 (CA); *R (LH) v Shropshire Council* [2014] EWCA Civ 404, [2014] PTSR 1052 and discussion in chapter 4.

the important question arises: does Miss A have a 'sufficient interest' to make this challenge?

As explained above, there are significant normative difficulties in the way of the conclusion that Miss A has standing to challenge the closure decision by invoking the assurance offered to Miss Coughlan. There is also an absence of case law in which applicants have been permitted to bring challenges of this kind. To suggest, however, that Miss A lacks standing to rely on her second ground is equally problematic; a statutory duty to consult users of a care facility prior to withdrawing funding from that facility would be designed to protect persons in precisely Miss A's position. To deny her standing, accordingly, would deny her the ability to enforce a legal duty recognised for the purpose of protecting a group to which she belongs. The most appropriate conclusion, therefore, would be that although Miss A lacks a 'sufficient interest' to rely on her first ground, she has standing to rely on her second.

It ought to be noted explicitly that this suggestion runs contrary to the Court of Appeal's judgment in *Kides*.[221] In this case, Laws LJ opined as follows:

> It seems to me that a litigant who has a real and genuine interest in challenging an administrative decision must be entitled to present his challenge on all available grounds.[222]

There are, however, reasons why the authority of this passage is doubtful. The first is that significant doubt has been cast on Laws LJ's line of reasoning in *Chandler*.[223] In this case, counsel for the public authority made the argument that this aspect of *Kides* was incorrect and 'contrary to authority'.[224] As full submissions had not been made on the argument, the Court of Appeal did not offer a conclusive view on the point but clearly left the issue open.[225]

The second is that there have also been decided cases in which the courts have recognised, at least the possibility, that an applicant may be found to have standing to rely on one legal duty, but lack standing to rely on another. In *McBride*[226] for instance Kerr J, as he was then, held that the applicant had standing to challenge the decision not to dismiss two soldiers who had been connected to the death of her son.[227] The applicant, however, was held to lack standing to argue that the decision violated the principle of equality on the basis that similar cases had resulted in dismissal.[228] Standing to bring this argument was said to be confined to the soldiers who had been treated less favourably. Another example is *Manson*.[229]

[221] *R (Kides) v South Cambridgeshire District Council* [2002] EWCA Civ 1370, Official Transcript.
[222] *Ibid* [134].
[223] *Chandler* (n 110).
[224] *Chandler* (n 110) [76].
[225] *Chandler* (n 110) [78].
[226] *McBride's Application for Judicial Review* [1999] NI 299.
[227] *Ibid*, 311.
[228] *Ibid*, 312.
[229] *R v Dyfed CC, ex parte Manson* [1995] Env LR 83 (QB).

Here, counsel for the public authority was prepared to accept that the applicant had standing to rely on two of the three grounds on which he sought to rely. However it challenged his standing to rely on a third legal duty.[230] The Court ultimately concluded that the applicant had standing to rely on all grounds. In the course of doing so, however, the Court clearly recognised the legitimacy of the authority's argument.

The third and final reason is that the conclusion reached in *Kides* itself could have been reached without making use of the idea that standing to rely on one legal duty logically entails standing to rely on all.[231] Laws LJ's proposition, in other words, was not clearly central to the determination of that case.

D. The 'Ground-Dependence' of Standing

This section has sought to address an important question raised in section I: if the courts are not making use of a 'rights-based'[232] approach to standing, nor one grounded in the promotion of the public interest, how do they determine whether an applicant has a 'sufficient interest in the matter to which [their] application relates'?[233] Answering this question categorically is very difficult for reasons articulated above. This part has, however, drawn attention to three important but often overlooked aspects of the standing jurisprudence.

First, the courts do not make use of a monolithic approach to standing in this field; different approaches are used in different contexts depending on the legislative background, the normative considerations in play and the legal relationships at stake in a case. Second, contrary to the suggestions of some, there is limited room in administrative law for something akin to the rights-based approach to standing used in fields such as private law. The courts have, for good reason, rejected a generalised approach to standing requiring the applicant to show a personal legal right to relief. There are, however, certain significant legal duties arising in this field in relation to which the courts either do, or there is good reason to think the courts would, treat standing as confined to the individual who holds the right correlative to the public authority's legal duty. Third, contrary to Laws LJ's suggestion in *Kides*,[234] it is a perfectly logical possibility that an applicant may have standing to rely on one or more legal ground but lack standing to rely on others.

[230] *Ibid*, 102.

[231] The Court, for instance, could have explained that the duty to consider existing affordable housing was an obligation created for the benefit of the public at large and that the applicant ought to be recognised as having standing in a representative capacity.

[232] Varuhas (n 5) 101.

[233] Senior Courts Act 1981, s31(3).

[234] *Kides* (n 221).

These three themes in the judicial approach can be aptly summarised by reference to the idea that standing, in English and Welsh administrative law, is 'ground-dependent'. One way of explaining this is to begin with the wording of the Senior Courts Act 1981. Section 31(3) provides that:

> … the court shall not grant leave to make such an application unless it considers that the applicant has a sufficient interest *in the matter to which the application relates*.[235]

Most important, for present purposes, is the phrase 'the matter to which the application relates'. There has been little, if any, explicit consideration of what constitutes 'the matter' of an application for judicial review. There are, however, a number of ways of thinking. Perhaps the most widespread assumption is that the 'matter' refers to the *decision* under challenge. On this view, what the applicant must demonstrate is that the relevant decision impacts her interests in a sufficient way such that she should be permitted to challenge it. This results in a focus on either the consequence of the decision for her interests, or the reasons for which she is interested in challenging the decision.

What this part shows, however, is that the *grounds* on which the applicant seeks to rely also form at least part of the 'matter'. The courts will think carefully about the nature of the legal arguments the applicant seeks to make and whether she ought to be permitted to make them. As explained in this section, different legal arguments result in different approaches to standing, and in the case of some, standing may be confined to only one individual. It is also perfectly possible that while an applicant may have standing to rely on one ground, she will lack a 'sufficient interest' to rely on others.

IV. Conclusion

It is useful to conclude this chapter with some reflections on its relationship with the book's broader themes. As the introductory chapter explained, this book has three main aims. The arguments of this chapter are important because they significantly advance each aim in turn.

First, this book seeks to further understanding of administrative law's legal 'anatomy'. It does so by emphasising three core senses in which the basic legal structures in play in adjudication are complex and varied: (i) administrative law doctrine interacts closely with a variety of legislative frameworks; (ii) the courts seek to accommodate a plurality of legal values, interests and purposes; and (iii) administrative law adjudication concerns legal relationships of different kinds. This chapter continues to illustrate this point. Thus, as section II explained, these three core senses of complexity and variety characterise the standing case law as

[235] Senior Courts Act 1981, s31(3) (emphasis added).

much as they do administrative law adjudication more broadly. The standing case law, in other words, provides a further illustration of administrative law's complex and varied anatomy.

Second, the book also argues that it is important to recognise this complexity and variety, not only for its own sake, but because it helps to shed light on a series of important doctrinal issues within the field. The book uses three case studies by which to show this. Chapter four discussed procedural review and chapter five legitimate expectations. This chapter has discussed the third and final case study: standing. Recognition of administrative law's anatomy, it has argued, significantly illuminates this area. It draws attention to a series of reasons why a singular approach to standing has not emerged in the administrative law context.[236] Reflecting on these issues also draws attention to a number of important, but often overlooked, aspects of the judicial approach to standing. These features can be encapsulated by the idea that standing in England and Wales is 'ground-dependent' in nature.

Third and finally, the book also seeks to raise an important but under-addressed question: is it plausible or useful to explain administrative law by reference to a singular, structuring 'master idea or principle'?[237] This issue will be discussed in full in the next chapter. Broadly, however, the overarching message of the book is one of cynicism. While 'monistic' accounts of administrative law doctrine often draw attention to important themes, the basic legal structures in play in administrative law adjudication are complex and varied. There is therefore a significant concern that explanations which rely on an overriding 'organising concept'[238] will obscure important aspects of the law. The discussion in this chapter provides an illustration of why there is reason for cynicism. Attempts have been made to characterise the courts' approach to standing as being guided by an overarching 'meta-value'.[239] An influential narrative, for instance, suggests that, over time, a 'rights-based' approach has been replaced with a focus on promoting the public interest.[240] Nonetheless, the case law has not settled on a monolithic approach to standing. For the reasons discussed in this chapter, furthermore, it is likely that this will continue to be the case.

[236] *Walton* (n 64) [92]–[94].

[237] Stephen Smith, *Contract Theory* (Oxford University Press, 2004) 11.

[238] Christopher Forsyth, 'The Rock and the Sand: Jurisdiction and Remedial Discretion' (2013) 18(4) *Judicial Review* 360 [27].

[239] Joe Tomlinson, 'The Narrow Approach to Substantive Legitimate Expectations and the Trend of Modern Authority' (2017) 17(1) *Oxford University Commonwealth Law Journal* 75, 81 (citing from Paul Daly, 'A Pluralist Account of Deference and Legitimate Expectations' in Matthew Groves and Greg Weeks (eds), *Legitimate Expectations in the Common Law World* (Hart Publishing, 2017)).

[240] Varuhas (n 18).

7

Monism

The introductory chapter explained that this book has three core aims. The first and second are positive in nature in that they aim to add something to the collective understanding of administrative law. The first aim of the book has been to highlight the complexity and variety of the legal structures in play in administrative law adjudication – what the book terms administrative law's 'anatomy'. The second has been to demonstrate the importance of recognising this complexity across a number of specific doctrinal areas: procedural review, legitimate expectations and standing.

The book's third and final aim, by contrast, is negative in nature. The core of the argument is that the complexity and variety of administrative law gives reason to question the continued utility of 'monistic' analysis in administrative law.

In order to explain this aim in more detail, it is useful to return again to a monologue offered by Nobel prize-winning physicist Richard Feynman, discussed in chapter one.[1] Feynman's 'Ode to a Flower' tells the story of a disagreement Feynman had with a friend of his who worked as an artist. Feynman's artist friend argues that, in order to understand a flower, it is sufficient to grasp only the single, most important thing about it: that it is beautiful. Feynman, however, fundamentally disagrees. The problem is not that Feynman thinks his friend is wrong in saying that the flower is beautiful. His issue, rather, is that emphasising the beauty of the flower alone leads to the smaller details of the flower, which are necessary to understanding it, being overlooked.

As explained in the Introduction, the approach of Feynman's artist friend has its analogues in the administrative law literature. The commentary is replete with attempts to makes sense of administrative law doctrine by isolating a singular 'master idea or principle'[2] which lends the field unity. The book has begun to demonstrate this at the level of particular doctrines across chapters four, five and six. Chapter four, for example, explained how the search for understanding in the procedural review context has often proceeded as the search for a singular normative goal which guides the courts.[3] In the standing context, similarly,

[1] Professor Richard Feynman, 'The Pleasure of Finding Things Out' (*BBC*, 1981–1982) available at: www.bbc.co.uk/programmes/p018dvyg.

[2] Stephen Smith, *Contract Theory* (Oxford University Press, 2004) 11.

[3] Denis Galligan, *Due Process and Fair Procedures* (Oxford University Press, 1997); Trevor Allan, 'Procedural Fairness and the Duty of Respect' (1998) 18(3) *OJLS* 497.

a particular narrative has dominated. According to it, the courts have replaced a rights-based approach to standing with one which determines whether an applicant has a 'sufficient interest'[4] by considering whether hearing from them would enhance the public interest. Monism's influence is not confined to the level of particular administrative doctrines. As will be seen shortly, the search for unifying concepts has also been present in attempts to make sense of administrative law as a whole.

The third aim of this book, however, is to cast doubt on the plausibility of explaining administrative law in such singular terms. Monistic accounts of administrative law are likely to offer only partial pictures of the field. Just as Feynman believes his friend has a point in emphasising the flower's beauty, there are often elements of truth in monistic accounts. Ultimately, however, the brushstrokes with which they paint are too broad.

This chapter will use two main strategies in order to make that argument. Section I discusses two significant examples of attempts to explain administrative law as a whole by reference to an 'organising principle'[5] – the 'public interest conception'[6] and jurisdiction theory. After mapping the basic contours of these ways of thinking, section I points to a series of deficiencies in the accounts of administrative law they offer. The overarching aim of this section is to suggest through a series of concrete illustrations that, while monistic accounts of administrative law often contain important kernels of truth, by purporting to reduce administrative law to a singular set of explanatory tools they fail to capture the whole.

Section II takes a different approach. In order to make a convincing case against monism, it is necessary to do more than just identify the deficiencies in leading monistic ways of thinking about administrative law. It is important also to explore whether there are good and convincing reasons for attempting to understand administrative law by reference to an 'organising concept'.[7] In light of this, section II discusses the *appeals* of monism. It argues that there are at least four considerations which can help to explain why scholars have been drawn to the idea that administrative law is best explained in monistic terms. Introduced briefly, they are:

a) the kernel of truth which lies at the centre of many of the major monistic approaches to administrative law;

[4] Senior Courts Act 1981, s31(3).

[5] Christopher Forsyth, 'Blasphemy against Basics: Doctrine, Conceptual Reasoning and Certain Decisions of the UK Supreme Court' in John Bell, Mark Elliott, Jason Varuhas and Philip Murray (eds), *Public Law Adjudication in Common Law Systems: Process and Substance* (Hart Publishing, 2016) 155.

[6] Jason Varuhas, 'The Public Interest Conception of Public Law: Its Procedural Origins and Substantive Implications' in Bell, Elliott, Varuhas and Murray (eds), *ibid.*

[7] Christopher Forsyth, 'The Rock and the Sand: Jurisdiction and Remedial Discretion' (2013) 18(4) *Judicial Review* 360 [27].

b) the tendency to equate the ideas of intelligibility, coherence and unity;[8]
c) the assumption that locating an 'organising principle'[9] which grounds administrative law is the most effective way to ensure that judges are properly constrained; and
d) the long-standing sense in which administrative law has suffered from an 'identity crisis'.[10]

The argument of section II, however, is that while these considerations provide superficially appealing arguments for explaining administrative law in monistic terms, their force weakens under closer consideration.

I. Two Monistic Accounts of Administrative Law and their Deficiencies

This aim of this section is to consider two major attempts to explain administrative law in monistic terms and to highlight that, while they capture important truths about the field, they are also tainted by certain explanatory deficiencies. The two accounts which have been chosen are – 'the public interest conception'[11] and jurisdiction theory.

These are far from the only examples of attempts by scholars or judges to explain administrative law in singular terms. 'Ultra vires',[12] 'abuse of power',[13] rationality,[14] the protection of fundamental rights[15] and the promotion of a

[8] Ernest Weinrib, *The Idea of Private Law* (Oxford University Press, 1995).

[9] Forsyth (n 5) 155.

[10] Something which is often said of the study of public administration but which also applies to the study of administrative law. See, for instance, Kent Aiken Kirawn, 'The Crisis of Identity in the Study of Public Administration' (1977) 9(3) *Polity* 321; Gerald Frug, 'The Ideology of Bureaucracy in American Law' (1983) 97 *Harvard Law Review* 1276; Jos CN Raadschelders, *Public Administration: The Interdisciplinary Study of Government* (Oxford University Press, 2011) Ch 1.

[11] Varuhas (n 6).

[12] Christopher Forsyth, 'Of Fig Leaves and Fairy Tales: The Ultra Vires Doctrine, The Sovereignty of Parliament and Judicial Review' (1996) 55(1) *CLJ* 12; Mark Elliott, 'The Ultra Vires Doctrine in a Constitutional Setting: Still the Central Principle of Administrative Law' (1999) 58(1) *CLJ* 129; Mark Elliott, 'The Demise of Parliamentary Sovereignty? The Implications for Justifying Judicial Review' (1999) 115 *LQR* 119; Mark Elliott, *The Constitutional Foundations of Judicial Review* (Bloomsbury, 2001); Christopher Forsyth, 'The Legitimacy of Judicial Review' [2003] *PL* 286.

[13] *R v Secretary of State for Education and Employment, ex parte Begbie* [2000] 1 WLR 115 (CA) 1129; Stephen Sedley, *Law and the Whirligig of Time* (Hart Publishing, 2018) Ch 178. See further Paul Daly, 'Administrative Law: Characteristics, Legitimacy, Unity' in Mark Elliott, Jason Varuhas and Shona Wilson Stark (eds), *The Unity of Public Law?* (Hart Publishing, 2018) 21. For critical discussion see Paul Daly, 'The Language of Administrative Law' (2016) 94 *Canadian Bar Review* 519.

[14] Adam Perry, 'Plan B: A Theory of Judicial Review' (22 November 2017) Oxford Legal Studies Research Paper No 66/2017. Available at SSRN: https://papers.ssrn.com/sol3/papers.cfm?abstract_id=3075886.

[15] Ronald Dworkin, *Taking Rights Seriously* (Duckworth, 1977); Ronald Dworkin, *Law's Empire* (Harvard University Press, 1986); Trevor Allan, *Constitutional Justice: A Liberal Theory of the Rule of Law* (Oxford University Press, 2001); Michael Taggart, 'Reinventing Administrative Law' in

'culture of justification'[16] have, for instance, all been put forward as candidates for administrative law's 'organising principle'[17] in recent years. The public interest conception and jurisdiction theory, however, represent two of the most developed attempts to explain administrative law by reference to a 'master principle or idea'.[18] They have also both experienced something of a resurgence in the academic literature in recent years.[19] They are therefore especially worthy of consideration.

A. 'The Public Interest Conception'

i. *The Content of the Public Interest Conception*

The public interest conception represents an approach to administrative law which is both old and new. It is relatively old in the sense that some of its basic ideas can be traced in commentary[20] and case law[21] from at least the 1980s. It is new in the sense that it is a way of thinking which has experienced a significant resurgence in recent years. The writings of Jason Varuhas[22] in particular have sought to place the public interest conception firmly at the centre of thinking about administrative law.

Nicholas Bamforth and Peter Leyland, *Public Law in a Multi-Layered Constitution* (Hart Publishing, 2003); Thomas Poole, 'The Reformation of English Administrative Law' (2009) 68(1) *CLJ* 142; Sian Elias, 'Righting Administrative Law' in David Dyzenhaus, Murray Hunt and Grant Huscroft (eds), *A Simple Common Lawyer: Essays in Honour of Michael Taggart* (Hart Publishing, 2009). For critique see: Thomas Poole, 'Legitimacy, Rights and Judicial Review' (2005) 25(4) *OJLS* 697; Jason Varuhas, 'The Reformation of English Administrative Law? "Rights", Rhetoric and Reality' (2013) 72 *CLJ* 369.

[16] See especially David Dyzenhaus, Murray Hunt and Michael Taggart, 'The Principle of Legality in Administrative Law: Internationalisation as Constitutionalisation' (2001) 1(1) *Oxford University Commonwealth Law Journal* 5; Thomas Poole, 'Between the Devil and the Deep Blue Sea: Administrative Law in an Age of Rights' in Linda Pearson (ed), *Administrative Law in a Changing State: Essays in Honour of Mark Aronson* (Hart Publishing, 2008); Murray Hunt, 'Sovereignty's Blight: Why Public Law Needs a Concept of Due Deference' in Bamforth and Leyland (eds), *ibid*; Michael Taggart, 'The Tub of Public Law' in David Dyzenhaus (ed), *The Unity of Public Law* (Hart Publishing, 2004); David Dyzenhaus, 'Dignity in Administrative Law: Judicial Deference in a Culture of Justification' (2012) 17(1) *Review of Constitutional Studies* 87.

[17] Forsyth (n 5) 155.

[18] Smith (n 2) 11.

[19] In the case of the public interest conception, this way of thinking has received considerable attention in the writings of Jason Varuhas. In the case of jurisdiction theory, the approach has been drawn on by a number of authors in order to develop a critique of the Supreme Court decisions in *R (Cart) v Upper Tribunal* [2011] UKSC 28, [2012] 1 AC 663 and *R (Jones) v First-tier Tribunal* [2013] UKSC 19, [2012] 2 AC 48. Both developments will be discussed below.

[20] Harry Woolf, *Protection of the Public – A New Challenge* (Stevens and Sons, 1990); Harry Woolf, 'Public Law – Private Law: Why the Divide? A Personal View' [1986] *PL* 220.

[21] *R v Somerset CC, ex parte Dixon* [1998] Env LR 111 (QB).

[22] Varuhas (n 6); Varuhas (n 15) and citations below.

The essence of the public interest concept is encapsulated by the following passage:

> … whereas private law was conceptualised as individual-regarding, [administrative law] was public-regarding. Private law was concerned principally with enforcement of the personal rights of individuals, while [administrative law] was concerned with ensuring public power was exercised properly – that is, in accordance with precepts of good administration – for the good of the public as a whole.[23]

As this passage makes clear, the public interest conception presupposes a binary between two different normative goals a body of law may have.[24] On the one hand, an area of law may be 'individual-regarding'[25] in the sense that its focus is on 'ensuring strong protection and vindication of personal, individual interests'.[26] On the other hand, a body of law may be 'public-regarding'[27] in the sense that its focus is on 'the exercise of public power itself'[28] and on ensuring that 'it is exercised as it ought to be in the public interest'.[29] According to the public interest conception, modern domestic administrative law doctrine largely falls into the second category. Administrative law is, in other words, conceived of as an inherently 'public-regarding'[30] legal field. In this way, the public interest conception suggests that it is the 'near-complete inverse'[31] of other bodies of law, such as human rights law[32] and aspects of private law.[33] These aim centrally to provide strong legal protection for important individual interests, whereas the individual is a 'subsidiary'[34] concern in administrative law. While the individual may benefit from the enforcement of some of the legal duties which administrative law creates, these benefits are incidental. The real concern of administrative law is to ensure that public power is exercised in a manner which promotes the *public* interest.

Stemming from this central idea are a number of further important aspects of the public interest conception. This approach, for instance, offers a distinctive way of thinking about the nature of, and relationship between, the grounds of review. Jason Varuhas, for instance, has written that:

> One of the principal functions of judicial review is to ensure that administrators do not go 'off the rails' in exercising of their powers. From this premise it is a short step to the major grounds. Acting for improper purpose, taking into account extraneous

[23] Varuhas (n 6) 52.
[24] Jason Varuhas, 'Taxonomy and Public Law' in Elliott, Varuhas and Wilson Stark (eds) (n 13).
[25] Varuhas (n 6) 52.
[26] Jason Varuhas, 'Against Unification' in Elliott, Varuhas and Wilson Stark (eds) (n 13) 101.
[27] Varuhas (n 6) 52.
[28] Varuhas (n 26) 101.
[29] Varuhas (n 26) 101.
[30] Varuhas (n 6) 52.
[31] Varuhas (n 26) 101.
[32] Varuhas (n 26) 101.
[33] Jason Varuhas, *Damages and Human Rights* (Hart Publishing, 2016).
[34] Varuhas (n 26) 101.

> concerns, or acting with bias are all ways in which … administrators *cannot be said to have genuinely exercise their powers for the common good* …. Ensuring that 'all relevant facts have been considered,' that the defendant has taken 'reasonable steps to acquaint [itself] with the relevant information to enable [it] to answer [the question] correctly,'[35] acting without undue delay, ensuring that all relevant considers have been considered and irrelevant ones omitted from consideration, affording those who may be affected by a decision notice, consulting them or affording them an opportunity to be heard, decision-making unclouded by personal bias and holding to specific representations made to individuals or entrenched past practices, *are all basic expectations of good administrative practice, and make it more likely that decision-making processes will result in reliable outcomes.*[36]

Underlying this passage is a basic idea: the grounds of review are all emanations of the 'public-regarding'[37] nature of administrative law. They are, that is, legal doctrines which are unified around a concern to ensure that decision-making power is only exercised in ways which will promote the interests of the *public as a collectivity*.

In addition to offering a distinctive account of the grounds of review, the public interest conception is also closely related to a particular way of thinking about standing.[38] This understanding, often described using the language of 'public interest',[39] was discussed in chapter six. According to it, the normative orientations of administrative law necessitates that the courts make use of a different approach to standing than that used in other fields. In 'individual-regarding'[40] fields such as private law[41] and human rights law,[42] it is appropriate that standing is confined to individuals whose rights are at stake. The focus of administrative law, by contrast, is not on affording protection to the interests of any one individual but ensuring that power more generally is exercised in accordance with the public interest. As such, it would run counter to the normative goals of this area of law to confine standing to persons whose rights are at stake or who are acutely affected by a decision. On the contrary, any person or organisation that is willing and able to stand up for the interests of the public should be heard as long as they are able to make out an arguable case.[43]

[35] *R v Lancashire County Council, ex parte Huddleston* [1986] 2 All ER 941 (CA), 945.

[36] Varuhas (n 6) 64–65 (emphasis added).

[37] Varuhas (n 6) 52.

[38] Varuhas (n 26) 101–102. Varuhas describes standing in domestic administrative law as 'exceptionally liberal' in the sense that 'public-spirited individuals and pressure groups are routinely granted standing where they can demonstrate an arguable case that administrative action is lawful'.

[39] Mark Elliott and Jason Varuhas, *Administrative Law*, 5th edn (Oxford University Press, 2017) Ch 14.

[40] Varuhas (n 6) 52.

[41] See Varuhas (n 6) 52.

[42] See Varuhas (n 26).

[43] *Council of Civil Service Unions (CCSU) v Minister for the Civil Service* [1985] AC 374 (HL) 410; Farah Ahmed and Adam Perry, 'Standing and Civic Virtue' (2018) 134 *LQR* 239.

The public interest conception has also been said to have a number of important practical implications for the proper direction of travel of administrative law. Two are especially pertinent. The first concerns the contentious issue of whether compensation should be made available for breaches of administrative law doctrine.[44] In 2010 the Law Commission looked into the question and ultimately made a positive case for compensation.[45] Of most interest for present purposes, however, is that the Commission reported that in the course of its consultation process:

> … there were some consultees who disagreed vigorously with the proposal that a wider availability of monetary remedies could or should be introduced. They opposed the suggestion to allow individuals to claim damages where no private right had been infringed. Such responses drew a sharp distinction between the rights that arise from a *public duty*, which are *owed to the world at large*, and private rights.[46]

At the heart of this argument is the basic idea underlying the public interest conception. Due to the fact, it is argued, that administrative law is concerned with enforcing legal duties owed to the public as a collectivity, as opposed to vindicating the rights of one individual, there can be no room for monetary compensation. Monetary compensation, it is said, is logically confined to bodies of law which are concerned with the personal legal relationships between *individuals*, not between administrative decision-makers and the public at large.[47]

A second example of the practical implications said to flow from the public interest conception concerns the proportionality doctrine.[48] It is well-known that there is a fervent and ongoing debate concerning how the courts ought to structure substantive review.[49] One set of arguments suggests that the concept of

[44] Peter Cane, 'Damages in Public Law' (1999) 3 *Otago Law Review* 489; Michael Fordham, 'Reparations for Maladministration: Public Law's Final Frontier' [2003] *Judicial Review* 104; Yasser Vanderman, 'Ultra Vires Legitimate Expectation: An Argument for Compensation' [2012] *PL* 85.

[45] Law Commission, 'Administrative Redress: Public Bodies and the Citizen' (Law Comm No 322, 2010) 2.16.

[46] *Ibid* 8 (emphasis added).

[47] Varuhas (n 26) 102. Varuhas writes: 'damages are not available [in domestic administrative law] and would be out of place given they are concerned to remedy setbacks *personal* to specific individuals pursuant to breach of individual rights'.

[48] *Pham v Secretary of State for the Home Department* [2015] UKSC 19, [2015] 1 WLR 1591 (see discussion in Thomas Adams, 'Stumbling Towards the Constitution: *Pham v Secretary of State for the Home Department*' (2016) 75(1) *CLJ* 1); *R (Keyu) v Secretary of State for Foreign and Commonwealth Affairs* [2015] UKSC 69, [2016] AC 1355; *Browne v Parole Board of England and Wales* [2018] EWCA Civ 2024, [2018] 9 WLUK 246 (see discussion in Christopher Knight, 'Proportionality at Common Law: Another False Dawn' (2019) C78(1) *CLJ* 5).

[49] Anthony Lester and Jeffrey Jowell, 'Beyond Wednesbury: Substantive Principles of Administrative Law' [1987] *PL* 368; Lord Irvine, 'Judges and Decision-Makers: The Theory and Practice of *Wednesbury* Review' [1996] *PL* 59; Johns Laws, '*Wednesbury*' in Christopher Forsyth and Ivan Hard (eds), *The Goldern Metwand and the Crooked Cord* (Oxford University Press, 1998); Murray Hunt, 'Against Bifurcation' in Dyzehaus, Hunt and Huscroft (eds) (n 15); Michael Taggart, 'Proportionality, Deference, *Wednesbury*' [2008] *New Zealand Law Reports* 423; Tom Hickman, 'Problems for

proportionality,[50] which the domestic courts have come to be comfortable with applying in the context of the Human Rights Act 1998,[51] is apt to play at least a partial[52] role in domestic administrative law. Relying on the public interest conception, however, Jason Varuhas has strongly resisted this suggestion. In the context of adjudication under the Human Rights Act, Varuhas argues, the proportionality doctrine serves as a 'defence'[53] to a claim that an *individual right* has been violated. Given, however, that administrative law is normatively oriented towards the promotion of the *public's* interest, there can logically be no room for proportionality to play a role, at least without a significant normative reconfiguration of the area.[54]

ii. The Deficiencies of the Public Interest Conception

The public interest conception offers a clear and simple account of the nature of administrative law. According to it, the essence of administrative law adjudication lies in the promotion of the interests of the public as opposed to those of any one individual. There is undoubtedly an element of truth in this idea. As chapter two explained, an important strand of administrative law's modern history has seen the courts assuming a greater role in enforcing statutory duties designed to benefit the public as a collectivity.[55] There is, therefore, explanatory value in the public interest conception. By stressing the important role that the interests of the public play in adjudication, this account emphasises that judges play a greater role in overseeing duties of this kind than they were once able to.[56]

Proportionality' [2010] *New Zealand Law Reports* 303; Paul Daly, 'Wednesbury's Reason and Structure' [2011] *PL* 238; Mark Elliott, 'From Bifurcation to Calibration: Twin-Track Deference and the Culture of Justification' and Jeffrey Jowell, 'Proportionality and Unreasonableness: Neither Merger Not Takeover' both in Mark Elliott and Hanna Wilberg (eds), *The Scope and Intensity of Substantive Review: Traversing Taggart's Rainbow* (Hart Publishing, 2015); Rebecca Williams, 'Structuring Substantive Review' [2017] *PL* 99.

[50] *Smith v United Kingdom* (2000) 29 EHRR 493; *Bank Mellat v HM Treasury* [2014] UKSC 39, [2014] AC 700; Julian Rivers, 'Proportionality and Variable Intensity Review' (2006) 65(1) *CLJ* 174; David Mead, 'Outcomes Aren't All: Defending Process-Based Review of Public Authority Decisions under the Human Rights Act 1998' [2012] *PL* 61.

[51] *R (Daly) v Secretary of State for the Home Department* [2001] 2 AC 532 (HL).

[52] Paul Craig, for example, argues that proportionality can suitably serve as a general ground of review, replacing reasonableness review in all cases (see especially Paul Craig, 'Proportionality, Rationality and Review' [2010] *New Zealand Law Reports* 303) whereas Jeff King envisages a much more limited role for domestic proportionality review (see Jeff King, 'Proportionality: A Halfway House' [2010] *New Zealand Law Reports* 327).

[53] Varuhas (n 26).

[54] Varuhas (n 26).

[55] See discussion in chapter 2 of *R v Guardians of the Lewisham Union* [1897] 1 QB 498 (DC) and *R v Secretary of State for Foreign and Commonwealth Affairs, ex parte World Development Movement* [1995] 1 WLR 386 (QB).

[56] Although emphasised in chapters 2 and 6, it is a mis-description to say that, prior to 1977, the courts *only* intervened in cases where the individual applicant's rights were at stake. See for instance *R v Greater London Council, ex parte Blackburn* [1976] 1 WLR 550 (CA).

That said, there are also important explanatory deficiencies in the public interest conception. These deficiencies have been explored in depth by Paul Craig in an illuminating article.[57] For present purposes, it suffices to call attention to three.

The first issue with the public interest conception is historical in nature and has been explored in depth in chapter two. It was seen there that the public interest conception generates a distinctive historical narrative of the development of administrative law. According to it, a cluster of leading judges[58] used the opportunities presented by the procedural reforms of the late-1970s[59] to reject Diceyan orthodoxy[60] and to carve out a new vision of administrative law. The public interest conception therefore paints a picture of administrative law as a deliberately crafted product of a series of landmark decisions from the 1980s onwards.[61]

Chapter two identified some of the major difficulties with this way of thinking. The overarching problem is that, as was seen, the modern history of administrative law is not the linear tale of the subject developing around a singular 'organising concept'.[62] It is, rather, both multifaceted and messy. As a result, it is important to be cynical of any attempt to paint administrative law's history in neat terms.[63] There are further, more specific, issues. One, for instance, is that by presenting the grounds of review as logical extensions of a central administrative law logic which was established in the 1980s, the public interest conception obscures the rather more complex way in which the grounds of review evolved. As chapter two emphasised, the grounds of review were not developed at a particular moment in time in order to comply with a unifying logic. Some, such as procedural review, evolved from case law across many centuries.[64] Others, such as legitimate expectations, are of more recent origin.[65]

A second major problem with the public interest conception is its reliance on a purported division between the interests of the individual, said to be the concern of human rights and private law, and the interests of the public, said to be the

[57] Paul Craig, 'Taxonomy and Public Law: A Response' [2019] *PL* 281.

[58] Lord Diplock, 'Judicial Review Revisited' (1974) 33(2) *CLJ* 233; Lord Wilberforce, 'Lord Diplock and Administrative Law' [1986] *PL* 6; Woolf, 'Public Law – Private Law' (n 20).

[59] Rules of the Supreme Court (Amendment No 3) 1977 (SI 1977/1955).

[60] Albert Venn Dicey (edited by John Allison), *The Law of the Constitution (Oxford Edition of Dicey)* (Oxford University Press, 2013). See further chapter 2 of this book.

[61] *R v Inland Revenue Commissioners, ex parte National Federation of Self-Employed* [1982] AC 617 (HL); *O'Reilly v Mackman* [1983] 2 AC 237; *CCSU* (n 43).

[62] Forsyth (n 7) [27].

[63] Stephen Sedley, 'Judicial Politics' (2012) 34 *London Review of Books* 15 and Stephen Sedley, 'In Time of Meltdown' (2019) 41(17) *London Review of Books* 4 (responding to Jonathan Sumption, 'The Limits of Law' reproduced in Richard Ekins, Paul Yowell and Nick Barber (eds), *Lord Sumption and the Limits of Law* (Hart Publishing, 2016) and Jonathan Sumption, *Trials of the State: Law and the Decline of Politics* (Profile, 2019) respectively).

[64] See discussion in chapter 2.

[65] *R v North & East Devon Health Authority, ex parte Coughlan* [2001] QB 213 (CA).

primary focus of administrative law. Paul Craig has emphasised a number of issues with this way of thinking. One is that the line between individual and public interest is often blurred, especially in the administrative law context.[66] As Craig has put it, there is a sense in which 'all legislation is designed to enhance the public interest, since it reflects the view of a duly elected legislature as to what rules should govern the polity'.[67] However, this does not prevent legislative schemes, especially in the 'social welfare'[68] context, from also being centrally concerned with improving conditions for individuals. In these contexts, the line between the public and individual interest becomes highly blurred: it might be said that the legislature has formed the view that the public interest lies in a particular way of treating of individuals.

A further problem emphasised by Craig is that consideration of the public interest is often of central importance in human rights adjudication.[69] As Craig explains, some of the most contentious issues in human rights case law concern the application of the proportionality doctrine.[70] Here the courts often grapple with the question of how to reconcile the individual's rights with broader public concerns.

Most difficult, from the perspective of this book, however, is the suggestion that the individual is of only secondary importance in domestic administrative law. The earlier chapters of this book show that the protection of the rights and interests of the individual is often of central importance in administrative law adjudication. As emphasised throughout this book, legislative frameworks play a highly significant role in judicial reasoning. These frameworks are not of one kind, and create different kinds of legal relationship. While some create institutional structures for protecting aspects of the public interest,[71] others specify relationships of individual right-duty correlativity between the applicant and the administrative decision-maker. When litigation occurs in these areas, therefore, it often raises questions about what the individual is legally entitled to from the decision-maker.[72] There are also areas of administrative law where the common law affords strong protection to the individual. Chapter four, for instance, discussed the

[66] Craig (n 57) 283–91.

[67] Craig (n 57) 284.

[68] Craig (n 57) 284.

[69] As Craig puts it, the public interest conception 'ignores … the fact that the great majority of HRA cases are concerned precisely with public interest defences to rights-based actions (Craig (n 57) 288).

[70] *R (Begum) v Denbigh High School Governors* [2006] UKHL 15, [2007] 1 AC 100; *Belfast CC v Miss Behavin' Ltd* [2007] UKHL 19, [2007 1 WLR 1420; *Huang v Secretary of State for the Home Department* [2007] UKHL 11, [2007] 2 AC 167.

[71] As emphasised in chapters 2 and 3, this is true of much environmental legislation, including nature conservation legislation. See, eg, National Parks and Access to the Countryside Act 1949; Wildlife and Countryside Act 1981; Natural Environment and Rural Communities Act 2006. See also The Conservation of Habitats and Species Regulations 2017 (SI 2017/1012) which implement European Union Directives.

[72] *R (Conville) v Richmond-upon-Thames LBC* [2006] EWCA Civ 718, [2006] 1 WLR 2808 (discussed in chapter 3).

strong common law presumption that individuals are entitled to be given notice of decisions that significantly impact on their interests.[73]

A third and final difficulty is that the public interest conception generates accounts of particular doctrines within administrative law which are deficient. Two examples will suffice to illustrate. The first concerns how the public interest conception explains procedural review. Jason Varuhas has suggested that there are two broad ways of thinking about procedural review.[74] According to the first, procedural review is centrally concerned with ensuring the dignified treatment of the individual. According to the second, its focus is on making sure that decision-making power is exercised in accordance with basic precepts of good administration, in order to promote the interests of the public. Unsurprisingly, Varuhas' preference is for the latter. The analysis in chapter four, however, clearly demonstrates the difficulties with understanding procedural review in this way. Procedural review is made up of both individual-regarding and public-regarding aspects. On the issue of notice, for instance, the courts have developed strong protection for the individual through a common law presumption that notice must be given to significantly affected individuals.[75] This presumption, however, gives way when insisting on it would significantly undermine the public-orientated aims of a statutory scheme.[76]

To suggest, in other words, that judges face a choice between understanding procedural review in either 'individual-regarding'[77] or 'public-regarding'[78] terms, does not accord with the procedural review case law. This case law can only be explained by recognising that this is an area of law in which the courts seek to accommodate both the interests of the individual and those of the public, and have developed a series of specific legal techniques in order to do so.

A further example of a particular explanatory deficiency concerns standing. As explained above, the public interest conception suggests that administrative law's 'public-regarding'[79] nature necessitates a distinctive approach to standing. There is, according to the public interest conception, no room for the courts to confine standing to applicants whose rights are affected,[80] meaning that an 'exceptionally liberal'[81] approach must be taken. This account of standing, however, overlooks a number of important arguments discussed in chapter six. Chapter six emphasised that there is not, in English and Welsh administrative law, a singular 'test' of standing which is applied in all contexts. Rather, the legislative framework,

[73] *Bank Mellat* (n 50).
[74] Jason Varuhas, 'Judicial Review at a Crossroads' (2015) 74(2) *CLJ* 215. See also Varuhas (n 15).
[75] See discussion of *Bank Mellat* (n 50) in chapter 4.
[76] See *R (Haralambous) v St Alban's Crown Court* [2018] UKSC 1, [2018] AC 236 and discussion in chapter 4.
[77] Varuhas (n 6) 52.
[78] Varuhas (n 6) 52.
[79] Varuhas (n 6) 52.
[80] Varuhas (n 26) 101–102.
[81] Varuhas (n 26) 101.

values at stake and legal relationships in issue leads the courts to adopt distinct understandings of 'sufficient interest'[82] in different contexts. Importantly, there are categories of challenge where there is reason to think the courts would confine standing to the individual who holds the right correlative to the duty relied on. These categories include challenges based on legislative provisions which confer rights on individuals and cases in which an individualised decision is challenged for want of notice.

The public interest conception, then, suffers from a series of explanatory drawbacks. It offers a misleading picture of the modern history of administrative law, relies on an unsustainable dichotomy between the public and individual interest and generates deficient explanations of particular doctrines. These deficiencies are important. They highlight a series of reasons to be cautious in accepting the public interest conception, and the alleged practical consequences which have been said to flow from it,[83] too lightly. There is also a lesson of broader significance here. The public interest conception endeavours to explain administrative law by emphasising one normative role the courts play. It has been seen, however, that the complexity and variety of the legal structures which are in play in administrative law adjudication prevents the field from being explained in such terms. Variety in terms of the legislative frameworks in play, the legal interests the courts aim to protect and the legal relationships with which they grapple mean that the public interest conception, while capturing an important truth about the field, obscures a series of other aspects which are essential to a full understanding of administrative law's nature.

B. Jurisdiction Theory

i. *The Content of Jurisdiction Theory*

The public interest conception is not a lone example of the difficulties of monistic analysis. A number of other accounts suffer from similar issues. This part focuses on a second example: jurisdiction theory.

Jurisdiction theory represents a long-standing and traditional way of thinking about the subject, which has been developed over a number of decades by leading thinkers including William Wade[84] and Christopher Forsyth.[85] It is also an

[82] Senior Courts Act 1981, s31(3).

[83] Varuhas (n 26).

[84] William Wade, 'Unlawful Administrative Action: Void or Voidable?' (1967) 83 *LQR* 499; William Wade, 'Unlawful Administrative Action: Void or Voidable?' (1968) 84 *LQR* 95.

[85] Forsyth (n 5); Forsyth (n 7); Christopher Forsyth, 'The Metaphysics of Nullity' in Christopher Forsyth and Ivan Hare (eds), *The Golden Metwand and the Crooked Cord* (Oxford University Press, 1998); Christopher Forsyth, 'The Legal Effect of Unlawful Administrative Acts: The Theory of the Second Actor Explained and Developed' (2001) 35 *Amicus Curiae* 20.

approach which continues to be referred to by some as offering the 'standard'[86] or 'orthodox'[87] way of thinking about the field.[88] Its essence is neatly captured in the following passage, taken from Wade and Forsyth's leading textbook:[89]

> When subjecting some administrative act or order to judicial review, the court is concerned with its legality: *is it within the limits of the power granted?* … Judicial control, therefore, means primarily review and is based on a fundamental principle, inherent throughout the legal system, that powers can be validly exercised *only within their true limits. The doctrines by which those limits are ascertained and enforced form the very marrow of administrative law.*[90]

Two points are especially worth drawing out from this passage. First, according to jurisdiction theory, in any given administrative law case, the Court has a single legal task: to determine whether the decision is tainted by a legal error, the effect of which is to deprive the decision-maker of power or 'jurisdiction'. Second, and relatedly, the grounds of review are therefore thought to play a particular role in adjudication. As Wade and Forsyth put it, they are understood as the 'doctrines by which th[e] limits [of administrative power] are ascertained and enforced'.[91] The grounds of review, in other words, are presented by jurisdiction theory as a singular cluster – they are the 'power-constraining'[92] legal standards which, taken collectively, identify the boundaries of what administrative decision-makers do and do not have power to do.

Jurisdiction theory is closely related to a number of other well-established ways of thinking within administrative law. Especially important is the idea of automatic nullity. There is a long-standing debate in English and Welsh administrative law concerning the legal consequences of contravening a ground of review.[93]

[86] Thomas Adams, 'The Standard Theory of Administrative Unlawfulness' (2017) 76(2) *CLJ* 289.

[87] Philip Murray, 'Process, Substance and the History of Error of Law Review' in Bell, Elliott, Varuhas and Murray (eds) (n 5) 108–109.

[88] On the evolution of jurisdiction theory, see: DM Gordon, 'The Observance of Law as a Condition of Jurisdiction' (1913) *LQR* 386; DM Gordon, 'The Relation of Facts to Jurisdiction' (1929) *LQR* 459; *R v Northumberland Compensation Appeal Tribunal, ex parte Shaw* [1952] 1 KB 338 (CA); Diplock (n 58); *Pearlman v Keepers and Governors of Harrow School* [1979] QB 56 (CA); *O'Reilly* (n 61); *Re Racal Communications Ltd* [1981] AC 374 (HL); Jack Beatson, 'The Scope of Judicial Review for Error of Law' (1984) 4(1) *OJLS* 22; *R v Lord President of the Privy Council, ex parte Page* [1993] AC 682 (HL); Murray (n 87); Rebecca Williams, 'When is an Error not an Error? Reform of Jurisdictional Review of Error of Law and Fact' [2007] *PL* 793; Philip Murray, 'Judicial Review of the Upper Tribunal: Appeal, Review and the Will of Parliament' (2011) 70(3) *CLJ* 487.

[89] William Wade and Christopher Forsyth, *Administrative Law*, 11th edn (Oxford University Press, 2014).

[90] *Ibid* 26 (emphasis added). See also Elliott and Varuhas (n 39) Ch 2 which explains that 'in a sense, all of judicial review is about jurisdiction'.

[91] Wade and Forsyth (n 89).

[92] For discussion, see Joanna Bell, 'The Doctrine of Legitimate *Expectations*: Power-Constraining or Right-Conferring Legal Standard' [2016] *PL* 437, 439–41.

[93] See especially citations at (n 84) and (85); Adams (n 86); David Feldman, 'Error of Law and Flawed Administrative Action' (2014) 73 *CLJ* 275; Veena Srirangam Nadhamuni, 'Suspending Invalidity while Keeping Faith with Nullity' [2015] *PL* 596; Chris Himsworth, 'Escape from Nullity? Readdressing the Consequences of Unlawfulness in Administrative Law' (2018) 3 *Judicial Review* 151.

As Thomas Adams has noted, jurisdiction theory has long presented itself as supplying the 'standard'[94] way of thinking about this issue. The basic idea is this: because, according to jurisdiction theory, the grounds of review function by placing legal boundaries, which demarcate the line between that which an administrative decision-maker has, and that which it lacks power to do, the consequence of a decision-maker violating one or more of these grounds must logically be that it steps outside of its jurisdiction. In such circumstances, the determination is therefore one which the decision-maker had no legal power to make and from a legal point of view[95] must have been void *ab initio*:[96] it must never have existed in the legal sphere.

Jurisdiction theory is also said to have implications for other doctrinal issues. It is said, for instance, that the possibility of collateral challenge is contingent on the idea of automatic nullity and therefore jurisdiction theory.[97] The line of thinking runs as follows. Imagine that an individual is criminally prosecuted for an offence committed under an administrative order.[98] They wish to defend themselves on the basis that the order is unlawful in administrative law terms. Merely establishing that the order is unlawful will not be of any significant utility: an unlawful order is still a legally effective order which continues to bind unless quashed by a court and the criminal courts do not have jurisdiction to issue quashing orders.[99] The defendant, therefore, must go further. She must show that the order is not only unlawful but void *ab initio*. In this way, jurisdiction theory and its counterpart, the idea of automatic nullity, are thought to facilitate collateral challenge. Only by adhering to the idea that breach of administrative law principle robs a decision of validity, it is said, can a defendant in criminal or civil proceedings raise administrative unlawfulness as an effective defence.[100]

Finally, jurisdiction theory is also said to have important implications for ouster clauses.[101] Because an unlawful administrative act is void *ab initio*, it has been argued, it cannot constitute a 'determination' and is merely a 'purported' determination.[102] In light of this, ouster clauses which purport to immunise

[94] Adams (n 86).

[95] On the purported distinction between validity as a matter of law and existence as a matter of fact, see both Wade refs in (n 84). For critique see Adams (n 86).

[96] As opposed to being 'voidable': *R v Central London County Court, ex parte London* [1999] QB 1260; *R v Wicks* [1998] AC 92; Paul Craig, *Administrative Law*, 8th edn (Sweet & Maxwell, 2017) Ch 25.

[97] See especially: Mark Elliott, 'Boddington: Rediscovering the Constitutional Logic of Administrative Law' [1998] *PL* 92; Elliott and Varuhas (n 39) Ch 3.

[98] *Boddington v British Transport Police* [1999] 2 AC 143 (HL).

[99] Senior Courts Act 1981, s29 confers the power to make a quashing order (and mandatory and prohibiting order) on the High Court.

[100] Elliott and Varuhas (n 39) Ch 3.

[101] Robert Craig, 'Ouster Clauses, Separation of Powers and the Intention of Parliament: from *Anisminic* to *Privacy International*' [2018] *PL* 570.

[102] See discussion of *Straatspresident en andere v United Democratic Front* 1988(4) SA 830(A) in Forsyth, 'Of Fig Leaves and Fairy Tales' (n 12).

'determinations' from judicial oversight will not be effective in ousting the courts' abilities to check whether a ground of review has been breached.[103]

ii. Deficiencies of Jurisdiction Theory

Much like the public interest conception, jurisdiction theory suffers from a number of deficiencies.[104] A recent useful discussion of these deficiencies can be found in Lord Carnwath's judgment in *Privacy International*.[105] A particular difficulty for his Lordship is the reliance of jurisdiction theory on 'highly artificial'[106] and 'elusive concepts'[107] such as 'jurisdiction (wide or narrow), ultra vires [and] nullity'.[108] At the heart of this judgment is the suggestion that the 'discussion [of administrative law issue] needs to move beyond'[109] these ideas.

A detailed discussion of every aspect of jurisdiction theory lies beyond the scope of this section.[110] For present purposes, it is sufficient to highlight two core ways in which the account of administrative law it offers is partial only.

A first problem with jurisdiction theory concerns the central idea that, in any given administrative law case, the courts are faced with a singular question: does the authority have, or does it lack, jurisdiction to take the decision at hand? This significantly oversimplifies the array of legal questions which can be raised in administrative law adjudication. Part of the issue is that, as has been emphasised throughout this book, the legislative framework in the background of a case plays a key role in shaping the issues. There are undoubtedly cases where the relevant legislative provisions confer power subject to conditions (both explicit and implicit[111]) and the central question raised is whether those conditions have been met.[112] In other cases, however, the background legislation may do something different. Many legislative provisions function by placing legal duties on administrative decision-makers designed to benefit the public as a collectivity.[113] Others, especially in the housing and social security contexts, confer entitlements on individuals.[114] Where legal challenges arise in such contexts, the central question

[103] *Anisminic Ltd v Foreign Compensation Commission* [1969] 2 AC 147 (HL);

[104] Joanna Bell, 'Rethinking the Story of *Cart v Upper Tribunal* and its Implications for Administrative Law' (2019) 39(1) *OJLS* 74.

[105] *R (Privacy International) v Investigatory Powers Tribunal* [2019] UKSC 22, [2019] 2 WLR 1219.

[106] *Ibid* [82] and [129].

[107] *Ibid* [132].

[108] *Ibid.*

[109] *Ibid* [128].

[110] Adams (n 86); Feldman (n 93); David Feldman, '*Anisminic Ltd v Foreign Compensation Commission* [1968]: In Perspective' in Maurice Sunkin and Satvinder Juss (eds), *Landmark Cases in Public Law* (Hart Publishing, 2017).

[111] See citations at n 12.

[112] A well-known example is *R (Evans) v Attorney General* [2015] UKSC 21, [2015] AC 1787.

[113] Many of the duties created in nature conservation legislation fit this description: see citations at n 71; Andrew Harding, *Public Duties and Public Law* (Oxford University Press, 1989).

[114] See, eg, Jobseekers Act 1995, s1(2): 'a claimant is entitled to a jobseeker's allowance if he (a) is available for employment, (b) has entered into a jobseeker's agreement which remains in force …'.

will often be one distinct from that of whether the decision-maker had the legal power to take the decision at hand. It may, rather, be a question of whether the decision-maker has failed to comply with a statutory obligation,[115] or whether it has failed to deliver the statutory right of an individual applicant.[116]

A second important problem is that, much like the public interest conception, jurisdiction theory generates problematic accounts of particular administrative law doctrines. A clear example is the idea of automatic nullity. As already explained, jurisdiction theory offers a very rigid and traditional way of thinking about the legal consequences of administrative unlawfulness: because breach of administrative law doctrine takes a decision-maker outside of its jurisdiction, its decision must be regarded as void *ab initio*. As Paul Daly has written, however, 'the proposition that unlawful administrative decisions are nullities … [which] never existed in the eyes of the law'[117] is 'flatly inconsistent with judicial practice',[118] at least beyond a small handful of well-known cases.[119] This is because judicial practice makes central use of the idea that remedies in administrative law are discretionary.[120] The proper remedy in a given case, in other words, is not thought of by the courts as being dictated by jurisdiction theory, which would generally demand that the courts make an order denoting the invalidity of the decision.[121] Judges, rather, conceive of themselves as having discretion to identify an appropriate remedy in light of the particular legal and factual contours of the case.[122]

A striking example of this can be seen through a comparison of the Court of Appeal decision in *Richardson*[123] and the Supreme Court judgment in *Dover DC*.[124] Both of these cases concerned a clear breach of a legislative provision requiring planning authorities to make publicly available a statement of their reasons for granting planning permission following an environmental impact assessment.[125]

[115] A good example, albeit with a European Union law dimension, is the ClientEarth litigation. See especially *R (ClientEarth) v Secretary of State for the Environment, Food and Rural Affairs* [2013] UKSC 25, [2013] 2 All ER 982; *R (ClientEarth) v Secretary of State for the Environment, Food and Rural Affairs* [2015] UKSC 28, [2015] 4 All ER 724.

[116] See discussion of *Conville* (n 72) (discussed in chapter 3).

[117] Paul Daly, 'Teaching *Anisminic* in a Foreign Language' published on *Administrative Law Matters* blog (22 April 2018). See further Feldman (n 93); *R v Monopolies and Mergers Commission, ex parte Argyll* [1986] 1 WLR 763; *Walton v Scottish Ministers* [2012] UKSC 44, [2013] PTSR 51; *R (Champion) v North Norfolk DC* [2015] UKSC 52, [2015] 1 WLR 3710.

[118] Daly, *ibid.*

[119] *Anisminic* (n 103); *Page* (n 88); *Boddington* (n 98); *Ahmed v HM Treasury* [2010] UKSC 5, [2012] 2 AC 534 (discussed in Forsyth (n 5)).

[120] Senior Courts Act 1981, s29 and s31; Civil Procedure Rules 1998, Part 54, especially 54.19.

[121] This could most obviously be done by issuing a quashing order.

[122] *Glynn v Keele University* [1971] 1 WLR 487 (Ch); *Agricultural, Horticultural and Forestry Industry Training Board v Aylesbury Mushrooms* [1972] 1 WLR 190 (QB); *R v Chief Constable of North Wales, ex parte Evans* [1982] 1 WLR 1155 (HL); *Salvesen v Riddell* [2013] UKSC 22, 2013 SC (UKSC) 236.

[123] *R (Richardson) v North Yorkshire CC* [2003] EWCA Civ 1860, [2004] 1 WLR 1920.

[124] *R (CPRE Kent) v Dover DC* [2017] UKSC 79, [2018] 1 WLR 108.

[125] Town and Country Planning (Environmental Impact Assessment) Regulations 2011 (SI 2011/1824), reg 24(1)(c) (since re-enacted as Town and Country Planning (Environmental Impact Assessment) Regulations 2017 (SI 2017/571), reg 30(1)(c)).

From the perspective of jurisdiction theory, the courts might have been expected to issue quashing orders denoting the invalidity of the resulting decisions.[126] This was not, however, the approach taken. Thus in *Richardson*, the Court of Appeal refused to quash the decision to grant planning permission, preferring to order that the reasons for the decision be disclosed subsequently. In *Dover DC*, by contrast, the Supreme Court reached the conclusion that 'the only appropriate remedy [was] to quash the permission'.[127]

Lord Carnwath has explained the difference between the two cases as turning on the extent to which the failure to give reasons undermined the purposes of the background legislation on the facts. In *Richardson*, all the benefits of requiring a statement of reasons to be issued had been achieved in another way.[128] Quashing the planning decision was not therefore necessary to promote the underlying aims of requiring the decision-maker to give reasons. In *Dover DC*, by contrast, the Supreme Court was of the view that breach of the duty to give reasons in the form stipulated had, on the facts, meant that one of the aims of the requirement had been undermined. Specifically, one of the purposes of requiring the publication of a statement of reasons was to make clear whether the decision-maker had 'properly understood the key issues … [and] reached a rational conclusion on them'.[129] Dover DC's conduct[130] had given rise to 'substantial doubt'[131] as to whether this had been done.

Automatic nullity is not the only specific problematic aspect of jurisdiction theory. There are also difficulties with the accounts jurisdiction theory offers of both collateral challenge and ouster clauses. In the case of collateral challenge, one issue is that the courts' approach to the availability of collateral challenge is considerably more nuanced than regarding collateral challenge as being generally available because administrative unlawfulness always results in nullity. In a number of cases, for instance, the courts have denied a defendant the opportunity to raise administrative unlawfulness collaterally on the basis of the defendant's failure to make use of an alternative statutory route of challenge at an earlier stage.[132]

[126] Mark Elliott, 'Has the Common Law Duty to Give Reasons Come of Age Yet?' [2011] *PL* 56, 68–74. The author suggests the proper remedial response to a failure to give adequate reasons is to quash, unless there are 'wholly disproportionate negative consequences'.

[127] *Dover DC* (n 124) 68–74.

[128] The local planning authority had made publicly available both the detailed report of a planning officer and the minutes of a council meeting straightforwardly approving his recommendations. The public had therefore been given straightforward access to the reasons for the decision.

[129] *Dover DC* (n 124) [68].

[130] Unlike the planning authority in *Richardson*, Dover DC had disapproved of the officer's recommendations and the minutes from the committee meeting left its reasons for doing so ambiguous in a number of respects.

[131] *Dover DC* (n 124) [68].

[132] *Crown Prosecution Service v T* [2006] EWHC 728 (Admin), [2007] 1 WLR 209. See also *R (TN (Vietnam)) v Secretary of State for the Home Department* [2018] EWCA Civ 2838, [2019] 1 WLR 2647.

In the case of ouster clauses, the recent Supreme Court decision in *Privacy International*[133] is a clear illustration that the judicial approach to interpreting ouster clauses is considerably more complex than jurisdiction theory suggests. As explained above, according to jurisdiction theory, an administrative decision which violates the grounds of review is a nullity. When interpreting ouster clauses, therefore, the central question is whether the clause protects only valid determinations or also extends to 'purported'[134] decisions. In different ways, however, the judgments of the Supreme Court in *Privacy International* cast doubt on this way of thinking. As indicated earlier, Lord Carnwath (with the agreement of Lady Hale, Lord Kerr and, on some issues, Lord Lloyd-Jones) emphasised the importance of 'moving beyond'[135] analysis based on notions such as jurisdiction and nullity, and instead recognising that:

> … the courts have not adopted a uniform approach [to determining the availability of judicial review, including in the context of an ouster clause] but have felt free to adapt or limit the scope and form of judicial review, so as to ensure respect on the one hand for the particular statutory context and the inferred intention of the legislature, and on the other for the fundamental principles of the rule of law, and to find an appropriate balance between the two.[136]

Lord Sumption (with the agreement of Lord Reed), while dissenting from the conclusion that the ouster clause in question[137] did not prevent the courts from considering the legal question raised by the applicant,[138] also offered analysis which is difficult to square with jurisdiction theory. According to his Lordship, review on certain legal grounds is far more difficult to exclude than review on others, if it is capable of exclusion at all. This is because some of the grounds of review[139] are centrally aimed at giving effect to Parliament's own stipulations. To read a generally worded ouster clause as excluding these iterations of review would therefore undermine Parliamentary intent on a grander scale. As his Lordship put it:

> If Parliament on the true construction of an enactment has created a tribunal of legally limited jurisdiction, then it must have intended that those limits should have effect in law. The only way in which a proposition can have effect in law, is for it to be recognised and applied by the courts. Parliament's intention that there should be legal limits to the tribunal's jurisdiction is not therefore consistent with the courts lacking the capacity to enforce the limits.[140]

[133] *Privacy International* (n 105).
[134] See *Anisminic* (n 103).
[135] *Privacy International* (n 105) [128].
[136] *Privacy International* (n 105) [130].
[137] Regulation of Investigatory Powers Act 2000, s67(8) (since amended by Investigatory Powers Act 2016, s242(1) which introduces a right of appeal).
[138] Namely, whether Intelligence Services Act 1994, s5 empowered the Government to issue 'general warrants'.
[139] *Privacy International* (n 105) [205].
[140] *Privacy International* (n 105) [210].

Lord Sumption's judgment, and the other judgments in *Privacy International* more broadly, are in need of close analysis.[141] For present purposes, the important point is that current judicial approaches to interpreting ouster clauses are being shaped by something other than the idea that administrative unlawfulness of all kinds renders a decision null and void.

Like the public interest conception, then, jurisdiction theory suffers from a number of explanatory drawbacks. It glosses over the variety of legal questions which can arise in administrative law adjudication and offers accounts of specific doctrinal issues, including the consequences of unlawfulness, collateral challenge and judicial interpretation of ouster clauses, which are too simplistic. Again, these deficiencies indicate something of broader importance: administrative law is not easily explained in monistic terms. The 'anatomy' of this field is deeply complex and varied. Accounts which rely on singular concepts therefore tend to place emphasis on important aspects of the field but fail to capture the whole picture.

II. The Appeals of Monism

The aim of the previous section was to begin to cast doubt on the plausibility of monism by highlighting the deficiencies of two leading accounts. Both the public interest conception and jurisdiction theory offer singular accounts of administrative law. The picture they paint of administrative law is, however, lacking in a number of respects. This is not especially surprising. This book has stressed throughout that the legal structures in play in administrative law adjudication are both complex and varied. It is unlikely that a monolithic account of administrative law will therefore be able to supply all of the intellectual tools needed to understand the field.

In order to make a convincing case against monism, however, it is necessary to do more than just point out some of the deficits in leading monistic accounts. It is important also to consider whether there *are good and convincing reasons* to continue to search for 'singular, superior constructs'[142] in administrative law. In order to explain why this task is important, it is helpful to return again to Feynman's 'Ode to a Flower'. As explained, this monologue tells the story of an argument between two friends about how to understand a flower. For Feynman's artist friend, simplicity is key; it is sufficient to understand only the most important thing about the flower, namely that it is beautiful. Feynman, by contrast, believes

[141] For discussion of the Court of Appeal decision (*R (Privacy International) v Investigatory Powers Tribunal* [2017] EWCA Civ 1868, [2018] 1 WLR 2572) see: Craig (n 101); Tom Hickman, 'The Investigatory Powers Tribunal: A Law unto Itself?' [2018] *PL* 584.

[142] Mark Elliott, 'From Heresy to Orthodoxy: Substantive Legitimate Expectations in the United Kingdom' in Matthew Groves and Greg Weeks, *Legitimate Expectations in the Common Law World* (Hart Publishing, 2017).

it is important not to allow the flower's beauty to obscure the many more intricate details of the flower which are important to an understanding of its nature.

At this stage, it is useful to point out a further dimension to this monologue which has not so far been unpacked. Feynman and his artist friend work in different intellectual fields. It is likely, therefore, that they have different priorities in observing and rendering an account of the flower. To put this point another way, artistic representation and scientific study have different purposes and commitments. To vastly oversimplify,[143] Kant defined the role of the artist as being that of promoting the 'free play of the cognitive faculties'.[144] By contrast, scientific research is centred around a commitment to 'systemic scepticism, transparency, quality control by peer review, professional independence and accountability and an emphasis on learning'.[145] Variation in the way an object is studied does not simply occur across disciplines but within them. This is as true of legal research as it is elsewhere. The methodology which underlies any piece of legal scholarship will be driven by a particular set of ideas about what the purpose(s) of legal writing is[146] and what constitutes good scholarly method(s).[147]

[143] The purposes and nature of artistic representation are, of course, deeply contentious. For an accessible introduction, see Cynthia Freeland, *Art Theory: A Very Short Introduction* (Oxford University Press, 2003).

[144] Immanuel Kant, *Critique of Judgement* (1790), First Part 'Critique of the Aesthetical Judgement'.

[145] Andrew Stirling, 'The Precautionary Principle in Science and Technology' in Tim O'Riordan, James Cameron and Andrew Jordan (eds), *Reinterpreting the Precautionary Principle* (Cameron May, 2011) 64 (discussed in Elizabeth Fisher, Bettina Lange and Eloise Scotford, *Environmental Law: Text, Case and Materials*, 2nd edn (Oxford University Press, 2019) 36).

[146] Kenneth Lasson, 'Scholarship Amok: Excesses in Pursuit of Truth and Tenure' (1990) 103(4) *Harvard Law Review* 926; Harry Edwards, 'The Growing Disjunction between Legal Education and the Legal Profession' (1992) 91(1) *Michigan Law Review* 34; Harry Edwards 'The Growing Disjunction between Legal Education and the Legal Profession: A Postscript' (1993) 91(8) *Michigan Law Review* 2191; Robert Gordon, 'Lawyers, Scholars and the Middleground' (1993) 91(8) *Michigan Law Review* 2075; Edward Rubin, 'Law and the Methodology of Law' (1997) *Wisconsin Law Review* 521; Deborah Rhode, 'Legal Scholarship' (2002) 115(5) *Harvard Law Review* 1327; Richard Posner, 'Legal Scholarship Today' (2002) 115(5) *Harvard Law Review* 1314; Lord Rodger, 'Judges and Academics in the UK' (2010) 29 *University of Queensland Law Journal* 29; Mark Tushnet, 'Academics as Lawmakers?' (2010) 29 *University of Queensland Law Journal* 19; Richard Posner, 'The Judiciary and the Academy: A Fraught Relationship' (2010) 29 *University of Queensland Law Journal* 13; Susan Bartie, 'The Lingering Core of Legal Scholarship' (2010) 30(3) *Legal Studies* 345.

[147] Carol Harlow and Richard Rawlings, *Law & Administration*, 3rd edn (Cambridge University Press, 2009) Ch 1; Carol Harlow, 'Changing the Mindset: The Place of Theory in English Administrative Law' (1994) 14(3) *OJLS* 419; Adam Tomkins, 'In Defence of the Political Constitution' (2002) 22(1) *OJLS* 157; Denis Galligan, 'Judicial Review and the Textbook Writers' (1982) 2 *OJLS* 257; Peter Cane, 'Theory and Values in Public Law' and Paul Craig, 'Theory and Values in Public Law: A Response' both in Paul Craig and Richard Rawlings, *Law and Administration in Europe: Essays in Honour of Carol Harlow* (Oxford University Press, 2003). For discussion in the field of general jurisprudence see: HLA Hart, *The Concept of Law*, 3rd edn (Oxford University Press, 2012) postscript; John Finnis, *Natural Law and Natural Rights*, 2nd edn (Oxford University Press, 2011) Ch 1; Julie Dickson, *Evaluation and Legal Theory* (Hart Publishing, 2001). For helpful discussion in the environmental law context see: Elizabeth Fisher, Bettina Lange, Eloise Scotford and Cinnamon Carlarne, 'Maturity and Methodology: Starting a Debate about Environmental Law Scholarship' (2009) 21(2) *Journal of Environmental Law* 213.

All of this means that it is important not to dismiss the monistic project too lightly and without understanding what motivates it. It is not enough simply to point out that the accounts it renders of administrative law are incomplete or misleading. An attempt must be made to understand *what drives* the search for singular 'organising principles'[148] and to consider whether those motivations supply good and convincing reasons for continuing to do so. To that end, this section will discuss four considerations which help to explain the appeal of monism. Its core, critical argument is that, while each provides a superficially appealing case for seeking to explain administrative law in singular terms, the force of these arguments breaks down under further consideration.

A. The Kernel of Truth in Monistic Accounts

A first consideration which can help to explain the considerable influence of monism is that many of the major monistic accounts of administrative law contain an important kernel of truth. As explained above, neither the public interest conception, nor jurisdiction theory, can be said to be 'wrong' in the sense that they reveal nothing of value about administrative law. On the contrary, both accounts usefully capture a significant theme which does indeed characterise aspects of administrative law adjudication or has characterised its development.

Thus, consider again the public interest conception. As explained in chapter three, across the course of the nineteenth[149] and twentieth centuries,[150] and for a variety of reasons,[151] the courts struggled to provide a remedy in circumstances where an administrative decision-maker failed to fulfil a statutory duty enacted to benefit the public as a collectivity.[152] One of the most important achievements of the courts, following the procedural reforms of the late-1970s, has been the creation of the notion of representative standing which enables the provision of a remedy in such circumstances.[153] Part of the appeal of the public interest conception is undoubtedly that it calls attention to this important development.

A similar point can be made about other influential monistic accounts of administrative law. Consider, for instance, Thomas Poole's suggestion in 2009[154] that administrative law was undergoing a 'reformation' in which 'rights and substantive review, like Cinderella, ha[d] escaped a subservient position to take

[148] Forsyth (n 5) 155.

[149] *Lewisham Union Guardians* (n 55).

[150] *Boyce v Paddington BC* [1903] 1 Ch 109 (Ch); *Gregory v Camden LBC* [1966] 1 WLR 899 (QB) 909; *Gouriet v Union of Post Office Workers* [1978] AC 435 (HL).

[151] JDB Mitchell, 'The Causes and Effects of the Absence of a System of Public Law in the United Kingdom' [1965] *PL* 95; Law Commission, 'Report on Remedies in Administrative Law' (Law Comm No 73, 1976).

[152] *R v Secretary of State for the Environment, ex parte Rose Theatre* [1990] 1 QB 504 (QB).

[153] *World Development Movement* (n 55); *R v Inspectorate of Pollution ex parte Greenpeace (No 2)* [1994] 2 CMLR 548 (QB).

[154] Poole, 'Reformation' (n 15). See also Taggart (n 15).

centre stage'.[155] Jason Varuhas has drawn attention to a series of ways in which, explaining administrative law by reference only to rights-based considerations obscures many of its important features which are not 'individual-regarding'[156] by nature. At the same time, rights-based accounts of administrative law contained an important kernel of truth. In particular, they draw attention to the increased role being played by concepts such as 'anxious scrutiny'[157] and proportionality in judicial reasoning from the 1990s onwards. Poole's writings also in some ways foreshadowed the 'resurgence'[158] of common law constitutional rights in more recent years.[159]

To what extent does this consideration supply a good and convincing reason for adhering to these monistic accounts of administrative law, or continuing to search for a 'master principle or idea'[160] more broadly? The answer is surely that a kernel of truth is not enough to accept an account wholesale. While the leading monistic accounts often accord with important themes in administrative law and this helps to explain why scholars and practitioners have found them appealing, this cannot justify the overlooking of other themes of equal relevance.

The point can be put another way. A good account of an area of the law will equip the reader with the intellectual tools she needs to understand the issues which are raised in litigation and the processes which are used by judges to resolve them. Many of the major monistic accounts of administrative law doctrine equip the reader with *some* of the relevant tools. The public interest conception, for instance, helps to explain why the applicants in *World Development Movement*[161] and *Greenpeace*[162] had a 'sufficient interest'[163] to bring their claim even though they could not show that their personal legal rights were affected. The problem, however, is that monistic accounts provide only *a part* of the necessary intellectual toolbox.

B. The Equation of Intelligibility, Coherence and Unity

A second consideration which can help to explain the appeals of monism is the tendency among some scholars to equate three notions: intelligibility, coherence

[155] Poole, 'Reformation' (n 15) 144.
[156] Varuhas (n 6) 52.
[157] *Bugcayday v Secretary of State for the Home Department* [1987] AC 514; Paul Craig, 'Judicial Review and Anxious Scrutiny: Foundations, Evolution and Application' [2015] *PL* 60;
[158] Roger Masterman and Se-Shauna Wheatle, 'A Common Law Resurgence in Rights Protection?' (2015) 1 *European Human Rights Law Review* 57.
[159] *Kennedy v Information Commissioner* [2014] UKSC 20, [2015] AC 455; *R (UNISON) v Lord Chancellor* [2017] UKSC 51, [2017] 3 WLR 409; Richard Clayton, 'The Empire Strikes Back: Common Law Rights and the Human Rights Act' [2015] *PL* 3.
[160] Smith (n 2) 11.
[161] *World Development Movement* (n 55).
[162] *Greenpeace* (n 153).
[163] Senior Courts Act 1981, s31(3).

and unity. This is a tendency which is especially prominent in certain strands of the literature on private law theory. Ernest Weinrib[164] and Allan Beever,[165] for instance, have famously developed arguments to the effect that intelligibility in the law can only be achieved by an account which reveals the field to be both coherent and unified.[166] The tendency to equate intelligibility, coherence and unity can also be seen in certain aspects of the public law literature. Consider, for instance, the following passage from Dean Knight's recent monograph:[167]

> The focus of non-contradiction and coherence is the *schematic unity of the system* … Coherence contrasts law as a seamless web with law as a patchwork quilt … coherence raises broader questions about the meta-architecture of a schema, that is, its organising theory or manner in which it is systematised. The focus extends to matters such as its comprehensiveness, connectedness and *internal unity*.[168]

In this passage, Knight introduces a metric[169] against which he suggests the appropriateness of approaches to structuring administrative law can be tested. He terms this metric 'coherence'. What is most important about this passage for present purposes is that, in explaining what is meant by coherence, Knight appears to naturally equate the notion with that of unity.

Why is this tendency important in explaining the appeals of monism? Accounts of administrative law are naturally informed by the writer's understanding, explicit or assumed, of what a good account of the law *should do*.[170] Many scholars would probably assume without difficulty that one facet of a successful account of the law is intelligibility. That is, they would regard a major part of their role to be the elucidation of the law in a way which is capable of being comprehended. But if intelligibility is the same as coherence, and coherence is the same as unity, then there is only one successful way of achieving this task: one must locate the 'master idea or principle'[171] which unites administrative law.

This perhaps helps to explain why some scholars have sought to locate an 'organising concept'[172] which holds administrative law together. But to what degree is it acceptable to fuse together intelligibility, coherence and unity? In exploring this question, it is useful to begin by mapping the argument offered by

[164] Weinrib (n 8) Chs 1–2.
[165] Allan Beever, 'Formalism in Music and Law' (2011) 61(2) *University of Toronto Law Journal* 213.
[166] For critique see Roderick Bagshaw, 'Tort Law, Concepts and What Really Matters' in Andrew Robertson and Hang Wu Tang, *The Goals of Private Law* (Hart Publishing, 2009).
[167] Dean Knight, *Vigilance and Restraint in the Common Law of Judicial Review* (Cambridge University Press, 2018).
[168] *Ibid*, 29–30 (emphasis added).
[169] Lon Fuller, *The Morality of Law* (Yale University Press, 1964).
[170] See citations at nn 146 and 147).
[171] Smith (n 2) 11.
[172] Forsyth (n 7) [27].

scholars such as Weinrib and Beever for equating these notions. The argument, on my understanding of it, can be encapsulated in five main propositions:

1) Accounts of the law are inevitably interpretative.
2) A good interpretation of the law will render it intelligible.
3) An account which shows the law to be incoherent does not render, or is less capable of rendering, the law intelligible.
4) The most important kind of coherence for an account of the law is 'moral' or 'justificatory' coherence.
5) Moral coherence can (only) be achieved through an explanation of the law which reveals it to be a unified whole.

Propositions (1), (2) and (3) can be usefully unpacked by drawing on the writings of Stephen Smith.[173] In relation to proposition (1), Smith has explained that, while accounts of the law sometimes present themselves as 'descriptions', rather than interpretations, the line between the two endeavours is heavily blurred:

> … there is no sharp break between description and interpretation; the difference is a matter of degree. A purely descriptive account would be entirely useless, if not impossible. It would amount to little more than a randomly collated list of data. This is why all textbooks engage in interpretation to some degree; for example, all textbooks impose an order or schema on the material they discuss.[174]

In a similar way, Elizabeth Fisher, Pasky Pascual and Wendy Wagner have explained that when an actor seeks to 'model' a subject-matter, something which administrative law scholars sometimes understand themselves as doing,[175] what they offer is a 'simplification of reality for a purpose'.[176] They go on to emphasise that, inherent in this definition, is the important point that:

> … a model is constructed for a purpose or set of purposes … [and that] the purpose or purposes for which a model is developed will directly influence how reality is simplified.[177]

A series of choices, in other words, will always underlie any account of a subject-matter, legal or otherwise.[178] Compiling an account of the law is not a mechanical exercise in gathering and presenting data but will always be informed by a scholar's understanding of their role and of what makes an explanation of the law useful or satisfactory.

[173] Smith (n 2).
[174] Smith (n 2) 6.
[175] Richard B Stewart, 'The Reformation of Administrative Law' (1974–1975) 88 *Harvard Law Review* 1667; Paul Craig, 'Competing Models of Judicial Review' [1999] *PL* 428, Richard Rawlings, 'Modelling Judicial Review' (2008) 61(1) *Current Legal Problems* 95.
[176] Elizabeth Fisher, Pasky Pascual and Wendy Wagner, 'Understanding Environmental Models in their Legal and Regulatory Context' (2010) 22(2) *Journal of Environmental Law* 251.
[177] *Ibid*, 266–67.
[178] Note that Fisher et al are discussing the creation of environmental models, especially to inform policy-making. Much of what the authors say, however, has resonance in legal scholarship.

Proposition (2) is fairly straightforward. According to this idea, a major goal in producing an account of the law is to render the subject matter intelligible. This is related to David Feldman's definition of legal scholarship as an attempt 'to discover more about whatever is being considered, and to understand it better'.[179]

Smith has explained the basic idea underlying (3) as follows:

> … a theory satisfies the coherence criteria to the extent that it presents [an area of law] as consistent or non-contradictory … A theory that reveals the law as inconsistent is less successful at achieving what was described earlier at the basic goal of interpretation: that of revealing an intelligible order in the law. Consistency in the sense of non-contradictoriness is a basic requirement of intelligibility.[180]

In essence, the argument is that if the goal is to promote intelligibility, then it is important that an account is able to explain how the various components of an area of law fit together in a way which is non-contradictory. Consider, for instance, the point made in chapter four that the courts in procedural review cases seek to accommodate both the underlying policy of the background legislation and afford protection to rights and interests which are 'highly regarded by the [common] law'.[181] At first sight, these disparate aspects of the law might seem contradictory. According to proposition (3), therefore, in order for an account of procedural review to be coherent and, by extension, intelligible, it is essential that it explains the relationship between these two rationales, revealing how any apparent tensions can be resolved.

Accepting, for a moment, proposition (3), an important question then arises: if it is essential to explain how the various parts of a subject-matter fit together, how should one go about building such an explanation? Ought one, for instance, focus primarily on the case law in order to understand how the courts have viewed the relationship between them? Should their interrelationship be explored from an historical perspective? Proposition (4) responds to this issue. The thinking of authors such as Weinrib and Beevers on this issue is implicit in the following passage:

> Not only is coherence and unity necessary for intelligibility; it is necessary for justification … Purported justifications that are inconsistent with others do not justify. Moreover, even if the justifications offered are consistent, they do not justify unless they cohere.[182]

For these scholars, in explaining the relationship between potentially conflicting parts of a legal field, the focus must be on *justification*. What one is seeking, in other words, is a *moral* account of the relationship between the subject-matters. To return to the example of procedural review, for instance, for Weinrib and

[179] David Feldman, 'The Nature of Legal Scholarship' (1989) 53(4) *MLR* 498, 498.

[180] Smith (n 2) 11.

[181] *R v Higher Education Funding Council, ex parte Institute of Dental Surgery* [1994] 1 WLR 242 (DC), 263.

[182] Beever (n 165) 235–36.

Beever the aim in explaining the relationship between the 'instrumental' and 'non-instrumental'[183] aspects of the ground is not just to offer any kind of explanation. It is, rather, to develop a morally sound justification of why the courts ought to be concerned with, and play a role in, both ensuring that administrative decision-makers promote the aims of the background legislative scheme and protecting important individual interests.

Proposition (5), finally, posits that in developing a moral explanation or justification of how the various aspects of the law fit together, *unity* will be essential for success. For Weinrib and Beever, an account of the law which does not reveal it to be a unified whole will not have accomplished the task of justification. Consider, for instance, an explanation of procedural review which explains that the courts give priority to the background policy aims of legislation in certain contexts, but the protection of the individual in others. For Weinrib and Beever, this account does not offer a consistent explanation of how cases are treated and therefore fails to justify the law. The only way, for scholars such as Weinrib and Beever, to satisfactorily deal with such issues would be to dig deeper and to find a unifying moral philosophy which can explain why we ought to care about *both* promoting Parliamentary ordained policy aims *and* protecting certain individual rights and interests. On identifying an underlying moral theory of this kind, it would then become possible to elucidate the relationship between these considerations.

To what degree does this, fairly lengthy and complex, line of thinking provide a convincing argument for continuing to search for 'organising concepts'[184] in administrative law? Answering this question in full would require the chapter to venture into very deep and complex methodological territory.[185] For present purposes it is sufficient to highlight that a number of the propositions expounded above, especially (3), (4) and (5), are open to question, at least in the administrative law context.

Take proposition (3). This supposition posits that there is an essential link between intelligibility and coherence; in order to offer a coherent account of the law one must be able to explain how apparently inconsistent aspects of the law fit together without contradiction. It is far from clear, however, that the link between intelligibility and coherence is as clear as this account assumes. It is surely possible that an account of the law might reveal the law to be incoherent, in the sense that it accepts that there are aspects of the law which do not neatly fit together, but at the same time render it intelligible. This might be said to apply to much environmental law scholarship. The focus here is often on drawing attention to various sources of

[183] Elliott and Varuhas (n 39) Ch 10 and discussed in chapter 4 of this volume.

[184] Forsyth (n 7) [27].

[185] Bagshaw (n 166); James Goudkamp and John Murphy, 'Tort Statutes and Tort Theories' (2015) 131(1) *LQR* 133; James Goudkamp and John Murphy, 'The Failure of Universal Theories of Tort Law' (2016) 21(2) *Legal Theory* 47; John Murphy, 'The Heterogeneity of Tort Law' (forthcoming in OJLS; available as an advance access article from: https://academic.oup.com/ojls/advance-article-abstract/doi/10.1093/ojls/gqz008/5479993?redirectedFrom=fulltext).

complexity in the law, while also striving to promote intelligibility by explaining the causes and nature of these complexities.[186] It might be possible, in other words, to construct an intelligible account of the law which helps the reader to make sense of how and why the law is *not* coherent in the sense described by Smith.

It is also open to question whether any scholar should begin with the presupposition that the law in an area *is* coherent. Such an assumption might be thought to cut off from the outset an important possibility, namely that aspects of the law do not neatly fit together. The assumption of coherence might be thought particularly inappropriate in administrative law. As chapter three explained, the administrative state has developed on a piecemeal basis, driven to a large degree by social change and political priorities;[187] administrative schemes are constituted by many layers of law and soft law[188] and the origins of the grounds of review can be traced back to different legal contexts[189] and historical periods.[190] All of this calls into question the plausibility of beginning from an assumption that all aspects of the law in this field must neatly fit together.

Proposition (4) posits that, in attempting to explain how apparently conflicting aspects of the law fit together, a particular kind of account should be prioritised above others. In particular, scholars should search for a *moral* explanation which is capable of *justifying* why the law should encompass those two ideas. One difficulty with this proposition is that there are arguably other ways of explaining the relationship between two apparently conflicting ideas which are, at least, equally important. To return again to the procedural review example, it is far from clear why we should assume that the best explanation of the relationship between the 'instrumental' and 'non-instrumental'[191] rationales is a justificatory one. Another variety of explanation, for instance, might focus on the role these ideas play in legal reasoning and would attempt to map the ways in which these considerations interact across the case law.[192] Rather than promoting 'moral' coherence, such an account might be said to further '*doctrinal* coherence'.

The importance of doctrine coherence, in the sense of a thorough understanding of how judges make use of legal materials in order to reason through to

[186] Fisher, Lange and Scotford (n 145) Ch 1; Elizabeth Fisher, 'Environmental Law as "Hot" Law' (2013) 25 *Journal of Environmental Law* 347; Eloise Scotford and Jonathan Robinson, 'UK Environmental Legislation and Its Administration in 2013 – Achievements, Challenges and Prospects' (2013) 25 *Journal of Environmental Law* 383.

[187] Derek Fraser, *The Evolution of the British Welfare State*, 4th edn (Palgrave Macmillan, 2009).

[188] Greg Weeks, *Soft Law and Public Authorities* (Hart Publishing, 2018). In the planning context, for instance, see Ministry of Housing, Communities and Local Government (hereafter, MHCLG), 'National Planning Policy Framework' (24 July 2018); William Upton QC, 'What is the Purpose of Planning Policy? Reflections on the Revised National Planning Policy Framework 2018' (2019) 31 *Journal of Environmental Law* 136.

[189] For instance, important case law on procedural review can be found in the context of claims for prerogative writs and in private law settings. For discussion, see Lord Reid's judgment in *Ridge v Baldwin* [1964] AC 40 (HL).

[190] See chapter 2.

[191] Language used in Elliott and Varuhas (n 39) ch 10 and discussed in chapter 4 of this volume.

[192] See discussion in chapter 4, section IV.

conclusions, ought not to be underestimated. It is essential to both legal practice and academia in a number of ways. Practitioners must have a deep understanding of judicial reasoning processes in order to know how to most convincingly build arguments. An important goal of the law student is surely to understand the nature of legal reasoning both for its own sake and so that they may engage in it. It is also essential that legal academics understand how courts make use of legal materials to resolve cases in order to both engage with and critique the law. Furthermore, legal scholars are perhaps uniquely placed to be able to promote doctrinal coherence. Legal scholars have the institutional space to read large bodies of case law, unhampered by the need to ensure that they are acting in a client's interests or to deliver timely judgment in a case.[193] They also have the legal expertise to bring to bear in a way that academics from other disciplines do not.

None of this is to say, of course, that moral explanations of the law are unimportant. The point, rather, is that the assumption should not be made too easily that the best or only way to explain the relationship between apparently disparate parts of the law is by seeking a justification of them. Doctrinal explanations of how legal ideas interact in legal reasoning is also illuminating and of significant utility across both academia and practice.

Turning to the final stage in the argument, there are numerous plausible routes to challenging proposition (5). Weinrib and Beever's writings, for instance, arguably overlook the existence of incommensurable values. For these scholars, an account of the law which draws on two or more explanatory rationales is too shallow an explanation: one must probe further in order to understand the underlying reason *why* these rationales are deemed valuable. The assumption is that a deep enough probing will turn out a singular, illuminating moral philosophy and that, from this standpoint, it will be possible to understand the relationship between the two rationales. Timothy Endicott, however, has warned against ignoring the incommensurability of values.[194] For Endicott, the assumption that all goods can be reduced to 'equivalent units of gravity'[195] cannot be sustained. This point has particular force in administrative law where, as argued throughout this book, the courts seek to accommodate values, policies and interests of various legal origins and which are both 'individual-regarding' and 'public-regarding'[196] in content.

A further possible difficulty with proposition (5) is the assumption that abstract moral theories are capable of justifying particular doctrinal solutions. This is a particularly acute difficulty in administrative law. Throughout earlier chapters this book has drawn attention to the diversity of legal components to be explained by an account of administrative law and the resulting tendency of

[193] Fisher (n 186).

[194] Timothy Endicott, 'Proportionality and Incommensurability' in Grant Huscroft, Bradley Miller and Gregoire Webber (eds), *Proportionality and the Rule of Law: Rights, Justification, Reasoning* (Cambridge University Press, 2014).

[195] *Ibid* 316.

[196] Varuhas (n 6) 52.

purportedly unifying theories to rely on 'thin' ideas or principles.[197] A difficulty with this, however, is that the more abstractly framed an 'organising concept'[198] is, the less capable it is of providing a meaningful justification for a particular doctrinal approach over another.

Overall, then, scholars such as Weinrib and Beever have offered a methodological argument in favour of searching for a unified account of an area of law. Their argument, however, arguably collapses three arguably distinct notions into one. The broad notion of intelligibility is collapsed into the narrower one of coherence. This in turn is then narrowed further into unity. By following this line of thinking, however, the broader notions of intelligibility and coherence are cut back significantly and there is a risk of losing sight of other varieties of intelligibility and coherence which are important in an account of law. This is important in thinking about the broader question of this chapter: should we continue to search for a 'master idea or principle'[199] in administrative law? The analysis above demonstrates that there is reason to be careful in assuming too easily that an account of the law can only be characterised as intelligible and coherent if it is also unified, especially in the administrative law context.

C. Constraining Judges

A third factor which can shed light on monism's influence is a concern to place constraints on judicial reasoning. Judicial restraint has been a hot topic in recent years,[200] especially in light of the rise of the 'Judicial Power Project'.[201] The movement warns about the dangers of 'judicial overreach'[202] and highlights a series of famous administrative law cases which are characterised as 'problematic'[203] in this regard. There may be a link between these concerns about judicial overreach and the prevalence of monism. There seem, in particular, to be two broad senses in which it has been assumed that isolating an 'organising principle'[204] can place meaningful constraints on legal reasoning.

First, some have assumed or argued that simply having *an* 'organising concept'[205] which the courts consistently treat as the launch-pad for deciding issues in this field will help to ensure that all legal actors are on the same page.

[197] See discussion in chapter 5.
[198] Forsyth (n 7) [27].
[199] Smith (n 2) 11.
[200] Ekins, Yowell and Barber (eds) (n 63).
[201] Paul Craig, 'Judicial Power, The Judicial Power Project and the UK' (2017) 36 *University of Queensland Law Journal* 355; Richard Ekins and Graham Gee, 'Putting Judicial Power in its Place' (2017) 36 *University of Queensland Law Journal* 375.
[202] See https://judicialpowerproject.org.uk/about/.
[203] See http://judicialpowerproject.org.uk/50-problematic-cases/.
[204] Forsyth (n 5) 155.
[205] Forsyth (n 7) [27].

This, in turn, will avoid the phenomenon of different judges proceeding to decide the same case by framing the central question in different terms. This assumption, for instance, underlies Forsyth's criticism of the *Cart* decision.[206] Forsyth suggests that had the Supreme Court in this case proceeded from the basis of 'orthodox' jurisdiction theory, the question of whether the Upper Tribunal had jurisdiction to make errors of law 'would [have been taken as] the starting point in any inquiry into whether the Upper Tribunal was subject to judicial review'. Forsyth goes on to explain that:

> … this starting point is important because everyone else – the parties, their counsel, others involved in cases raising the same point, etc – would know that this was the starting point. If [judges] have a common starting point they are more likely to arrive at the same destination.[207]

One of the virtues of recognising an 'organising principle'[208] within administrative law, in other words, is thought to be that it provides a clear and singular way of framing legal questions. That all judges frame the question in a given case in the same way will ensure that they are subjected to proper constraint in terms of both how they reason and the solutions open to them.

Second, it also seems to have been assumed that the content of *particular* monistic approaches to administrative law reflect appropriate allocations of power between the judiciary and the administration. Take, for instance, the public interest conception. Jason Varuhas has written that:

> The core concern here is that it is difficult to locate any convincing justification for the radical shift in the focus of public power, away from the public interests for which the power was conferred by a democratically-elected legislature, to judge-made fundamental values over which the judges exercise determinative judgment.[209]

On one reading, what is underlying this passage is a belief that the public interest conception reflects a desirable understanding of what judicial power may be legitimately deployed in order to protect. Varuhas seems to regard it as self-evident[210] that it is proper for the courts to develop doctrine so as to ensure that administrative decision-makers are better able to perform the 'public-regarding'[211] tasks allocated to them by Parliament. By contrast, he is much more cynical about the idea that the courts may also develop administrative law doctrine so as to protect the rights and interests of the individual. Part of the appeal of the public interest conception, in other words, might be that it is thought by some to send an appropriate message to the courts concerning the proper boundaries of their own role.

[206] *Cart* (n 19).
[207] Forsyth (n 7) 152–53.
[208] Forsyth (n 5) 155.
[209] Varuhas (n 26) 125.
[210] Craig (n 57).
[211] Varuhas (n 6) 52.

To what extent does a concern to ensure that judges are sufficiently constrained provide a convincing reason for continuing to understand administrative law in monistic terms? The broader arguments of this book suggest at least three reasons for cynicism.

First, it cannot be assumed that inability to identify a guiding 'meta-value'[212] or idea in a legal field necessarily means that courts are therefore ineffectively restrained. To give an example, chapter five focused on legitimate expectations.[213] It was seen in that chapter that legitimate expectations have been thought of as a particular area of concern. Mark Elliott, for instance, has noted a tendency to regard the ground as capable of becoming 'an unnecessary envelope capable of being placed around intervention on any ground'.[214] A close reading of recent case law, however, demonstrated a number of things. In the first place, applicants succeed far less in legitimate expectations challenges that might be assumed. In the second, it is possible to trace clear patterns in how the courts treat particular cases. In the third, it is also clear from this case law that the courts are very reluctant to make use of the doctrine in a way which would effectively prevent an administrative decision-maker from implementing a decision to change policy direction.[215] Although an 'organising concept'[216] has proven elusive in this field, therefore, the case analysis in chapter five suggests that administrative decisions are not lightly overturned on the basis of a breach of legitimate expectations.

Second, to return to a previous point, the complexity and variety of legal structures in play in administrative law means that purported unifying explanations often rely on very thin or abstractly framed ideas. Subection B above explained how this undermines the idea that they are able to justify particular doctrinal approaches. For present purposes, there is another consequence: it is very difficult to see how an abstractly framed idea is capable of providing meaningful constraints on judicial reasoning.

Jurisdiction theory is a case in point. As explained earlier, Christopher Forsyth has strongly criticised the Supreme Court judgments in *Cart*[217] for neglecting to frame the central legal question in terms of the extent of the Upper Tribunal's ('UT') jurisdiction.[218] At the heart of Forsyth's argument is the supposed importance of

[212] Joe Tomlinson, 'The Narrow Approach to Substantive Legitimate Expectations and the Trend of Modern Authority' (2017) 17(1) *Oxford University Commonwealth Law Journal* 75, 81 (citing from Paul Daly, 'A Pluralist Account of Deference and Legitimate Expectations' in Groves and Weeks (eds) (n 142)).

[213] Examples can also be found in chapters 4 and 6.

[214] Mark Elliott, 'Legitimate Expectations, Consistency, and Abuse of Power: The *Rashid* Case' (2005) 10 *Judicial Review* 281, 283.

[215] See, for instance, the discussion of *Walapu v HMRC* [2016] EWHC 658 (Admin), [2016] 4 All ER 955 in chapter 5.

[216] Forsyth (n 7) [27].

[217] *Cart* (n 19).

[218] Forsyth (n 5); Murray (n 87); Philip Murray, 'Judicial Review of the Upper Tribunal: Appeal, Review and the Will of Parliament' (2011) 70(3) *CLJ* 487; Janina Boughey, 'Reconsidering *R (Cart) v Upper Tribunal* and the Rationale for Jurisdictional Error' [2017] *PL* 592.

all legal actors framing the legal question in the same way from the beginning. Had the Court understood the question as being whether the UT had jurisdiction to make errors of law, Forsyth argues, the options open to the Court would have been restrained and it would have been 'more likely' that all legal actors 'arrive[d] at the same destination'.[219]

It is far from clear, however, that the notion of jurisdiction is capable of performing the sort of restraining role Forsyth seeks. It is notable, for example, that critics of *Cart* who have made arguments to this effect have all reached different conclusions about the proper solution to the *Cart* problem. For Forsyth himself the appropriate approach would have been for the Supreme Court to reach back to Lord Diplock's suggestion in *Re Racal*[220] that, when what is in issue is judicial review of an inferior court (which, for Forsyth, the UT is), the task of the court must be to ask whether Parliament intended that court to be able to make errors of law.[221] Had the Supreme Court addressed this issue, Forsyth suggests, they would have concluded that Parliament intended the UT to be able to make errors of law while remaining within jurisdiction. (Note, however, that Forsyth offers no clearer explanation as to how the line between jurisdictional and non-jurisdictional errors would be drawn.) Other critics of *Cart*, however, have envisaged the Supreme Court reasoning in other ways. Philip Murray, for instance, has argued that, beginning with the notion of jurisdiction, the Supreme Court ought to have looked back to the 1841 decision in *Bolton*[222] and deployed the idea that the UT would fall into jurisdictional error if it made a mistake of law prior to embarking on an inquiry.[223]

What all of this shows is that any argument that an organising concept is necessary in the administrative law sphere because it will help to constrain judicial reasoning ought not to be accepted too easily. The commentators discussed in the previous paragraph began from the same starting point in reasoning through the issue in *Cart*, but they took divergent paths. Part of the difficulty is surely that, in order to capture the complex and varied array of legal structures in play in administrative law, a purported 'organising principle'[224] will often be framed at a very high level of abstraction. The resulting breadth of these concepts limits the role they can go on to play in guiding legal reasoning.

A third and final problem with some influential monistic accounts of administrative law is that they propose 'organising principles'[225] which are not capable of being carried through in the realities of the English and Welsh legislative and administrative landscape. This point is rather abstract and so it is useful to explain with an example. The public interest conception[226] posits that there

[219] Forsyth (n 7) 153.
[220] *Re Racal* (n 88).
[221] Forsyth (n 7).
[222] *R v Bolton* (1841) 1 QB 66.
[223] Murray (n 87).
[224] Forsyth (n 5) 155.
[225] Forsyth (n 5) 155.
[226] Varuhas (n 6).

is a 'fundamental'[227] difference between 'individual-regarding'[228] areas of law, such as private law and human rights law, and the 'public-regarding'[229] nature of domestic administrative law. On this view, the focus of a court in an administrative law challenge is on the quality of 'the exercise of power itself'[230] with the aim of ensuring that it is 'exercised for the benefit of all … [and not] for the benefit of a select few'.[231]

As the discussion above demonstrated, however, the idea that administrative law is inherently 'public-regarding' as opposed to 'individual-regarding'[232] in focus is very difficult to carry through in the English and Welsh legal context. A particular problem is that, as this book has emphasised, administrative law issues do not arise in a legislative vacuum. Rather they arise against the background of a broad variety of legislative and policy frameworks. These frameworks create legal relationships, and pursue policy aims, of different kinds. As Craig has explained, this poses a significant difficulty for the plausibility of understanding administrative law in wholly or even primarily 'public-regarding'[233] terms because:

> … where the statute is framed in terms of specific rights of individuals it is untenable to regard judicial review as being purely public-regarding, designed to secure some collective interest, detached from the rights of the individuals that are the express beneficiaries of the statutory duties. Parliament has chosen to give statutory rights to the individuals that fall within its ambit. Judicial review framed in terms of, for example, error of law, mistake of fact, or impropriety of purpose is designed to ensure that the rights Parliament has granted are duly protected.[234]

The point is that, while understanding administrative law by reference to an overarching concern to promote the public interest may seem plausible in the abstract, when one moves down to the level of particular cases and legislative provisions the idea becomes extremely hard to maintain. In practice administrative law doctrine becomes closely entangled with legislative and policy provisions. Variety in the detail and aims of these provisions makes it difficult to see how the case law can be explained in singular terms.

D. Solving Administrative Law's 'Identity Crisis'

A fourth and final factor worthy of consideration concerns what might be thought of as administrative law's 'identity crisis'.[235] There has long been a sense that

227 Varuhas (n 26).
228 Varuhas (n 6) 52.
229 Varuhas (n 6) 52.
230 Varuhas (n 26) 101.
231 Varuhas (n 26) 101.
232 Varuhas (n 6) 52.
233 Varuhas (n 6) 52.
234 Craig (n 57) 287.
235 See n 10.

administrative law is an academic field of study persistently plagued by questions about its own necessity. These questions have changed in nature over time and three main varieties of challenge can be observed.

The first is the 'Diceyan challenge'. As explained in chapter two, Dicey famously questioned the need to recognise a branch of administrative law. A major reason for this was that, for Dicey, the preference of the English and Welsh courts as opposed to those of other states was to control the exercise of power through 'ordinary' legal techniques.[236] For Dicey, this meant that there was no need to carve out and study a separate branch of administrative law. The law which regulated public bodies could be studied as part of the law of property, contract and tort.

A second challenge can be labelled the 'functionalist challenge'. As Martin Loughlin has observed,[237] functionalism is a broad church which 'cannot be presented as a clear and singular legal philosophy'.[238] The dictionary definition of functionalism, however, offers a clue to its essence. The Oxford English Dictionary defines functionalism as 'the theory that the design of an object should be determined by its function'.[239] This goes some way to explaining the role of functionalism in thinking about administrative law. For functionalists, it is important always to remember that institutions of public administration are set up to perform particular functions and to achieve particular social goals. The aim of scholarship, accordingly, ought to be on exploring mechanisms by which these institutions could become more adept at promoting these social ends.

Functionalist thinking gave rise to questions about the necessity of studying administrative law in two main ways. In the first place, focusing on the *law* aspect of the phrase, many functionalists doubted the capacity of *courts* to contribute meaningfully to the realisation of the new social goals which states set out to achieve across the twentieth century.[240] Particularly notable in this regard were the writings of Allan Hutchinson,[241] Patrick MacAuslan[242] and John Willis,[243] each of whom argued that traditional legal techniques would hinder rather than help the implementation of ambitious and socially progressive administrative schemes. In the second place, functionalist thinking has sometimes given rise to questions concerning the appropriateness of studying *generalist* administrative law. If the

[236] Dicey (n 60); Harry W Arthurs, 'Rethinking Administrative Law: A Slightly Dicey Business' (1979) 17(1) *Osgoode Hall Law Journal* 1.

[237] Martin Loughlin, 'The Functionalist Style in Public Law' (2005) 55 *Toronto Law Journal* 361.

[238] *Ibid* 367.

[239] See https://en.oxforddictionaries.com/definition/functionalism.

[240] See chapter 3.

[241] Allan C Hutchinson, 'The Rise and Ruse of Administrative Law and Scholarship' (1985) 48(3) *MLR* 293.

[242] Patrick McAuslan, *Ideologies of Planning Law* (Pergamon Press, 1980).

[243] John Willis (ed), *Canadian Boards at Work* (MacMillan, 1941); John Willis, 'What I like and What I Don't Like About Lawyers' (1969) 76 *Queen's Q* 1.

focus of the academic must be on finding techniques for the realisation of the social goals of administrative schemes, then it may make little sense to think broadly about these issues.[244] Why not break the subject up by subject-matter and think specifically about how the policy aims underlying, for instance, housing administration,[245] tax administration,[246] planning administration[247] and health administration,[248] can best be realised?

Third and finally, is the 'constitutional challenge'. This takes the form of the prevalent idea that administrative law is properly understood as a sub-branch of constitutional law. As Tom Ginsburg has provocatively suggested, in the eyes of some:

> Administrative law is the poor relation of public law; the hard-working, unglamorous cousin labouring in the shadow of constitutional law. Constitutional law, it is generally believed resolves the great issues of state and society, while administrative law, in its best moments merely refines those principles for dealing with the administrative state.[249]

Ginsburg was writing in the context of the US academy but his suggestion that administrative law continues to struggle to escape the 'shadow of constitutional law' has some resonance in the UK. Despite the calls of Griffiths and Street in 1952[250] to make administrative law a compulsory subject of study in law schools, in many English and Welsh universities administrative law continues to be taught as a unit on a broader constitutional law course.[251]

Administrative law's struggles against these challenges may suggest a further reason for the appeal of monism: a successful monistic account of administrative law would confer on the field a clear identity and provide a straightforward way of explaining the importance of its study.

[244] Carol Harlow and Richard Rawlings, 'Administrative Law in Context: Restoring a Lost Connection' [2014] *PL* 28; Carol Harlow and Richard Rawlings, *Law and Administration*, 3rd edn (Cambridge University Press, 2009) especially Ch 1.

[245] Ian Loveland, 'Reforming the Homelessness Legislation? Exploring the Constitutional and Administrative Legitimacy of Judicial Law-Making' [2018] *PL* 299.

[246] Stephen Daly, 'Recent Developments in Tax Law: Vires Revisited' [2016] *PL* 190.

[247] Joanna Bell, '*Dover DC v CPRE Kent:* Legal Complexity and Reason-Giving in Planning Law' (2018) 23(1) *Judicial Review* 25.

[248] Daniel Wei L Wang, 'From *Wednesbury* Unreasonableness to Accountability for Reasonableness' (2017) 76(3) *CLJ* 642.

[249] Tom Ginsburg, 'Written Constitutions and the Administrative State: On the Constitutional Character of Administrative Law' University of Chicago Public Law & Legal Theory Working Paper, No 331 (2010) available at http://chicagounbound.uchicago.edu/cgi/viewcontent.cgi?article=1391&context=public_law_and_legal_theory.

[250] TCT, 'Reviewed Works: Principles of Administrative Law by JAG Griffith & H Street' (1953) 11(3) *CLJ* 501.

[251] Reflected in some of the leading textbooks in the field. See, for instance, Ian Loveland, *Constitutional Law, Administrative Law and Human Rights: A Critical Introduction*, 7th edn (Oxford University Press, 2015) in which four of 24 chapters engage with administrative law and Mark Elliott and Robert Thomas, *Public Law*, 3rd edn (Oxford University Press, 2017) of which four of 21 chapters deal with administrative law issues.

Consider, for example, the 'functionalist challenge' and the question of whether administrative law ought to be studied in general terms, or broken down by subject-matter into fields such as 'planning law' and 'tax law'. Perhaps part of the appeal of jurisdiction theory is that it appears to provide a straightforward solution to this challenge: if administrative law is an exercise in patrolling the boundaries of jurisdiction then, across all of these areas, the courts are performing the same task. It is therefore important to trace the approaches the courts are using across all of these areas. Consider, by way of another example, the 'constitutional challenge'. This challenge raises the question of whether administrative law is best understood as a sub-branch of constitutional law. Perhaps part of the allure of the public interest conception is that it would seem to offer a straightforward answer to this challenge. In the view of Jason Varuhas it seems to.[252] According to Varuhas, the 'public-regarding'[253] nature of administrative law reveals it to be a discrete legal field, characterised by its own internal logic. This logic is distinct from that of other branches of public law, such as human rights and European Union law. It is therefore important to recognise public law as a field made up of a series of distinct branches, characterised by their own features.

To what degree does administrative law's 'identity crisis' provide an argument for explaining the field in monistic terms? The core issue is that there are more direct ways of overcoming these challenges.

Consider, for instance, the idea that administrative law is best understood as a series of discrete areas – housing law, planning law, tax law, etc – which ought to be studied as such. A case can be built for the study of *generalist* administrative law which does not rely on monistic analysis. As I have written elsewhere:

> … there are a number of considerations that can help to explain why … it is possible both to accept [the complex and varied nature of administrative law adjudication] and to believe that it is important to maintain a body of research and teaching that 'looks at the legal regulation of administrative generally. One important consideration is that the extent of the role played by the specific statutory scheme may vary depending on the 'legal ground' on which the applicant is seeking to rely … A second … is that, even in relation to those 'grounds' where the specific statutory framework is truly central, there is surely still an important role for general administrative law scholarship. [There are] a series of important and underexplored questions that *can only be* answered by looking across different areas of administration. How, for instance, do judges go about extracting the policy aims which underlie an administrative scheme …? Does legislation provide meaningful structure …? Have there been any major changes in the techniques used by courts over time? Do the courts deploy these techniques consistently across different areas of administration?[254]

[252] See especially Varuhas (n 6).
[253] Varuhas (n 6) 52.
[254] Bell (n 104) 98–99 (original emphasis).

The central point is that, even if administrative law lacks an 'organising concept',[255] it is important to maintain a body of scholarship which looks at how the courts oversee public administration across different areas. If scholarship were to lose this, it would lose the ability to identify important patterns in how the courts approach review, as well as the potential to identify outliers. Although it is important to recognise differences between areas of administration, courts are grappling with similar legal questions. Questions concerning, for instance, the procedural steps decision-makers must follow before reaching a conclusion and the manner in which they may decide to change policy direction, arise in planning, tax and professional discipline contexts alike. Fragmentation of administrative law scholarship would prevent a holistic understanding of those issues from forming.

Consider also the idea that administrative law is a sub-branch of constitutional law. An obvious objection to this view is that studying administrative law *through* the lens of constitutional law concepts represents only one way of exploring administrative law issues and not necessarily the most illuminating one. The idea of parliamentary sovereignty, for instance, may illuminate some of the reasons why the courts engage in vires and improper purpose review. The literature on parliamentary sovereignty, however, only takes us so far in understanding how the courts go about identifying the purposes which underlie a statutory scheme, and the ways in which administrative frameworks have evolved in recent decades.[256] Similarly, a rule of law explanation of administrative law would undoubtedly offer important insights into aspects of administrative law, most obviously the principle of legality.[257] There is a huge amount of day-to-day administrative law activity, however, which would not fall within its purview.[258]

To put this another way: not everything which is important about administrative law can be helpfully explained through broad notions of constitutional law such as parliamentary sovereignty, the rule of law and constitutional rights.[259] Administrative law adjudication is detailed. In this field, judges draw on many layers of law (Acts of Parliament; Regulations; common law precedents) and soft law (policy; guidance). They make use of grounds of review which are more or less directly connected with traditional constitutional concepts.[260] They are grappling with an ever-evolving administrative state, a quickly changing legislative and policy landscape and are therefore regularly faced with novel legal questions. This is all in need of careful study, separate from the more overarching concerns of constitutional law.

[255] Forsyth (n 7) [27].

[256] See chapter 2.

[257] *Evans* (n 112) and discussion in Mark Elliott, 'A Tangled Constitutional Web: The Black-Spider Memors and the British Constitution's Relational Architecture' [2015] *PL* 539.

[258] Varuhas (n 15); Sarah Nason, *Reconstructing Judicial Review* (Hart Publishing, 2017).

[259] Joanna Bell, 'Judicial Review of Executive Action & Common Law Constitutional Rights' in Mark Elliott and Kirsty Hughes, *Common Law Constitutional Rights* (forthcoming in Hart Publishing).

[260] *Ibid*. See also chapter 3.

III. Conclusion

The overarching aim of this chapter has been to raise an important, but underexplored, question: is it plausible and useful to explain administrative law in terms of a singular, unifying idea or principle? The ultimate message is one of cynicism: the complexity and variety of administrative law's 'anatomy' means that, while singular accounts of the field often capture important themes, they fail to supply the whole set of intellectual tools needed to understand administrative law adjudication.

The chapter has made use of two main techniques by which to cast doubt on the utility of monistic analysis. Section I critically explored two leading monistic accounts of administrative law: the public interest conception and jurisdiction theory. After mapping the basic contours of these ways of thinking, it drew attention to a series of explanatory deficiencies. Section II then considered the appeals of monism. It discussed four considerations which can help to explain why scholars have often been drawn to the idea that administrative law should be explained by reference to a 'master idea or principle'.[261] It also argued, however, that on closer consideration the strength of these arguments weakens.

None of this is especially surprising in light of the book's broader themes. The basic legal structures which are in play in administrative law adjudication are both complex and varied. It is difficult to see how a monistic account of administrative law could, therefore, be anything more than partial.

[261] Smith (n 2) 11.

8

Conclusion

This chapter offers the book's conclusion. It looks backwards, to the territory traversed in this book, and forwards, to some important future implications. The chapter has three short sections. The first briefly revisits the book's three main aims. The second draws out a handful of practical implications of the arguments for administrative law and its study in the future. The third offers some final words.

I. The Three Main Aims of the Book Revisited

The introductory chapter explained that this book has three main aims. Those aims were elucidated partly through a discussion of a monologue offered by Nobel prize-winning physicist Richard Feynman in the course of an interview which has come to be known as the 'Ode to a Flower'.[1] Feynman's monologue tells the story of two friends who disagree about the proper way to understand a flower. The first, an artist, favours a search for simplicity. His approach is reminiscent of the suggestion by American modernist[2] Georgia O'Keeffe[3] that 'details are confusing … [and that] it is only by selection, by elimination, by emphasis that we get to the real meaning of things'.[4] In order to understand the flower, therefore, it is important to understand the most important thing about it and, for the artist friend, that is its beauty. The second friend, Feynman himself, takes significant issue with this approach. Feynman's problem is not that he believed his friend to be wrong in emphasising that the flower is beautiful. Rather, for Feynman, the flower

[1] Professor Richard Feynman, 'The Pleasure of Finding Things Out' (*BBC*, 1981–1982) available at: www.bbc.co.uk/programmes/p018dvyg.

[2] As the Tate's website puts it, 'although many different styles are encompassed by the term, there are certain underlying principle that define modernist art' including 'innovation and experimentation with form with a tendency to abstraction' (see: www.tate.org.uk/art/art-terms/m/modernism).

[3] Hannah Johnston, *Tate Introductions: O'Keeffe* (Tate Publishing, 2016).

[4] Jonathan Stuhlman and Barbara Buhler Lynes, *Georgia O'Keeffe: Circling Around Abstraction* (Hudson Hill Press, 2007) 22. For discussion of this quotation, see the video recording of a presentation delivered by Pasky Pascual, at a Workshop on 'How Modelling Can Inform Strategies to Improve Population Health' organised by the National Academies of Science, Engineering and Medicine in 2015, available at: www.nationalacademies.org/hmd/Activities/PublicHealth/PopulationHealthImprovementRT/2015-APR-09/Videos/6-Pascual-Video.aspx.

is a complex object with a detailed 'structure and inner working'.[5] It is important that any understanding of the flower captures these complexities and Feynman is concerned that emphasising the flower's beauty alone unhelpfully obscures them.

The three main aims of this book can be elucidated by reference to this story. The first has been to argue that, just as for Feynman a flower is an inherently complex object, the legal structures in play in administrative law are both complex and varied. Throughout this book and especially in chapter three, the discussion has explored the 'anatomy' of administrative law, 'pulling apart' the case in order to reveal the nature of the legal structures which are in play. The first main argument of this book has been that these structures are both complex and varied in at least three core senses.

First, administrative law challenges arise against the background of legislative and policy frameworks, which are often, and perhaps increasingly, dense in detail. These frameworks vary significantly in terms of structure and purpose. They also play an important 'shaping' role in how the grounds of review are applied. Second, administrative law protects a variety of different values, interests and policies. In terms of origin, administrative law's values derive from different sources, and include both legislative purposes and values or interests highly regarded by the common law. In terms of beneficiaries, administrative law is neither wholly nor primarily 'public-regarding'[6] nor 'individual-regarding'.[7] Rather, the courts seek to accommodate both the public interest and 'highly regarded'[8] individual interests protected by both statute[9] and the common law. Third, administrative law challenges are characterised by different kinds of legal relationship between applicant and administrative decision-maker. In some cases, applicants seek to enforce legal duties created in order to benefit the public as a collectivity.[10] In others, the applicant argues that an obligation owed to her directly has been breached.[11]

The second main aim of the book has been to argue that recognition of these sources of complexity and variety matters deeply, not only for its own sake but also, because it sheds significant light on a series of doctrinal issues within the field. This argument was developed primarily across chapters four, five and six. These chapters sought to demonstrate the value of a better understanding of administrative law's 'anatomy' in the context of three doctrinal case studies.

[5] Feynman (n 1).

[6] Jason Varuhas, 'The Public Interest Conception of Public Law: Its Procedural Origins and Substantive Implications' in John Bell, Mark Elliott, Jason Varuhas and Philip Murray (eds), *Public Law Adjudication in Common Law Systems: Process and Substance* (Hart Publishing, 2016) 52.

[7] *Ibid.*

[8] *R v Higher Education Funding Council, ex parte Institute of Dental Surgery* [1994] 1 WLR 242 (DC), 263.

[9] Especially in the context of much social welfare legislation: Paul Craig, 'Taxonomy and Public Law: A Response' [2019] *PL* 281.

[10] *R v Guardians of the Lewisham Union* [1897] 1 QB 498 (DC); *R v Inspectorate of Pollution ex parte Greenpeace (No 2)* [1994] 2 CMLR 548 (QB); *R v Secretary of State for Foreign and Commonwealth Affairs, ex parte World Development Movement* [1995] 1 WLR 386 (QB).

[11] *R (Conville) v Richmond-upon-Thames LBC* [2006] EWCA Civ 718, [2006] 1 WLR 2808.

Chapter four considered procedural review. Post-*Ridge*,[12] the most influential and successful account of procedural review characterises the courts as applying a 'flexible notion of overarching fairness'.[13] Laying significant emphasis on 'fairness', however, has its drawbacks. In particular it risks perpetuating an image of procedural review as involving an 'essentially intuitive'[14] judgment as to what 'feels'[15] fair in a given context. Attempts to identify a thicker 'organising concept'[16] at the heart of procedural review, such as by pinpointing an 'irreducible core'[17] of process rights applicable in all contexts, have not, however, been borne out consistently in case law.[18] A better understanding of administrative law's anatomy helps to shed light on these difficulties. In the first place, recognition of the three core senses in which administrative law's basic legal structures are complex and varied helps to explain why procedural review cannot be easily explained by reference to an overarching 'master idea or principle'.[19] In the second, a close reading of the modern procedural review case law with the complex and varied anatomy of administrative law reveals that there is considerably more legal structure to judicial reasoning in this context than the fairness account tends to suggest.

Chapter five explored legitimate expectations. Post-*Coughlan*,[20] many attempts have been made to explain the case law on legitimate expectations. Much like procedural review, however, a general and universally accepted account has proven elusive. These difficulties have in turn given rise to a cynical view of the law. Many have expressed concern that the law on legitimate expectations lacks structure,[21] insufficiently constraints judges[22] and is need of significant reform.[23] A richer understanding of administrative law's 'anatomy' can usefully illuminate these issues. In the first place, recognition of the three core senses of complexity and variety across administrative law's structures explains why it is not especially surprising that it has proven difficult to explain the case law on legitimate

[12] *Ridge v Baldwin* [1964] AC 40 (HL).

[13] *R (L) v West London Mental Health NHS Trust* [2014] EWCA Civ 47, [2014] 1 WLR 3103 [69].

[14] *R (Forest Heath DC) v Electoral Commission Boundary Committee* [2009] EWCA Civ 1296 [39].

[15] To borrow an idea, from a different context, from Core Hoexter, 'A Matter of Feel? Public Powers and Functions in South Africa' in Mark Elliott, Jason Varuhas and Shona Wilson Stark (eds), *The Unity of Public Law?* (Hart Publishing, 2018).

[16] Christopher Forsyth, 'The Rock and the Sand: Jurisdiction and Remedial Discretion' (2013) 18(4) *Judicial Review* 360 [27].

[17] *Secretary of State for the Home Department v AF (No 3)* [2009] UKHL 28, [2010] 2 AC 269.

[18] *Tariq v Home Office* [2011] UKSC 35, [2012] 1 AC 452; *R (Haralambous) v St Alban's Crown Court* [2018] UKSC 1, [2018] AC 236.

[19] Stephen Smith, *Contract Theory* (Oxford University Press, 2004) 11.

[20] *R v North & East Devon Health Authority, ex parte Coughlan* [2001] QB 213 (CA).

[21] Swati Jhaveri, 'The Doctrine of Substantive Legitimate Expectations: The Significance of *ChiuTeng@Kallang Pte Ltd v Singapore Land Authority*' [2016] *PL* 1.

[22] Cameron Stewart, 'The Doctrine of Substantive Unfairness and the Review of Substantive Legitimate Expectations' in Matthew Groves and HP Lee (eds), *Australian Administrative Law* (Cambridge University Press, 2007) 282.

[23] Rebecca Williams, 'The Multiple Doctrines of Legitimate Expectations' (2016) 132(3) *LQR* 639, 655.

expectations by reference to an overarching 'meta-value'[24] or idea. In the second, a reading of the modern case law on legitimate expectations with the broader themes of this book in mind tends to suggest that there are greater levels of predictability and judicial restraint in the legitimate expectations case law than has sometimes been assumed.

Chapter six focused on the final of the book's three case studies: standing. This chapter explored the development of standing in English and Welsh administrative law.[25] It argued that standing evolution has been beset by a tension. On the one hand, scholars and judges have sometimes sought to explain the courts' approach by reference to general propositions. It is a common view, for instance, that the procedural reforms of 1977[26] prompted the courts to replace a 'rights-based'[27] approach to standing to a 'liberal'[28] one, grounded in a concern to promote the public interest. On the other hand, the case law is not easily explained in such general terms. The courts, that is, have made use of different approaches to standing in different sorts of case,[29] and the leading case law continues to emphasise that the sufficient interest test is variable.[30] Again, chapter six argued that recognition of the complex and varied anatomy of administrative law sheds considerable light on these issues. In the first place, appreciating the complex and varied legal structures which are in play in adjudication helps to explain why the courts continue to insist that sufficiency of interest is a variable concept, which applies differently in different contexts.[31] In the second, exploring standing with the book's broader themes in mind also draws attention to an overlooked aspect of the English and Welsh approach to standing. Chapter six termed this characteristic the 'ground-dependent' nature of standing and explored some of its most important iterations.

The first and second aims of this book are positive in nature. The third main aim of the book, by contrast, is negative. The aim has been to raise the question of, and ultimately cast doubt on, the plausibility and utility of a popular way of thinking in administrative law scholarship.

It is helpful to return again to Feynman's monologue. Just as Feynman's artist friend believed the key to understanding the flower was to identify its single most important feature, the literature is replete with attempts to make sense of

[24] Joe Tomlinson, 'The Narrow Approach to Substantive Legitimate Expectations and the Trend of Modern Authority' (2017) 17(1) *Oxford University Commonwealth Law Journal* 75, 81 (citing from Paul Daly, 'A Pluralist Account of Deference and Legitimate Expectations' in Matthew Groves and Greg Weeks (eds), *Legitimate Expectations in the Common Law World* (Hart Publishing, 2017)).

[25] Mark Elliott and Jason Varuhas, *Administrative Law*, 5th edn (Oxford University Press, 2016) 565.

[26] Rules of the Supreme Court (Amendment No 3) 1977 (SI 1977/1955).

[27] Jason Varuhas, 'Against Unification' in Mark Elliott and Hanna Wilberg, *The Intensity and Scope of Substantive Review: Traversing Taggart's Rainbow* (Hart Publishing, 2015) 101.

[28] John McGarry, 'The Importance of an Expansive Test of Standing' (2014) 19(1) *Judicial Review* 60.

[29] Law Commission, 'Report on Remedies in Administrative Law' (Law Comm No 73, 1976).

[30] *AXA General Insurance Ltd v HM Advocate* [2011] UKSC 46, [2012] 1 AC 868 [170].

[31] *Walton v Scottish Ministers* [2012] UKSC 44, [2013] PTSR 51 [92]–[94].

administrative law by isolating an 'organising concept'[32] which lends the field unity. This is true on both general and specific levels. At the general level, a number of different concepts have been put forward as candidates for the administrative law's overarching 'master principle or idea'.[33] Chapter seven introduced two in particular – jurisdiction theory[34] and the 'public interest conception'[35] – but others – including ultra vires,[36] abuse of power,[37] the protection of fundamental rights[38] and the promotion of a culture of justification[39] – could be added to the list. At the specific level, it has been common for explanations of particular administrative law doctrines to proceed via an attempt to isolate a singular guiding 'meta-value'[40] or idea. As explained above 'fairness'[41] has often played this role in discussions of procedural review. Similarly, the literature on both legitimate expectations and standing is littered with attempts to find a 'singular, superior construct'[42] which guides the case law.

The final aim of the book is to bring to the forefront the question of whether, in attempting to understand administrative law doctrine, it is plausible or useful

[32] Forsyth (n 16) [27].

[33] Smith (n 19) 11.

[34] Forsyth (n 16); Christopher Forsyth, 'Blasphemy against Basics: Doctrine, Conceptual Reasoning and Certain Decisions of the UK Supreme Court' in Bell, Elliott, Varuhas and Murray (eds) (n 6).

[35] Varuhas (n 6).

[36] Christopher Forsyth, 'Of Fig Leaves and Fairy Tales: The Ultra Vires Doctrine, the Sovereignty of Parliament and Judicial Review' (1996) 55(1) *CLJ* 12; Mark Elliott, 'The Ultra Vires Doctrine in a Constitutional Setting: Still the Central Principle of Administrative Law' (1999) 58(1) *CLJ* 129; Mark Elliott, 'The Demise of Parliamentary Sovereignty? The Implications for Justifying Judicial Review' (1999) 115 *LQR* 119; Mark Elliott, *The Constitutional Foundations of Judicial Review* (Bloomsbury, 2001); Christopher Forsyth, 'The Legitimacy of Judicial Review' [2003] *PL* 286.

[37] *R v Secretary of State for Education and Employment, ex parte Begbie* [2000] 1 WLR 115 (CA), 1129; Stephen Sedley, *Law and the Whirligig of Time* (Hart Publishing, 2018) Ch 178. See further Paul Daly, 'Administrative Law: Characteristics, Legitimacy, Unity' in Elliott, Varuhas and Wilson Stark (eds) (n 15) 21.

[38] Michael Taggart, 'Reinventing Administrative Law' in Nicholas Bamforth and Peter Leyland, *Public Law in a Multi-Layered Constitution* (Hart Publishing, 2003); Thomas Poole, 'The Reformation of English Administrative Law' (2009) 68(1) *CLJ* 142; Sian Elias, 'Righting Administrative Law' in David Dyzenhaus, Murray Hunt and Grant Huscroft (eds), *A Simple Common Lawyer: Essays in Honour of Michael Taggart* (Hart Publishing, 2009). For a cogent critique see: Jason Varuhas, 'The Reformation of English Administrative Law? "Rights", Rhetoric and Reality' (2013) 72 *CLJ* 369.

[39] David Dyzenhaus, Murray Hunt and Michael Taggart, 'The Principle of Legality in Administrative Law: Internationalisation as Constitutionalisation' (2001) 1(1) *Oxford University Commonwealth Law Journal* 5; Thomas Poole, 'Between the Devil and the Deep Blue Sea: Administrative Law in an Age of Rights' in Linda Pearson (ed), *Administrative Law in a Changing State: Essays in Honour of Mark Aronson* (Hart Publishing, 2008); Murray Hunt, 'Sovereignty's Blight: Why Public Law Needs a Concept of Due Deference' in Bamforth and Leyland (eds) (n 38); Michael Taggart, 'The Tub of Public Law' in David Dyzenhaus (ed), *The Unity of Public Law* (Hart Publishing, 2004); David Dyzenhaus, 'Dignity in Administrative Law: Judicial Deference in a Culture of Justification' (2012) 17(1) *Review of Constitutional Studies* 87.

[40] Tomlinson (n 24).

[41] *West London Mental Health NHS Trust* (n 13) [69].

[42] Mark Elliott, 'From Heresy to Orthodoxy: Substantive Legitimate Expectations in the United Kingdom' in Groves and Weeks (n 24); Joe Tomlinson, 'Do We Need a Theory of Legitimate Expectations?' (26 August 2019. Legal Studies (Forthcoming). Available at SSRN: https://ssrn.com/abstract=3442761).

to search for a singular 'organising concept'[43] in this way. The ultimate message of the book is one of cynicism. Chapter seven used two main techniques to cast doubt on the plausibility and utility of monistic analysis. First, it explored the deficiencies in two leading, monistic accounts of administrative law. Although the 'public interest conception'[44] and 'jurisdiction theory' capture important themes in administrative law's development, the accounts of administrative law they offer obscure a great deal of important detail. Chapter seven suggested that this is not a coincidence: the complexity and variety of the legal structures which are in play in administrative law adjudication make it very likely that monolithic accounts of the field will unhelpfully obscure at least some of the important features of the law. Second, chapter seven also explored the appeals of monism. Although, it argued, there are numerous considerations which can help to explain why scholars have sometimes sought to explain administrative law doctrine by reference to an overarching 'master idea or principle', on further reflection these considerations do not provide good and convincing reasons to continue to seek to understand the field in this way. Overall, then, there is considerable reason to doubt that 'monistic' analysis is the best or most useful way of making sense of administrative law doctrine.

II. Practical Implications

Having looked backwards by briefly outlining the arguments of the earlier chapters, it is useful in this section to look forwards and to draw out some of the practical implications of these arguments for administrative law and its study in the future. Three sets of practical implications are especially worthy of discussion.

The first are the implications for students of administrative law. Making sense of administrative law case law, especially for the first time, is challenging. Judgments in this field are often very lengthy and are commonly made up of a series of parts. It is common for judgments to begin with a detailed discussion of the legislative and policy background to a case, before proceeding to an extended discussion of the particular legal grounds on which the applicant relies. Students may be tempted, when reading these judgments, to skirt over the discussion of the legislative framework and to focus only or primarily on those aspects which speak to the grounds. This temptation is entirely understandable. Students will often be directed to administrative law case law from reading lists with headings such as 'procedural fairness' and 'legitimate expectations' and therefore make the natural assumption that the parts of judgments which use this language are the most important. Furthermore, textbooks sometimes might be understood as

[43] Forsyth (n 16) [27].
[44] Varuhas (n 6).

encouraging students to read case law in this way. William Wade and Christopher Forsyth's leading textbook,[45] for instance, introduces the reader to administrative law by explaining:

> … administrative law may be said to be the body of general principles which govern the exercise of powers and duties by public authorities. This is only one part of the mass of law to which public authorities are subject. *All the detailed law about their composition and structure, though clearly related to administrative law, lies beyond the scope of the subject* … The essence of administrative law lies in judge-made doctrines which apply right across the board and which therefore set legal standards of conduct for public authorities generally.[46]

Wade and Forsyth, of course, are making an important point in this passage: it would be a folly to aim to cover in a singular forum every aspect of law and 'soft law'[47] which touches on the activities of administrative decision-makers. The mass of legislation, Regulations, policy, guidance which has accumulated is simply not capable of coverage in a single textbook or course, nor would a course which attempted to overview all of this be illuminating or interesting. Students, however, should resist the temptation to read passages such as this as an invitation to focus only on the aspects of legal judgments which speak directly to the grounds of review. Administrative law doctrine interacts closely, and in a variety of ways, with the legislative and policy framework in the background of the case. One of the aims of studying law is to understand how courts use the legal materials before them to reason through to conclusions. Engagement with legislation and policy is often a crucial part of this process in administrative law. It is important, in other words, not to think of the legislative framework as merely part of the factual 'background' to a case. This framework will often set up the legal contours in which administrative law doctrine operates and play an important role in shaping the courts' legal conclusions.

A second, related, set of practical implications concerns the teaching of administrative law in universities. The short point is that this book brings to the forefront a series of challenges in course design and highlights the need to give serious consideration to them.

One challenge is identifying the proper balance to be struck between the general and the particular.[48] Traditionally, much thinking about administrative law in England and Wales[49] is organised around generally-applying grounds of review.

[45] William Wade and Christopher Forsyth, *Administrative Law*, 11th edn (Oxford University Press, 2014).

[46] *Ibid* 5 (emphasis added).

[47] Greg Weeks, *Soft Law and Public Authorities* (Hart Publishing, 2018).

[48] Dame Sian Elias, 'The Unity of Public Law?' in Elliott, Varuhas and Wilson Stark (eds) (n 15); David Stratas, '"It All Depends on the Circumstances": The Decline of Doctrine on the Grounds and Intensity of Review' in Elliott, Varuhas and Wilson Stark (eds) (n 15).

[49] Dean Knight, *Vigilance and Restraint in the Common Law of Judicial Review* (Cambridge University Press, 2018) especially Ch 3.

As Sarah Nason has noted, however, there is something of a tension between this generalist focus and the realities of legal practice where practitioners,[50] tribunals[51] and courts[52] seem to be increasingly specialising into fields such as 'planning law', 'education law' and 'health law'. This book has drawn attention to a series of ways in which administrative context shapes legal doctrine. Certain types of legal question, such as whether the applicant's right to be given notice has been breached for instance, tend to arise in particular fields of public administration which are centrally preoccupied with making decisions about individuals, such as tax[53] and parole decisions.[54] The courts' approach to standing also varies depending on the administrative context.[55]

Another related challenge is how to develop students' abilities to read legislation and understand the role it plays in legal reasoning. Again, there is a balance to be struck here. On the one hand, if an important aim of legal education is to enable students to understand how legal challenges are argued and decided,[56] then it is important that students engage carefully with the legislative detail in the background of a case. On the other, too much legislative detail can overwhelm and cause students to lose sight of broader, important issues.

Challenges such as these are not easily solved. It might be tempting to conclude that, as both the administrative state and the mass of court and tribunal decisions dealing with it continue to grow and diversify, it becomes less plausible to maintain generalist administrative law as a field of study. For reasons discussed in chapter seven[57] and elsewhere[58] it is important to resist this temptation. There is a need, however, for a deeper conversation about whether and how these challenges are best met within traditional administrative law courses.

A third and final cluster of implications concerns future directions in academic research. It is very difficult to speak generally about administrative law scholarship, which is both rich and methodologically diverse. What follows should not therefore be read as a criticism, nor as indicating some sort of widespread crisis. This book, however, suggests at least two possible directions for future research which could be usefully pursued to a greater degree than they are at present.

[50] Sarah Nason, *Reconstructing Judicial Review* (Hart Publishing, 2017), especially Ch 4.

[51] Tribunals, Courts and Enforcement Act 2007.

[52] Mr Justice Lindblom, 'The Planning Court: One Year On' [2015] *Journal of Planning and Environment Law* OP3

[53] *R (Rowe) v Revenue and Customs Commissioners* [2017] EWCA Civ 2105, [2018] 1 WLR 3039.

[54] *R (Osborn) v Parole Board* [2013] UKSC 61, [2014] AC 1115.

[55] Chapter 6; *R v Inland Revenue Commissioners, ex parte National Federation of Self-Employed* (*Fleet Street Casuals*) [1982] AC 617 (HL).

[56] The purposes of legal education are of course deeply controversial: Kenneth Lasson, 'Scholarship Amok: Excesses in Pursuit of Truth and Tenure' (1990) 103(4) *Harvard Law Review* 926; Harry Edwards, 'The Growing Disjunction between Legal Education and the Legal Profession' (1992) 91(1) *Michigan Law Review* 34; Harry Edwards 'The Growing Disjunction between Legal Education and the Legal Profession: A Postscript' (1993) 91(8) *Michigan Law Review* 2191.

[57] Chapter 7, section II, D.

[58] Joanna Bell, 'Rethinking the Story of *Cart v Upper Tribunal* and its Implications for Administrative Law' (2019) 39(1) *OJLS* 74.

First of all, it is important to ask more questions about legislation and policy. One overarching theme of this book has been the central role played by legislation in administrative law adjudication. Despite this, there is much which remains unknown about legislation. Understanding of how the legislative frameworks which structure administration evolved across the twentieth and twenty-first centuries, for instance, is relatively thin. Relatedly, not much has been written about how changes in these legislative frameworks potentially change the nature of the legal questions which arise in adjudication.[59] Chapter three also pointed to a further related development: the apparently increasing role being played by published policy and guidance.[60] Legal scholarship is beginning to grapple directly with the doctrinal and normative questions to which this gives rise.[61] This book emphasises the importance of doing so and suggests the need for more thought.

A second practical implication for legal scholarship is highlighting the utility of getting beyond the 'leading' cases which deal with a doctrine. Academic analysis of administrative law doctrine commonly, and understandably, focuses primarily on the, usually appellate level, decisions which explicitly articulate the contours of the grounds of review. One broader lesson of this book, however, is that doing so can produce a misleading impression of the day-to-day reality.

Chapter five offered a good example. As explained, there is a widespread view that the law on legitimate expectations suffers from a serious lack of predictability and judicial restraint. It is likely that a major reason for the influence of this view is that analysis commonly focuses on a handful of leading Court of Appeal judgments which articulate legitimate expectations in broad terms such as 'abuse of power'[62] and 'good administration'.[63] Chapter five, however, demonstrated that 'getting beyond' these cases and exploring the legitimate expectations case law in a more systematic way produces a rather different picture.[64] According to this picture, it is possible to see patterns in how courts tend to respond to different kinds of legitimate expectation challenge. It also appears that the courts are considerably more concerned with preserving the autonomy of decision-makers to change policy direction than is commonly thought.

Although, in other words, leading cases are important, it is also important for scholarship to recognise that they offer only a partial picture. Part of the issue is that, given the various sources of diversity in play in administrative law,

[59] For an example see Joanna Bell, 'Reason-Giving in Administrative Law: Where Are We and Why Have the Courts Not Embraced the "General Common Law Duty to Give Reasons?"' (forthcoming in *MLR*) (an early access version is available at: https://onlinelibrary.wiley.com/doi/10.1111/1468-2230.12457).

[60] Elliott and Varuhas (n 25) Ch 5; *Nzolameso v Westminster CC* [2015] UKSC 22, [2015] PTSR 549, [39]–[41].

[61] Weeks (n 47); Aileen McHarg, 'Administrative Discretion, Administrative Rule-Making and Judicial Review' (2017) 70(1) *Current Legal Problems* 267.

[62] *Coughlan* (n 20).

[63] *R (Nadarajah) v Secretary of State for the Home Department* [2005] EWCA Civ 1363.

[64] Chapter 5, section IV.

leading cases will commonly offer guidance in broad and general terms. In order to evaluate that guidance, including its ability to generate appropriate outcomes and to adequately constrain lower courts, it is necessary to go beyond the leading judgments and to explore how it is applied in practice.

III. Final Words

Carol M Rose has written in the US environmental law context that:

> A mature environmental law is not pretty. It is past the stage of grand theory and well into the stage of acronyms and statutory sections. It bristles with code numbers and code names … None of the this makes the environmental novice happy. She wants to keep the air sparkling, and what she finds are the PSD70 requirements. She wants to save the whales, and all she gets is the MMPA.71.[65]

Although she was discussing environmental law, Rose's point has much resonance in the administrative law context. Administrative law adjudication is far from pretty. This is not, if it ever was,[66] an area in which judges are usually faced with 'skeleton legislation'[67] and decide cases primarily by looking back to ancient precedents in order to uncover basic principles of common law. In order to understand an administrative law case, the reader must often navigate section upon section of legislation, a cluster of detailed Regulations and masses of accompanying policy. As Felix Frankfurter is reported to have said,[68] the best advice which can be given to an administrative lawyer is therefore '(1) read the legislation; (2) read the legislation and (3) read the legislation'.[69] Common law principle, of course, is deeply important in this field, but it is not common for courts to articulate it from scratch. The live common law questions, rather, usually concern the application of well-established principles to rich legislative contexts. The courts' task is to determine how common law interacts with the detail of often highly particularised legislative and policy frameworks.

Beyond this, the legal structures in play in administrative law cases are varied and complex in other ways. There is no singular paradigm of an administrative law case. In some cases, individuals raise legal questions about the proper construction of their statutory rights or the application of the terms of the statute to the facts.[70]

[65] Carol Rose, 'Environmental Law Grows Up (More or Less), and What Science Can Do to Help' (2005) 9(2) *Lewis & Clark Law Review* 273.

[66] Although some cases can be characterised in this way (for example *Cooper v Wandsworth Board of Works* (1863) 143 ER 414), it is important to remember that the law prior to 1977 was characterised by a good deal of legal complexity: see chapter 2.

[67] House of Lords Select Committee on the Constitution, *The Legislative Process: The Delegation of Powers* (16th Report of Session 2017–2019) 17–19.

[68] Henry J Friendly, *Benchmarks* (University of Chicago Press, 1967) 196.

[69] *Ibid.*

[70] *Conville* (n 11).

In others, non-governmental organisations, public bodies[71] or 'public-spirited citizens'[72] seek to enforce legislative duties enacted to benefit the public at large.[73] There are also cases which do not fit neatly into these camps.[74]

All of this makes administrative law a difficult subject to understand, to study and to write about. The difficulties arise not only because administrative law cases often make for lengthy and hard-going reads. Understanding administrative law case law also requires an appreciation of many different types of legal frame.[75] If this book has one core message, however, it is that the legally complex and varied nature of administrative law is something to be embraced, rather than explained away. A grasp of the complex and varied anatomy of administrative law is essential to a rounded understanding of the nature of adjudication. It also necessary to endeavours to make meaningful sense of legal doctrine and case law.

[71] *R v Secretary of State for Employment, ex parte Equal Opportunities Commission* [1994] 2 WLR 409 (HL).

[72] *Fleet Street Casuals* (n 55); *Walton* (n 31).

[73] *Lewisham Union Guardians* (n 10).

[74] For instance systematic review cases: *R (Medical Justice) v Secretary of State for the Home Department* [2011] EWCA Civ 1710; *R (Tabbakh) v Staffordshire and West Midlands Probation Trust* [2014] EWCA Civ 827, [2014] 1 WLR 4620; *R (S) v Director of Legal Aid Casework* [2016] EWCA Civ 464, [2016] 1 WLR 4733; *R (Howard League for Penal Reform) v Lord Chancellor* [2015] EWCA Civ 819.

[75] In this way, it might be described as a 'hot' legal context: Elizabeth Fisher, 'Environmental Law as "Hot" Law' (2013) 25 *Journal of Environmental Law* 347–58.

INDEX